G000274923

STRE

Bedfordshire

Bedford, Biggleswade, Dunstable, Leighton Buzzard, Luton

www.philips-maps.co.uk

First published in 2000 by

Philip's, a division of
Octopus Publishing Group Ltd
www.octopusbooks.co.uk
2–4 Heron Quays, London E14 4JP
An Hachette Livre UK Company
www.hachettelivre.co.uk

Third edition 2009
First impression 2009
BEDCA

ISBN 978-0-540-09210-9 (pocket)

© Philip's 2009

 Ordnance Survey®

This product includes mapping data licensed
from Ordnance Survey®, with the permission of
the Controller of Her Majesty's Stationery Office.

© Crown copyright 2009. All rights reserved.
Licence number 100011710

Data for the speed cameras provided by
PocketGPSWorld.com Ltd.

Ordnance Survey and the OS symbol are
registered trademarks of Ordnance Survey, the
national mapping agency of Great Britain

Printed and bound in China by Toppan

Contents

II **Mobile safety cameras**

III **Key to map symbols**

IV **Key to map pages**

VI **Route planning**

VIII **Administrative and Postcode boundaries**

1 **Street maps** at 2⅔ inches to 1 mile

133 **Index** of towns, villages, streets, hospitals, industrial
estates, railway stations, schools, shopping centres
universities and places of interest

Digital Data

The exceptionally high-quality mapping found in this atlas is available as digital data in
TIFF format, which is easily convertible to other bitmapped (raster) image formats.

The index is also available in digital form as a standard database table. It contains all the
details found in the printed index together with the National Grid reference for the map
square in which each entry is named.

For further information and to discuss your requirements, please contact
victoria.dawbarn@philips-maps.co.uk

II

Mobile safety cameras

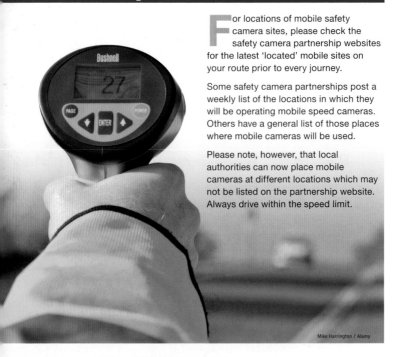

Mike Harrington / Alamy

For locations of mobile safety camera sites, please check the safety camera partnership websites for the latest 'located' mobile sites on your route prior to every journey.

Some safety camera partnerships post a weekly list of the locations in which they will be operating mobile speed cameras. Others have a general list of those places where mobile cameras will be used.

Please note, however, that local authorities can now place mobile cameras at different locations which may not be listed on the partnership website. Always drive within the speed limit.

Useful websites

Bedfordshire and Luton Casualty Reduction Partnership
www.drivesafely.org

Bedfordshire Police Online
www.bedfordshire.police.uk

Luton Borough Council
www.luton.gov.uk

Bedfordshore County Council
www.bedscc.gov.uk

Further information
www.dft.gov.uk
www.dvla.gov.uk
www.highways.gov.uk
www.road-safe.org
www.thinkroadsafety.gov.uk

Key to map symbols

III

	Motorway with junction number
	Primary route – dual/single carriageway
	A road – dual/single carriageway
	B road – dual/single carriageway
	Minor road – dual/single carriageway
	Other minor road – dual/single carriageway
	Road under construction
	Tunnel, covered road
	Speed cameras - single, multiple
	Rural track, private road or narrow road in urban area
	Gate or obstruction to traffic (restrictions may not apply at all times or to all vehicles)
	Path, bridleway, byway open to all traffic, restricted byway
	Pedestrianised area
DY7	**Postcode boundaries**
	County and unitary authority boundaries
	Railway, tunnel, railway under construction
	Tramway, tramway under construction
	Miniature railway
Walsall	**Railway station**
	Private railway station
South Shields	**Metro station**
	Tram stop, tram stop under construction
	Bus, coach station

	Ambulance station
	Coastguard station
	Fire station
	Police station
	Accident and Emergency entrance to hospital
H	**Hospital**
+	**Place of worship**
i	**Information Centre** (open all year)
	Shopping Centre
P	**Parking**
P&R	**Park and Ride**
PO	**Post Office**
Ⓧ	**Camping site**
	Caravan site
	Golf course
	Picnic site
Prim Sch	**Important buildings, schools, colleges, universities and hospitals**
	Built up area
	Woods
River Medway	**Water name**
	River, weir, stream
	Canal, lock, tunnel
	Water
	Tidal water
Church	**Non-Roman antiquity**
ROMAN FORT	**Roman antiquity**
87 / **58**	**Adjoining page indicators**

Acad	**Academy**	Inst	**Institute**	Recn Gd	**Recreation Ground**
Allot Gdns	**Allotments**	Ct	**Law Court**		
Cemy	**Cemetery**	L Ctr	**Leisure Centre**	Resr	**Reservoir**
C Ctr	**Civic Centre**	LC	**Level Crossing**	Ret Pk	**Retail Park**
CH	**Club House**	Liby	**Library**	Sch	**School**
Coll	**College**	Mkt	**Market**	Sh Ctr	**Shopping Centre**
Crem	**Crematorium**	Meml	**Memorial**	TH	**Town Hall/House**
Ent	**Enterprise**	Mon	**Monument**	Trad Est	**Trading Estate**
Ex H	**Exhibition Hall**	Mus	**Museum**	Univ	**University**
Ind Est	**Industrial Estate**	Obsy	**Observatory**	W Twr	**Water Tower**
IRB Sta	**Inshore Rescue Boat Station**	Pal	**Royal Palace**	Wks	**Works**
		PH	**Public House**	YH	**Youth Hostel**

■ The small numbers around the edges of the maps identify the 1 kilometre National Grid lines

■ The dark grey border on the inside edge of some pages indicates that mapping does not continue onto the adjacent page

The scale of the maps on the pages numbered in blue is 4.2 cm to 1 km • 2⅔ inches to 1 mile • 1: 23810

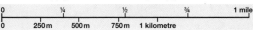

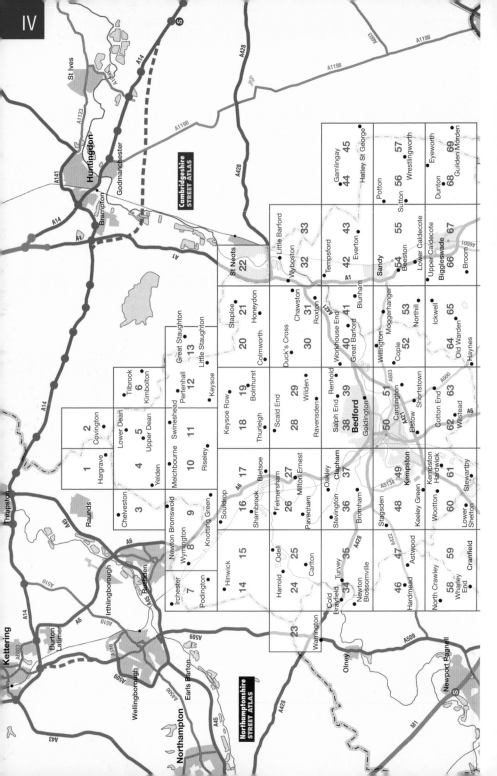

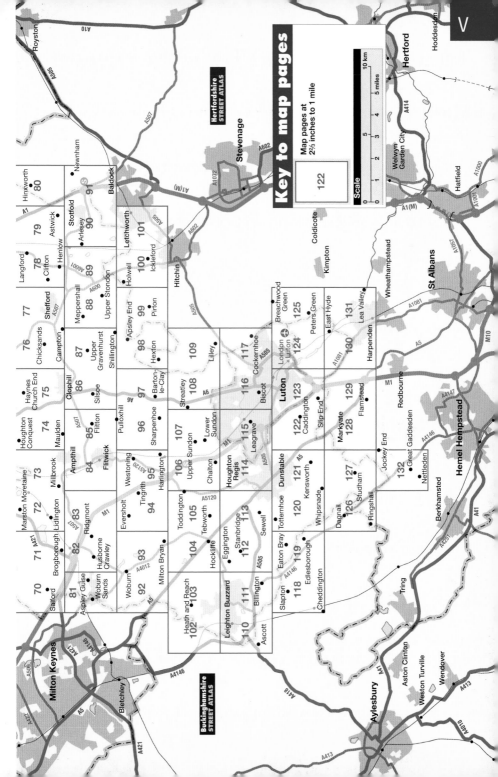

V

Key to map pages

Map pages at
2⅔ inches to 1 mile

122

Scale

0 1 2 3 4 5 miles
0   5   10 km

Hertfordshire STREET ATLAS

Buckinghamshire STREET ATLAS

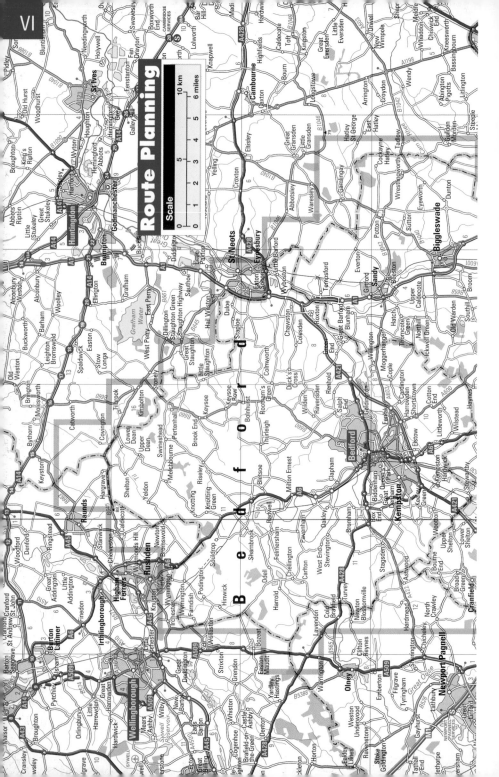

Route Planning

Scale

10 km

6 miles

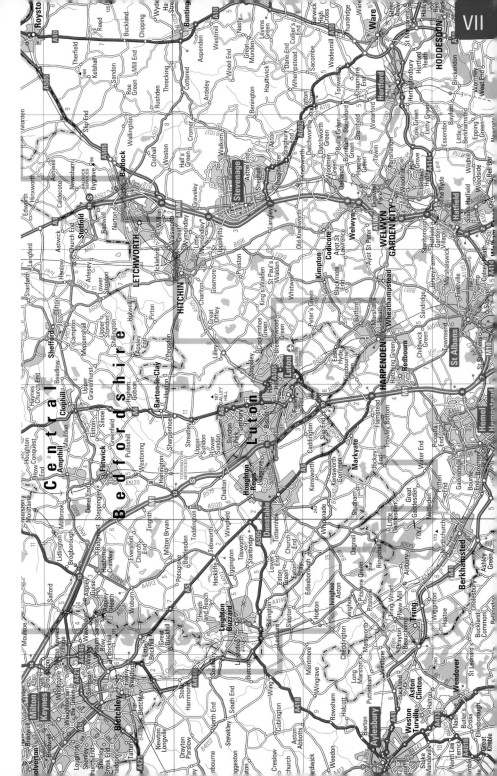

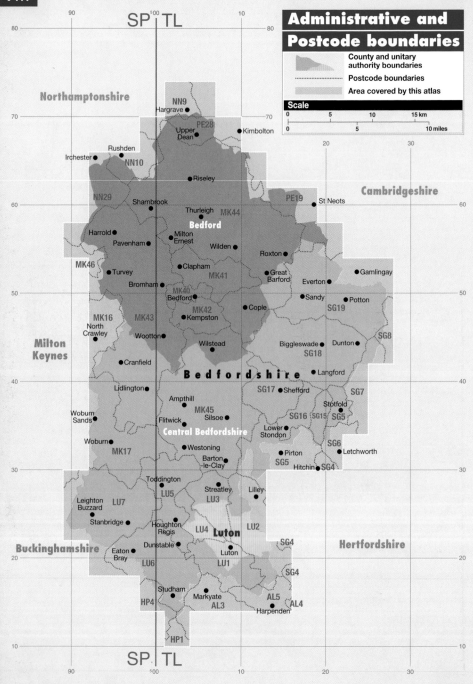

VIII

SP TL

500

Administrative and
Postcode boundaries

County and unitary
authority boundaries

Postcode boundaries

Area covered by this atlas

Scale

| 0 | 5 | 10 | 15 km |

| 0 | 5 | 10 miles |

Northamptonshire

NN9
Hargrave

PE28

Upper
Dean

Kimbolton

Rushden

Irchester
NN10

Riseley

Cambridgeshire

NN29
Sharnbrook

Thurleigh
MK44

PE19
St Neots

Bedford

Harrold
Milton
Ernest

Pavenham
Wilden

Roxton

MK46

Clapham
MK41

Great
Barford

Everton

Gamlingay

Turvey

Bromham

MK40
Bedford

Sandy

Potton

Cople

SG19

MK16
North
Crawley

MK43

MK42
Kempston

SG8

Wootton

Milton
Keynes

Cranfield

Wilstead

Biggleswade

Dunton

SG18

Langford

Lidlington

SG17
Shefford

SG7

Ampthill

MK45

Stotfold

Woburn
Sands

Flitwick

Silsoe

SG16
SG15
SG5

Woburn

Central Bedfordshire

Lower
Stondon

SG6

MK17

Westoning

Pirton

Letchworth

Barton
-le-Clay
SG5

Hitchin
SG4

Toddington

Bedfordshire

Streatley

Lilley

Leighton
Buzzard
LU7

LU5
LU3

Stanbridge

Houghton
Regis

LU4
Luton

LU2

Buckinghamshire

Eaton
Bray

Dunstable

SG4

Hertfordshire

LU6

Luton
LU1

Studham

SG4

HP4

Markyate
AL3

AL5

AL4

Harpenden

HP1

SP TL

500

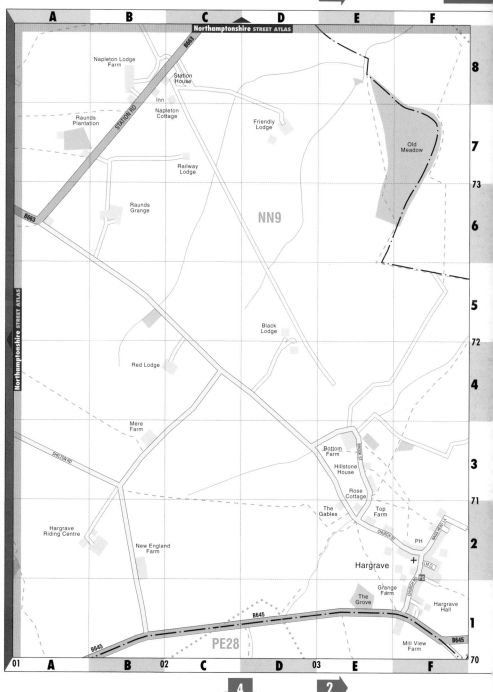

Napleton Lodge Farm

Station House

B663

STATION RD

Inn

Napleton Cottage

Raunds Plantation

Railway Lodge

Friendly Lodge

Raunds Grange

B663

NN9

Old Meadow

Black Lodge

Red Lodge

Mere Farm

Bottom Farm

BROOK ST

Hillstone House

Rose Cottage

The Gables

Top Farm

CHURCH ST

PH

MAIN RD LA

SHELTON RD

Hargrave Riding Centre

New England Farm

Hargrave

ELM CL

CHURCH LA

PO

Grange Farm

The Grove

B645

B645

PE28

Hargrave Hall

Mill View Farm

B645

Northamptonshire STREET ATLAS

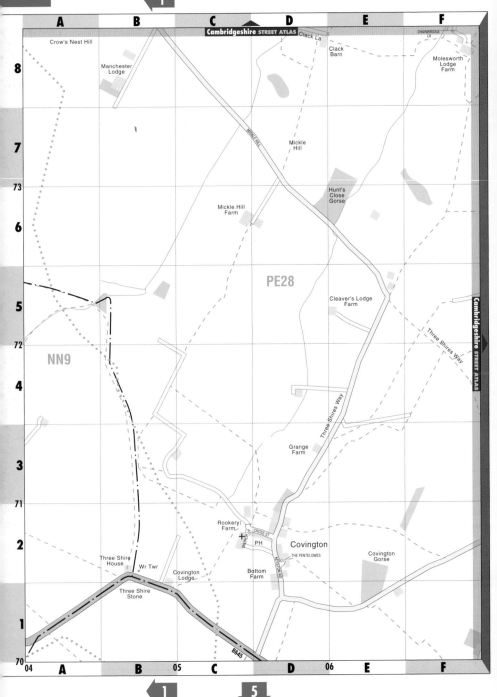

Cambridgeshire STREET ATLAS

Crow's Nest Hill

Manchester Lodge

Clack La

Clack Barn

Molesworth Lodge Farm

CHAINBRIDGE LA

Mickle Hill

MICKLE HILL

Hunt's Close Gorse

Mickle Hill Farm

PE28

Cleaver's Lodge Farm

NN9

Three Shires Way

Cambridgeshire STREET ATLAS

Three Shires Way

Grange Farm

Three Shires Way

Rookery Farm

CROSS ST

PH

Covington

THE PENTELOWES

Covington Gorse

Three Shire House

Wr Twr

Covington Lodge

KEYSTON RD

Bottom Farm

Three Shire Stone

B645

04   05   06

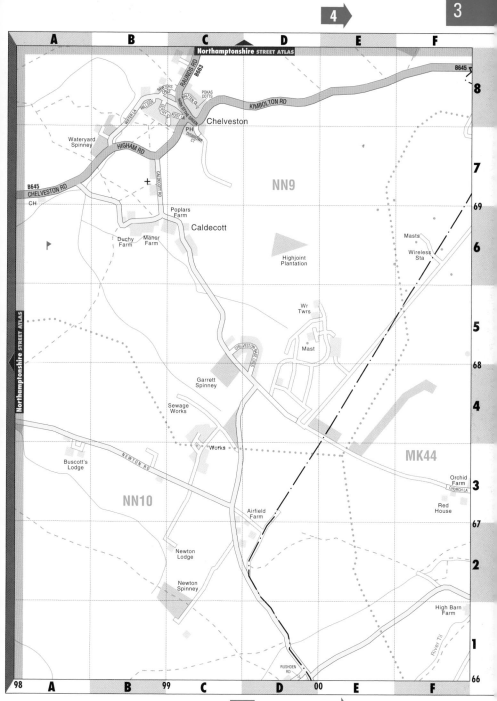

3

4

9

4

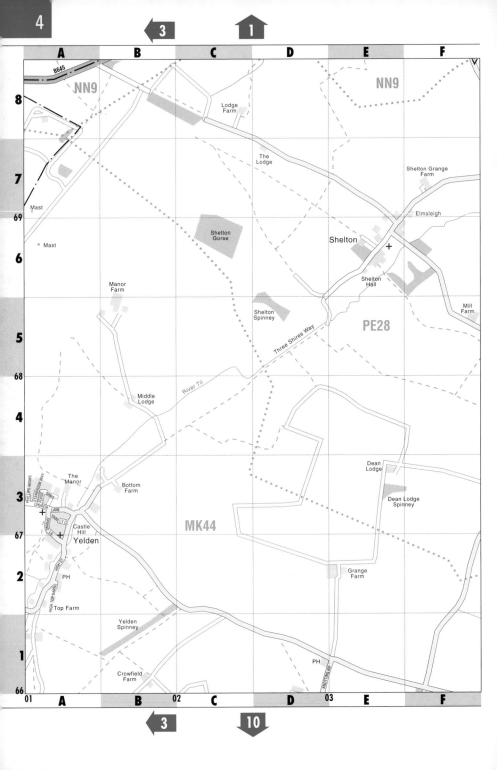

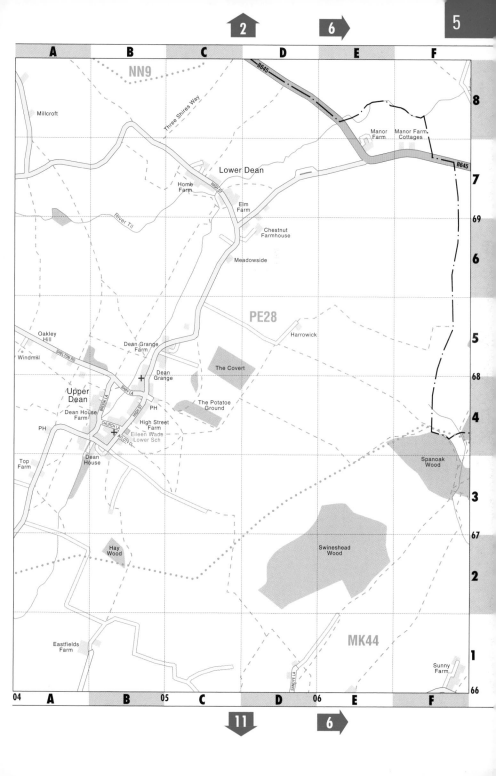

5

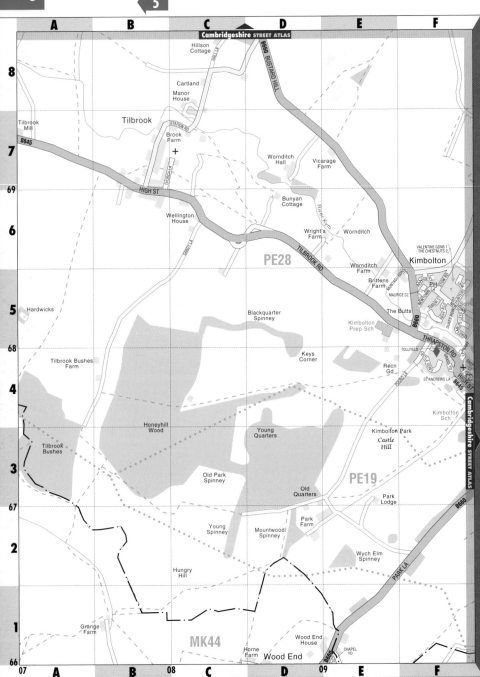

A   B   C   D   E   F

8

Hillson
Cottage

Cartland

Manor
House

Tilbrook

Tilbrook
Mill

B645

7

Brook
Farm

STATION RD

HIGH ST

69

Wellington
House

Wornditch
Hall

Vicarage
Farm

Bunyan
Cottage

6

Wright's
Farm

Wornditch

PE28

TILBROOK RD

Wornditch
Farm

River Kym

VALENTINE GDNS 1
THE CHESTNUTS 2

Kimbolton

Brittens
Farm

PH

MAURICE CL

5

Hardwicks

Blackquarter
Spinney

The Butts

Kimbolton
Prep Sch

B660

THRAPSTON RD

68

Tilbrook Bushes
Farm

Keys
Corner

Tollfield

Recn
Gd

HIGH ST

B645

St ANDREWS LA

4

Honeyhill
Wood

Young
Quarters

Kimbolton Park

Kimbolton
Sch

Tilbrook
Bushes

Castle
Hill

3

Old Park
Spinney

Old
Quarters

PE19

Park
Lodge

67

Young
Spinney

Park
Farm

Mountwood
Spinney

B660

2

Wych Elm
Spinney

Hungry
Hill

PARK LA

1

Grange
Farm

MK44

Horne
Farm

Wood End
House

Wood End

CHAPEL
YD

B660

66

07   A   B   08   C   D   09   E   F

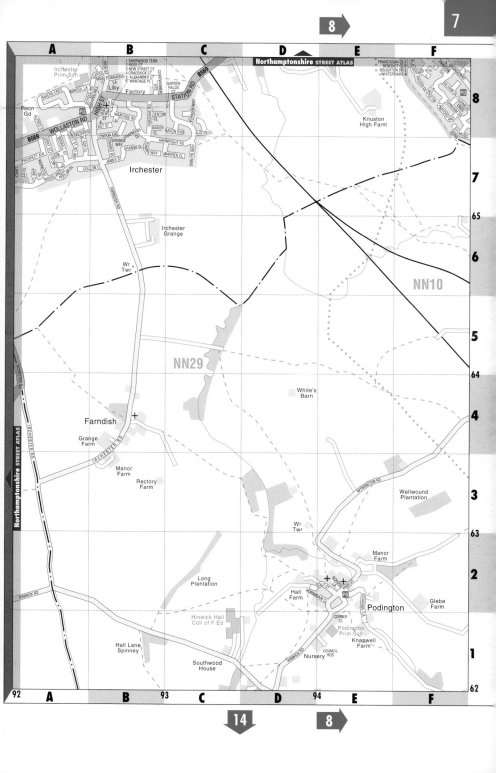

A **B** **C** **D** **E** **F**

8

1 SHERWOOD TERR
2 ROSE CT
3 NEW STREET CT
4 CRADDOCK CT
5 ALEXANDER CT
6 WANTAGE PL

FRANCISCAN CL 1
BENEDICT CL 2
BOUGHTON DR 3
WHITEFRIARS 4

Irchester
Prim Sch

Factory

Liby

GARDEN
FIELDS
CT

Knuston
High Farm

STATION RD   B569

PO

BAKERS CRES
SCHOOL LA
HIGH ST
TOWNWELL LA
NORMAN WAY
DENTON CL
SAXON RISE
AUSTIN CL

Recn
Gd

WOLLASTON RD

B569

WANTAGE RD

ARKWRIGHT RD

WARREN CL
EVELYN WAY
WAY CL

PROSPECT AVE

LONDON END

GRANGE CL
CHAPMANS CL
MANOR CL

COULON CL

JAMES ST

Irchester

7

65

NN10

Irchester
Grange

6

Wr
Twr

FARNDISH RD

5

NN29

64

White's
Barn

4

Farndish

Grange
Farm

IRCHESTER RD

Manor
Farm

Rectory
Farm

Wellwound
Plantation

3

63

Wr
Twr

Manor
Farm

WYMINGTON RD

2

Long
Plantation

Hall
Farm

HINWICK RD

HINWICK RD

Hinwick Hall
Coll of F Ed

Hall Lane
Spinney

Southwood
House

Nursery

COUNCIL
HOS

Glebe
Farm

Podington

HORNBEAM CL
SCHOOL LA
HIGH ST
VICARAGE LA

PO

CORNER
CL

Podington
Prim Sch

Knapwell
Farm

1

62

A
B   **C**
D   **E**   **F**

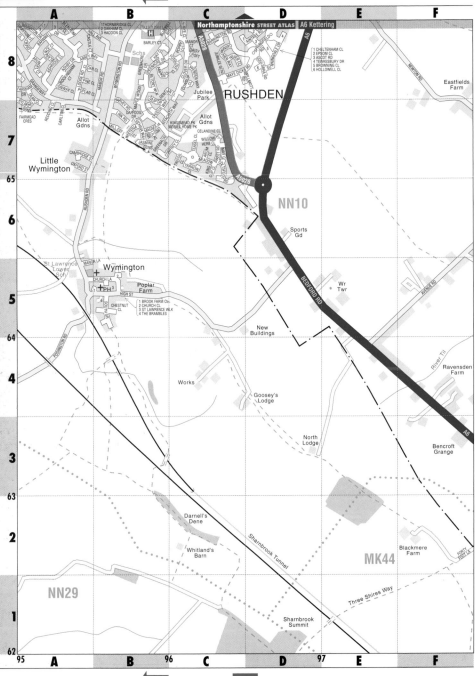

Northamptonshire STREET ATLAS A6 Kettering

1 CHELTENHAM CL
2 EPSOM RD
3 ASCOT RD
4 TEWKESBURY DR
5 BROWNING CL
6 HOLLOWELL CL

RUSHDEN

NN10

Eastfields
Farm

Jubilee
Park

Little
Wymington

Allot
Gdns

Sports
Gd

Wr
Twr

River Til

Ravensden
Farm

A6

Wymington

Poplar
Farm

1 BROOK FARM Cl
2 CHURCH CL
3 ST LAWRENCE WLK
4 THE BRAMBLES

New
Buildings

BEDFORD RD

Works

Goosey's
Lodge

North
Lodge

Bencroft
Grange

Darnell's
Dene

Whitland's
Barn

Sharnbrook Tunnel

MK44

Blackmere
Farm

FORTY FOOT LA

NN29

Three Shires Way

Sharnbrook
Summit

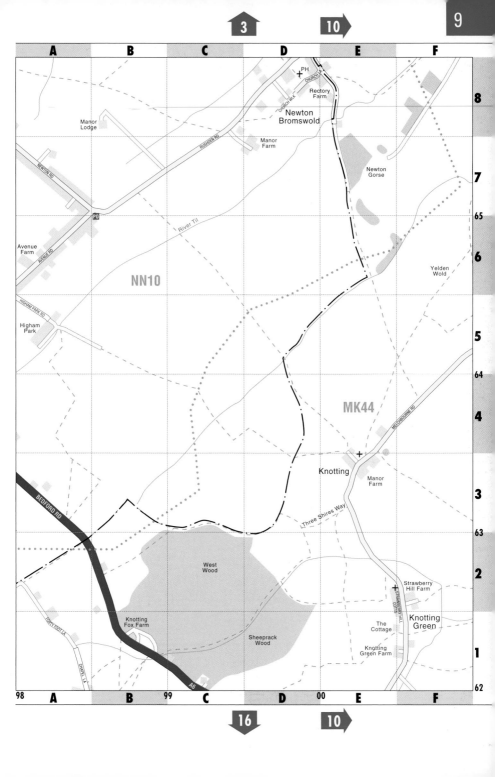

A B C D E F

8

7

65

6

5

64

4

3

63

2

1

62

Manor
Lodge

RUSHDEN RD

CHURCH WAY

+PH

Rectory
Farm

Newton
Bromswold

Manor
Farm

Newton
Gorse

NEWTON RD

PO

Avenue
Farm

AVENUE RD

River Til

NN10

Yelden
Wold

HIGHAM PARK RD

Higham
Park

MK44

MELDBOURNE RD

Knotting

+

Manor
Farm

BEDFORD RD

Three Shires Way

West
Wood

Strawberry
Hill Farm

+

STRAWBERRY HILL COTTS

Knotting
Green

FORTY FOOT LA

Knotting
Fox Farm

Sheeprack
Wood

The
Cottage

Knotting
Green Farm

CHAPEL LA

A6

98 A B 99 C D 00 E F

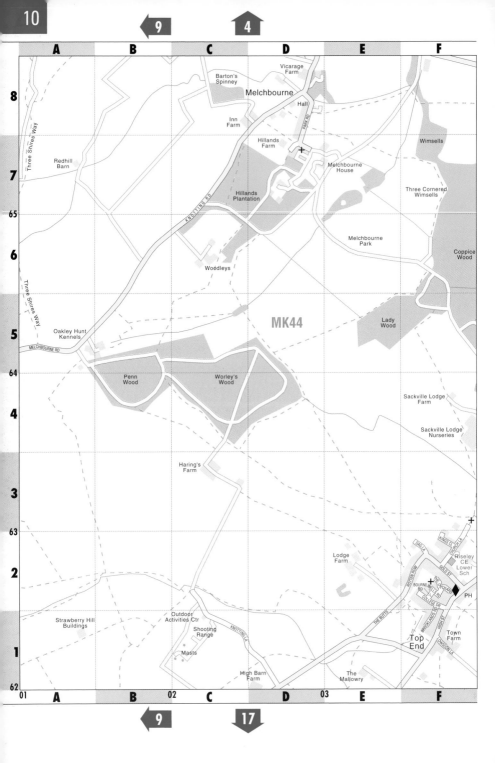

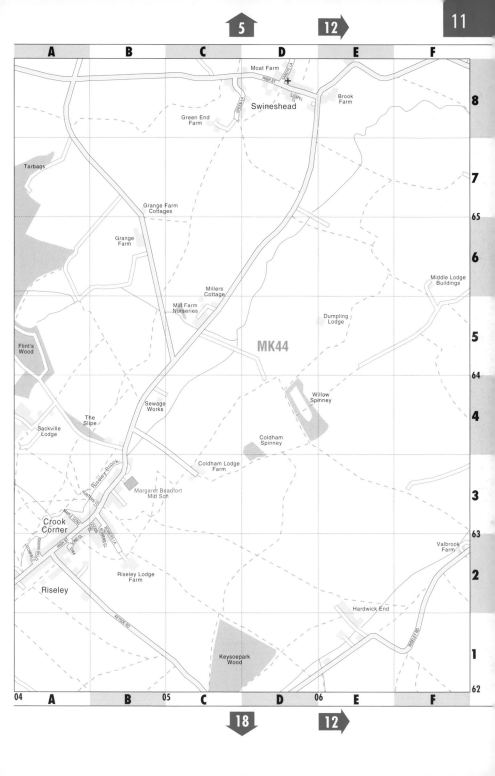

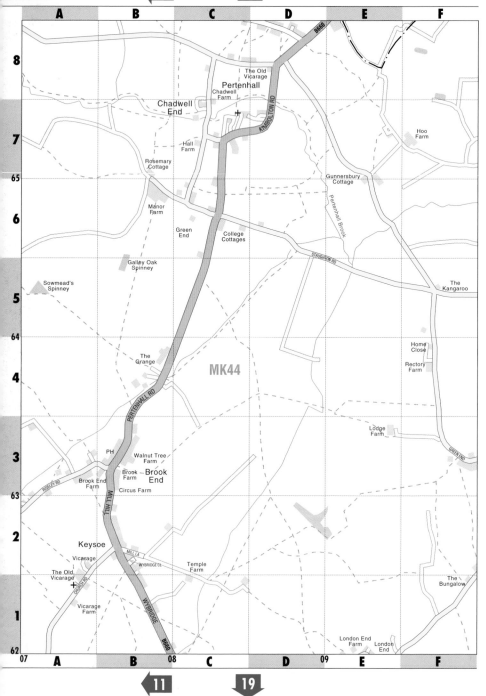

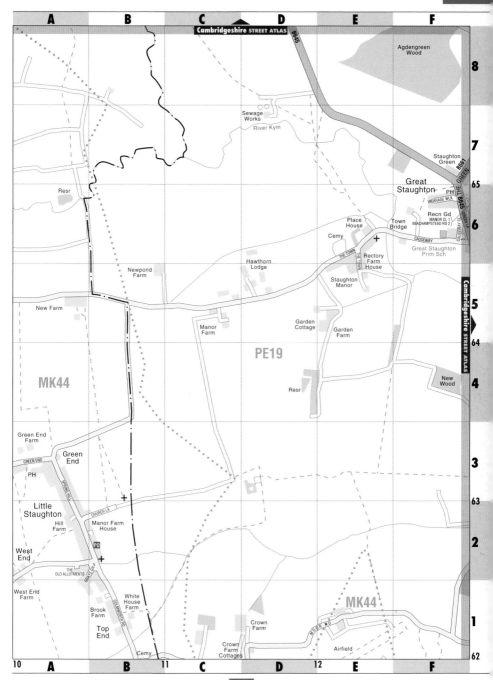

Cambridgeshire STREET ATLAS

8

Agdengreen Wood

River Kym

Sewage Works

7

Staughton Green

65

Great Staughton

Resr

VICARAGE WLK
PH

Recn Gd
MANOR CL 1
BEACHAMPSTEAD RD 2

6

Place House

Town Bridge

CAUSEWAY

Cemy

Great Staughton Prim Sch

Newpond Farm

Hawthorn Lodge

THE TOWN

Staughton Manor

Rectory Farm House

New Farm

5

Manor Farm

Garden Cottage

Garden Farm

64

MK44

PE19

4

Resr

New Wood

Green End Farm

GREEN END

Green End

3

63

PH

SPRING HILL

Little Staughton

CHURCH LA

Hill Farm

Manor Farm House

PO

2

West End

THE OLD ALLOTMENTS

BROOK SPA

West End Farm

Brook Farm

White House Farm

Crown Farm

MK44

MOOR RD

1

Top End

Cemy

Crown Farm Cottages

Airfield

62

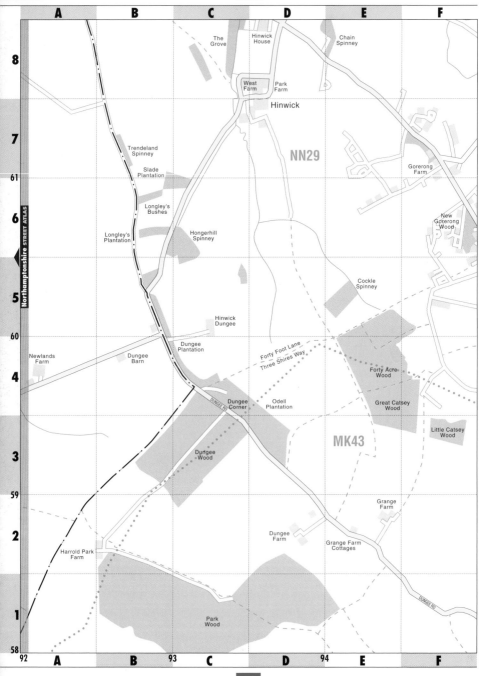

8

7

61

6

5

60

4

3

59

2

1

58

A B C D E F

Northamptonshire STREET ATLAS

92 93 94

The Grove

Hinwick House

Chain Spinney

West Farm

Park Farm

Hinwick

NN29

Gorerong Farm

Trendeland Spinney

Slade Plantation

Longley's Bushes

New Gorerong Wood

Longley's Plantation

Hongerhill Spinney

Cockle Spinney

Hinwick Dungee

Dungee Plantation

Forty Foot Lane

Three Shires Way

Forty Acre Wood

Newlands Farm

Dungee Barn

Dungee Corner

DUNGEE RD

Odell Plantation

Great Catsey Wood

Little Catsey Wood

MK43

Dungee Wood

Grange Farm

Harrold Park Farm

Dungee Farm

Grange Farm Cottages

DUNGEE RD

Park Wood

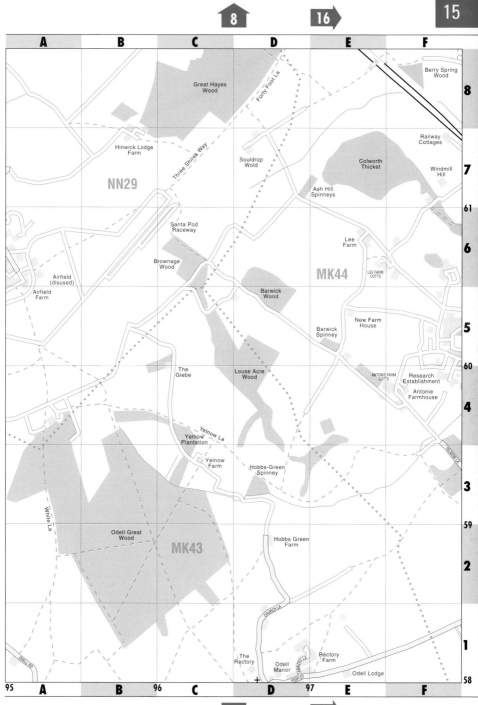

Berry Spring Wood

Great Hayes Wood

Forty Foot La

8

Railway Cottages

Hinwick Lodge Farm

Three Shires Way

Souldrop Wold

Colworth Thicket

Windmill Hill

7

NN29

Ash Hill Spinneys

61

Santa Pod Raceway

Lee Farm

Brownage Wood

MK44

LEE FARM COTTS

6

Airfield (disused)

Barwick Wood

New Farm House

Airfield Farm

Barwick Spinney

5

The Glebe

Louse Acre Wood

ANTONIE FARM COTTS

Research Establishment

60

Antonie Farmhouse

4

YELNOW LA

Yelnow La
Yelnow Plantation

Yelnow Farm

Hobbs-Green Spinney

3

White La

Odell Great Wood

MK43

Hobbs Green Farm

59

2

CHURCH LA

The Rectory

Odell Manor

Rectory Farm

HIGH ST

HANGER LA

1

ODELL RD

Odell Lodge

58

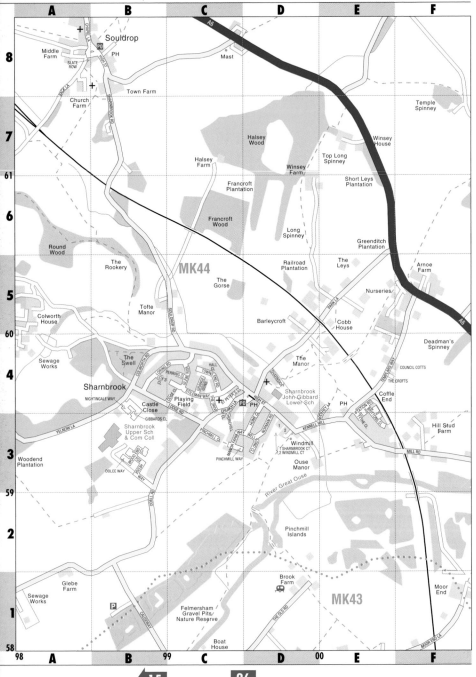

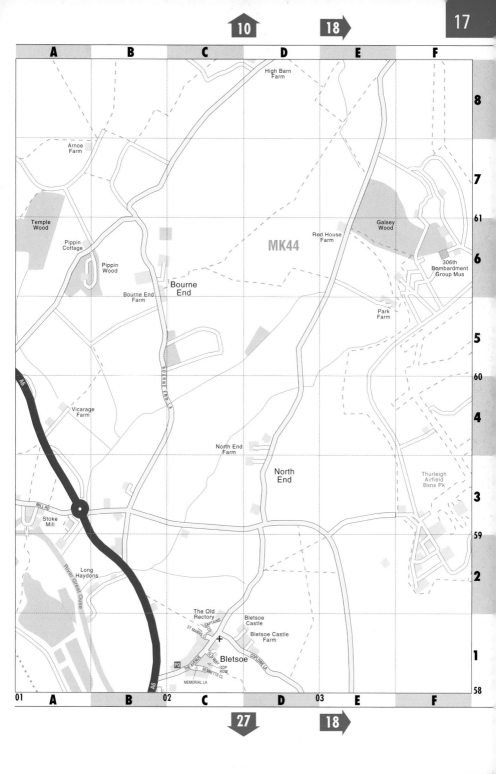

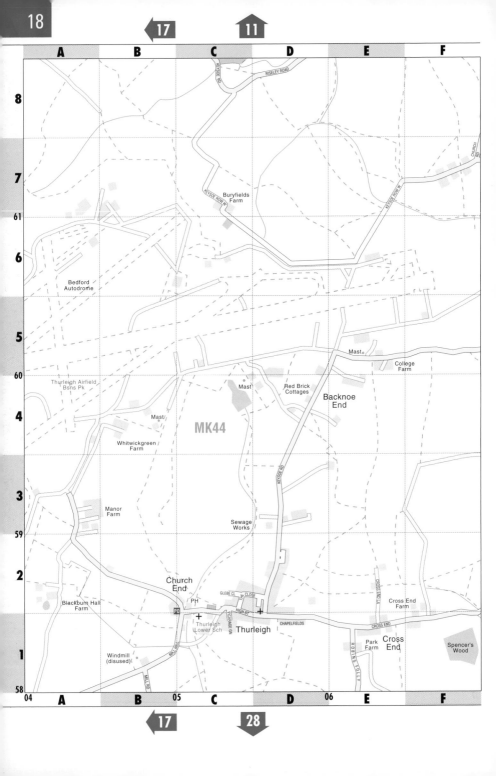

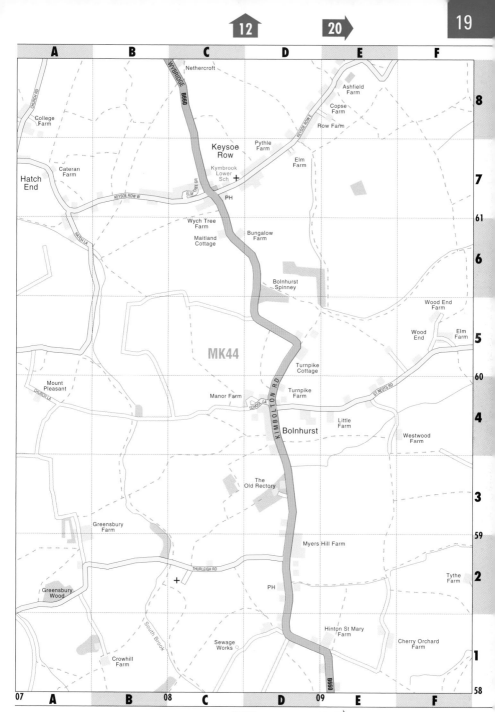

19
13

A B C D E F

8

PE19

Top End

Top End Farm

MOOR RD

Little Staughton Airfield

Works

Staughton Moor

The Wickey Farm

7

Works

PE19

61

Berrywood Farm

Dulae Brook

6

Bushmead Priory

Sewage Works

Garden Wood

The Camps

Bushmead Big Wood

5

Steeple Wood

BUSHMEAD CROSS

Home Farm

Wood Corner

ST NEOTS RD

60

Honeydon Brook

Bushmead

4

MK44

Upper Honeydon Farm

3

City Farm

CITY LA

The City

SHELFORD LA

LITTLE STAUGHTON RD

59

THE TUDORS

QUEENS RD

PO

Church End

Colmworth

2

SCHOOL LA

HONEYDON RD

Kennels Farm

CHURCH LA

Jewsfield

Lower Goodwick Farm

Manor Farm

1

CHAPEL LA

COX LA CL

CHURCH RD

Mast

Colley Hill

Coxfield

Chapel End

Chapel Farm

58

10 **A** **B** 11 **C** **D** 12 **E** **F**

19
30

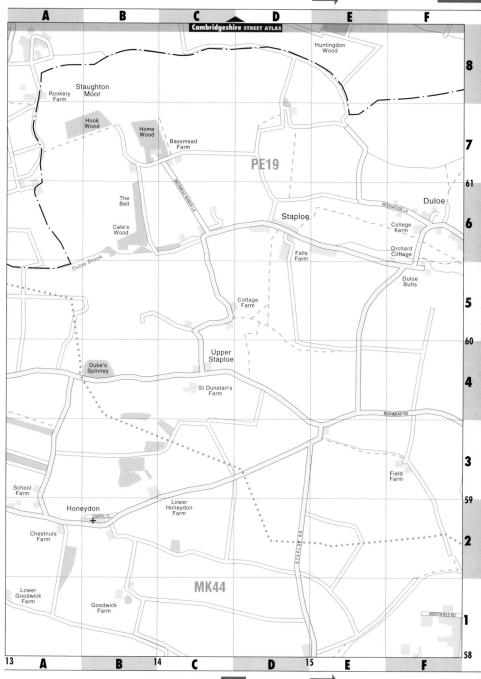

Cambridgeshire STREET ATLAS

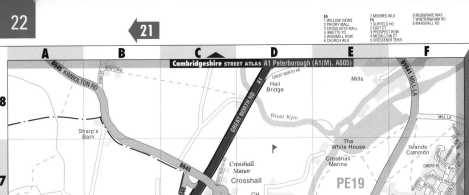

E5
1 WILLOW VIEWS
2 PRIORY MALL
3 CROSS KEYS MALL
4 IBBETTS YD
5 WINDMILL ROW
6 CHURCH WLK

7 MOORES WLK

F5
1 SUFFIELD HO
2 EAST CT
3 PROSPECT ROW
4 MEDALLION CT
5 CRESSENER TERR

6 MUSGRAVE WAY
7 WINTRINGHAM RD
8 MARSHALL RD

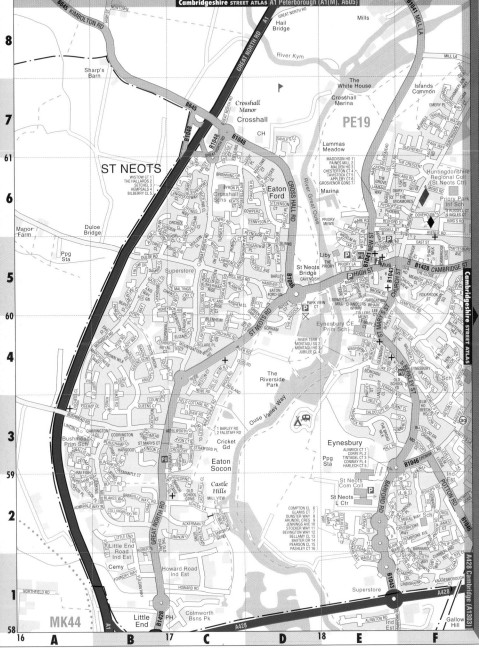

CAMBRIDGESHIRE STREET ATLAS A1 Peterborough (A1(M), A605)

ST NEOTS

PE19

Eaton Ford

Crosshall

Crosshall Manor

Eynesbury

Eaton Socon

Castle Hills

The Riverside Park

MK44

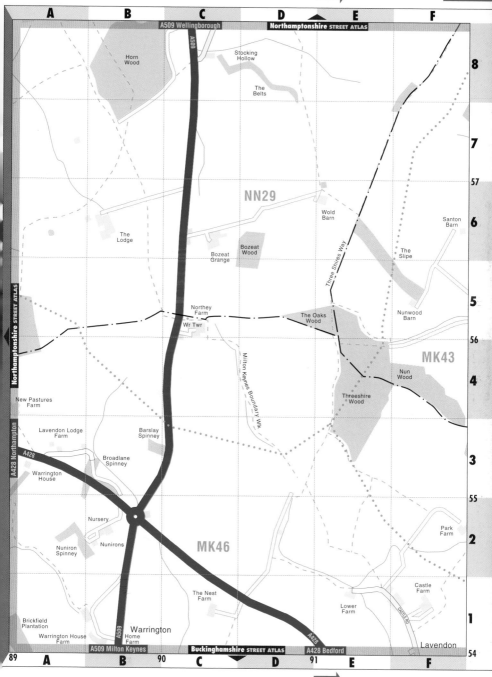

A   B   C   D   E   F

8

Horn
Wood

Stocking
Hollow

A509

The
Belts

7

57

NN29

Wold
Barn

Santon
Barn

6

The
Lodge

Bozeat
Wood

Three Shires Way

The
Slipe

Nunwood
Barn

Bozeat
Grange

5

Northey
Farm

The Oaks
Wood

Wr Twr

56

MK43

Milton Keynes Boundary Wlk

Nun
Wood

4

New Pastures
Farm

Threeshire
Wood

Lavendon Lodge
Farm

Barslay
Spinney

3

A428 Northampton

Broadlane
Spinney

55

Warrington
House

A428

Park
Farm

2

Nursery

MK46

Nuniron
Spinney

Nunirons

Castle
Farm

Brickfield
Plantation

The Nest
Farm

Lower
Farm

CASTLE RD

1

Warrington House
Farm

Warrington
Home
Farm

A509

Warrington

Lavendon

54

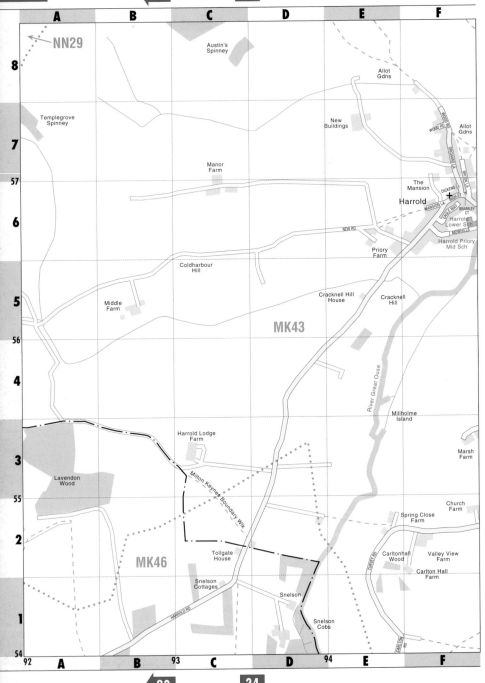

NN29

Templegrove
Spinney

Austin's
Spinney

Allot
Gdns

New
Buildings

Manor
Farm

Allot
Gdns

The
Mansion

Harrold

WOOD RD

ORCHARD LA

BRICK LA

DICKENS CT

MANSION LA

ROSE WAY

MILL ST

BRAMLEY
CT

Harrold
Lower Sch

MOWHILLS

Harrold Priory
Mid Sch

NEW RD

Priory
Farm

Coldharbour
Hill

Cracknell Hill
House

Cracknell
Hill

MK43

Middle
Farm

River Great Ouse

Millholme
Island

Marsh
Farm

Harrold Lodge
Farm

Lavendon
Wood

Milton Keynes Boundary Wlk

Church
Farm

Spring Close
Farm

MK46

Tollgate
House

Carltonhall
Wood

Valley View
Farm

Carlton Hall
Farm

TURVEY RD

Snelson
Cottages

HARROLD RD

Snelson

Snelson
Cobs

CARLTON RD

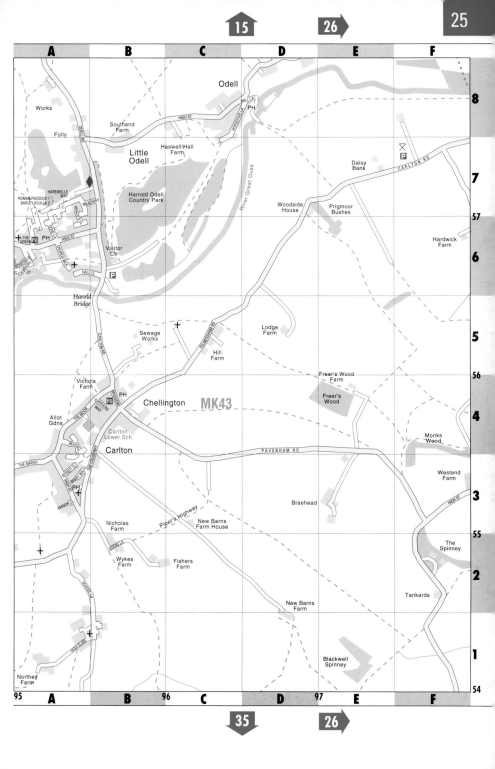

Odell

Works

Folly

Southend
Farm

Little
Odell

Haswell Hall
Farm

HIGH ST

MILL LA

HORSEFAIR LA

ODELL RD

PH

Daisy
Bank

CARLTON RD

HAREWELLE
WAY

ROMAN PADDOCK 1
BARLEY KILN LA 2

Harrold Odell
Country Park

River Great Ouse

Woodside
House

Prigmoor
Bushes

Hardwick
Farm

THE
GREEN

PH

HIGH ST

MEADOW

FIELD CL

CHURCH WK

PRIORY

PO

MONTGU
Sch Cl

Visitor
Ctr

HALL CL

P

6

Harold
Bridge

CARLTON RD

FELMERSHAM RD

Sewage
Works

Hill
Farm

Lodge
Farm

5

56

Victoria
Farm

BRIDGEND

PH

PO

Chellington

MK43

Freer's Wood
Farm

Freer's
Wood

4

Allot
Gdns

THE MOOR

CASSIOBURY
WAY

REC

Carlton
Lower Sch

Carlton

Monks
Wood

THE CAUSEWAY

THE MARSH

STREET CL

BEVEL CL

HIGH ST

PH

MANOR CL

PAVENHAM RD

Westend
Farm

HIGH ST

3

Braehead

55

Piper's Highway

Nicholas
Farm

New Barns
Farm House

The
Spinney

STEVENS LA

Wykes
Farm

Fishers
Farm

2

SCHOOL LA

Tankards

New Barns
Farm

HIGH CT MS

Northey
Farm

Blackwell
Spinney

1

54

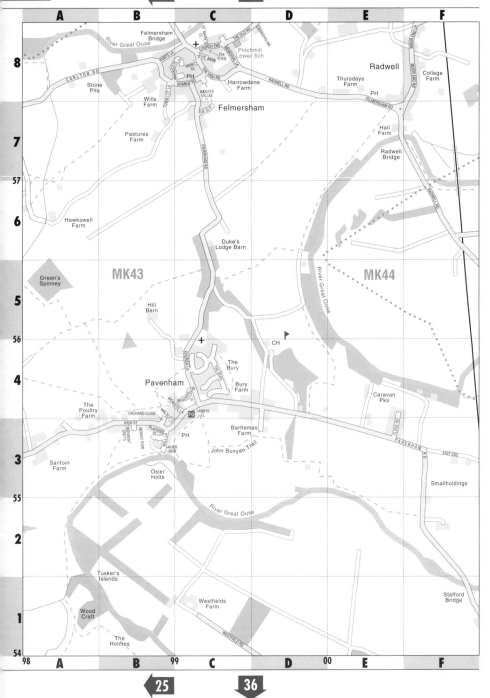

A B C D E F

8

7

57

6

5

56

4

3

55

2

1

54

River Great Ouse

Felmersham Bridge

BUNYS LA

CARLTON RD

Stone Pits

Wills Farm

Pastures Farm

Hawkswell Farm

Green's Spinney

Hill Barn

The Poultry Farm

ORCHARD CLOSE

HIGH ST

Sanfoin Farm

Osier Holts

Tusker's Islands

Wood Craft

The Holmes

ST MARY'S LA

CHURCH END

TRINITY CL

GRANGE RD

PH

BAILEYS VILLAS

THE SLIP

TOWN CL LA

PAVENHAM RD

Felmersham

Duke's Lodge Barn

CHURCH LA

THE BURY

Pavenham

WEAVERS LA

BROOK CLOSE

MONKS ROW

DERWENT CROFTS

PLAITERS END

MILL LA

PO

TANDYS CL

PH

RIVER ROW

Bartlemas Farm

John Bunyan Trail

River Great Ouse

Westfields Farm

WESTFIELD RD

THE OLD RD

THE HIGH RD

TITHE BARN

THE TITHE

MEADWAY LA

STRANTON AVE

Pinchmill Lower Sch

Harrowdene Farm

RADWELL RD

Thursdays Farm

FELMERSHAM RD

PH

Radwell

Hall Farm

Radwell Bridge

MK43

MK44

River Great Ouse

CH

The Bury

Bury Farm

Caravan Pks

CLOSE RD

PAVENHAM RD

EAST END

Smallholdings

Stafford Bridge

MOOR END LA

MOOR END RD

College Farm

PACKHILL RD

A B C D E F

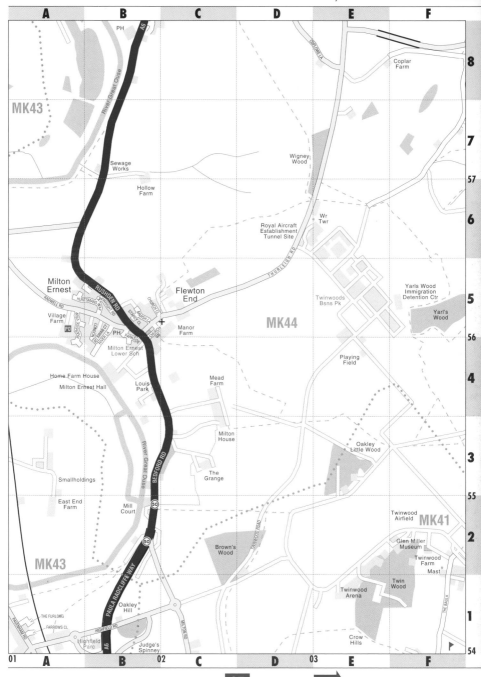

PH

River Great Ouse

Diddington La

Coplar Farm

MK43

Sewage Works

Hollow Farm

Wigney Wood

Wr Twr

Royal Aircraft Establishment Tunnel Site

Milton Ernest

RUSHDEN RD

Radwell Rd

Huntsmans Rd

Village Farm

PO

PH

Flewton End

Manor Farm

CHURCH ST

Milton Ernest Lower Sch

Twinwoods Bsns Pk

MK44

Yarls Wood Immigration Detention Ctr

Yarl's Wood

THURLEIGH RD

Playing Field

Home Farm House

Milton Ernest Hall

Louis Park

Mead Farm

Milton House

BEDFORD RD

River Great Ouse

Oakley Little Wood

Smallholdings

The Grange

East End Farm

Mill Court

50

Brown's Wood

TWINWOOD ROAD

Twinwood Airfield

MK41

Glen Miller Museum

Twinwood Farm Mast

MK43

50

PAULA RADCLIFFE WAY

Oakley Hill

HIGHFIELD RD

Twin Wood

Twinwood Arena

THE BAULK

THE FURLONG

FARROWS CL

Highfield Parc

A6

Judge's Spinney

MILTON RD

Crow Hills

27
18

A
B
C
D
E
F
8
7
57
6
5
56
4
3
55
2
1
54
04
05
06
OLD MILTON RD
Romp Hall
Scald End Farm
Scald End
MILL RD
ROBINS FOLLY
Robins Folly Farm
Park End Farm
Short Wood
Waterfall Farm
Rutter's Farm
Tilwick Wood
Red Gate Farm
MK44
Brook Farm
Little Wood
Great Wood
Traylesfield Farm
Manor Farm
Wood End
Ravensden House
Brook Farm
Outfields Farm
Ravensden Brook
THURLEIGH RD
GRAZE HILL
B660
SUNDERLAND HILL
Gray's Hill Farm
Highfield Farm
Graze Hill House
Willow Farm
SUNDERLAND CL
BUTLER ST
PO
PH
NEW CL
OLDWAYS RD
BEDFORD RD
B660
Fairfield Farm
MK41
Highfield House

27
38

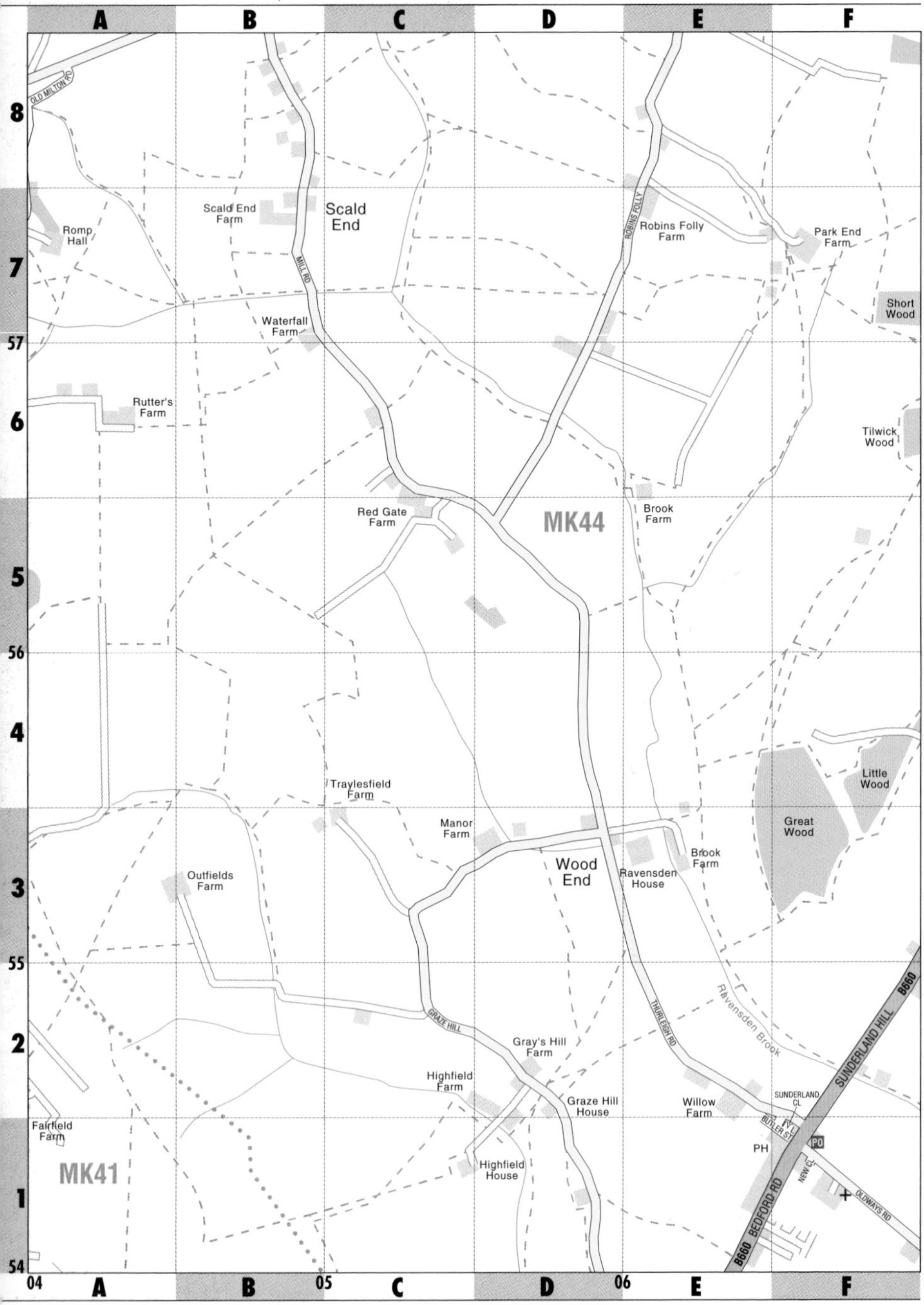

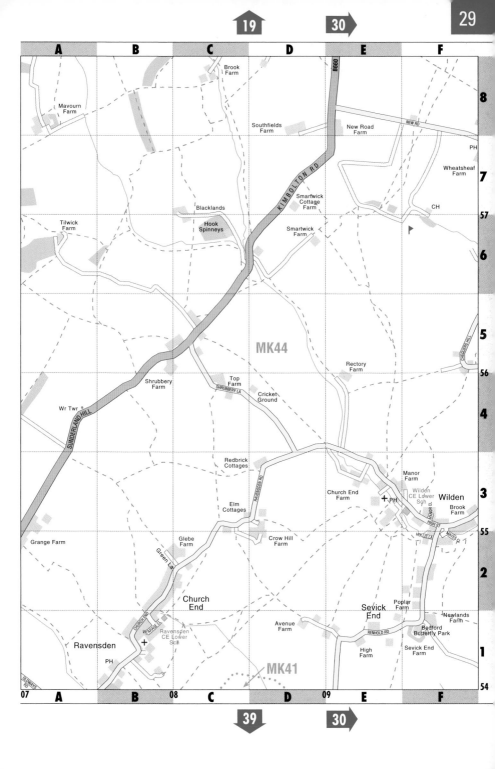

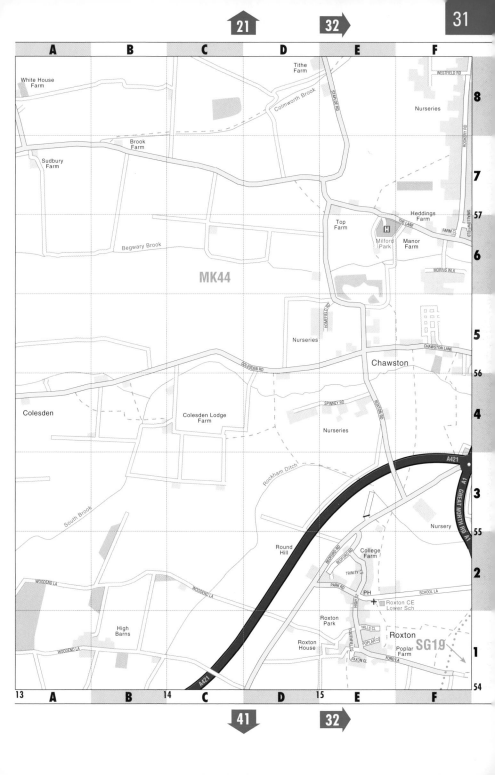

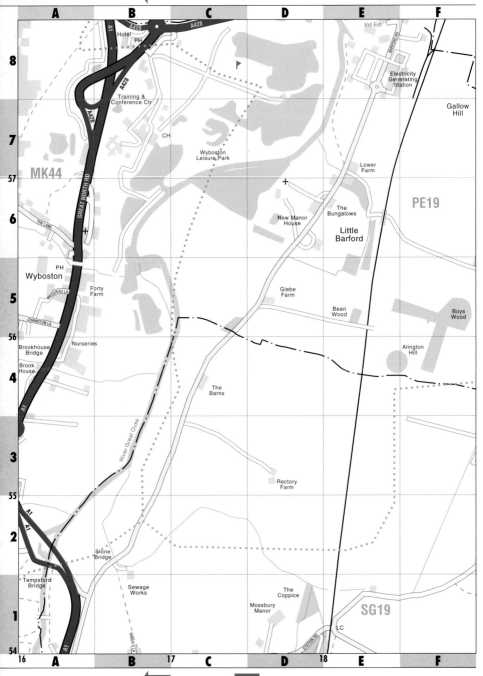

A · B · C · D · E · F

8

7

57

6

MK44

Wyboston

PH

Forty
Farm

Brookhouse
Bridge

Brook
House

Nurseries

5

56

4

River Great Ouse

3

55

2

A1

Stone
Bridge

Tempsford
Bridge

Sewage
Works

1

54

16 · 17 · 18

Hotel
PH

A428

A1

A428

Training &
Conference Ctr

CH

Wyboston
Leisure Park

GREAT NORTH RD

THE LANE

KNOTSHEAD LA

CHAWSTON LA

BAKER'S LA

STATION RD

BARFORD RD

Ind Est

Electricity
Generating
Station

Gallow
Hill

Lower
Farm

PE19

New Manor
House

The
Bungalows

Little
Barford

Glebe
Farm

Bean
Wood

Boys
Wood

Alington
Hill

The
Barns

Rectory
Farm

The
Coppice

Mossbury
Manor

SG19

LC

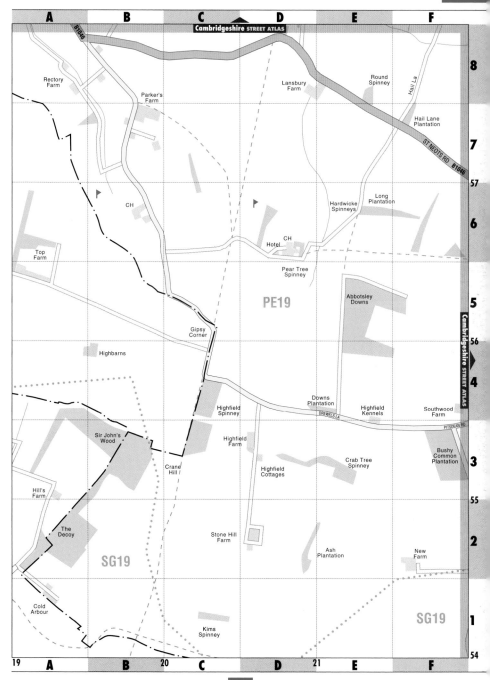

PE19

SG19

SG19

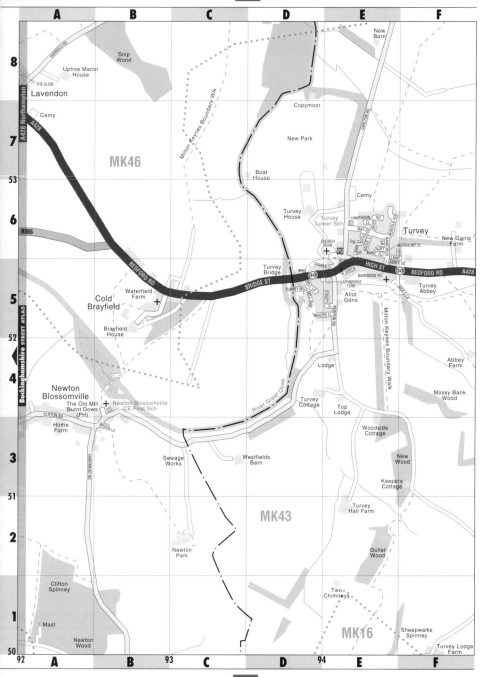

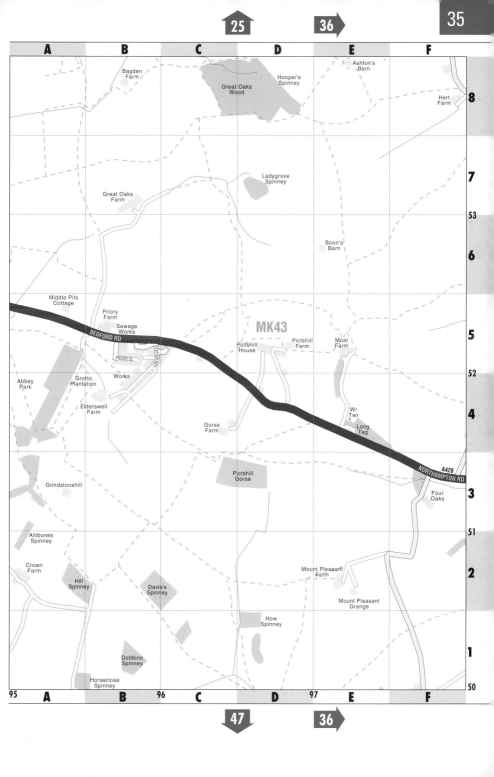

A   B   C   D   E   F

8

Bagden Farm

Great Oaks Wood

Hooper's Spinney

Ashton's Barn

Hart Farm

7

Ladygrove Spinney

Great Oaks Farm

53

Boon's Barn

6

Middle Pits Cottage

MK43

5

Priory Farm

BEDFORD RD

Sewage Works

Pictshill House

Pictshill Farm

Moat Farm

PRIORY CL

STANDEN RD

52

Abbey Park

Grotto Plantation

Works

Elderswell Farm

Gorse Farm

Wr Twr

Long Tag

4

NORTHAMPTON RD

A428

Grindstonehill

Pictshill Gorse

Four Oaks

3

51

Allibones Spinney

Mount Pleasant Farm

2

Crown Farm

Hill Spinney

Davis's Spinney

Mount Pleasant Grange

How Spinney

1

Dobbins Spinney

Horseclose Spinney

50

95   A   B   96   C   D   97   E   F

35
26

A **B** **C** **D** **E** **F**

8

Meeting Farm
West End
WEST END
Langcroft Farm
Westend Farm
Manor Farm
Church End

Fox Covert

FARSANDS
QUEENS CL
HIGH ST
PO
Town Farm
TOWN FARM COURT
PH
THE CAUSEWAY
FIRST CL

7

Stevington
PH
SILVER ST
AVE
BAKERY
FOXBROOK
CHURCH RD
FOX RD
WAY

River Great Ouse

Oakley House

53

Duck End Farm
Park End
Stevington Belt
Oakley Bridge

6

Duck End
Mill Farm
MILL LANE
Stevington Windmill
Park Farm
PARK RD
Bromham Plantation
Mushroom Hill

5

Skylark Cottage
MK43
John Bunyan Trail
P
OAKLEY RD

52

4

Tithe Farm
1 RED OAK CL
2 BLUE SPRUCE CL
Molliver's Wood
WOODLAND DR
WIND FIELD RD
AVOCA
MOLLIVERS LA
HO CL
WILLOW CL
THE GREEN

Salem Thrift
Wr Twr
ST CECILIA RD
CHESTNUT AVE
STONE PINE RD
2
Rainbow Special Sch
THE GLADE
Bowels Wood
SPINNEYS
ARUNDELS
SPENFIELD
AVE
LOOK CL
Bromham
Bromham CE Lower Sch

3

A428
NORTHAMPTON RD
A428
London Barn Farm
West Lodge
NORTHAMPTON RD
TULIP TREE CL
PARKLAND
CHESTNUT AVE
East Lodge
NORTHAMPTON RD
Liby
GRANGE LA
VILLAGE RD

51

Salem Cottages
BROWNING CL 1
PEACOCK RD 2
BARKER DR 3
WISDOM CL 4
HOWKIN CL 5
GRANGE CT
NEVILLE CL
NEVILLE CRES
GODWIN CL
RANDALLS CL
ROSEMARY DR

2

Burdelys Manor
White's Wood
NORTHAMPTON CRES
TREVOR DR
BROOK WAY
WEBBS CL
BUCKS CL
MILL END

Bury End
Kinsbourne Farm
PH
BERRY DR
STAGSDEN RD
HERONS MEAD
PADDOCKS

PH
Brookside Caravan Park
Bridge End
A5134
A428
BOX END RD
A5134

1

How Wood
Becks Ash Spinney
A22
BEDFORD RD
Wick End Farm
Dropshort Farm
CARTWRIGHT DR

50

98 **A** **B** 99 **C** **D** 00 **E** **F**

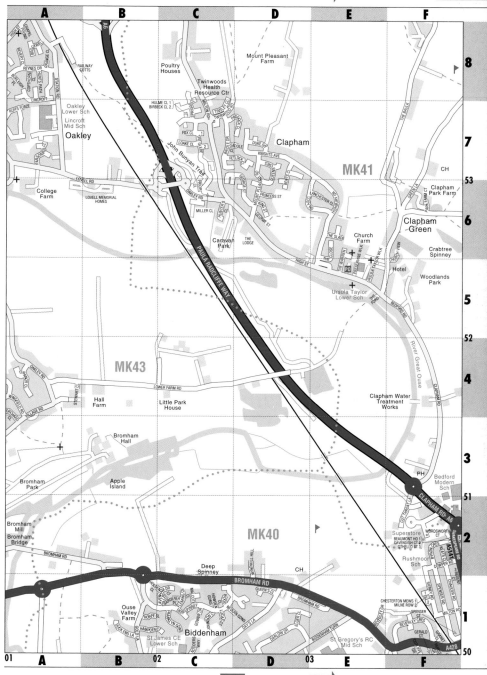

A B C D E F

8

MK44

College Farm

GREEN LA

7

BREAMISH WLK 1
PETTERIL WLK 2
THE GELT 3
SWALE PATH4

Cleat Hill

CLEAT HILL

CH

Mowsbury Hill

Clapham Park Wood

53

Clapham Park

6

MK41

Little Park Farm

St Thomas More RC Upper Sch

GLENROSE AVE
WAGBURY CL
WAGSTAFFE CL

Putnoe Wood

Mowsbury Park

1 IRVINE CT
2 MEDWAY CT
3 WELLAND CT

John Bunyan Trail

AELFRIC CT 1
MERSEY WLK 2
WESTBURY CT 3
LEIGHTON CT 4
HIGHFIELD 5
EVESHAM CT 6
UPTON CT 7
FRAMPTON CT 8

Beauchamp Mid Sch

Scott Lower Sch

1 SUNNINGDALE WLK
2 TURNBERRY WLK
3 LOWTHER RD
4 PENSHORE CL

WENTWORTH DR
CLARE RD

5

52

Laboratory

Ind Est

MURDOCK RD

Mast

Brickhill

Brickhill Lower Sch

1 LIBRARY WLK
2 LITTLE HEADLANDS
3 GREYSTONE WLK

WOODMERE

4

The Manton Ctr

Mast

Pilgrims Pre-Prep Sch

Pilgrim Ctr

Schs

3

Cemy Crem

1 BRANGWYN GDNS
2 ROMNEY WLK

NEWBURY HO 1
ST MICHAEL'S CTS 2
KIMBOLTON CT 3
RODEAN CT 4

Putnoe

51

Bedford Modern Sch

Bedford Park

Edith Cavell Lower Sch

1 LINDEN CT
2 CULVER HO
3 WARWICK HO
4 STRETFORD CT

Newnham Mid Sch

Univ of Bedfordshire

1 MELBURY CT
2 WENDOVER CT
3 RISBBOROUGH CT

2

A6

CLAPHAM RD

Livingstone Lower Sch

Robinson Pool

3 KENWORTH CT

SIDMOUTH CL 1
SHALDON CT 2 SALTASH

Goldington Mid Sch

A5141

SHAKESPEARE RD

Univ

TAVISTOCK ST

UNION ST

Bedford Park

Bedford (North Wing)

The Place Theatre

Univ of Bedfordshire

A428

1

Univ

TREVOR ST

BROMHAM RD

HM Prison

MK40

ST PETER'S ST

GOLDINGTON RD

A5140

A428

50

A428

DAME ALICE ST

P
A428

Bedford RFC

Bedford Lower Sch

04 A 05 B C 06 D E F

A1
1 REGENT CT
2 MILTON RD
3 STOKE ALBANY MEWS
4 PADBURY HO
5 BEECH CT
6 CYMBELINE CT
7 LANSDOWNE TERR
8 SALISBURY HO
9 BEAUCHAMP CT

B1
1 PRIORY CT
2 NORTH PAR
3 ROISE CT
4 PRIORY TERR
5 GWYN ST
6 BALSALL ST E
7 PEEL ST
8 BOSWELL PL
9 PRINCES ST

10 ALBERT ST
11 COBDEN SQ
12 QUEEN'S CT
13 BOSWELL CT
14 CHANDOS CT
15 ARLINGTON CT

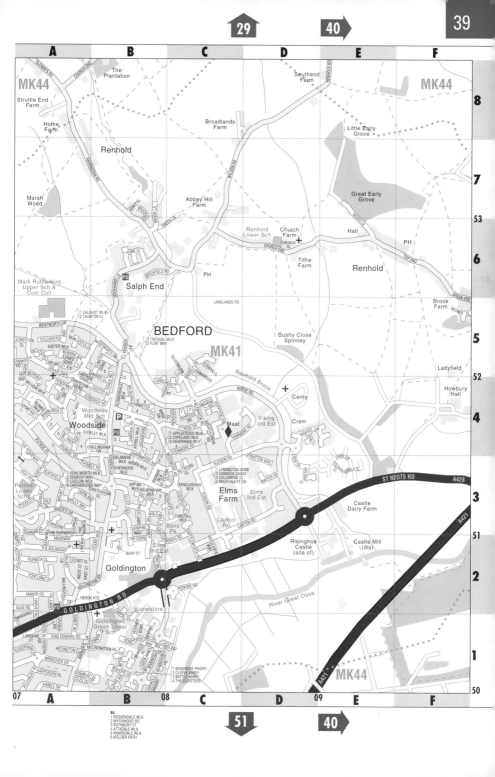

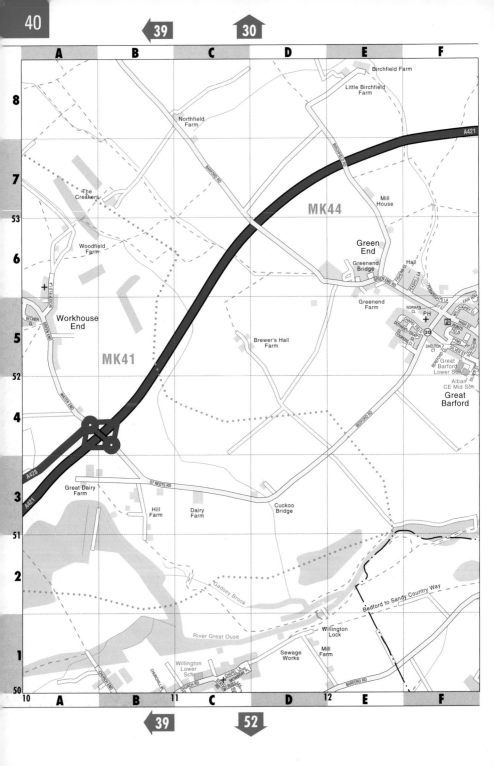

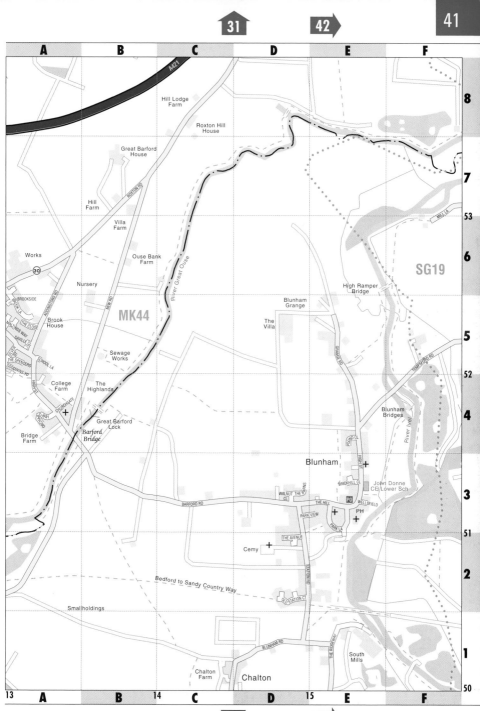

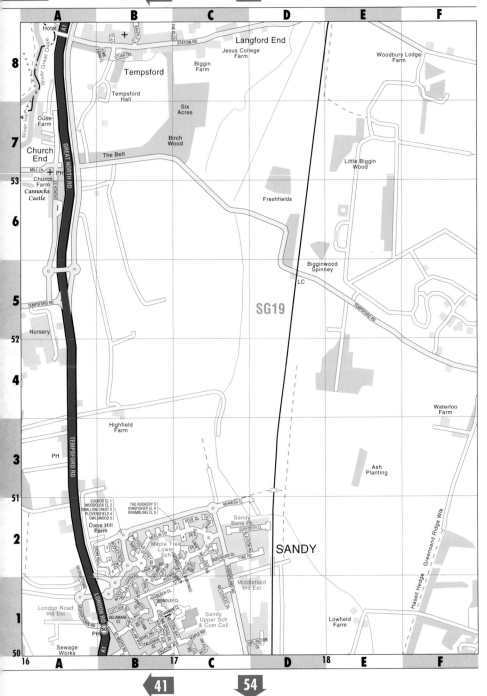

A B C D E F

8

Hotel

Langford End

Jesus College Farm

Woodbury Lodge Farm

Biggin Farm

Tempsford

STATION RD

Tempsford Hall

Six Acres

Birch Wood

7

River Great Ouse

Church End

The Belt

Little Biggin Wood

53

Church Farm
Cannocks Castle

Freshfields

6

GREAT NORTH RD

Bigginwood Spinney

5

TEMPSFORD RD

SG19

LC

TEMPSFORD RD

Nursery

52

4

Highfield Farm

Waterloo Farm

3

PH

Ash Planting

51

CUCKOO CL 1
WOODDOCK CL 2
SWALLOW CREST 3
PLOVERSFIELD 4
OWLSWOOD 5.

BEAMISH CL

THE ROOKERY 3
KINGFISHER CL 4
BRAMBLING CL 5.

DOVE CL

Sandy Bsns Pk

Dane Hill Farm

Maple Tree Lower Sch

GOSFORTH CL

SANDY

2

TYNE RD

Greensand Ridge Wlk

Middlefield Ind Est

Hasell Hedge

1

London Road Ind Est

50

Sandy Upper Sch & Com Coll

DARLINGTON

Lowfield Farm

PH

LONDON RD

Sewage Works

50

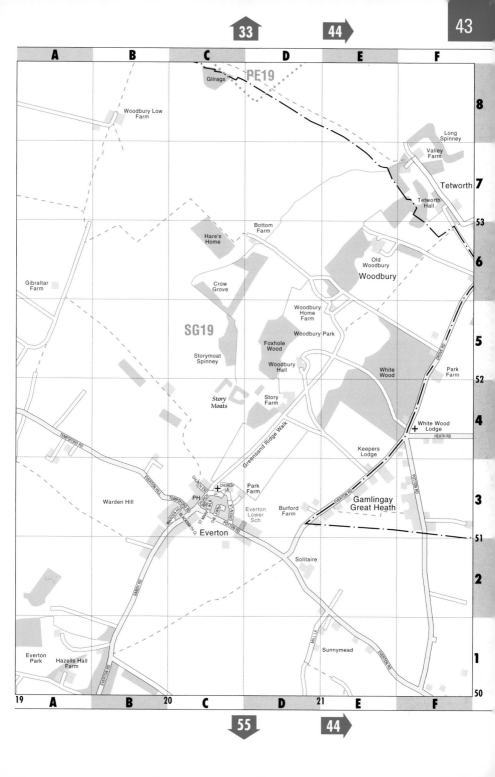

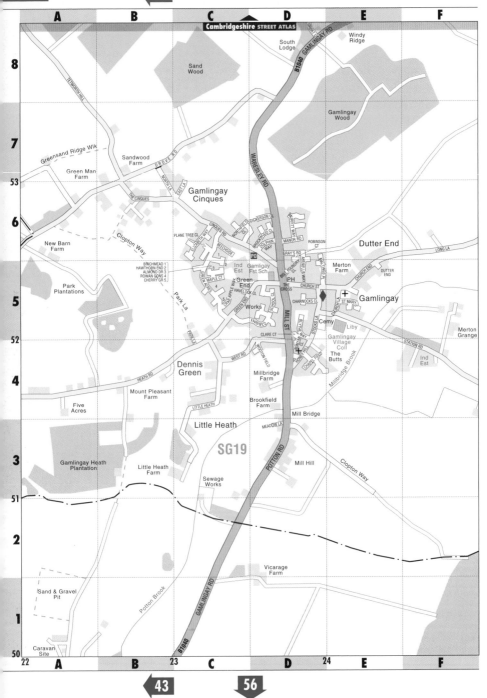

Cambridgeshire STREET ATLAS

8

South Lodge

B1040 GAMLINGAY RD

Windy Ridge

Sand Wood

7

WARESLEY RD

Gamlingay Wood

Greensand Ridge Wlk

53

Green Man Farm

Sandwood Farm

GROVE RD

NORTH LA

CASTLE LA

Gamlingay Cinques

6

THE CINQUES

Clopton Way

PLANE TREE CL

CINQUES RD

ELIZABETH WAY

NORTH END

DICKERSON CL

BROOKEND CL

DOLPHIN WAY

NORTH WAY

MANOR RD

ROBINSON CT

Dutter End

LONG LA

New Barn Farm

BEECHSIDE

P.O

GRAY'S RD

Merton Farm

CHURCH END

DUTTER END

Park Plantations

BIRCHMEAD 1
HAWTHORN END 2
ALMOND DR 3
ROWAN GDNS 4
CHERRY GR 5

JOHN MAPLE CT

Ind Est

Gamligay Fst Sch

Green End

HAVELOCK CL

THE CROSS

PH

CHURCH ST

AVENELL'S WAY

HASTINGS PL

Gamlingay

Park La

PARK LA

CRAB APPLE WAY

GREEN END

Works

4

Merton Grange

5

CLARE CT

FAIRLY

Cemy

ST MARY

CHARNOCKS CL

Liby

STATION RD

52

WEST RD

POTTON FIELD

Gamlingay Village Coll

Ind Est

Dennis Green

HEATH RD

MILL ST

The Butts

Millbridge Brook

Millbridge Farm

Mount Pleasant Farm

Five Acres

LITTLE HEATH

Brookfield Farm

Mill Bridge

4

Little Heath

MEADOW LA

Gamlingay Heath Plantation

Little Heath Farm

SG19

POTTON RD

Mill Hill

Clopton Way

3

Sewage Works

51

2

Sand & Gravel Pit

Vicarage Farm

Potton Brook

GAMLINGAY RD

1

B1040

Caravan Site

50

22

A

B

23

C

D

24

E

F

Cambridgeshire STREET ATLAS

SG19

B1046

Model Farm

B1046

Airfield

Ash Tree Cottage

Fuller's Hill Farm

Crooked Billet Farm

LONG LA

Millbridge Brook

HATLEY RD

Castle Farm

Newlands Buildings

Newlands Cottages

West Lodge

North Lodge

Church Farm

Stud Bungalow

Hatley Park

Hatley St George

ST GEORGES TOWER

MAIN ST

Stud Cottage

Dower House

Hatley Park

Wood Farm

Cockayne Hatley Wood

Potton Wood

Pincote Barn

BUFF LA

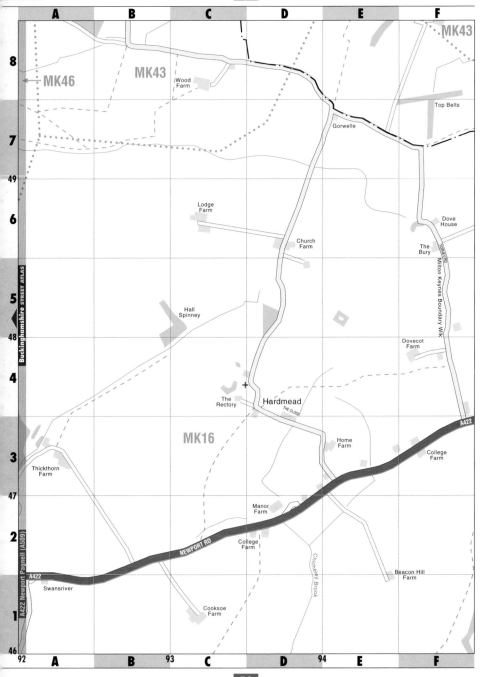

MK43

MK46

MK43

Wood Farm

Top Belts

Gorwelle

Lodge Farm

Dove House

The Bury

Church Farm

Hall Spinney

Dovecot Farm

The Rectory

Hardmead

THE CLOSE

MK16

Home Farm

College Farm

Thickthorn Farm

Manor Farm

College Farm

Chicheley Brook

Beacon Hill Farm

NEWPORT RD

A422

Swansriver

A422

Cooksoe Farm

Milton Keynes Boundary Wlk

TURVEY RD

A422 Newport Pagnell (A509)

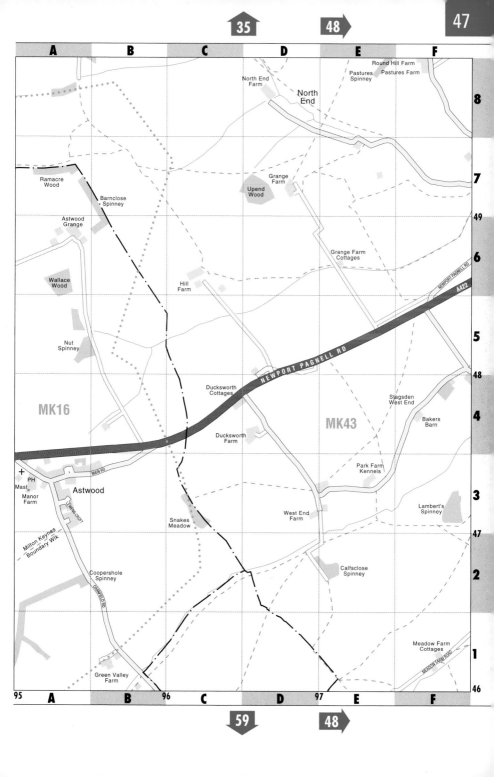

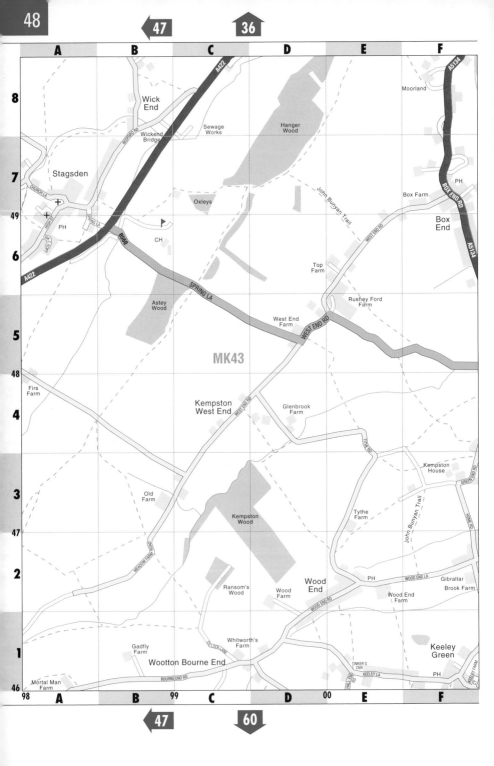

A   B   C   D   E   F

8

Moorland

A422

Wick End

Wickend Bridge

Sewage Works

Hanger Wood

A5134

7

Stagsden

Oxleys

John Bunyan Trail

Box Farm

PH

BOX END RD

49

PH

CH

Box End

SPRING LA

WEST END RD

A5134

6

B560

A422

Astey Wood

Top Farm

Rushey Ford Farm

West End Farm

WEST END RD

5

MK43

48

Firs Farm

Kempston West End

WEST END RD

Glenbrook Farm

4

Kempston House

GREEN END RD

3

Old Farm

Kempston Wood

Tythe Farm

John Bunyan Trail

RIDGE RD

47

MEADOW FARM RD

2

Ransom's Wood

Wood Farm

Wood End

PH

WOOD END LA

Wood End Farm

Gibraltar Brook Farm

KEELEY FARM LA

1

Gadfly Farm

Whitworth's Farm

DILLOCK LANE

Wootton Bourne End

BOURNE END RD

TINKER'S CNR

HALL END RD

KEELEY LA

Keeley Green

PH

46

Mortal Man Farm

98 A   B 99 C   D 00 E   F

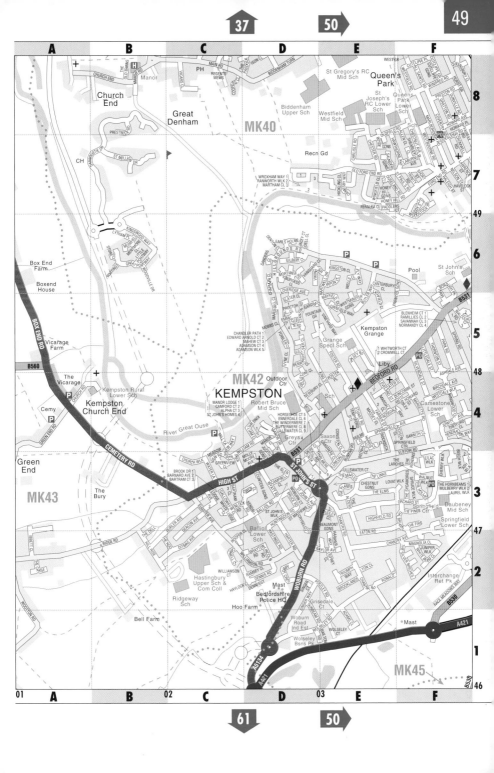

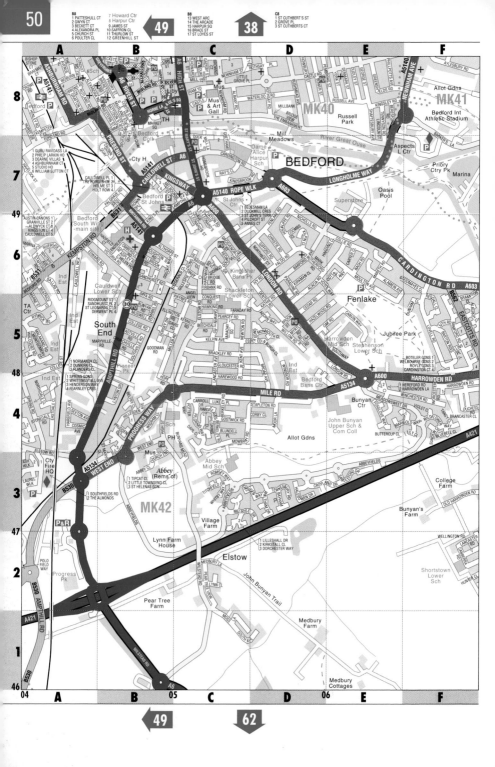

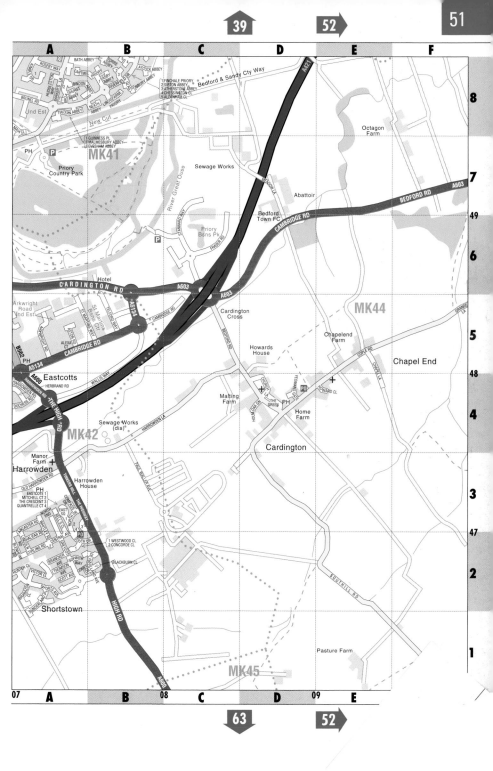

51
40

8

Works

Manor
Farm

Dovecote

CHURCH END

CHURCH RD

Willington

PH

GOSTWICK PL

STATION RD

BALES LA

GRANGE

Nursery

BARFORD RD

Willowhill
Farm

Willowhill
Cottages

PO

SANDY RD

A603

7

Dog
Farm

BEDFORD RD

A603

Nurseries

Gravel Pit
Spinney

WOOD LA

49

ALL SAINTS RD

WILLINGTON RD

Home
Farm

Hill
Farm

Conduit
Grove

6

PYE CROS

Cople

Grange
Farm

Cople
Lower Sch

BURA C CO T

GRANGE LA

PH

5

WOODLANDS CL

48

MK44

4

WATER RD

Water
End

Middle
Farm

3

NORTHILL RD

Hoo
Farm

47

2

Wood End
Farm

Mox Hill

SG18

Oak
Farm

1

Moxhill
Farm

Sweetbrier
Cottage

46

10   A   B   11   C   D   12   E   F

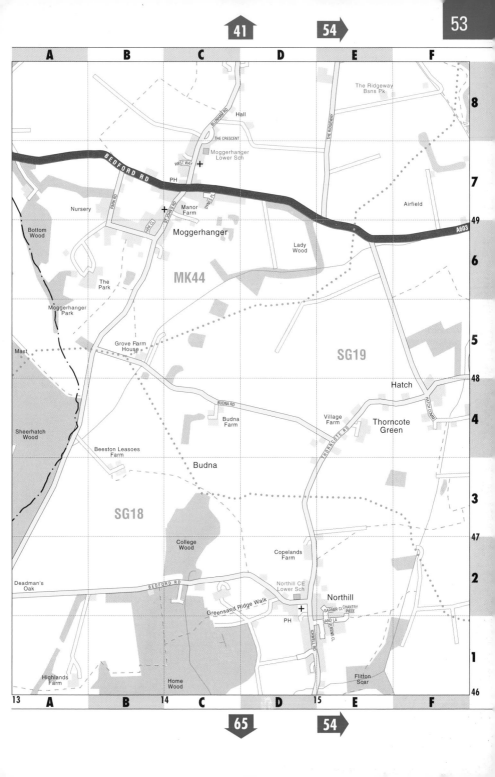

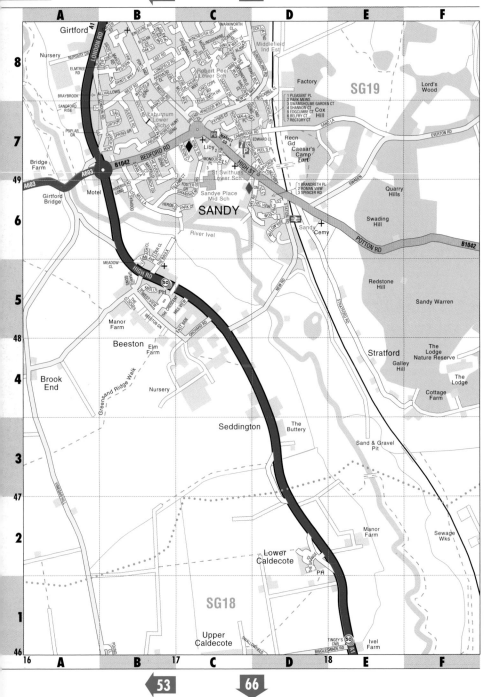

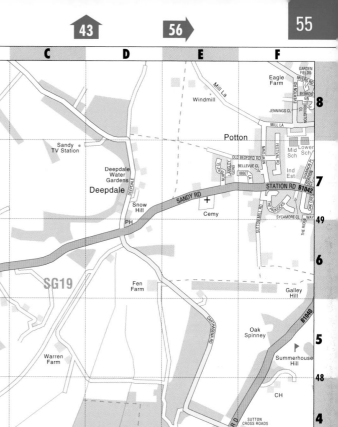
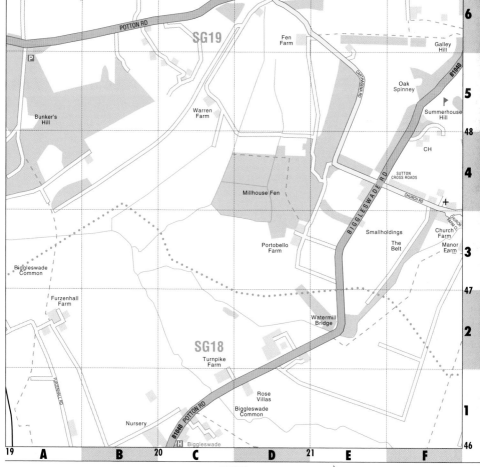

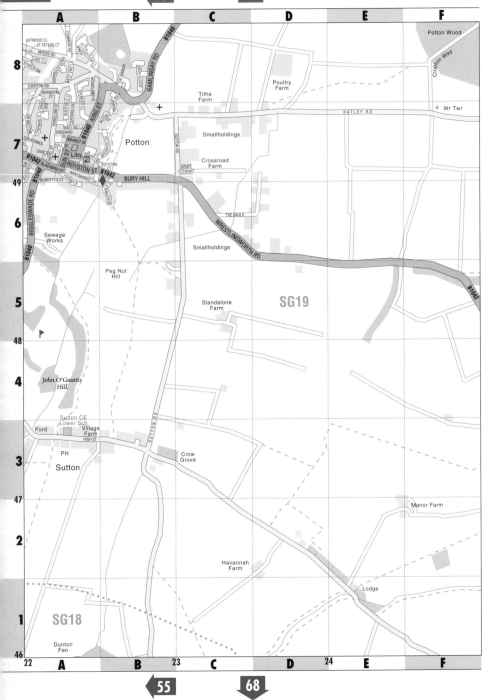

A B C D E F

8

ASTWOOD CL
ST PETERS CT
MYERS RD
COMMON RD
BYARDS GM

GAMLINGAY RD
B1040

Potton Wood

CLOPTON WAY

EVERTON RD
BURGOYNE
CT

WOODLAND CT

JUDITH GDNS
THE MANOR

Tithe
Farm

Poultry
Farm

7

CATHERINES
ORCHARD
MEETING LA
MARKET SQ
BULL ST

Potton

SUTTON RD

Smallholdings

HATLEY RD

Wr Twr

Liby

ROYSTON ST

Crossroad
Farm

CROFT
STEWART

ROYSTON

49

B1042
BLACKBIRD ST

BRAYBROOKE LA
BURDETT'S CT

BURY HILL

B1042

THE BAULK

6

B1040

Sewage
Works

WRESTLINGWORTH RD

BIGGLESWADE RD

Smallholdings

Peg Nut
Hill

5

SG19

Standalone
Farm

48

4

John O'Gaunts
Hill

SUTTON RD

Sutton CE
Lower Sch

3

Ford

Village
Farm
HIGH ST

Crow
Grove

PH

Sutton

47

Manor Farm

2

Havannah
Farm

Lodge

1

SG18

Dunton
Fen

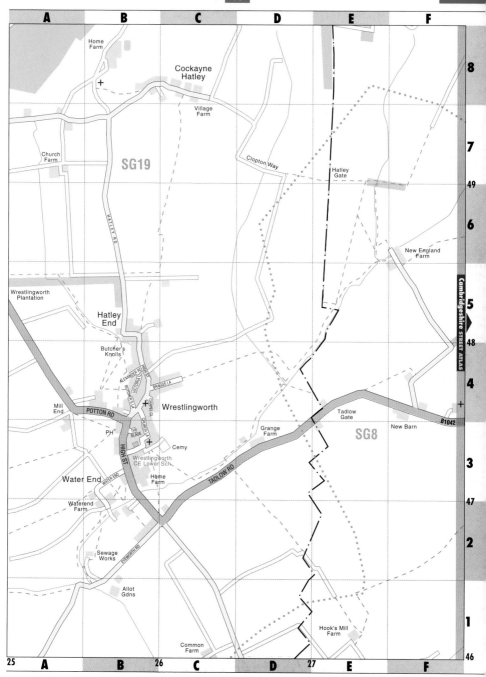

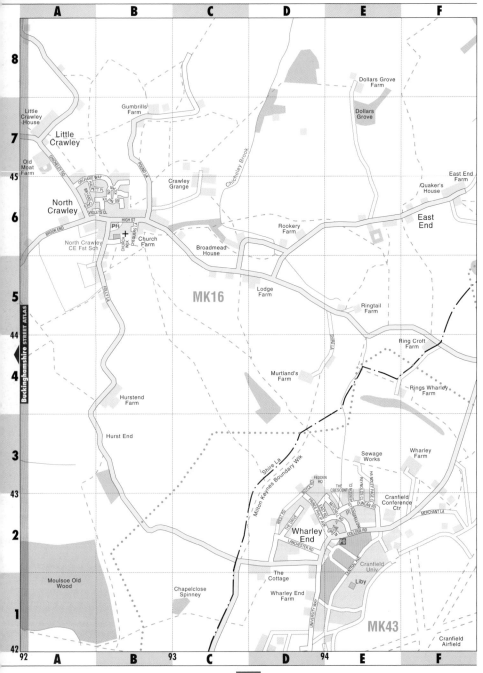

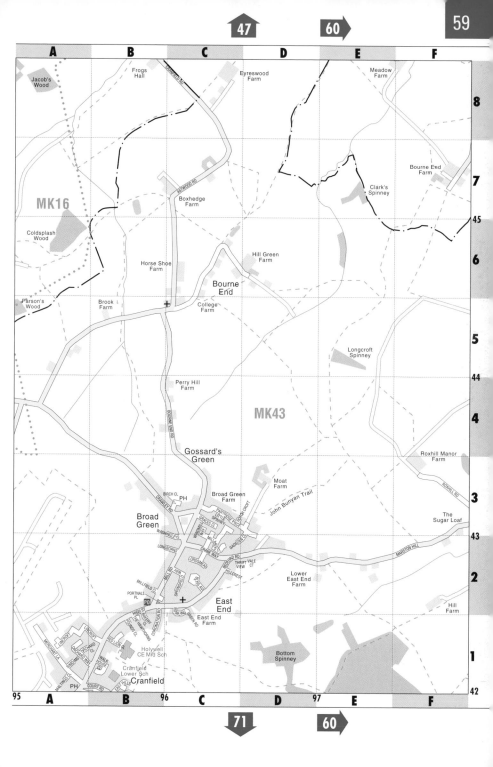

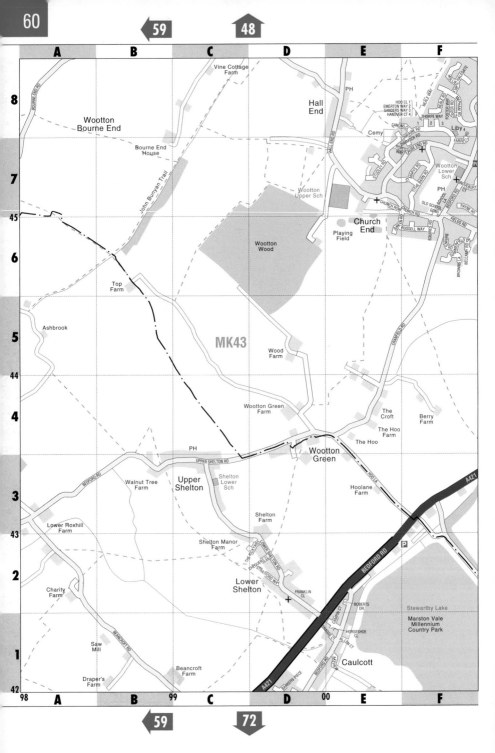

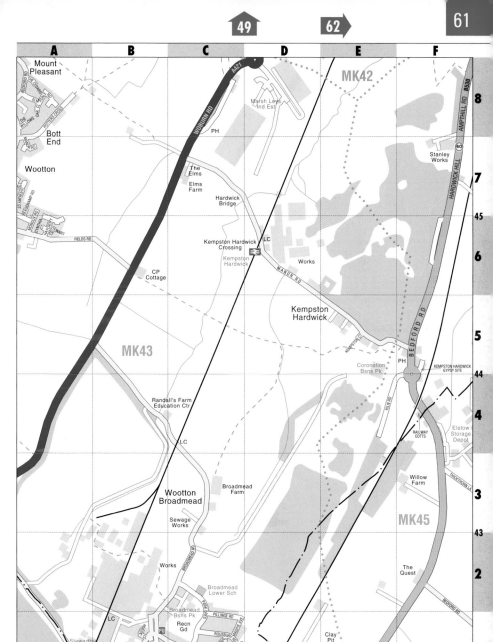

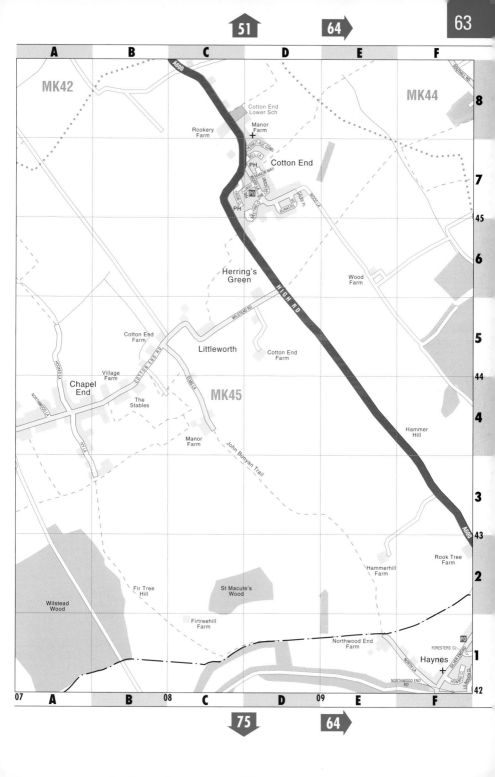

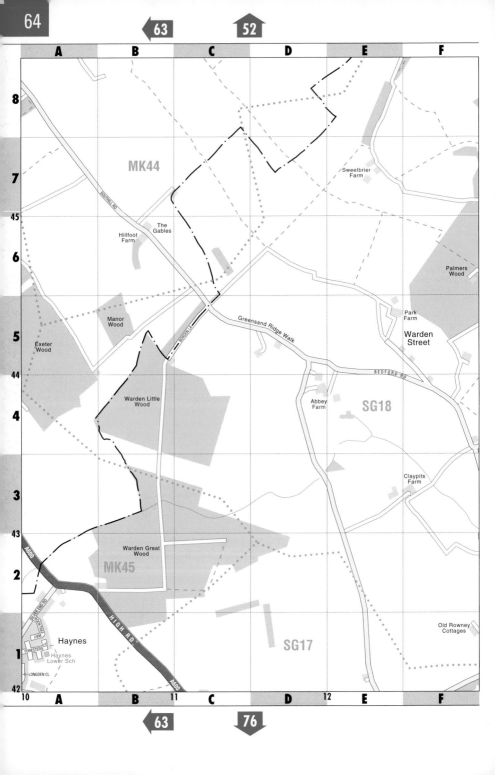

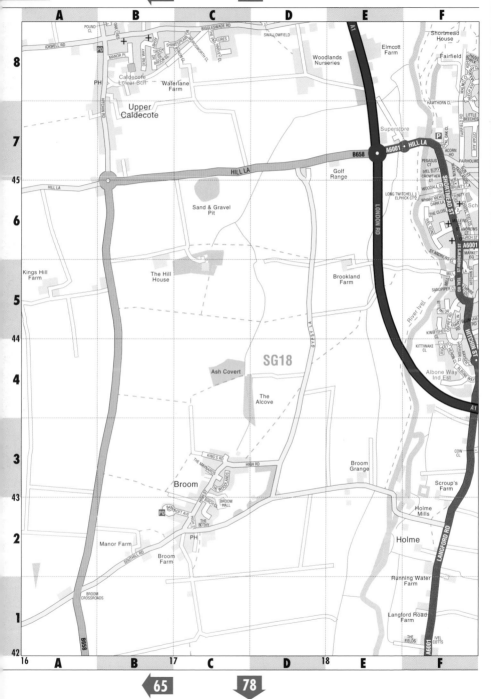

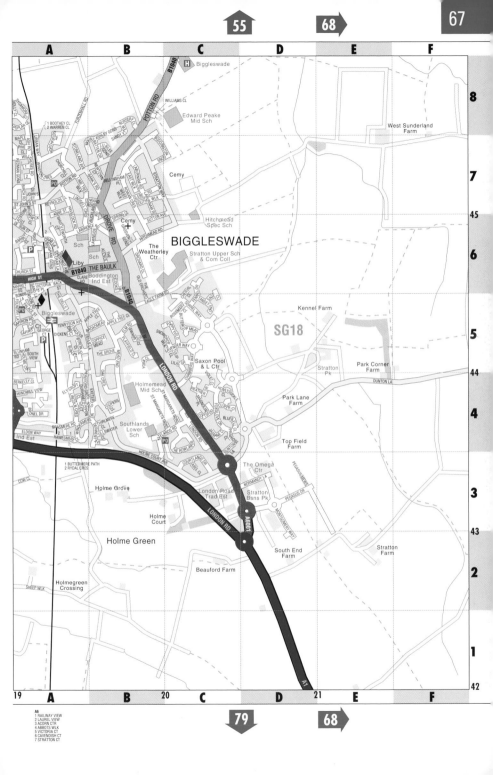

67
56

A **B** **C** **D** **E** **F**

8

Dunton Fen

Sunderland Hall
Farm

SUTTON RD

Eyeworth

SG19

SUTTON RD

HIGH ST

Church Farm

7

45

6

CAMBRIDGE RD

Water
Works

Newton

Newton Grove
Farm

Sewage
Works

Middlesex
Farm

GREENFIELD
WAY

KINGS POND CL

OLD
BAKERY
YD

HORSESH CL

HALLSIDE

Dunton
Lower Sch

PO

HIGH ST

PH

CHURCH ST

CHAPEL

LIME TREE

RD CL

SPRINGFIELD

Dunton

Church
Farm

5

BIGGLESWADE RD

44

SG18

4

Millow Hall
Farm

Millow Lodge
Farm

Millow

Millow Hill
Farm

River Cam or Rhee

3

43

Millowbury
Farm

Plantation
Farm

SG7

2

1

Green La

42

22 **A** **B** 23 **C** **D** 24 **E** **F**

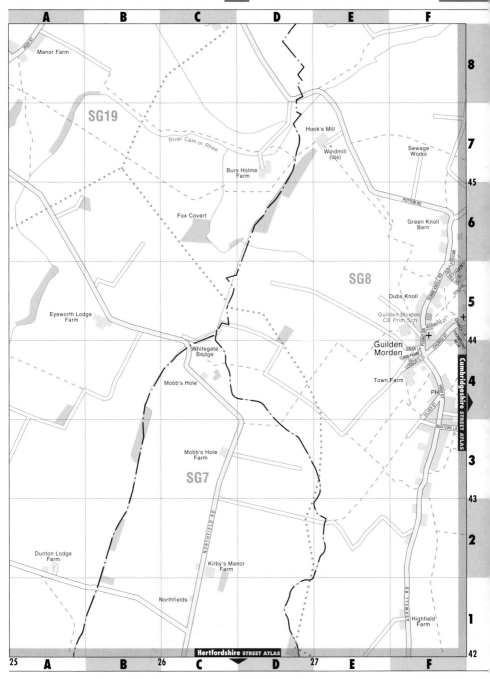

A B C D E F

8

7

45

6

SG19

River Cam or Rhee

Manor Farm

Hook's Mill

Windmill (dis)

Sewage Works

Bury Holme Farm

POTTON RD

Green Knoll Barn

Fox Covert

SG8

Dubs Knoll

5

44

Eyeworth Lodge Farm

Guilden Morden CE Prim Sch

Guilden Morden

SWAN LA
TOWN FARM
CONDUIT ST

Whitegate Bridge

Town Farm

4

Mobb's Hole

PH

SILVER ST

BUXTONS LA

Mobb's Hole Farm

3

SG7

43

NORTHFIELD RD

2

Dunton Lodge Farm

Kirby's Manor Farm

ASHWELL RD

Northfields

Highfield Farm

1

42

25 A B 26 C D 27 E F

Cambridgeshire STREET ATLAS

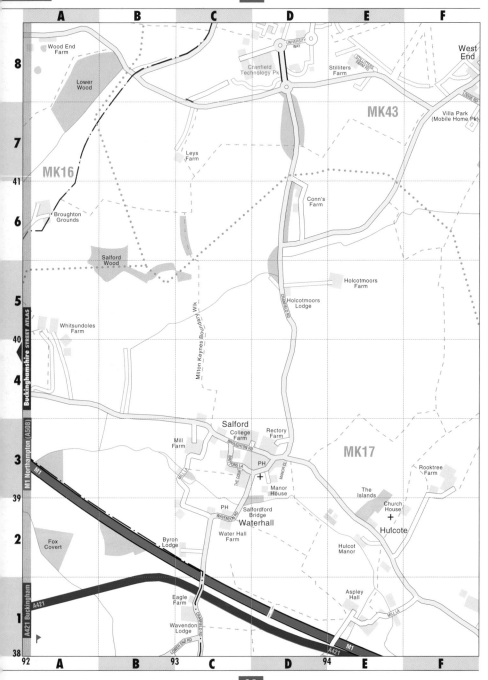

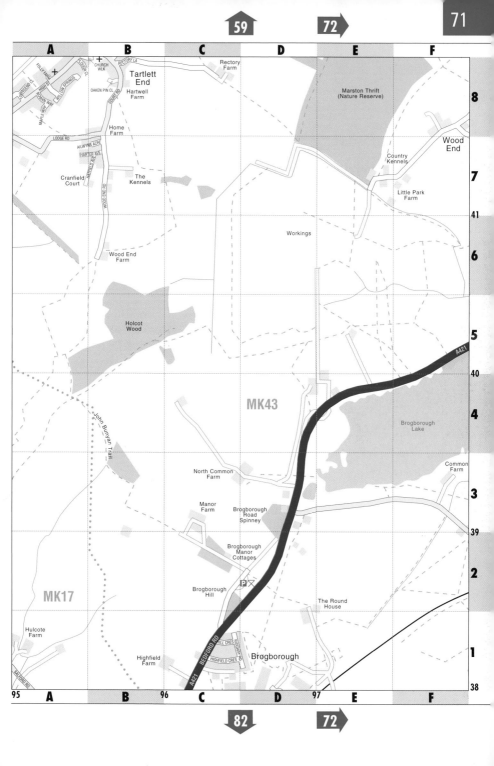

A B C D E F

8

Marston Thrift
(Nature Reserve)

Wood
End

Rectory
Farm

Rectory La

Church
Wlk

Folly Farm

Oaken Pin Cl

Tartlett
End

Hartwell
Farm

Home
Farm

Lodge Rd

Ailwyns Acre

Harter Ave

Cranfield
Court

The
Kennels

Country
Kennels

7

Little Park
Farm

41

Workings

6

Wood End
Farm

5

Holcot
Wood

A421

40

MK43

4

Brogborough
Lake

John Bunyan Trail

North Common
Farm

Common
Farm

3

Manor
Farm

Brogborough
Road
Spinney

39

Brogborough
Manor
Cottages

2

MK17

Brogborough
Hill

The Round
House

P

Hulcote
Farm

Highfield
Farm

Bedford Rd

Hill Cres

Highfield Cres

Brogborough

1

Salford Rd

A421

38

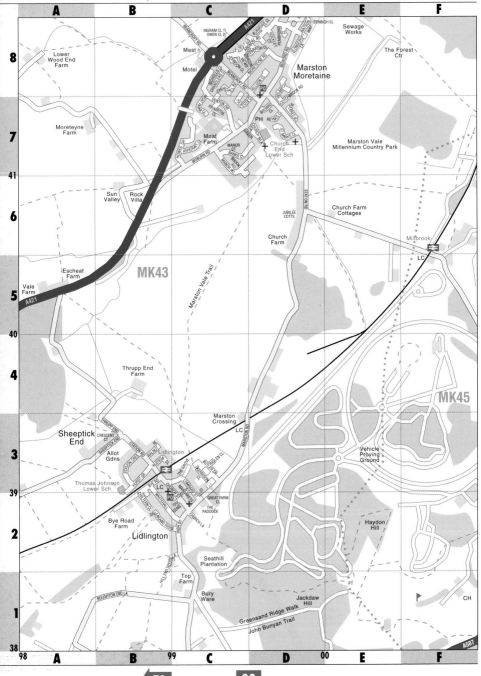

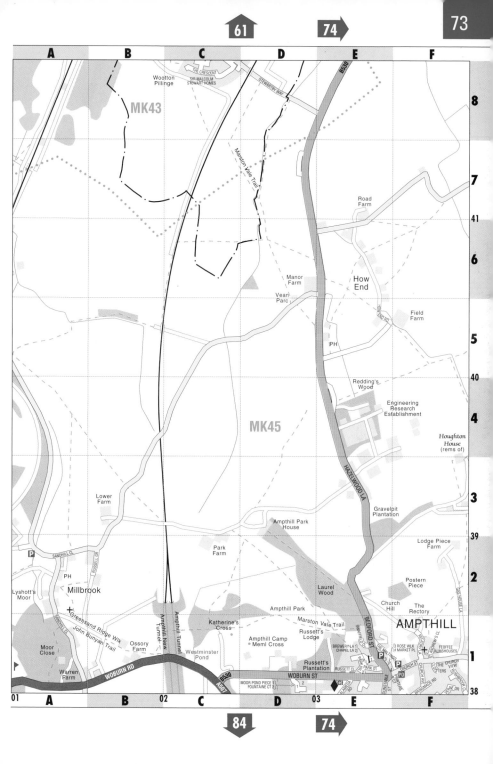

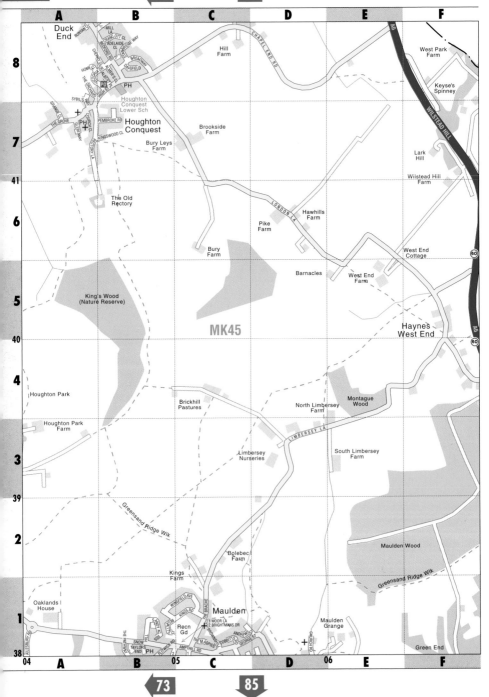

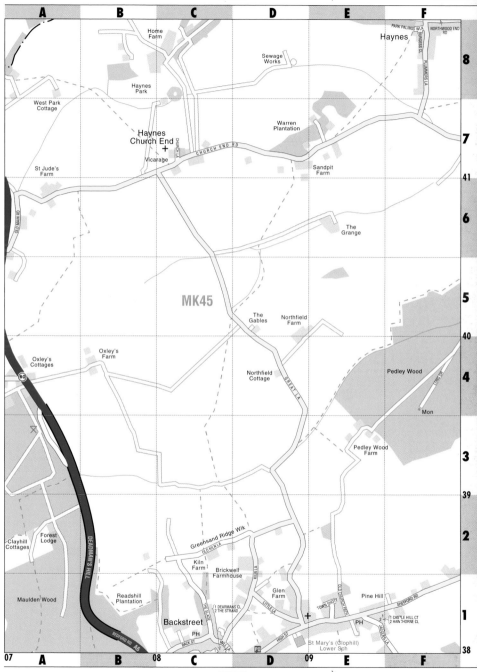

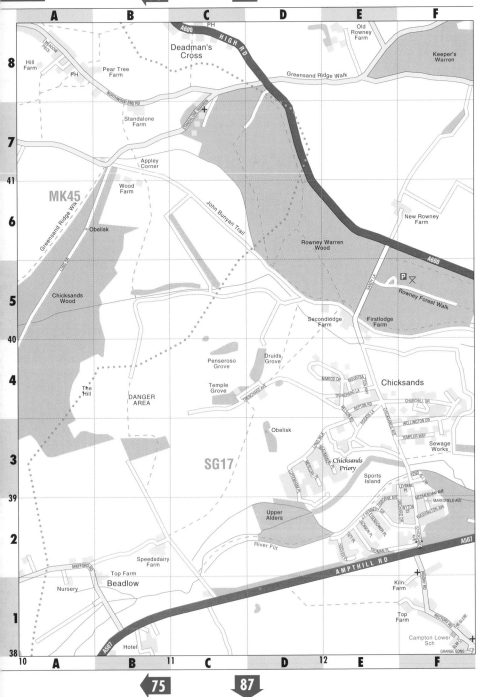

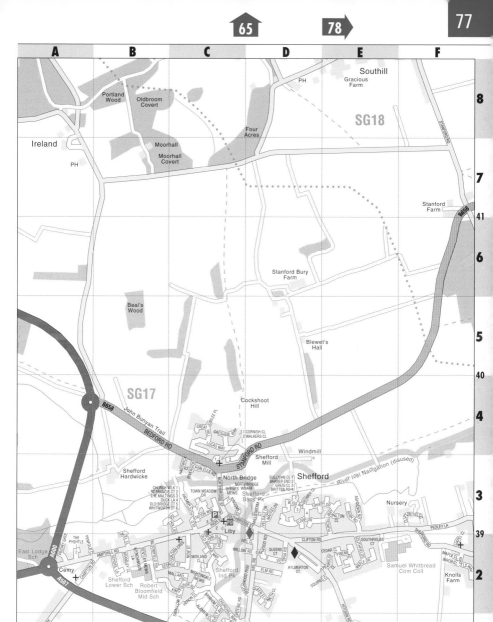

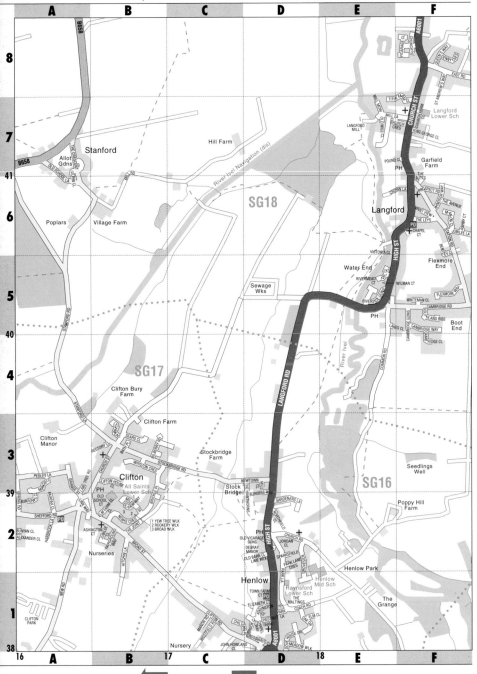

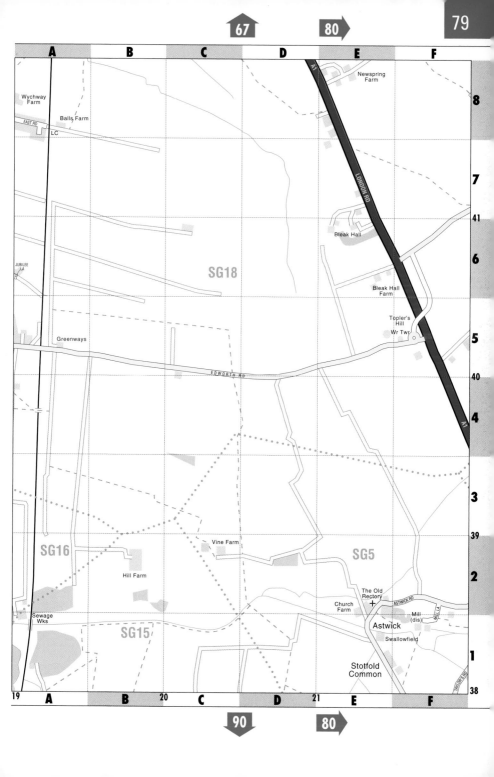

A B C D E F

8
7
41
6
5
40
4
3
39
2
1
38

Newspring Farm

Wychway Farm

Balls Farm

EAST RD

LC

JUBILEE LA

SG18

Bleak Hall

Bleak Hall Farm

Topler's Hill

Wr Twr

LONDON RD

A1

Greenways

EDWORTH RD

SG16

Hill Farm

Vine Farm

SG5

The Old Rectory

Church Farm

ASTWICK RD

Mill (dis)

MILL LA

Astwick

Swallowfield

Sewage Wks

SG15

Stotfold Common

TAYLORS RD

19 20 21

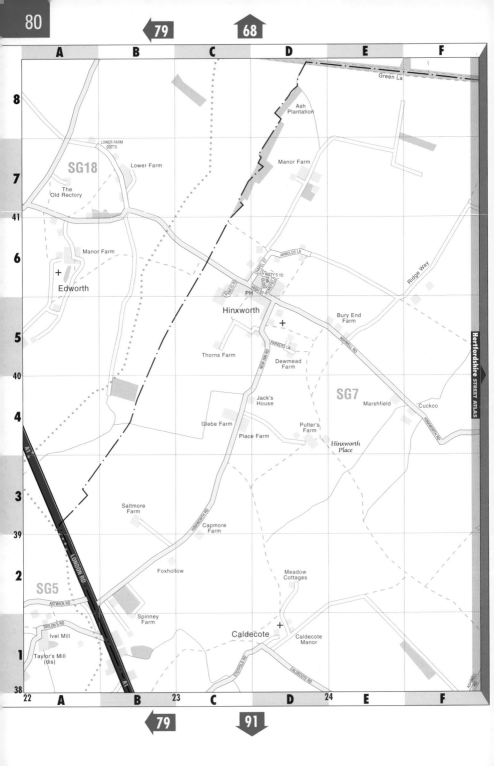

A B C D E F

8

7

SG18

Lower Farm

LOWER FARM
COTTS

The
Old Rectory

41

Ash
Plantation

Manor Farm

Green La

6

Manor Farm

Edworth

ARNOLDS LA

CHAPEL ST

CHRISTY'S YD

PANTERS RD

HIGH ST

PH

Hinxworth

Bury End
Farm

Ridge Way

ASHWELL RD

5

Thorns Farm

PARKERS LA

NEW INN RD

Dewmead
Farm

SG7

Marshfield

Cuckoo

HIXWORTH RD

40

Jack's
House

4

Glebe Farm

Place Farm

Pulter's
Farm

Hinxworth
Place

3

Saltmore
Farm

HINXWORTH RD

Capmore
Farm

39

2

SG5

LONDON RD

Foxhollow

Meadow
Cottages

ASTWICK RD

Spinney
Farm

Caldecote

Caldecote
Manor

1

TAYLOR'S RD

Ivel Mill

Taylor's Mill
(dis)

A1

STOTFOLD RD

CALDECOTE RD

ASHWELL RD

38

22 A B 23 C D 24 E F

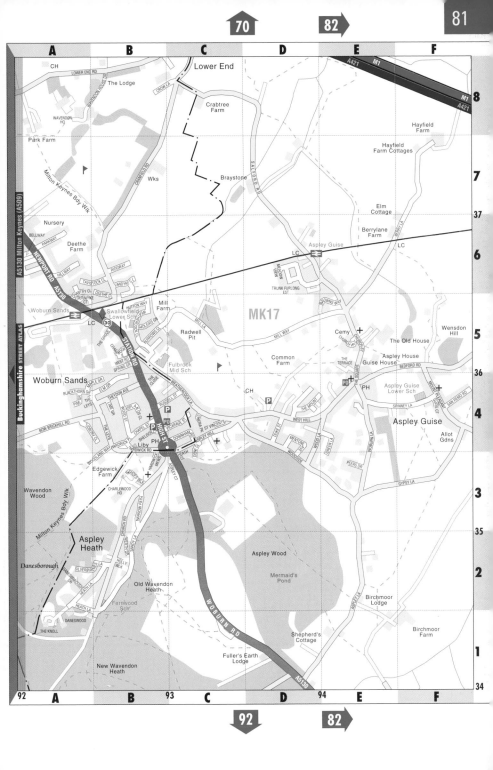

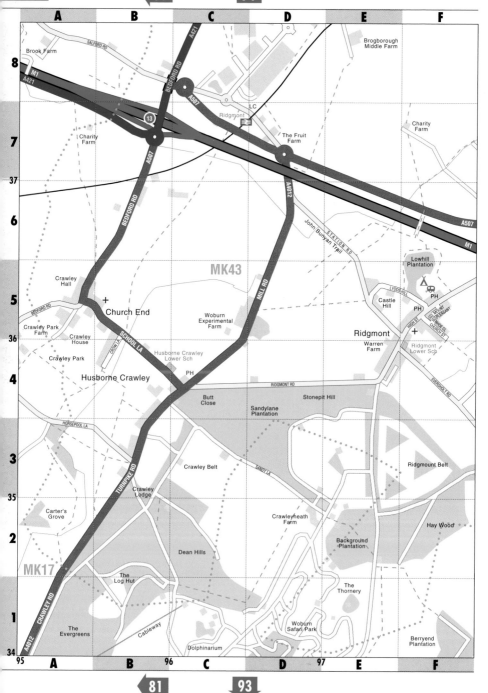

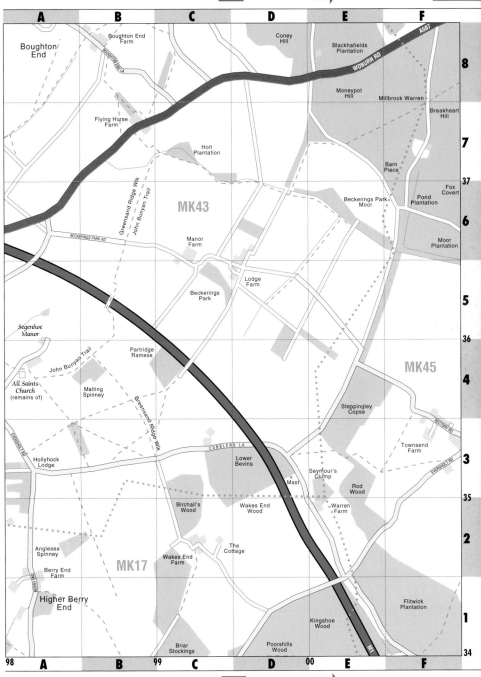

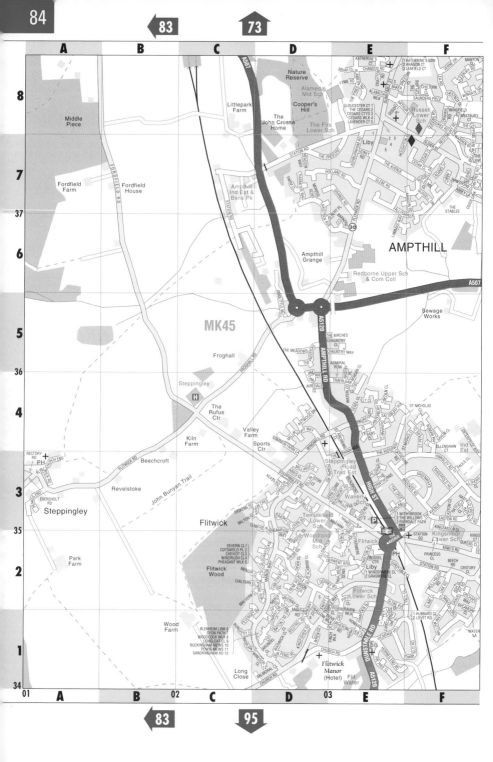

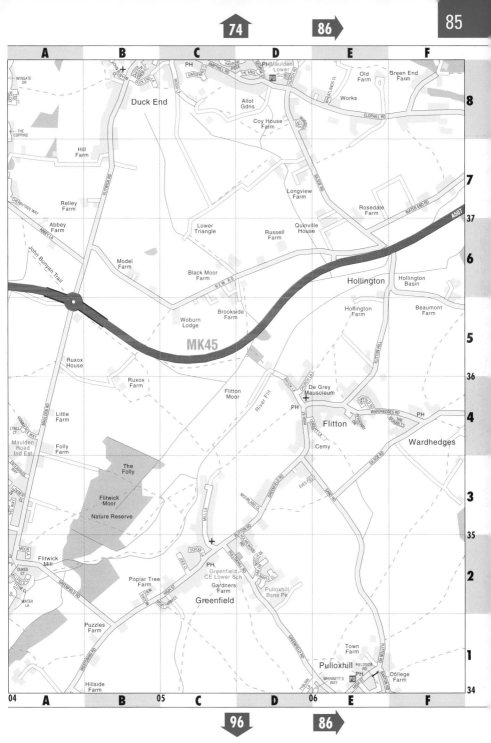

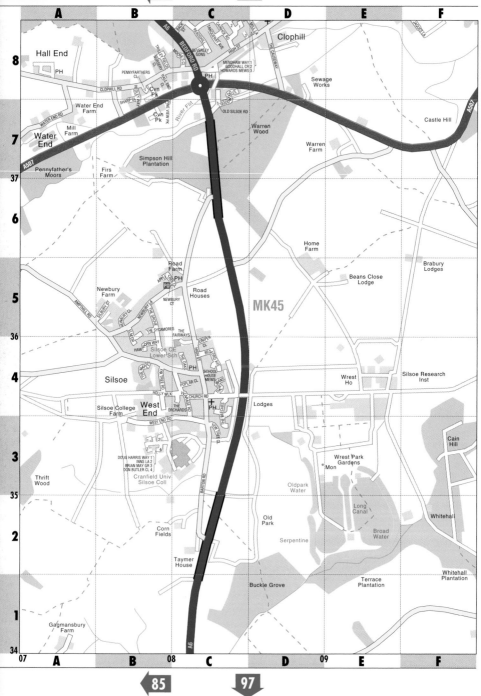

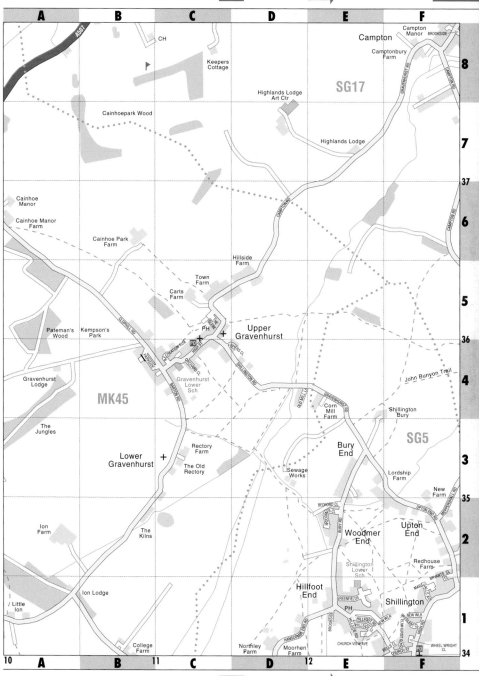

A507

CH
Keepers
Cottage

Campton
Campton Manor
BROOKSIDE

SG17

Campton Manor
Farm

Highlands Lodge
Art Ctr

8

Cainhoepark Wood

Highlands Lodge

7

37

Cainhoe
Manor

Cainhoe Manor
Farm

Cainhoe Park
Farm

Hillside
Farm

6

Pateman's
Wood

Kempson's
Park

CLOPHILL RD

Town
Farm

Carts
Farm

PH

CREATION RISE

Upper
Gravenhurst

5

36

Gravenhurst
Lodge

HIGH ST

ORCHARD CL

MAULDEN RD

PO

Gravenhurst
Lower
Sch

CRANFIELD CL

SHILLINGTON RD

John Bunyon Trail

4

MK45

GRAVENHURST RD

Corn
Mill
Farm

OLD MILL LA

Shillington
Bury

SG5

The
Jungles

Lower
Gravenhurst

Rectory
Farm

The Old
Rectory

Bury
End

Lordship
Farm

3

35

Ion
Farm

The
Kilns

Sewage
Works

BEDFORD CL

WOODMER

BURY RD

Woodmer
End

UPTON END

Upton
End

MEPPERSHALL RD

New
Farm

Redhouse
Farm

2

Ion Lodge

Shillington
Lower
Sch

Hillfoot
End

BRYANTS CL

MARSH

Shillington

1

Little
Ion

College
Farm

Northley
Farm

Moorhen
Farm

GREENFIELDS
PH

HAMECROFT RD

HILLFOOT RD

HILLSUCK

BROOKSIDE

CHURCH VIEW AVE

MILL LANE RD

NEW WLK

NEW WLK
ELMHURST RD

HILL ST

CHURCH ST

WHEEL WRIGHT
CL

PO

34

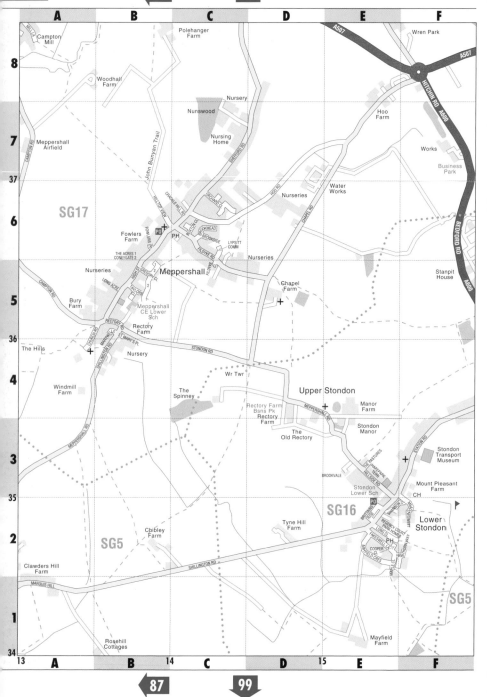

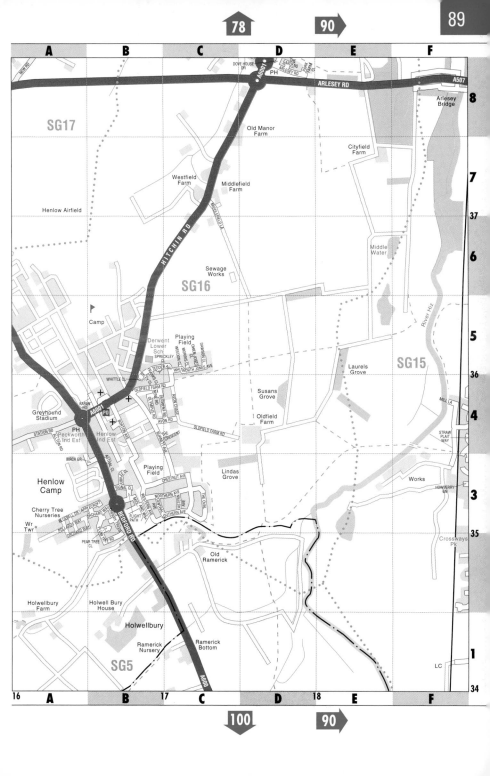

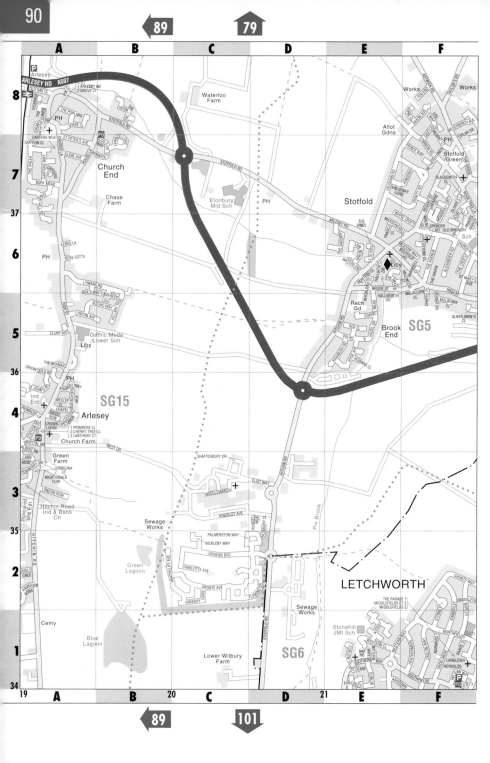

A **B** **C** **D** **E** **F**

8

ARLESEY RD A507
P Arlesey
OLD OAK CL
1 ARLESEY RD
2 GROVE CT

Works
Works

Waterloo
Farm

Allot
Gdns

THE POPLARS
CHASE CL
STOTFOLD RD
PH

PH
Stotfold
Green

7
Church
End

STOTFOLD RD

Etonbury
Mid Sch

PH

Stotfold

37
Chase
Farm

THE
VINES

BLACKSMITH

ARLESEY RD

6
PH
LEWIS LA
ROSE COTTS

WATERLOO
Liby

SG5

LYMANS RD
COX'S WAY EVEREST
GOTHIC WAY
LYNTON AVE

BROOK ST
HALLWORTH
Recn
Gd

Queen Anne's
Cl

5
CLUNY WAY
Gothic Mede
Lower Sch
Liby

Brook
End

36
THE GRANARY
CRICKETERS RD
PH

SG15
Ind
Est

4
Arlesey
1 PRIMROSE CL
2 CHERRY TREE CL
3 LANTHONY CT
Church Farm
WEST DR

Green
Farm
GEORGINA
CT
NIGHTINGALE
TERR
LONDON ROW

SHAFTESBURY DR
ELIOT WAY
HITCHIN RD

3
MIDDLEMARCH

Pix Brook

Hitchin Road
Ind & Bsns
Ctr

KINGSLEY AVE

Sewage
Works

PALMERSTON WAY

35

NICKLEBY WAY

2
JUBILEE
CRES

Green
Lagoon

DICKENS BLVD
CHARLOTTE AVE
BRONTE AVE

SG6

LETCHWORTH

THE PARADE
MIDDLEFIELDS CT
MIDDLEFIELDS

Cemy

FARADAY

Sewage
Works

Stonehill
JMI Sch

LANGLEIGH
REYNOLDS
P

1
Blue
Lagoon

Lower Wilbury
Farm

STOTFOLD RD

SG6

34

A **B** **C** **D** **E** **F**

19
20
21

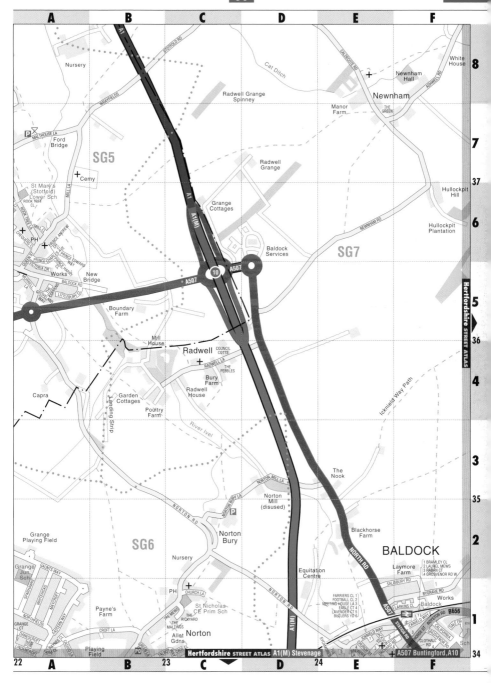

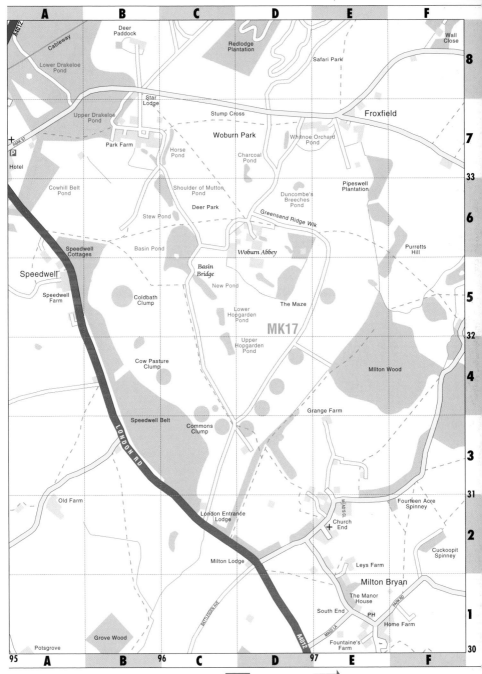

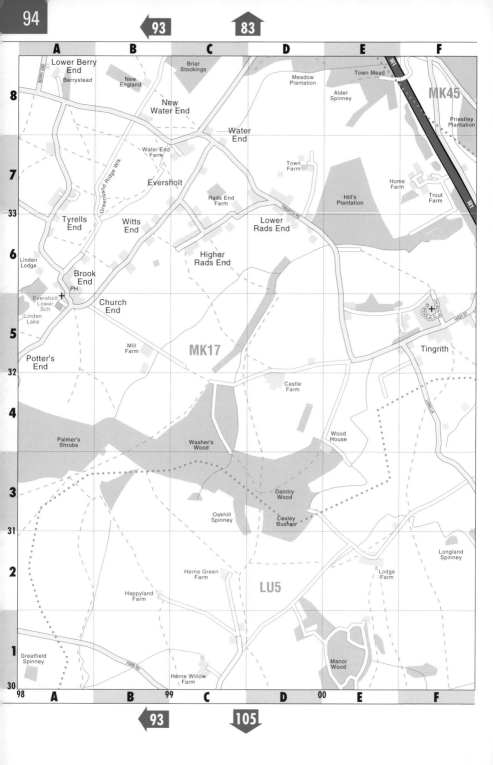

93
83

Lower Berry
End
Berrystead
New
England
Briar
Stockings
Meadow
Plantation
Town Mead
MK45

New
Water End
Alder
Spinney
Priestley
Plantation

Water End
Farm
Water
End
Town
Farm
Home
Farm
Trout
Farm

Greensand Ridge Wlk
Eversholt
Hill's
Plantation

Rads End
Farm
TINGRITH RD

Tyrells
End
Witts
End
Lower
Rads End

Linden
Lodge
Higher
Rads End

Brook
End
PH
Eversholt
Lower
Sch
Church
End
Tingrith
HIGH ST
CHURCH

Linden
Lake
MK17

Potter's
End
Mill
Farm
Tingrith

Castle
Farm
LODGE LA

Palmer's
Shrubs
Washer's
Wood
Wood
House

Daintry
Wood

Oakhill
Spinney
Cexley
Bushes

Longland
Spinney

Herne Green
Farm
LU5
Lodge
Farm

Happyland
Farm

Greatfield
Spinney
PARK RD
Manor
Wood

Herne Willow
Farm

93
105

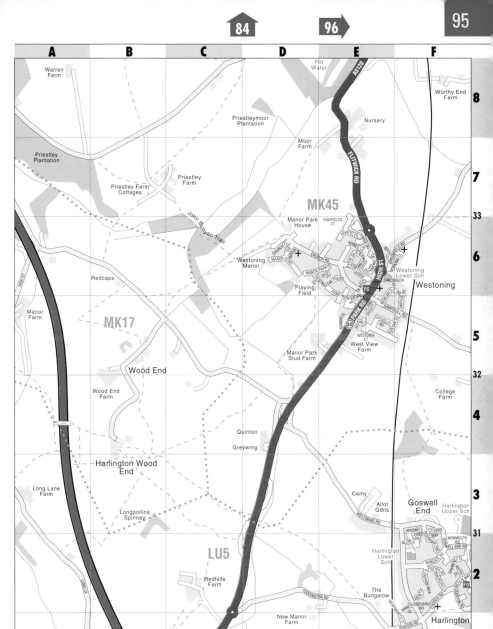

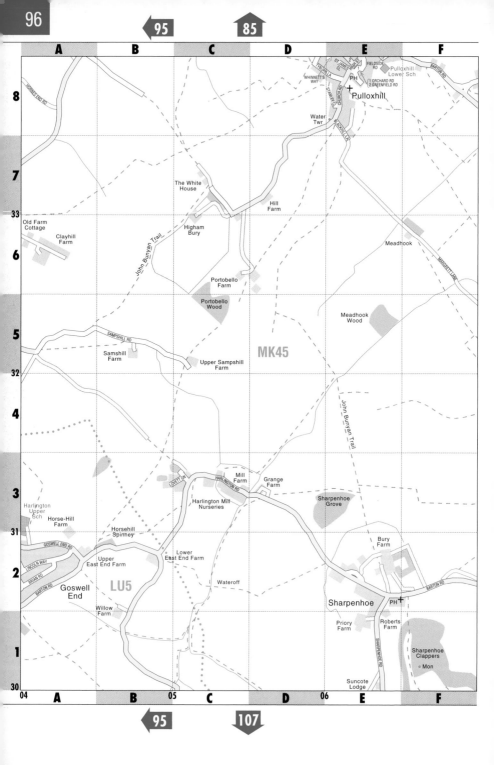

95
85

A **B** **C** **D** **E** **F**

8

7

33

6

5

32

4

3

31

2

1

30

HORSES END RD

Pulloxhill
PH
Water Twr

ST JAMES RD
FIELDSIDE RD
Pulloxhill Lower Sch
BARTON RD

WHINNETT'S WAY
GREENFIELD RD
STAIRWAY LA
CHURCH RD
1 ORCHARD RD
2 GREENFIELD RD
BLACKSHILL LA

The White House
Hill Farm

Old Farm Cottage
Clayhill Farm
Higham Bury

Meadhook
MARQUETTE LANE

John Bunyan Trail

Portobello Farm

Portobello Wood

MK45

Meadhook Wood

SAMPSHILL RD
Samshill Farm
Upper Sampshill Farm

John Bunyan Trail

Mill Farm
LYCETT CN
HARLINGTON RD
Grange Farm

Harlington Upper Sch
Horse-Hill Farm
Horsehill Spinney

Harlington Mill Nurseries

Sharpenhoe Grove

Bury Farm

GOSWELL END RD
LINCOLN WAY
Upper East End Farm
Lower East End Farm

Goswell End
LU5
BRIAN RD
BARTON RD

Willow Farm

Wateroff

Sharpenhoe
PH

BARTON RD

Priory Farm
Roberts Farm

SHARPENHOE RD

Sharpenhoe Clappers
Mon

Suncote Lodge

A **B** **C** **D** **E** **F**

04 05 06

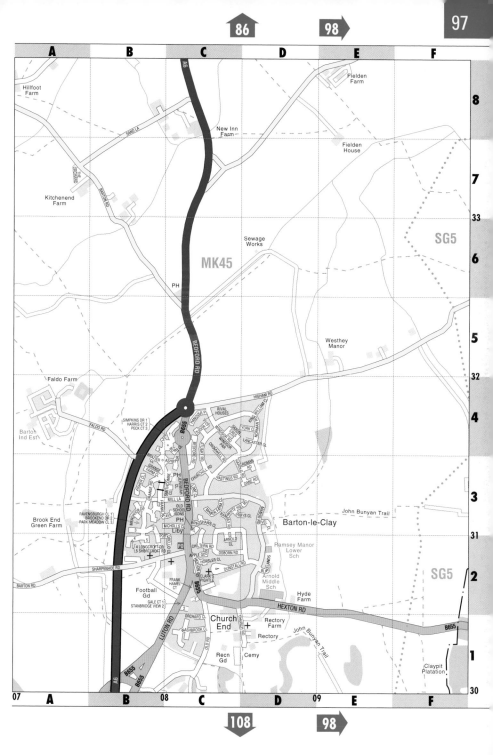

97
87

	A	B	C	D	E	F

8

Ion Bridge Farm

Archers Farm

PH

MK45

Hanscombe End Farm

Parsonage Farm

Hanscombe End

7

Chalkybush Farm

Apsley End

Manor Cottage

Higham Cottages

Green Farm

33

Manor Farm

Pirton Grange Farm

Pirton Hall

Manor Farm Bsns Pk

Pirton Grange

Wesley Spinney

6

Higham Gobion

Apsleybury Wood

PH

Lowerpiece Spinnies

Ravendale Farm

5

Apsley Bury Farm

Shillington Manor

32

Hexton Common

Common La

Kettledean Farm

4

John Bunyan Trail

SG5

3

The Mill

MILL LA

31

Sewage Works

Manor Farm

The Curl Paper

Pegsdon Common Farm

2

PH

Hexton

Green End Farm

Pegsdon Belt

Church Wood

PO

DAIRY COTTS

Hexton Manor

The Rookery

Bury Farm

Hexton JMI Sch

Pegsdon

B655

BARTON RD

PH

HITCHIN RD

PEGSDON WAY

1

The Butts

Bonfirehill Knoll

B655

30

10	A	B	11	C	D	12	E	F

97
109

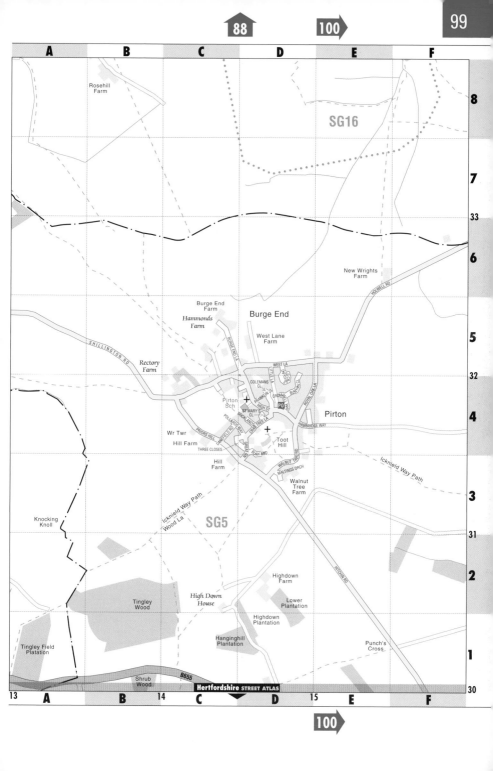

A   B   C   D   E   F

8

7

33

6

SG16

Rosehill Farm

New Wrights Farm

HOLWELL RD

Burge End Farm

Hammonds Farm

Burge End

West Lane Farm

SHILLINGTON RD

Rectory Farm

5

32

WEST LA

COLEMANS CL

LITTLE GN

FRANCIS W

BUNYAN CL

GROVE C

ROYAL OAK LA

Pirton

4

Pirton Sch

ST MARY HIGH ST

CRAB TREE LA

POLLARDS WAY

Wr Twr

Hill Farm

PRIORS HILL

DANEFIELD RD

BURY END

GREAT GN

SHAW GRN

Toot Hill

GREAT LA

HAMBRIDGE WAY

Icknield Way Path

Hill Farm

THREE CLOSES

WALNUT ORCH

MALTINGS ORCH

Walnut Tree Farm

3

31

Knocking Knoll

Icknield Way Path
Wood La

SG5

Highdown Farm

HITCHIN RD

2

Tingley Wood

High Down House

Lower Plantation

Highdown Plantation

Hanginghill Plantation

Punch's Cross

1

Tingley Field Platation

Shrub Wood

B655

Hertfordshire STREET ATLAS

30

13   A   B   14   C   D   15   E   F

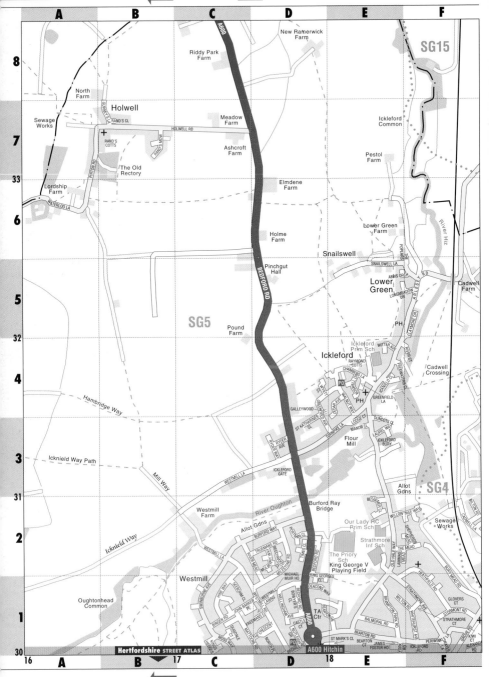

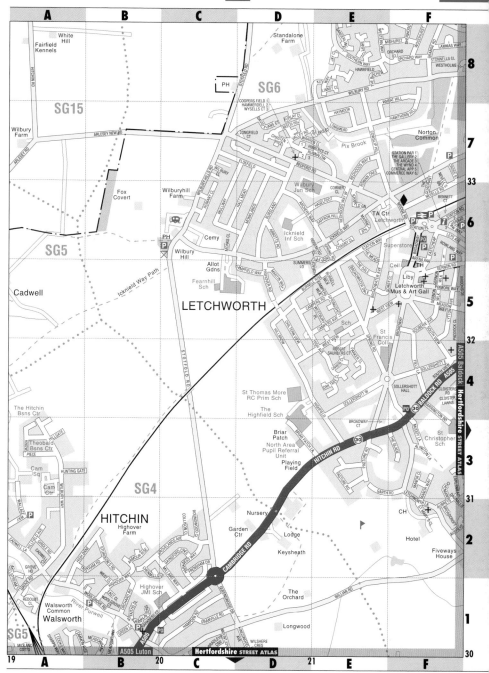

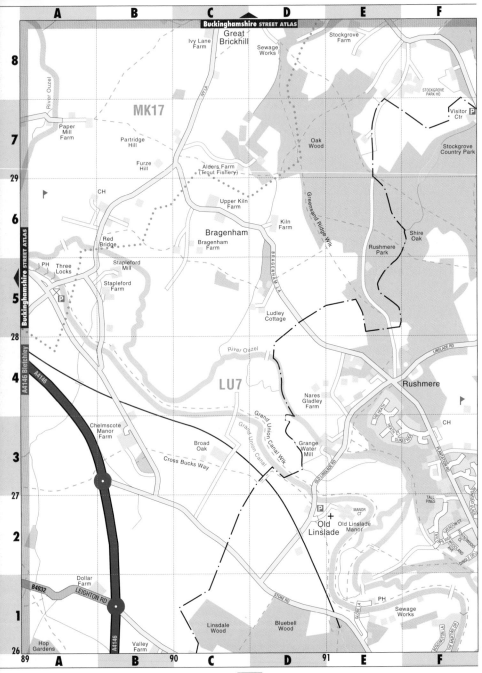

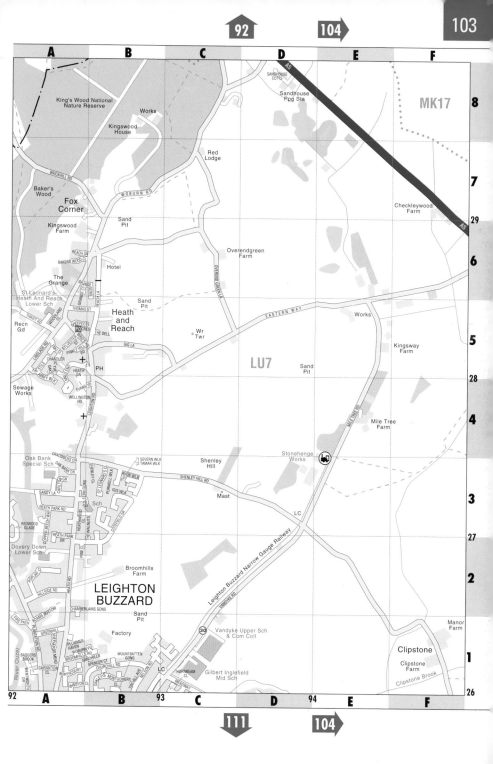

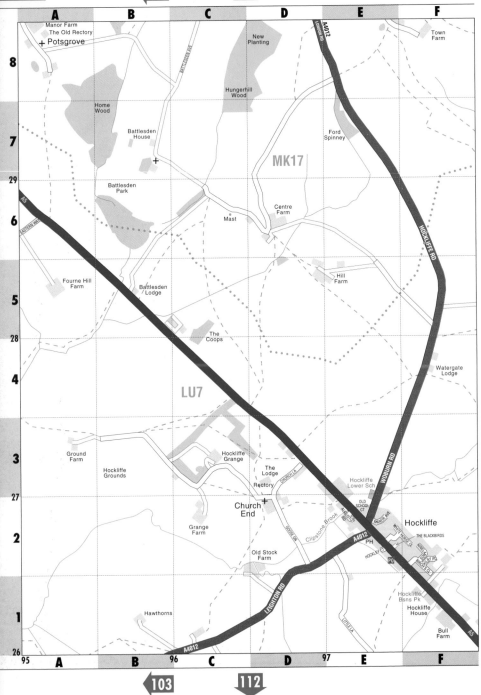

MK17

Toddington Manor

Toddington Park

Herne Manor Farm

The Lodge

Herne Farm

Herne Grange

PARK RD

Manor Lodge

LU5

WARREN CL
HERNE CL
WENTWORTH CL
MONMOUTH CL

PARK HILL
CHEYNEY

Parkfields Mid Sch

PO

Herne Poplar Farm

Alma Farm

CHURCH RD

HIGH ST

A5120

Toddington

LEIGHTON RD

MEADOW RD

ALMA LEIGH CL
ELM LEIGH CL
CHAPEL
CHALK HILL
ORCHARD
MARLBOROUGH
AYR CL

THE GRANGE
CRESCENT CT 1
CRESCENT CL 2
DALE CL
STOCKDALE

PRINCES ST
B579

Warmark Farm

Watergate Farm

HOLMFIELD CL 1
PEAR TREE CL 2
FRENCHMANS CL 3

Fairview Farm

ROSE DENE
WILLOW WAY

CLEARVIEW
THE DALES

RANDALL DR

BRADFORD WAY 1
KIMBERWELL CL 2
DE MONTFORT CT 3
MOUNT PLEASANT CL 4
SHELTON CL 5

MOUNT PLEASANT AVE
SHELTON AVE

THE LANE

Dropsholt Farm

Chalgrave

DUNSTABLE RD

LU7

TODDINGTON RD

CHALGRAVE RD

College Farm

PARK FARM

PO   PH

ST MARY'S CL

Tebworth

WOODLANDS

Upper Tithe Farm

Rose Farm

A5120

Icknield Way Path

Great Wood

Lords Hill Cottage

Hill Cottage

HOCKLIFE RD

TEBWORTH RD

THE ARCHWAYS

PH

HILL CL

Wingfield

LORD'S HILL

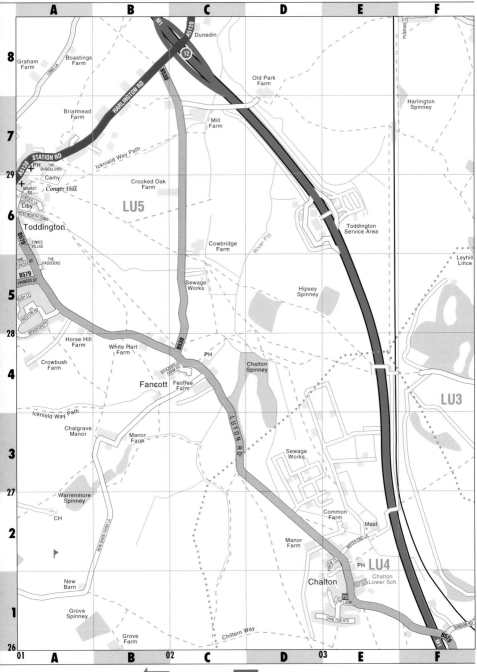

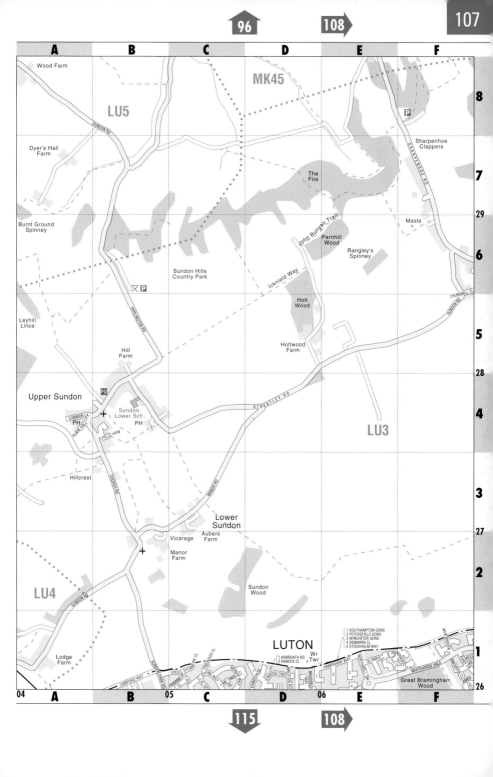

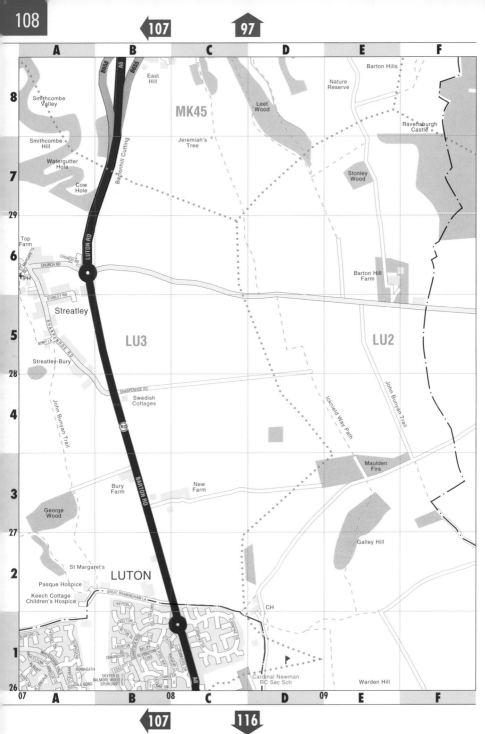

MK45

Barton Hills

Nature Reserve

Ravensburgh Castle

East Hill

Leet Wood

Stonley Wood

Smithcombe Valley

Smithcombe Hill

Watergutter Hole

Cow Hole

Jeremiah's Tree

Bartonhill Cutting

LUTON RD

Barton Hill Farm

Top Farm

CHURCH RD

PH

Church Rd

STANLEY RD

Streatley

SHAKER RD

BURY LA

Streatley-Bury

LU3

LU2

John Bunyan Trail

SHARPENHOE RD

Swedish Cottages

60

BARTON RD

Icknield Way Path

John Bunyan Trail

Maulden Firs

Bury Farm

New Farm

George Wood

Galley Hill

St Margaret's

LUTON

Pasque Hospice

Keech Cottage Children's Hospice

GREAT BRAMINGHAM LA

HAYTON

CH

SWAMPTON DR

A6

Cardinal Newman RC Sec Sch

Warden Hill

BURFORD CL

FERNHEATH

DEXTER CL 1
BALMORE WOOD 2
SPURCROFT 3

CHARD DR

	A	B	C	D	E	F	

Church Hole

Claypit Plantation

Lion Hill

Moor Hill

Butts Hill

Clark's Hill

Deacon Hill

8

Cank Hill

Burwell Platation

The Meg

Devil's Ditch

7

Claypit Hole

Gravel Hill

Hoo Bit

SG5

Wicks Spring

Pegdons Spring

29

Fairy Hole

Ickneild Way Path

Telegraph Hill

Nature Reserve

Muzzleford Wood

6

Wasgrove Wood

Mortgrove Farm

Staple Knoll

Brogsdell Plantation

Lilley Hoo

Newfield Wood

5

Brogsdell

28

Wasgrove Plantation

John Bunyan Trail

Walk Spring

LU2

Burnwell Spinneys

Lilley Manor Farm

Kingshill Plantation

Mazebeard Spring

4

HEXTON RD

Kingshill La

Ward's Spring

Stockinghill Plantation

3

Pond Farm

Ward's Farm

Lilley Hoo Farm

27

Ward's Wood

Wardswood La

John Bunyan Trail

RECTORY LA

Lilley

GREEN ACRES

RUEFLEY DELL RD

EAST ST

THE BRAUCK

LILLEYHOO LA

A505 Hitchin

2

Lilleypark Plantation

PH

Church Farm

Hollybush Hill

George's Plantation

Lilley Park

WEST ST

LILLEY BOTTOM

A505

SG5

1

Mushroom Elders

Lilleypark Wood

Allot Gdns

Ralphs Farm

26

Hertfordshire STREET ATLAS

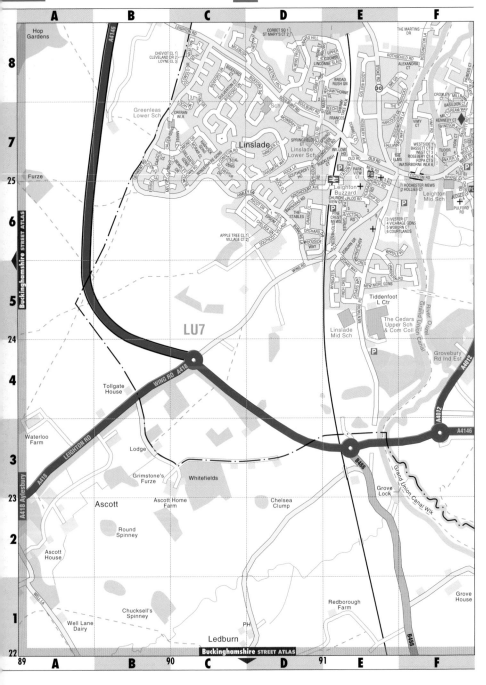

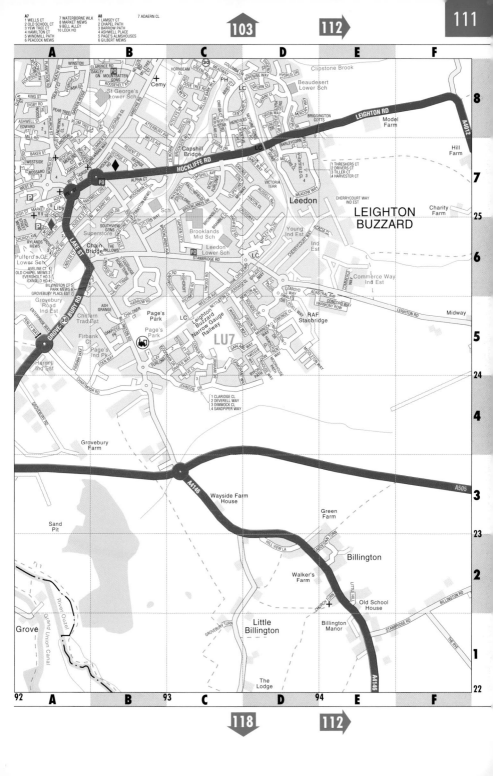

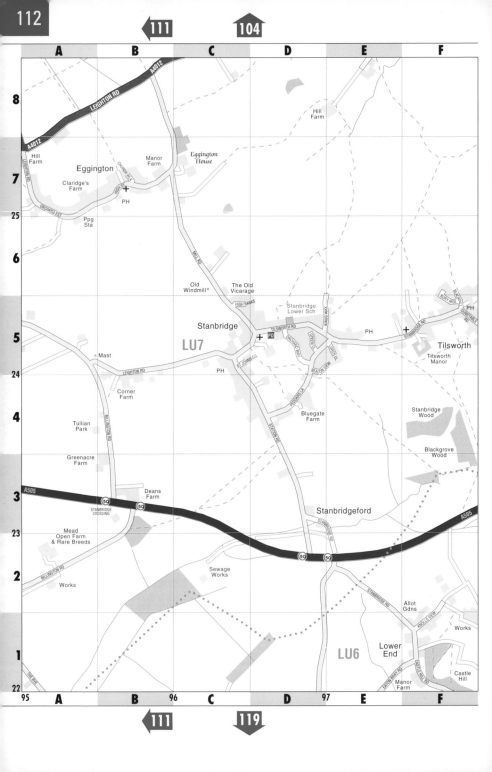

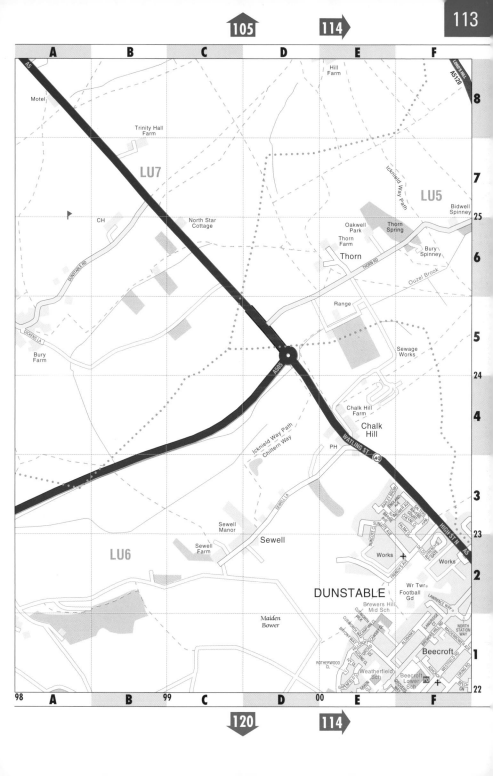

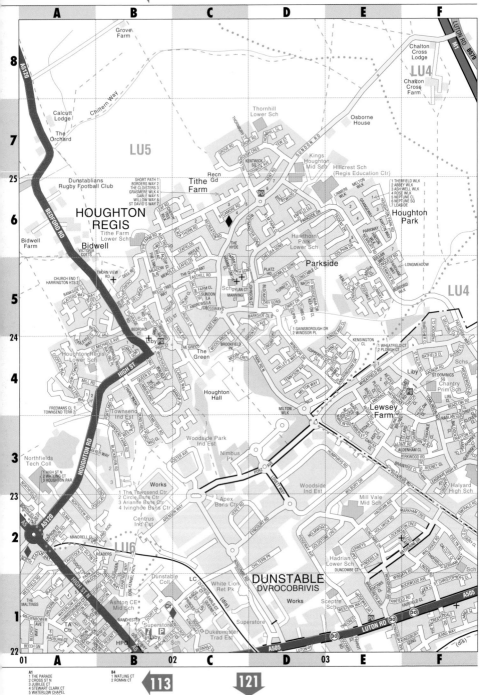

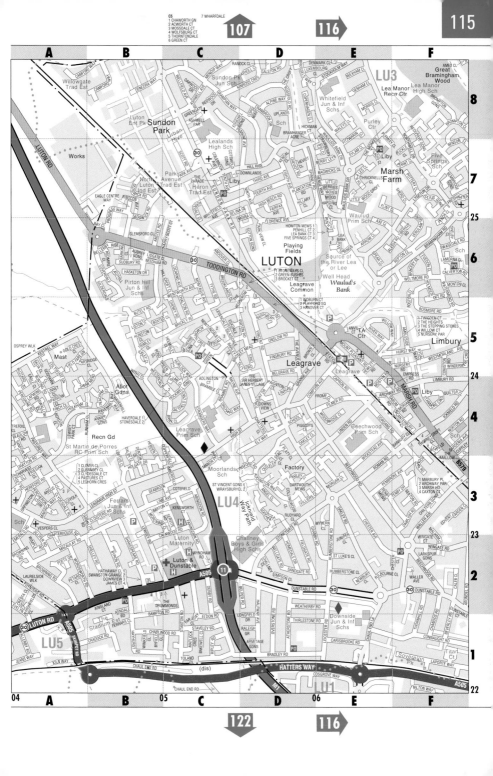

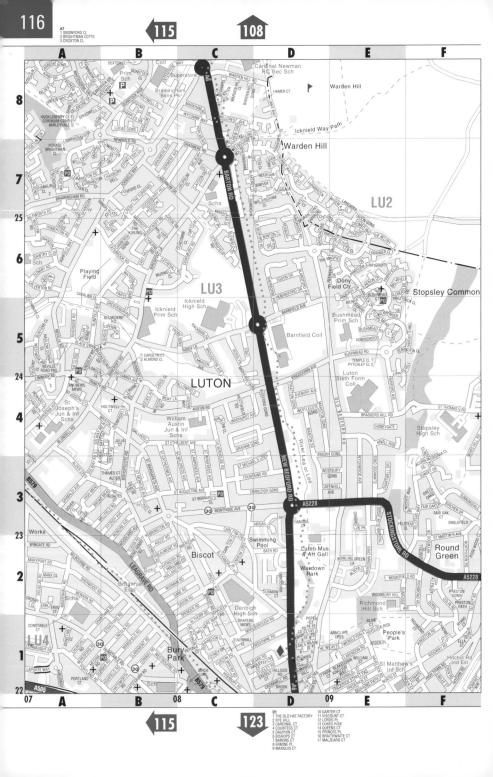

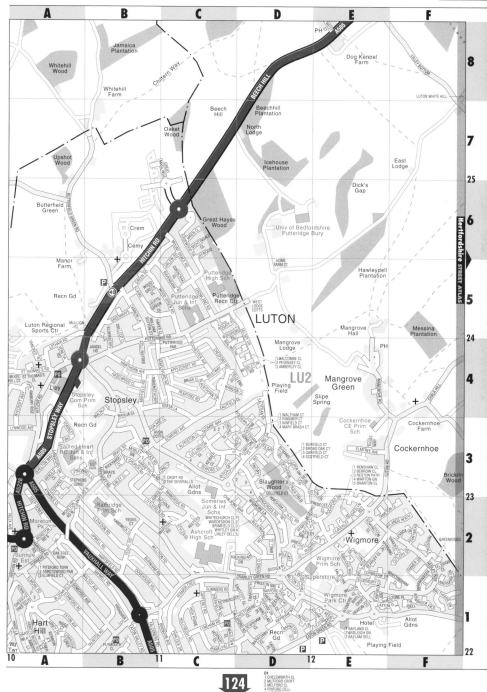

D1
1 CHELSWORTH CL
2 MUTFORD CROFT
3 MELFORD CL
4 PINFORD DELL
5 ALDERTON CL

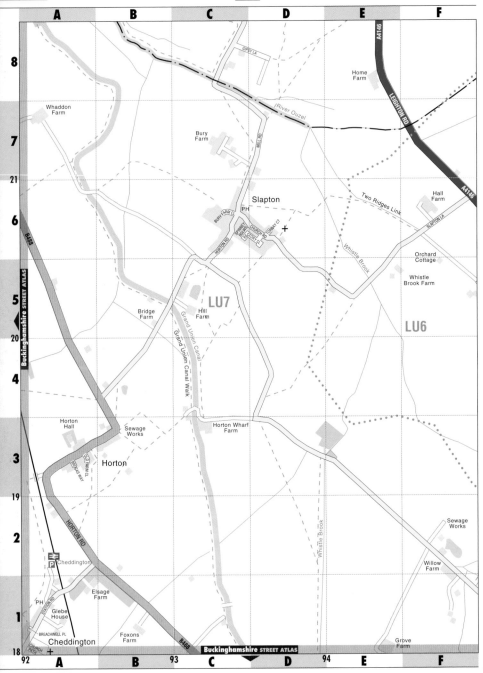

A B C D E F

8
7
21
6
5
20
4
3
19
2
1
18

92 93 94

A B C D E F

GIPSY LA

Home Farm

LEIGHTON RD

A4146

Whaddon Farm

River Ouzel

Bury Farm

MILL RD

Hall Farm

A4146

Two Ridges Link

SLAPTON LA

Slapton

PH

BURY HORM CL

HORTON RD

CHURCH RD

DORM-V CT

SPINNEY

PRIORY

RECTORY CL

Whistle Brook

Orchard Cottage

Whistle Brook Farm

Buckinghamshire STREET ATLAS

LU7

Bridge Farm

Hill Farm

Grand Union Canal

Grand Union Canal Walk

LU6

Horton Hall

Sewage Works

Horton Wharf Farm

Whistle Brook

Sewage Works

Horton

OLD FARM CL

BROOKS WAY

HORTON RD

STATION RD

Cheddington

Elsage Farm

Willow Farm

PH

Glebe House

BREACHWELL PL

Foxons Farm

B488

Cheddington

FOOTPATH

Grove Farm

Buckinghamshire STREET ATLAS

B488

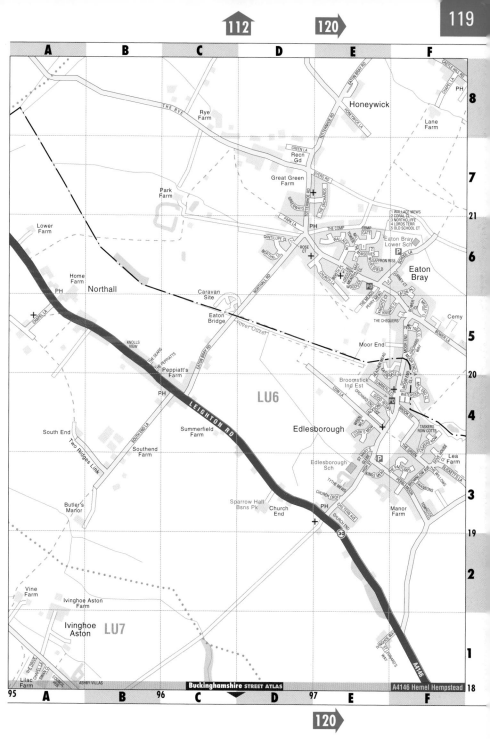

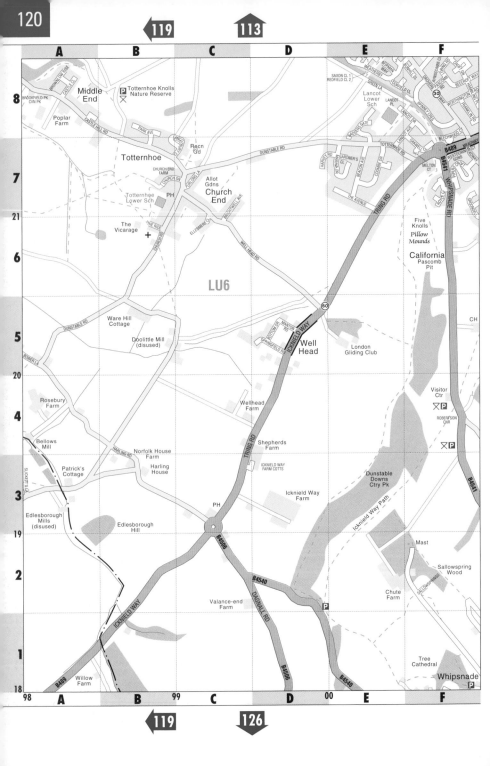

A B C D E F

8

Middle End

Totternhoe Knolls Nature Reserve

BROOKFIELD PK CVN PK

Poplar Farm

CASTLE HILL RD

PARK AVE

Lancot Lower Sch

Lancot Pk

SAXON CL 1 REDFIELD CL 2

30

Recn Gd

Totternhoe

DUNSTABLE RD

B489

7

CHURCH END FARM

Allot Gdns

Church End

Totternhoe Lower Sch

PH

B4541

WHIPSNADE RD

MELTON CT

21

The Vicarage

THE RIDE

ELLESMERE CLO

WINDMILL AVE

WELL HEAD RD

TRING RD

Five Knolls

Pillow Mounds

6

CHURCH RD

LU6

California

Pascomb Pit

5

DUNSTABLE RD

Ware Hill Cottage

Doolittle Mill (disused)

MANTON DR

SPRINGFIELD RD

ICKNIELD WAY

Well Head

60

London Gliding Club

CH

20

BOWER LA

Rosebury Farm

Wellhead Farm

Visitor Ctr

P

ROBERTSON CNR

4

Bellows Mill

HARLING RD

Norfolk House Farm

Harling House

TRING RD

Shepherds Farm

ICKNIELD WAY FARM COTTS

P

3

SLICKETTS LA

Patrick's Cottage

PH

Icknield Way Farm

Dunstable Downs Ctry Pk

Icknield Way Path

B4541

19

Edlesborough Mills (disused)

Edlesborough Hill

B4506

Mast

Sallowspring Wood

2

ICKNIELD WAY

B4540

DAGNALL RD

Valance-end Farm

SALLOWSPRINGS

Chute Farm

1

B489

Willow Farm

B4506

B4540

Tree Cathedral

Whipsnade

P

18

98 A B 99 C D 00 E F

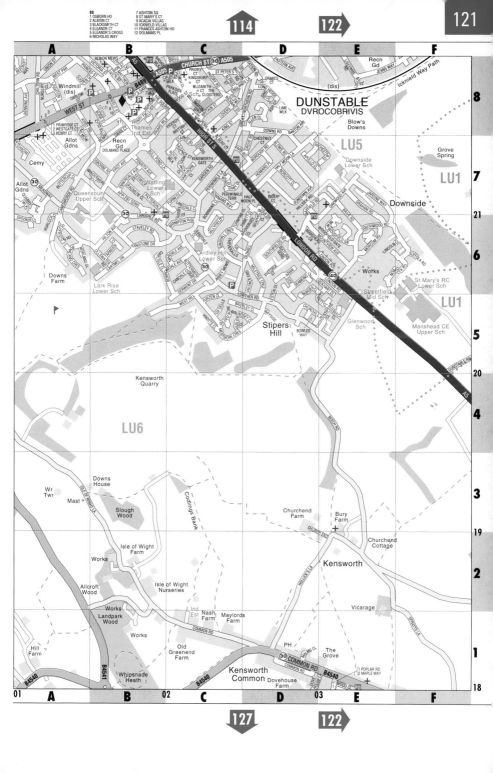

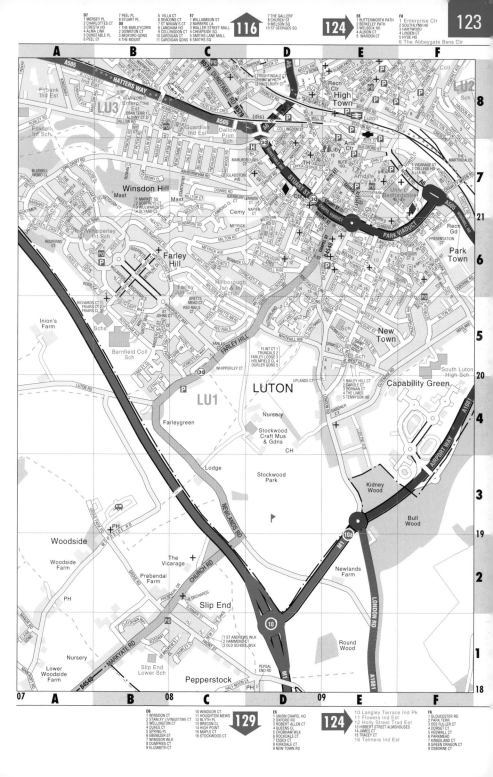

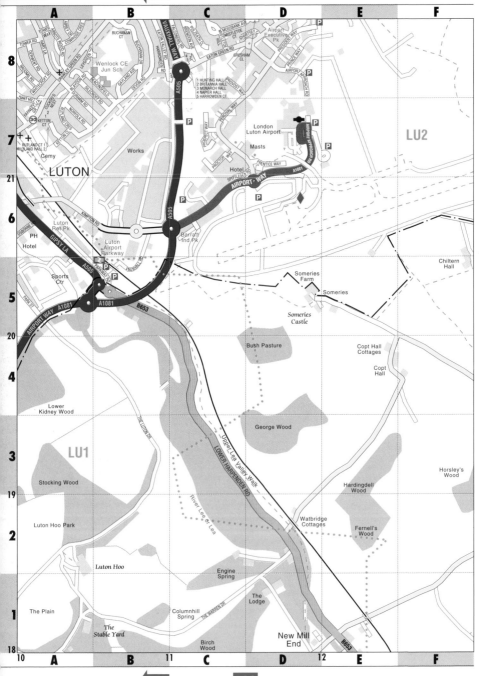

LU2

LUTON

Wenlock CE Jun Sch

London Luton Airport

Masts

1 HUNTING HALL
2 BRITANNIA HALL
3 MONARCH HALL
4 NAPIER HALL
5 HARROWDEN CT

Hotel

PRENTICE WAY

AIRPORT WAY

Works

Cemy

Luton Ret Pk

PH

Hotel

GIPSY LA

Luton Airport Parkway

Barratt Ind Pk

Sports Ctr

AIRPORT WAY A1081

A1081

B653

Someries Farm

Someries

Someries Castle

Chiltern Hall

Copt Hall Cottages

Copt Hall

Bush Pasture

Lower Kidney Wood

LU1

THE LUTON DR

Upper Lea Valley Walk

George Wood

LOWER HARPENDEN RD

Stocking Wood

Luton Hoo Park

River Lee or Lea

Horsley's Wood

Hardingdell Wood

Watbridge Cottages

Fernell's Wood

Luton Hoo

Engine Spring

The Plain

Columnhill Spring

THE WARDEN DR

The Lodge

New Mill End

B653

The Stable Yard

Birch Wood

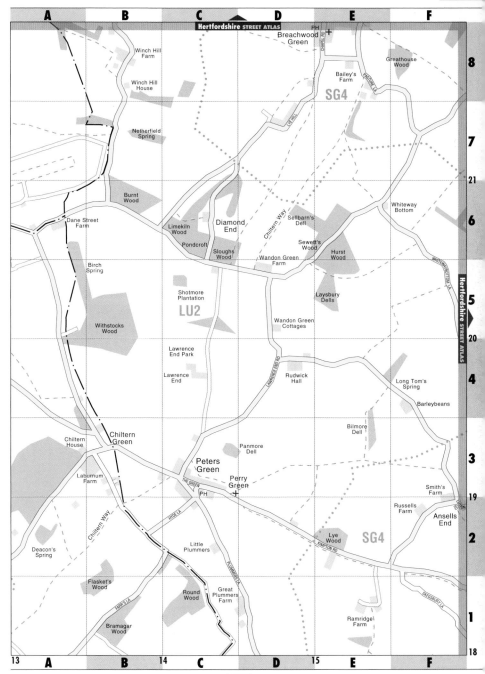

Breachwood Green

Winch Hill Farm

Winch Hill House

Greathouse Wood

Bailey's Farm

SG4

Netherfield Spring

Burnt Wood

Whiteway Bottom

Dane Street Farm

Limekiln Wood

Diamond End

Chiltern Way

Selbarn's Dell

Pondcroft

Sewett's Wood

Sloughs Wood

Wandon Green Farm

Hurst Wood

Birch Spring

Shotmore Plantation

LU2

Laysbury Dells

Withstocks Wood

Wandon Green Cottages

Lawrence End Park

Lawrence End

Rudwick Hall

Long Tom's Spring

Barleybeans

Bilmore Dell

Chiltern House

Chiltern Green

Panmore Dell

Peters Green

Laburnum Farm

Perry Green

Smith's Farm

Russells Farm

Ansells End

SG4

Chiltern Way

Deacon's Spring

Little Plummers

Lye Wood

Flasket's Wood

Round Wood

Great Plummers Farm

Ramridge Farm

Bramagar Wood

THE GREEN

PH

HYDE LA

PLUMMERS LA

FARR'S LA

KIMPTON RD

SKEGSBURY LA

LAWRENCE END RD

LYE HILL

CHAPEL RD

PASTURE LA

WHITEWAY BOTTOM LA

LUTON RD

8

21

7

6

5

20

4

3

19

2

1

18

13

A

B

14

C

D

15

E

F

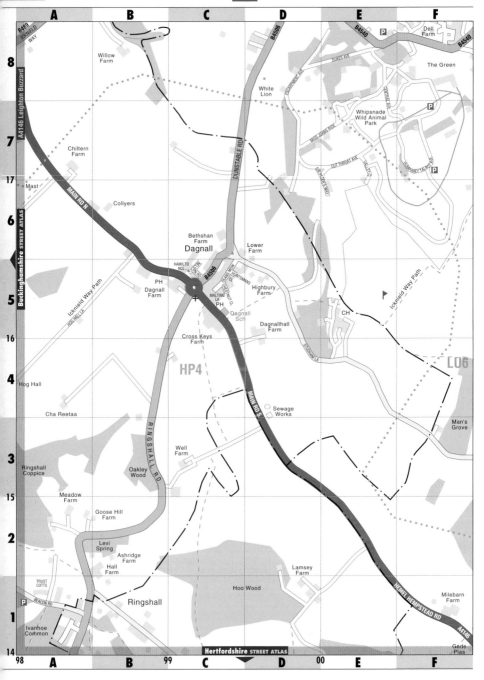

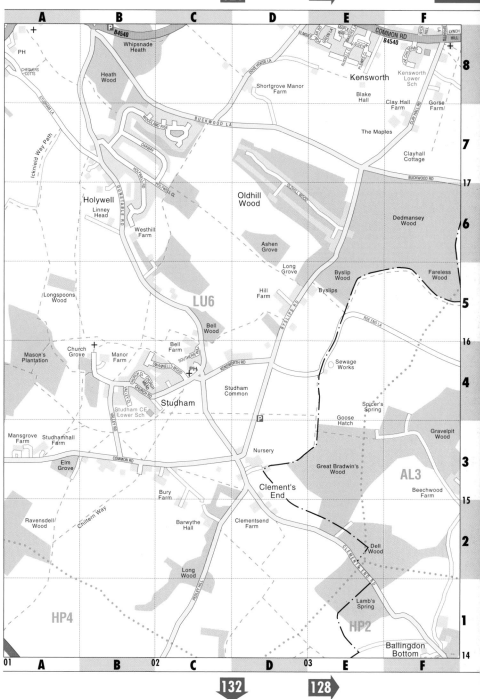

127
122

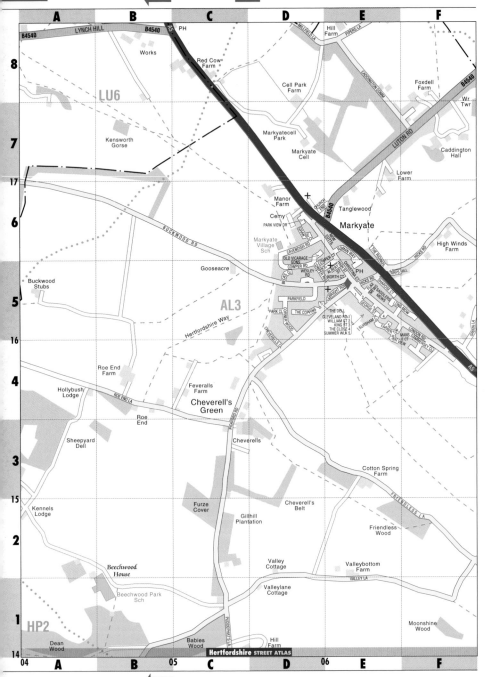

127

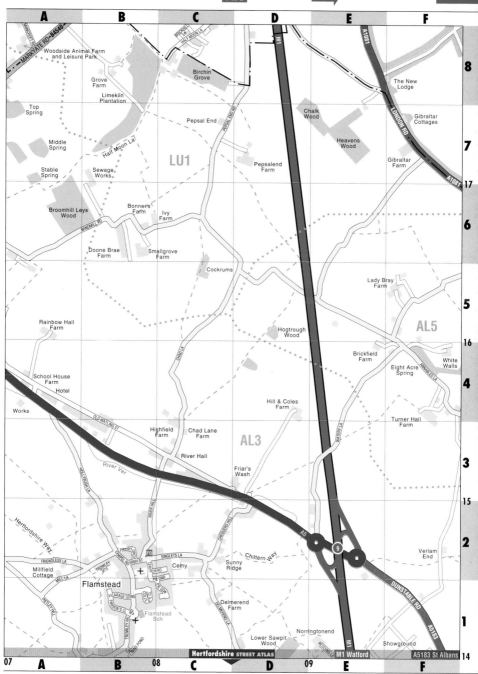

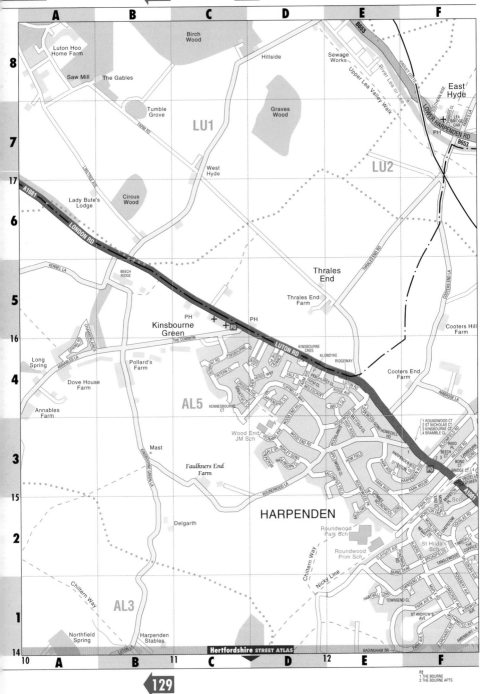

A   B   C   D   E   F

8

Luton Hoo
Home Farm

Saw Mill   The Gables

Birch
Wood

Hillside

Sewage
Works

B653

River Lea or Lee

East
Hyde

7

Tumble
Grove

LU1

Graves
Wood

Upper Lea Valley Walk

PH
B653

FARM RD

LOWER HARPENDEN RD

17

A1081

Lady Bute's
Lodge

Circus
Wood

West
Hyde

LU2

LIME TREE AVE

6

LONDON RD

KENNEL LA

BEECH
RIDGE

Thrales
End

THRALES END RD

COOTERS END LA

5

PH

Thrales End
Farm

Cooters Hill
Farm

16

Kinsbourne
Green

THE COMMON

PH
PO
PH

LUTON RD

Kinsbourne
Cres

Klondyke
Ridgeway

Cooters End
Farm

Long
Spring

GHARBEL LANE

Pollard's
Farm

KINGCROFT RD

TATTUN CL

VALE CL

PENACROFT

MOLESCROFT

WELLS LA

RIDGE AVE

LUTON RD

AMBROSE LA

4

ANNABLES LA

Dove House
Farm

HERONS WAY

CROSSFIELD

TUFTNELL WAY

Annables
Farm

AL5

KENNESBOURNE
CT

BRAMFIELD

CARLTON RD

1 ROUNDWOOD CT
2 ST NICHOLAS CT
3 KINSBOURNE CT
4 BRAMBLE CL

HOMEDELL
RD

3

Mast

Faulkners End
Farm

Wood End
JM Sch

WOOD END RD

WOODLANDS DR

WOODMANS RD

WOODMERE

HOW FIELD

OTTERTON CL

HARPENDEN RISE

REED
PL

BOND
CT

BRIDGE CT

PO

LAMBOURN
DR

15

KINSBOURNE GREEN LA

Delgarth

ROUNDWOOD LA

WALKERS FIELD

ROUNDWOOD DR

PARK RISE

PARK MOUNT

HARPENDEN

A1081

2

Chiltern Way

Nicky Line

Roundwood
Park Sch

Roundwood
Prim Sch

BARLING DENE

St Hilda's
Sch

CLAYCATE AVE

BROADFIELDS

TANGLEWOOD

AL3

Chiltern Way

HARTWELL GDNS

TOWNSEND CL

St Andrew's
Ave

PARK AVE N

THE
COPPICE

AMENBURY LA

1

Northfield
Spring

Harpenden
Stables

LUTON LA

PARK AVE

BADINGHAM DR

14

F2
1 THE BOURNE
2 THE BOURNE APTS

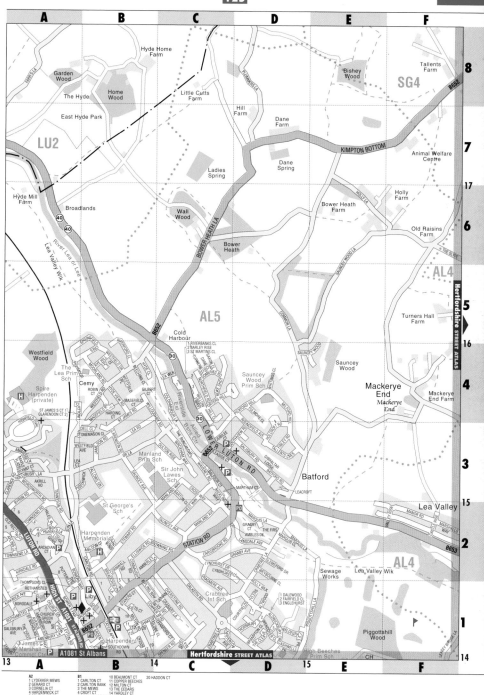

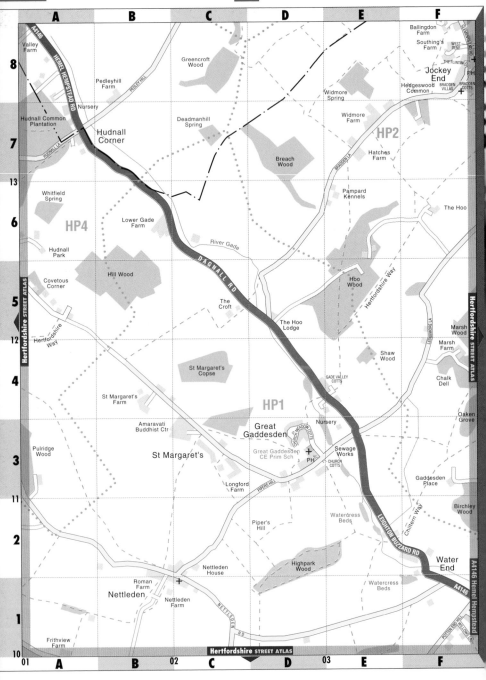

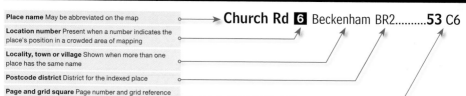

133

Place name May be abbreviated on the map

Location number Present when a number indicates the place's position in a crowded area of mapping

Locality, town or village Shown when more than one place has the same name

Postcode district District for the indexed place

Page and grid square Page number and grid reference for the standard mapping

Church Rd **6** Beckenham BR2.........**53** C6

Cities, towns and villages are listed in CAPITAL LETTERS   **Public and commercial buildings** are highlighted in magenta
Places of interest are highlighted in blue with a star ★

Abbreviations used in the index

Acad	**Academy**	Comm	**Common**	Gd	**Ground**	L	**Leisure**	Prom	**Promenade**
App	**Approach**	Cott	**Cottage**	Gdn	**Garden**	La	**Lane**	Rd	**Road**
Arc	**Arcade**	Cres	**Crescent**	Gn	**Green**	Liby	**Library**	Recn	**Recreation**
Ave	**Avenue**	Cswy	**Causeway**	Gr	**Grove**	Mdw	**Meadow**	Ret	**Retail**
Bglw	**Bungalow**	Ct	**Court**	H	**Hall**	Meml	**Memorial**	Sh	**Shopping**
Bldg	**Building**	Ctr	**Centre**	Ho	**House**	Mkt	**Market**	Sq	**Square**
Bsns, Bus	**Business**	Ctry	**Country**	Hospl	**Hospital**	Mus	**Museum**	St	**Street**
Bvd	**Boulevard**	Cty	**County**	HQ	**Headquarters**	Orch	**Orchard**	Sta	**Station**
Cath	**Cathedral**	Dr	**Drive**	Hts	**Heights**	Pal	**Palace**	Terr	**Terrace**
Cir	**Circus**	Dro	**Drove**	Ind	**Industrial**	Par	**Parade**	TH	**Town Hall**
Cl	**Close**	Ed	**Education**	Inst	**Institute**	Pas	**Passage**	Univ	**University**
Cnr	**Corner**	Emb	**Embankment**	Int	**International**	Pk	**Park**	Wk, Wlk	**Walk**
Coll	**College**	Est	**Estate**	Intc	**Interchange**	Pl	**Place**	Wr	**Water**
Com	**Community**	Ex	**Exhibition**	Junc	**Junction**	Prec	**Precinct**	Yd	**Yard**

Index of towns, villages, streets, hospitals, industrial estates, railway stations, schools, shopping centres, universities and places of interest

306th Bombardment Group
Mus★ MK44...............17 F6

A

Abbey Cl
Ampthill MK45...............84 F7
Elstow MK42...............50 B3
Renhold MK41...............39 B7
Abbey Dr LU2...............117 A1
Abbeyfields MK42...............50 C3
Abbeygate Bsns Ctr The **6**
LU2...............123 F8
Abbey Gr SG19...............54 C8
Abbey La MK45...............85 A6
Abbey Mews LU1...............121 C6
Abbey Rd MK41...............39 A2
Abbey Sq MK43...............34 E5
Abbey Way NN10...............2 A8
Abbey Wlk
Heath and Reach LU7...............103 A4
Houghton Regis LU5...............114 E6
Abbis Cl MK45...............84 D3
Abbis Orch SG5...............100 E5
Abbot Cres MK42...............49 D2
Abbots Ct LU2...............141 A1
Abbots Wlk 4 SG18...............67 A6
Abbotswood Par LU2...............117 A1
Abbots Wood Rd LU2...............124 A8
Abbotts Rd SG6...............101 D6
Abercorn Rd LU4...............114 F3
Abigail Cl LU3...............116 D3
Abigail Ct LU3...............116 D3
Abingdon Rd LU4...............115 D3
Abrahams Cl MK40...............38 E1
Acacia Cl LU7...............111 E6
Acacia Rd MK42...............50 D6
Acacia Villas 8 MK42...............50 D6
Ackerman Gdns PE19...............22 C2
Ackerman St PE19...............22 C2
Acorn Cl LU2...............116 F3
Acorn Ct 3 SG18...............67 A6
Acorn Ho SG18...............66 F7
Acorn Way MK42...............50 D5
Acres The LU7...............114 F3
Acworth Cres LU4...............115 C5
Acworth Ct 2 LU1...............115 C5
Adaern Ct 7 LU7...............111 A8
Adams Ct
Ampthill MK45...............84 F7

Adams Cl continued
Kempston MK42...............49 E1
Adamson Ct MK42...............49 D5
Adamson Wlk MK42...............49 D5
Adastral Ave LU7...............111 C6
Addington Cl
Bedford MK41...............39 A1
Henlow SG16...............78 D1
Addingtons Rd MK44...............41 A5
Addington Way LU4...............115 D3
Addington Wlk PE19...............22 C2
Addison Cl MK42...............49 F4
Adelaide Cl MK45...............74 B8
Adelaide Sq MK40...............38 B1
Adelaide St LU1...............123 D7
Adlington Ct LU4...............115 C4
Admiral Row MK45...............84 E4
Admirals Way PE19...............22 A2
Aelfric Ct MK41...............38 C5
Aidans Cl LU6...............113 E1
Ailesbury Rd MK45...............84 F8
Ailsworth Rd LU3...............116 A7
Ailwyns Acre MK43...............71 B7
Ainsland Ct LU4...............115 B2
Aintree Rd NN10...............8 D8
Airedale Cl MK45...............84 D4
Aire Wlk MK41...............38 C7
Airport Approach Rd
LU2...............124 D8
Airport Executive Pk
LU2...............124 D8
Airport Way LU1, LU2...............124 A5
Akrill Ho AL5...............131 A3
Alameda Mid Sch MK45...............84 E8
Alameda Rd MK45...............84 E8
Alameda Wlk MK45...............84 E8
Alamein Ave MK42...............50 E6
Alamein Cl SG17...............77 C1
Alamein Ct PE19...............22 C5
Alban CE Mid Sch MK44...............40 F5
Albany Cl LU1...............123 B8
Albany Rd
Bedford MK40...............50 C8
Leighton Buzzard LU7...............111 B7
Albert Cl LU6...............114 F3
Albert Ct LU6...............121 C7
Albert Pl
Ampthill MK45...............84 D6
Houghton Conquest MK45...............74 B8
Albert Rd
Arlesey SG15...............90 A4
Luton LU1...............123 E6

Albert St
10 Bedford MK40...............38 B1
Markyate AL3...............128 E5
Albion Ct
2 Dunstable LU6...............121 B8
4 Luton LU2...............123 E8
Sandy SG19...............54 C7
Albion Mews LU6...............121 B8
Albion Rd LU2...............123 E8
Albion St LU6...............121 B8
Albone Way SG18...............66 F4
Albone Way Ind Est SG18...............66 F4
Alburgh Cl MK42...............50 F5
Albury Cl LU3...............108 A1
Aldbanks LU6...............113 F1
Aldenham Cl
Bedford MK41...............51 B8
Luton LU4...............114 F3
Aldens Mead MK41...............38 F4
Alder Cl PE19...............22 B6
Alder Cres LU3...............116 A3
Alder Ct LU3...............116 B3
Alders End La AL5...............130 F2
Alders The MK42...............49 E3
Alderton Cl 6 LU2...............117 D1
Aldgate Cl SG19...............56 B7
Aldhous Cl LU3...............116 B5
Aldwickbury Cres AL5...............131 D1
Aldwyck Ct MK42...............50 A6
Alesia Rd LU3...............115 F6
Alexa Ct MK42...............51 A5
Alexander Cl
Clifton SG17...............78 A2
Stewartby MK43...............61 C1
Alexander Ct MK41...............38 C5
Alexander Rd
Stotfold SG5...............90 F6
Wrestlingworth SG19...............57 B4
Alexandra Ave LU3...............116 C2
Alexandra Ct LU7...............110 F8
Alexandra Pl 4 MK40...............50 B8
Alexandra Rd
Bedford MK40...............50 A8
Hitchin SG5...............100 F1
ALEY GREEN...............122 E1
Alfred Cope Rd SG19...............54 C8
Alfred St
Dunstable LU5...............121 C8
2 Luton LU2...............117 D4
Irchester NN29...............7 A8
Alfriston Cl LU2...............117 C3
Algar Cl SG19...............54 B4
Alington Pl MK40...............50 B8
Alington Rd PE19...............22 E1
Allenby Ave LU5...............115 A1

Allen Cl
Bedford MK40...............49 F8
Dunstable LU5...............121 D8
Allen Ct MK43...............60 E1
Allendale LU3...............108 A1
Allhallows
Bedford MK40...............50 B8
Sandy SG19...............54 B8
Allied Bsns Ctr AL5...............131 C3
All Saints CE Lower Sch
SG17...............78 B2
All Saints Rd
Bedford MK40...............49 F8
Cople MK44...............52 A7
Houghton Regis LU5...............114 B5
All Saints Way SG19...............54 B8
Allton Rd SG16...............89 A4
Alma Farm Rd LU5...............105 E6
Alma Link 4 LU1...............123 D7
Alma St LU1...............123 D7
Almer's Cl MK45...............74 B8
Almond Cl LU3...............116 B4
Almond Rd
Leighton Buzzard LU7...............111 C8
St Neots PE19...............22 F2
Almonds The MK42...............50 A3
Alnwick Cl SG19...............54 C8
Alnwick Ct PE19...............22 F2
Alpha Ct
Kempston MK42...............49 D3
Alpine Way LU3...............115 D8
Alsop Cl LU5...............114 B5
Althorp Cl MK45...............89 A4
Althorpe St MK42...............50 B6
Althorp Rd LU3...............116 B4
Alton Rd LU1...............123 F5
Attwood AL5...............131 D1
Alwen Wlk MK41...............38 C5
Alwins Field LU7...............110 D8
Alwyn Cl LU2...............116 E2
Amaravati Buddhist Ctr
HP1...............132 C3
Amberley Cl
Harpenden AL5...............131 B2
Luton LU2...............117 D4
Amberley Gdns MK40...............38 D2
Ambleside
Harpenden AL5...............131 D2
Luton LU3...............115 F5
Ambrose La AL5...............130 F4
Amenbury Ct AL5...............131 A1

306-Ara

Amenbury La AL5...............131 A1
Ames Cl LU3...............107 F1
Amhurst Rd LU4...............114 F3
AMPTHILL...............84 E6
Ampthill Ind Est & Bsns Pk
MK45...............84 C7
Ampthill Rd
Bedford MK42...............50 B5
Chicksands SG17...............76 E2
Silsoe MK45...............86 B5
Steppingley MK45...............84 D5
Ampthill St MK42...............50 C7
Andover Cl LU4...............115 C6
Andrew Rd PE19...............22 F2
Andrews Cl MK45...............74 C1
Angel Cl LU4...............115 D3
Angels La LU5...............114 B5
Angel View MK42...............50 C5
Angus Cl LU3...............115 A3
Anmer Gdns LU4...............115 B4
Annables La AL5...............130 A4
Annes Ct MK42...............50 C7
Anne St SG18...............67 A7
ANSELLS END...............125 F2
Anson Pl PE19...............22 A2
Anstee Rd LU4...............115 B6
Anthony Gdns LU1...............123 D6
Antonie Farm Cotts MK44...............15 F4
Anvil Cl LU3...............115 E5
Anvil Ho 8 AL5...............131 A2
Apex Bsns Ctr LU5...............114 C2
Aplins Cl AL5...............131 A2
Apollo Cl LU5...............121 D7
Appenine Way LU7...............111 D8
Appleby Cl PE19...............22 E6
Appleby Gdns LU6...............121 B7
Applecroft SG16...............89 B3
Applecroft Rd LU2...............117 C4
Applecross Wlk MK41...............38 C5
Appledore Rd MK40...............38 D1
Apple Glebe MK45...............97 C2
Apple Gr PE19...............22 C4
Apple Tree Cl
Biggleswade SG18...............67 B5
Leighton Buzzard LU7...............110 D6
Silsoe MK45...............86 B5
Appley End MK45...............130 C3
Appley End Rd SG5...............98 E6
Aquila Rd LU7...............111 D8
Aragon Ct MK45...............84 D4

Aragon Pl PE28 . . . . . 6 F5
Aragon Rd MK45 . . . . . 84 F7
Arbour Cl LU3 . . . . . 108 A1
Arbroath Rd LU3 . . . . . 107 D1
Arcade The
14 Bedford MK40 . . . . . 50 B8
Letchworth SG6 . . . . . 101 F6
Arcadian Ct AL5 . . . . . 131 A2
Archers Way SG6 . . . . . 101 D6
Archway Par LU3 . . . . . 115 F4
Archway Rd LU3 . . . . . 115 E4
Arden Gr AL5 . . . . . 131 B1
Arden Pl LU2 . . . . . 116 E1
Arden Wlk MK41 . . . . . 39 B3
Ardleigh Gn LU2 . . . . . 117 E1
Ardley Cl LU6 . . . . . 121 C5
Ardley Hill Lower Sch LU6 . . . . . 121 C6
Arena Par SG6 . . . . . 101 F6
Arenson Way LU5 . . . . . 114 C2
Argyll Ave LU3 . . . . . 116 C2
Argyll St MK40 . . . . . 38 B2
Arianne Bsns Ctr LU5 . . . . . 114 B3
Aries Ct LU7 . . . . . 111 C8
Arkwright Rd
Bedford MK42 . . . . . 51 A5
Irchester NN29 . . . . . 7 C7
Milton Ernest MK44 . . . . . 27 B5
Arkwright Road Ind Est MK42 . . . . . 51 A5
ARLESEY 90 A4
Arlesey Ho SG15 . . . . . 90 A8
Arlesey New Rd SG6, SG15 . . . . . 101 B7
Arlesey Rd
Church End SG16 . . . . . 89 E8
Henlow SG16 . . . . . 89 D8
Ickleford SG5 . . . . . 100 F5
Arlesey Sta SG15 . . . . . 90 A8
Arlington Ct 15 MK40 . . . . . 38 B1
Armitage Gdns LU4 . . . . . 115 D1
Armour Rise SG4 . . . . . 101 B2
Armstrong Cl MK45 . . . . . 62 F3
Armstrong Dr MK42 . . . . . 50 C6
Arnald Way LU5 . . . . . 114 A4
Arncliffe Cres LU2 . . . . . 116 E1
Arndale Ctr LU1 . . . . . 123 E7
Arnhem Cl PE19 . . . . . 22 C5
Arnhem Pl SG17 . . . . . 77 C2
Arnold Cl
Barton-le-C MK45 . . . . . 97 C2
Luton LU2 . . . . . 117 A3
Arnold Middle Sch MK45 . . 97 D2
Arnolds La SG7 . . . . . 80 D6
Arran Cl SG19 . . . . . 54 B8
Arran Ct LU1 . . . . . 123 D7
Arrow Cl LU3 . . . . . 115 E6
Arrow Leys MK41 . . . . . 38 F4
Arthur St
Ampthill MK45 . . . . . 84 E8
Luton, New Town LU1 . . . . . 123 E6
Arum Cl NN10 . . . . . 8 C7
Arun Cl MK41 . . . . . 38 D5
Arundel Cl MK45 . . . . . 84 D1
Arundel Cres PE19 . . . . . 22 E2
Arundel Ct NN10 . . . . . 8 A8
Arundel Dr MK41 . . . . . 39 A4
Arundel Rd
Luton LU4 . . . . . 115 F2
Marston Moretaine MK43 . . . 72 C8
Ascot Dr LU7 . . . . . 110 D6
Ascot Rd
Luton LU3 . . . . . 116 B2
Rushden NN10 . . . . . 8 D8
ASCOTT 110 B2
Ascott House* LU7 . . . . . 110 A2
Asgard Dr MK41 . . . . . 39 D4
Ashburnham Cres LU7 . . . 110 E6
Ashburnham Ct MK40 . . . . . 50 A8
Ashburnham Rd
Ampthill MK45 . . . . . 84 E7
Bedford MK40 . . . . . 50 A8
Luton LU1 . . . . . 123 C7
Ashby Ct SG18 . . . . . 78 F6
Ashby Dr
Barton-le-C MK45 . . . . . 97 C3
Rushden NN10 . . . . . 8 A8
Upper Caldecote SG18 . . . . . 66 B8
Ashby Villas LU6 . . . . . 119 A1
Ash Cl
Beeston SG19 . . . . . 54 B6
Flitwick MK45 . . . . . 84 F2
Irchester NN29 . . . . . 7 A7
Ashcraft Cl MK43 . . . . . 72 C7
Ashcroft LU6 . . . . . 113 F1
Ashcroft High Sch LU2 . . 117 C2
Ashcroft Rd LU2 . . . . . 117 B3
Ashdale Ave MK42 . . . . . 49 F5
Ashdale Gdns LU3 . . . . . 108 A1
Ashdown SG6 . . . . . 90 F1
Ashdown Rd SG17 . . . . . 77 E3
Ashfield PE28 . . . . . 6 F5
Ashfield Way LU3 . . . . . 116 A6
Ash Gr
Biggleswade SG18 . . . . . 66 F8
Dunstable LU5 . . . . . 121 D8
Leighton Buzzard LU7 . . . . . 111 A8
Wilstead MK45 . . . . . 62 F2
Ash Grange LU7 . . . . . 111 B5
Ashington Ct SG17 . . . . . 78 B2
Ashley Gdns
Biggleswade SG18 . . . . . 67 B7
Harpenden AL5 . . . . . 130 D3
Ashlong Cl LU7 . . . . . 111 C7
Ashmead Rd MK41 . . . . . 38 C7
Ash Rd
Biggleswade SG18 . . . . . 67 A7
Luton LU4 . . . . . 123 B8
Ashridge Cl NN10 . . . . . 8 A8
Ashridge Dr MK41 . . . . . 39 C4
Ashton CE Mid Sch LU6 . . 114 B1
Ashton Rd
Dunstable LU6 . . . . . 114 B1
Luton LU1 . . . . . 123 E5
Ashton St Peter CE Sch LU5 . . . . . 114 C1
Ashton Sq 7 LU6 . . . . . 121 B8
Ash Tree Rd LU5 . . . . . 114 B6
Ashwell Ave LU3 . . . . . 115 C8
Ashwell Par LU3 . . . . . 115 C8
Ashwell Pk AL5 . . . . . 131 D1
Ashwell Place 4 LU7 . . . 111 A8
Ashwell Rd
Guilden Morden SG8 . . . . . 69 F1
Hinxworth SG7 . . . . . 80 E5
Newnham SG7 . . . . . 91 F8
Ashwell St LU7 . . . . . 111 A8
Ash Well Wlk LU5 . . . . . 114 E6
Ash Wlk MK42 . . . . . 49 F3
Aspects L Ctr MK41 . . . . . 50 F7
Aspen Ave MK41 . . . . . 38 E4
Asplands Cl MK17 . . . . . 81 B4
Aspley Cl LU4 . . . . . 114 E3
Aspley Ct
Bedford MK40 . . . . . 38 A1
Woburn Sands MK17 . . . . . 81 C3
ASPLEY END 98 E7
ASPLEY GUISE 81 F4
Aspley Guise Lower Sch MK17 . . . . . 81 F4
Aspley Guise Sta MK17 . . . 81 D6
ASPLEY HEATH 80 B2
Aspley Hill MK17 . . . . . 81 C4
Aspley La MK17 . . . . . 81 E2
Aspley Rd MK42 . . . . . 50 B6
Astley Gn LU2 . . . . . 117 D2
Aston Rd MK42 . . . . . 51 A5
Astra Ct LU2 . . . . . 116 F2
Astral Cl SG16 . . . . . 89 B3
Astrey Cl LU5 . . . . . 95 F2
ASTWICK 79 E1
Astwick Rd SG5 . . . . . 79 F2
ASTWOOD 47 A3
Astwood Cl SG19 . . . . . 56 A8
Astwood Dr MK45 . . . . . 84 D4
Astwood Rd MK43 . . . . . 59 C7
Atherstone Abbey MK41 . . . 51 B8
Atherstone Rd LU4 . . . . . 115 D1
Atholl Cl LU3 . . . . . 115 D8
Atholl Wlk MK41 . . . . . 39 B4
Attadale Wlk 4 MK41 . . . . . 39 B4
Atterbury Ave LU7 . . . . . 111 B8
Aubrey Gdns LU4 . . . . . 115 B6
Aubreys SG6 . . . . . 101 F2
Auckland Rd SG18 . . . . . 67 B7
Augustus Rd LU7 . . . . . 104 E2
Austin Canons MK42 . . . . . 50 A6
Austin Cl NN29 . . . . . 7 C8
Austin Rd LU3 . . . . . 116 C4
Avebury Ave LU2 . . . . . 116 D4
Aveline Ct LU7 . . . . . 111 A6
Avenells Way SG19 . . . . . 44 D5
Avenue Rd
Rushden NN10 . . . . . 8 F5
St Neots PE19 . . . . . 22 F6
Avenue St Nicholas AL5 . 131 A1
Avenue The
Ampthill MK45 . . . . . 84 E7
Bedford MK40 . . . . . 50 A8
Biggleswade SG18 . . . . . 67 B6
Bletsoe MK44 . . . . . 17 C1
Blunham MK44 . . . . . 41 D2
Dunstable LU6 . . . . . 120 E7
Flitwick MK45 . . . . . 84 F3
Langford SG18 . . . . . 78 F6
Luton LU4 . . . . . 115 D5
Sandy SG19 . . . . . 54 B7
Stotfold SG5 . . . . . 90 F6
Aviary Wlk MK41 . . . . . 38 C5
Avoca Ho MK43 . . . . . 36 F3
Avocet SG6 . . . . . 90 E1
Avocet Cl
Biggleswade SG18 . . . . . 66 F4
Sandy SG19 . . . . . 42 B1
Avon Chase SG16 . . . . . 89 C4
Avon Cotts LU2 . . . . . 117 B3
Avon Ct
17 Harpenden AL5 . . . . . 131 B1
Luton LU1 . . . . . 123 C8
St Neots PE19 . . . . . 22 C3
Avondale Rd LU1 . . . . . 123 C8
Avon Dr MK41 . . . . . 38 C5
Avon Rd SG16 . . . . . 89 B4
Avon Rise MK45 . . . . . 84 D2
Avon Wlk LU7 . . . . . 103 B3
Axe Cl LU3 . . . . . 115 E6
Axis Way PE19 . . . . . 22 B5
Aydon Rd LU3 . . . . . 116 B6
Aylesbury Ct MK41 . . . . . 38 F1
Aylesbury Rd MK41 . . . . . 50 F8
Aylmerton Ct SG17 . . . . . 77 D2
Aylott Cl PE28 . . . . . 5 B4
Aynscombe Cl LU6 . . . . . 120 F8

B

Back La MK44 . . . . . 16 A8
BACKNOE END 18 E4
Back St
Biggleswade SG18 . . . . . 67 A6
Clophill MK45 . . . . . 75 C1
Luton LU2 . . . . . 123 E8
BACKSTREET 75 C1
Badgers Brook LU7 . . . . . 103 A1
Badgers Cl MK45 . . . . . 84 E3
Badgers Gate LU6 . . . . . 120 E8
Badingham Dr AL5 . . . . . 130 E1
Bagwicks Cl LU3 . . . . . 115 E7
Bailey Hill Ct LU1 . . . . . 123 E5
Bailey St LU1 . . . . . 123 F6
Baileys Villas MK43 . . . . . 26 C8
Baker Ave SG19 . . . . . 56 A7
Bakers Cl MK43 . . . . . 34 D5
Bakers Cres NN29 . . . . . 7 A8
Bakers La LU6 . . . . . 127 E8
Baker's La SG19 . . . . . 42 B8
Baker St
Ampthill MK45 . . . . . 84 E8
Leighton Buzzard LU7 . . . . . 111 A7
Luton LU1 . . . . . 123 E5
Bakers Wood Cl LU7 . . . . . 103 A6
Bakery Cl MK43 . . . . . 59 B1
Bakery The MK43 . . . . . 36 B7
Bakewell Cl LU4 . . . . . 115 C1
Balcombe Cl LU2 . . . . . 117 D4
BALDOCK 91 F2
Baldock Cl LU4 . . . . . 114 F3
Baldock Rd
Letchworth SG6 . . . . . 101 F4
Stotfold SG5 . . . . . 91 A5
Baldock Sta SG7 . . . . . 91 F1
Baldur Cl MK41 . . . . . 39 D3
Balfour Ct AL5 . . . . . 131 C3
Balham Cl NN10 . . . . . 7 F8
BALLINGDON BOTTOM . . . 127 F1
Ballinghall Ct MK41 . . . . . 39 A2
Balliol Lower Sch MK42 . . . 49 D3
Balliol Rd MK42 . . . . . 49 D3
Balls La MK44 . . . . . 52 B8
Balmoral Ave MK40 . . . . . 38 D2
Balmoral Cl
Flitwick MK45 . . . . . 84 D1
Sandy SG19 . . . . . 42 B1
Balmoral Rd SG5 . . . . . 100 E1
Balmoral Way PE19 . . . . . 22 F2
Balmore Wood LU3 . . . . . 108 B1
Balsall St E 6 MK40 . . . . . 38 B1
Balsall St W MK40 . . . . . 38 B1
Bamburgh Dr MK41 . . . . . 39 A4
Bamford Rd MK42 . . . . . 50 F5
Bamfords La MK43 . . . . . 34 E6
Bamfords Yd MK43 . . . . . 34 E5
Bampton Rd LU4 . . . . . 115 B2
Banbury Cl LU4 . . . . . 115 F4
Bancroft Ave SG18 . . . . . 66 B2
Bancroft Rd LU3 . . . . . 116 B5
Bank Cl LU4 . . . . . 115 C4
Banks Cl MK43 . . . . . 72 C7
Banks Dr SG19 . . . . . 54 B7
Bankside Cl LU5 . . . . . 114 A5
Bank's Rd SG18 . . . . . 67 B7
Barber End SG17 . . . . . 77 D3
Barbers La 2 LU1 . . . . . 123 E7
Barclay Ct LU2 . . . . . 123 F8
Barford Ave MK42 . . . . . 50 D6
Barford Rd
Blunham MK44 . . . . . 41 C3
St Neots PE19 . . . . . 22 E2
Willington MK44 . . . . . 40 C7
Barford Rise LU2 . . . . . 117 D1
Barker Dr MK43 . . . . . 36 D2
Barkers Cl MK45 . . . . . 84 E6
Barker's La MK41 . . . . . 51 A8
Barkers Piece MK43 . . . . . 60 D1
Barking Cl LU4 . . . . . 115 B6
Bar La SG19 . . . . . 45 E3
Barley Brow LU6 . . . . . 113 E3
Barleycorn Cl LU7 . . . . . 111 D7
Barleycorn The 1 LU3 . . 123 D8
Barley Ct
Rushden NN10 . . . . . 8 C8
St Neots PE19 . . . . . 22 D5
Barleyfield Way LU5 . . . . . 114 A4
Barley Kiln La MK43 . . . . . 25 A6
Barley La LU4 . . . . . 115 C5
Barley Rd PE19 . . . . . 22 C3
Barley Rise AL5 . . . . . 131 C4
Barleyvale LU3 . . . . . 116 A8
Barley Way MK41 . . . . . 39 A3
Barnabas Rd LU7 . . . . . 110 D6
Barnard Ave MK42 . . . . . 49 C3
Barnard Cl PE19 . . . . . 22 F1
Barnard Rd LU1 . . . . . 123 A7
Barncroft MK43 . . . . . 34 E6
Barndell Cl SG5 . . . . . 90 F6
Barnes Cl PE19 . . . . . 22 E6
Barnes Rd MK43 . . . . . 60 F6
Barnett Cl SG18 . . . . . 67 A6
Barnfield Ave LU2 . . . . . 116 D5
Barnfield Coll
Luton LU2 . . . . . 116 D5
Luton LU2 . . . . . 123 F8
Luton LU3 . . . . . 116 B8
Barnfield Coll South LU1 . . . . . 123 B5
Barnhill MK41 . . . . . 39 A2
Barns Dene AL5 . . . . . 130 E2
Barnstaple Rd MK40 . . . . . 38 E2
Barns The
Blunham MK44 . . . . . 41 D3
Riseley MK44 . . . . . 11 A2
Barnston Cl LU2 . . . . . 117 D1
Barnwell Dr NN10 . . . . . 8 A8
Baron Ct PE19 . . . . . 22 B4
Barons Ct 7 LU2 . . . . . 116 D1
Barratt Ind Pk LU2 . . . . . 124 C6
Barrie Ave LU6 . . . . . 113 E3
Barringer Way PE19 . . . . . 22 F7
Barrington Rd
Letchworth SG6 . . . . . 101 F4
Barrington Rd *continued*
Rushden NN10 . . . . . 8 C8
Barrowby Cl LU2 . . . . . 117 D1
Barrow Path 3 LU7 . . . . . 111 A8
Barton Ave LU5 . . . . . 121 D8
Barton Cl AL5 . . . . . 131 C3
Barton Ct LU4 . . . . . 115 B3
Barton Ind Est MK45 . . . . . 97 A4
BARTON-LE-CLAY 97 D3
Barton Rd
Barton-le-C MK45 . . . . . 97 B7
Bedford MK42 . . . . . 50 F5
Gravenhurst MK45 . . . . . 87 C4
Harlington LU5 . . . . . 96 A2
Hexton SG5 . . . . . 98 A1
Luton LU3 . . . . . 116 C7
Sharpenhoe MK45 . . . . . 96 F2
Silsoe MK45 . . . . . 86 C3
Bartram Cl MK42 . . . . . 49 C3
Bartram Ct MK42 . . . . . 49 C3
Basildon Ct LU7 . . . . . 110 F7
Bassett Ct LU7 . . . . . 110 F7
Bassett Rd LU7 . . . . . 110 F7
Bassie Cl MK42 . . . . . 50 C6
Bassmead Manor La PE19 21 C6
Batcheldor Gdns MK43 . . . . . 36 E1
BATFORD 131 D3
Batford Rd AL5 . . . . . 131 D3
Bath Abbey MK41 . . . . . 51 B8
Bath Pl SG17 . . . . . 78 B3
Bath Rd LU3 . . . . . 116 D2
Battison St MK40 . . . . . 50 B8
Battle Abbey MK41 . . . . . 39 B1
Battlesden Ave MK17 . . . . . 104 C8
Baulk The
Beeston SG19 . . . . . 54 B6
Biggleswade SG18 . . . . . 67 B6
Clapham MK41 . . . . . 37 F7
Lilley LU2 . . . . . 109 D2
Potton SG19 . . . . . 56 C6
Baxter Dr PE19 . . . . . 22 E2
Bay Cl LU4 . . . . . 115 B6
Bayham Cl MK42 . . . . . 50 D3
Baylam Dell LU2 . . . . . 117 E1
Beachampstead Rd PE19 . . 13 F6
Beacon Ave LU6 . . . . . 120 E7
Beacon Rd HP4 . . . . . 126 A1
Beaconsfield LU2 . . . . . 124 B8
Beaconsfield St MK41 . . . . . 38 B2
Beacon View LU7 . . . . . 112 D5
BEADLOW 76 B1
Beadlow Rd LU4 . . . . . 114 F4
Beale St LU6 . . . . . 114 A1
Beamish Cl SG19 . . . . . 42 C2
Beancroft Rd MK43 . . . . . 60 B1
Beanley Cl LU2 . . . . . 117 E2
Bearton Cl SG5 . . . . . 100 E1
Bearton Gn SG5 . . . . . 100 D1
Bearton Rd SG5 . . . . . 100 E1
Beatrice St MK42 . . . . . 50 A5
Beatty Rd PE19 . . . . . 22 B2
Beauchamp Cl PE19 . . . . . 22 B3
Beauchamp Ct 9 MK40 . . . 38 A1
Beauchamp Mid Sch MK41 . . . . . 38 C5
Beauchamp Rd MK43 . . . . . 61 A7
Beaudesert LU7 . . . . . 111 A7
Beaudesert Lower Sch LU7 . . . . . 111 D8
Beaufort Way MK41 . . . . . 38 C6
Beaulieu Way MK41 . . . . . 38 E5
Beaumanor Pl SG17 . . . . . 76 E3
Beaumont Ct
Flitwick MK45 . . . . . 84 E3
10 Harpenden AL5 . . . . . 131 B1
Beaumont Gdns MK42 . . . . . 49 E3
Beaumont Ho MK40 . . . . . 37 F2
Beaumont Rd
Flitwick MK45 . . . . . 84 E3
Luton LU3 . . . . . 116 B2
Beaver Cl PE19 . . . . . 22 B5
Becher Cl MK41 . . . . . 39 F5
Beckerings Park Rd MK43 83 A6
Beckett Ct 3 MK40 . . . . . 50 B8
Becketts Cl MK45 . . . . . 74 B1
Beckett St MK40 . . . . . 50 B8
Beckham Cl LU2 . . . . . 116 D7
Becks Cl AL3 . . . . . 128 D5
Bec Rd PE19 . . . . . 22 E5
Bedesman La MK42 . . . . . 50 C7
BEDFORD 50 D7
Bedford Autodrome MK44 . . . . . 18 A6
Bedford Ave MK45 . . . . . 86 C4
Bedford Bsns Ctr MK42 . . . 50 D4
Bedford Butterfly Pk* MK44 . . . . . 29 F1
Bedford Cl SG5 . . . . . 87 E2
Bedford Coll MK42 . . . . . 50 B7
Bedford Ct LU5 . . . . . 114 B5
Bedford Gdns 3 LU2 . . . 123 D8
Bedford High Sch MK40 . . . 38 B1
Bedford Hospl (North Wing) MK40 . . . . . 38 D1
Bedford Hospl (South Wing-main site) MK42 . . . . . 50 B6
Bedford Int Athletic Stadium MK41 . . . . . 50 F8
Bedford Modern Sch MK41 . . . . . 38 A3
Bedford Mus* MK40 . . . . . 50 C8
Bedford Rd
Aspley Guise MK17 . . . . . 81 F5
Barton-le-C MK45 . . . . . 97 C3
Brogborough MK43 . . . . . 82 C8
Cardington MK44 . . . . . 51 C5
Clapham MK41 . . . . . 37 F5
Clophill MK45 . . . . . 86 C8
Bedford Rd *continued*
Cold Brayfield MK46 . . . . . 34 B5
Cranfield MK43 . . . . . 59 C2
Cranfield MK43 . . . . . 60 A3
Great Barford SG18 . . . . . 40 E4
Haynes SG18 . . . . . 64 E5
Hitchin SG5 . . . . . 100 D2
Hitchin, Westmill SG5 . . . . . 100 D1
Houghton Conquest MK45 . . 62 A1
Houghton Regis LU5 . . . . . 114 A6
Kempston Hardwick MK45 . . 61 F5
Kempston MK42 . . . . . 49 E4
Letchworth SG6 . . . . . 101 D7
Lower Stondon SG16 . . . . . 89 B3
Marston Moretaine MK43 . . 72 D8
Milton Ernest MK44 . . . . . 27 B3
Moggerhanger MK44 . . . . . 53 B7
Northill SG18 . . . . . 53 B2
Ravensden MK44 . . . . . 28 E1
Roxton MK44 . . . . . 31 E2
Rushden NN10 . . . . . 8 D5
Sandy SG19 . . . . . 54 B7
Shefford SG17 . . . . . 77 B4
Stagsden MK43 . . . . . 36 C1
Turvey MK43 . . . . . 35 B5
Wick End MK43 . . . . . 48 B8
Willington MK44 . . . . . 52 B7
Wilstead, Duck End MK45 . . 62 C7
Wilstead MK45 . . . . . 62 D5
Wootton MK43 . . . . . 61 A8
Bedford RFC MK40 . . . . . 38 D1
Bedford Road Lower Sch MK42 . . . . . 49 E4
Bedford St Johns Halt MK42 . . . . . 50 B7
Bedford Sch MK40 . . . . . 38 C1
Bedford Sq LU5 . . . . . 114 B5
Bedford St
Ampthill MK45 . . . . . 73 E1
Leighton Buzzard LU7 . . . . . 111 A7
St Neots PE19 . . . . . 22 E6
Woburn MK17 . . . . . 92 F7
Bedford Sta MK40 . . . . . 50 A8
Beeby Way MK43 . . . . . 25 A3
Beech Ave
Biggleswade SG18 . . . . . 66 F8
Wilstead MK45 . . . . . 62 F2
Beech Cl
Dunstable LU6 . . . . . 121 E5
Greenfield MK45 . . . . . 85 D2
Beech Cres NN29 . . . . . 7 A7
Beech Ct
5 Bedford MK40 . . . . . 38 A1
Harpenden AL5 . . . . . 130 F3
Beechdale Rd MK42 . . . . . 50 C5
Beeches The MK45 . . . . . 86 C4
Beech Gn LU6 . . . . . 114 A1
Beech Gr
Leighton Buzzard LU7 . . . . . 110 E7
St Neots PE19 . . . . . 22 F6
Beech Hill
Letchworth SG6 . . . . . 101 D7
Luton LU2 . . . . . 117 D8
Beech Hill Com Prim Sch LU4 . . . . . 116 B1
Beech Ho PE19 . . . . . 22 F3
Beeching Cl AL5 . . . . . 131 B4
Beech Rd
Dunstable LU6 . . . . . 121 E4
Flitwick MK45 . . . . . 84 F2
Luton LU1 . . . . . 123 C8
Beech Ridge AL5 . . . . . 130 B5
Beechside SG19 . . . . . 44 C6
Beech Tree Way LU5 . . . . . 114 B5
Beech Wlk MK42 . . . . . 49 F3
Beechwood Cl SG5 . . . . . 100 D2
Beechwood Ct LU6 . . . . . 120 F7
Beechwood Park Sch AL3 . . . . . 128 B1
Beechwood Prim Sch LU4 . . . . . 115 E4
Beechwood Rd LU4 . . . . . 115 E3
Beechwood Rise SG17 . . . . . 77 D2
BEECROFT 113 F1
Beecroft Lower Sch LU6 . 113 F1
Beecroft Way LU6 . . . . . 121 A8
BEESTON 54 B4
Beeston Gn SG19 . . . . . 54 B5
Beezling Cl PE19 . . . . . 22 C6
Begwary Cl PE19 . . . . . 22 B5
Belam Way SG19 . . . . . 42 B1
Belfry Cl MK42 . . . . . 50 B4
Belfry Ct SG19 . . . . . 54 C7
Belfry The LU2 . . . . . 116 E6
Belgrave Rd LU4 . . . . . 115 D5
Bell Alley 9 LU7 . . . . . 111 A7
Bellamy Cl PE19 . . . . . 22 E2
Bellamy Rd MK43 . . . . . 60 F6
Bell Cl MK45 . . . . . 95 E6
Bellerby Rise LU4 . . . . . 115 B6
Bellevue Cl SG19 . . . . . 55 F7
Bell Foundry Cl SG19 . . . . . 44 D5
Bellingham Pl SG18 . . . . . 67 B7
Bell La MK45 . . . . . 63 D7
Bells Cl SG5 . . . . . 87 F1
Bell's Cl MK42 . . . . . 51 A3
Bellway MK17 . . . . . 81 A6
Belmont Rd LU1 . . . . . 123 C7
Belper Rd LU4 . . . . . 115 D2
Belsize Rd LU4 . . . . . 114 F3
Belvedere Rd LU3 . . . . . 116 B5
Belvoir Wlk MK41 . . . . . 39 A4
Bembridge Gdns LU3 . . . . . 115 F7
Benedict Cl NN10 . . . . . 7 F8
Benington Cl LU2 . . . . . 116 F5
Bennett Ct SG6 . . . . . 101 F6
Bennetts Cl
Bletsoe MK44 . . . . . 17 C1

Bennetts Cl continued
Dunstable LU6 . . . . 121 B7
Benning Ave LU6 . . . . 121 A8
Benson Cl LU3 . . . . 115 F7
Bentley Cl SG18 . . . . 78 F6
Bentley Ct LU1 . . . . 123 C8
Bentley Mews SG17 . . . . . . 77 B2
Bents Cl MK41 . . . . 37 D7
Berberry Dr MK45 . . . . 85 E4
Bereford Cl MK44 . . . . 40 F5
Beresford Rd
  Bedford MK40 . . . . 50 E8
  Luton LU4 . . . . 116 A1
Berkeley Cl SG18 . . . . 67 A4
Berkeley Ct AL5 . . . . 131 A2
Berkeley Path ☑ LU2 . . . . 123 E8
Berkeley Rd MK42 . . . . 50 C4
Berkley Ct PE19 . . . . 22 E4
Berkley St PE19 . . . . 22 F4
Bernard Cl LU5 . . . . 114 C1
Berrill St NN29 . . . . 7 A7
Berrow Cl LU2 . . . . 117 E2
Berry Dr MK43 . . . . 36 E2
Berry End MK17 . . . . 83 A1
Berry La MK17 . . . . 81 F6
Berry Leys LU3 . . . . 115 E7
Berwick Way SG19 . . . . 54 C8
Besford Cl LU2 . . . . 117 E2
Bessemer Cl SG5 . . . . 100 E2
Bethune Cl LU1 . . . . 123 B6
Betjeman Cl AL5 . . . . 131 C1
Betony Wlk NN10 . . . . 8 B8
Beverley Cres MK40 . . . . . . 37 F1
Beverley Gdns MK45 . . . . . . 96 C8
Beverley Gr MK40 . . . . 37 E1
Beverley Rd LU4 . . . . 115 F1
Bevery Cl MK43 . . . . 37 A8
Bevington Way PE19 . . . . . . 22 E2
Bewcastle Cl MK41 . . . . 39 A5
Bewdley Dr LU7 . . . . 110 C7
Bexhill Rd LU2 . . . . 117 D2
Bibshall Cres LU6 . . . . 121 C6
Bickerdikes Gdns SG19 . . . . 54 B8
BIDDENHAM 37 C1
Biddenham Turn MK40 . . . . . 37 E1
Biddenham Upper Sch
  MK40 . . . . 49 D8
Bideford Ct LU7 . . . . 110 C8
Bideford Gdns LU3 . . . . 116 D4
Bideford Gn LU7 . . . . 110 C8
BIDWELL 114 A6
Bidwell Hill LU5 . . . . 114 B5
Bidwell Path LU5 . . . . 114 B4
BIGGLESWADE 67 C6
Biggleswade Hospl SG18 . . 67 C8
Biggleswade Rd
  Dunton SG18 . . . . 68 B5
  Sutton SG19 . . . . 55 E4
  Upper Caldecote SG18 . . . 66 C8
Biggleswade Sta SG18 . . . . 67 A5
Bigthan Rd LU6 . . . . 121 C8
Bilberry Cl PE19 . . . . 22 C5
Bilberry Rd SG17 . . . . 78 B3
BILLINGTON 111 E2
Billington Cl MK45 . . . . 84 D3
Billington Ct LU7 . . . . 111 D1
Billington Rd
  Billington LU7 . . . . 112 A2
  Stanbridge LU7 . . . . 112 B4
Bilsdon Cl NN10 . . . . 7 B8
Bilton Rd SG4 . . . . 100 F2
Bilton Way LU1 . . . . 115 F1
Binder Cl LU4 . . . . 114 E4
Bindon Abbey MK41 . . . . . . 51 A8
Bingen Rd SG5 . . . . 100 C1
Binham Cl LU2 . . . . 116 D7
Birbeck Cl MK41 . . . . 37 C7
Birch Cl
  Broom SG18 . . . . 66 C2
  Clifton SG17 . . . . 78 A2
  Cranfield MK43 . . . . 59 C3
Birchdale Ave MK42 . . . . . . 49 F4
Birchen Gr LU2 . . . . 116 F3
Birches The
  Flitwick MK45 . . . . 84 D5
  Letchworth SG6 . . . . 111 D8
Birchfield Rd MK44 . . . . 40 E7
Birch Gr
  Lower Stondon SG16 . . . . . 89 B3
  Sandy SG19 . . . . 54 B6
Birch Link LU4 . . . . 116 C1
Birchmead SG19 . . . . 44 C6
BIRCHMOOR GREEN 92 E8
Birch Rd SG18 . . . . 67 A7
Birch's Cl LU7 . . . . 104 F2
Birch Side LU6 . . . . 121 D6
Bird Cl MK45 . . . . 62 E4
Birdsfoot La LU3 . . . . 116 B6
Bird's Hill LU7 . . . . 103 A5
Birds of Prey Ctr SG18 . . . . 65 D5
Birkdale Rd MK41 . . . . 38 E5
Birling Dr LU2 . . . . 117 C4
Birse Gn MK41 . . . . 39 B4
Birtley Croft LU2 . . . . 117 E1
BISCOT 116 C3
Biscot Rd LU3 . . . . 116 C2
Bishop Cl LU7 . . . . 111 D6
Bishopscote Rd LU3 . . . . . . 116 B3
Bishops Ct ☑ LU3 . . . . 116 D1
Bishops Rd
  Bedford MK40 . . . . 39 B1
  St Neots PE19 . . . . 22 F2
Bishopstone Ct MK40 . . . . . 50 A8
Bishops Wlk MK17 . . . . 81 B3
Bittern Dr SG18 . . . . 66 F5
Blackbird Cl MK45 . . . . 84 D2
Blackbird St SG19 . . . . 56 A7

Blackbirds The LU7 . . . . . . 104 E2
Blackburn Cl MK42 . . . . 51 B2
Blackburn Rd LU5 . . . . 114 B3
Blackfriars NN10 . . . . 7 F8
Black Hat Cl MK45 . . . . 62 E4
Blackhill LU7 . . . . 112 F5
Blackhill La MK45 . . . . 96 E8
Blacksmith Cl
  Everton SG19 . . . . 43 C3
  Stotfold SG5 . . . . 90 F7
Blacksmith Ct ☑ LU6 . . . . 121 B8
Black Swan La LU3 . . . . . . 116 A5
Blackthorn Dr LU2 . . . . 117 C4
Blackthorn Gr MK17 . . . . . . 81 A4
Black Thorn Rd LU5 . . . . . . 114 C6
Blackwood Rd PE19 . . . . . . 22 B3
Blair Way PE19 . . . . 22 E2
Blakedown LU2 . . . . 116 E1
Blakedown Rd LU2 . . . . 116 E1
Blakelands 97 D2
Blakeney Dr LU2 . . . . 116 C7
Blakes Way PE19 . . . . 22 B2
Blandford Ave LU2 . . . . 116 D6
Brackendale Gr
  Harpenden AL5 . . . . 130 D3
  Luton LU3 . . . . 116 B5
Bracken Pl MK41 . . . . 39 B1
Brackham Rd MK45 . . . . 62 E4
Blaydon Rd
  Luton LU2 . . . . 124 A8
  Sandy SG19 . . . . 42 C2
Blenheim Cl
  Rushden NN10 . . . . 8 A8
  St Neots PE19 . . . . 22 C4
Blenheim Cres LU3 . . . . . . 116 C2
Blenheim Link MK45 . . . . . . 84 D1
Blenheim Rd MK42 . . . . 51 B2
BLETSOE 17 C1
Bliss Ave
  Cranfield MK43 . . . . 59 C8
  Shefford SG17 . . . . 77 D3
Bloomfield Ave LU2 . . . . . . 117 A1
Bloomfield Ct LU7 . . . . 77 B2
Bloomfield Rd AL5 . . . . 130 F3
Bloomsbury Cl MK17 . . . . . . 92 F6
Bloomsbury Gdns LU5 . . . . 114 D5
Blows Rd LU5 . . . . 121 D7
Bluebell Cl
  Bedford MK40 . . . . 50 F4
  Biggleswade SG18 . . . . . . 67 C4
  Flitwick MK45 . . . . 84 D3
Bluebell Dr SG16 . . . . 89 A3
Bluebell Rise NN10 . . . . 8 B8
Bluebell Wood LU1 . . . . . . 123 A7
Blue Spruce Cl MK43 . . . . . 56 C4
Blundell Pl MK42 . . . . 50 C4
Blundell Rd LU3 . . . . 116 A4
BLUNHAM 41 E3
Blunham Rd
  Biggleswade SG18 . . . . . . 66 F5
  Moggerhanger MK44 . . . . . 53 C8
Blythe Way SG19 . . . . 44 D5
Blyth Pl ☑ LU1 . . . . 123 D6
Boddington Gdns LU6 . . . . . 67 C7
Boddington Ind Est SG18 . . 67 B6
Bodiam Way PE19 . . . . 22 B3
Bodmin Rd LU4 . . . . 115 F3
Bolingbroke Rd LU1 . . . . . . 123 B6
Bolney Gn LU2 . . . . 117 D3
BOLNHURST 19 D4
Bolton Rd LU1 . . . . 123 F7
Bond Ct AL5 . . . . 130 F3
Bonds La SG18 . . . . 67 A5
Bonnick Cl LU1 . . . . 123 C6
Boothey Cl SG18 . . . . 67 A7
Booth Pl LU6 . . . . 119 E6
Boot La SG18 . . . . 68 D5
Borden La SG18 . . . . 64 C5
Borders Way LU5 . . . . 114 C6
Bordale AL5 . . . . 131 A1
Borough Rd LU5 . . . . 121 D7
Borrowdale Ave LU6 . . . . . . 121 C6
Borton Ave SG16 . . . . 89 B4
Boscombe Rd LU2 . . . . 114 C2
Bosmore Rd LU3 . . . . 115 F5
Bossard Ct LU7 . . . . 111 A7
Bossington La
  Leighton Buzzard, Linslade
  LU7 . . . . 110 F7
  Leighton Buzzard LU7 . . . 110 F8
Boswell Ct ☑ MK40 . . . . . . 38 B1
Boswell Dr SG5 . . . . 100 C4
Boswell Pl ☑ MK40 . . . . . . 38 B1
Boteler Gdns MK42 . . . . 50 F5
Bothy The SG18 . . . . 66 C2
BOTT END 61 A7
Bottom Dr LU6 . . . . 120 D5
Boughton Dr NN10 . . . . 8 A8
BOUGHTON END 83 A8
Boughton End La MK43 . . . . 72 B1
Boundary The MK41 . . . . . . 39 A2
Bourne Apts The ☑ AL5 . . 130 F2
BOURNE END
  MK43 . . . . 59 C6
  MK44 . . . . 17 C6
Bourne End La MK44 . . . . . 17 B4
Bourne End Rd
  Cranfield MK43 . . . . 59 C4
  Kempston MK43 . . . . 48 B1
Bourne Rd MK44 . . . . 10 F2
Bourneside MK41 . . . . 38 D6
Bourne The ☑ AL5 . . . . . . 130 F2
Bow Brickhill Rd MK17 . . . . 81 A4
Bowbrook Vale LU2 . . . . . . 117 F1
Bower Cl LU6 . . . . 119 F5
Bower Heath La AL5 . . . . . 131 C6
Bower La LU6 . . . . 119 F5
Bowers Cl MK44 . . . . 11 B3
Bowers La MK44 . . . . 11 B3
Bower's Mill PE19 . . . . 22 E5
Bower's Par AL5 . . . . 131 A1
Bower St MK40 . . . . 50 D8
Bowers Way AL5 . . . . 131 A1

Bowhill MK41 . . . . 38 F3
Bowland Cres LU4 . . . . 121 A6
Bowles Way LU6 . . . . 121 D5
Bowling Green La LU2 . . . . 116 E2
Bowling Green Rd MK43 . . . 59 C1
Bowmans Cl LU6 . . . . 121 C7
Bowmans Way LU6 . . . . . . 121 C7
Bowyer's Cl SG5 . . . . 100 D1
BOX END 48 F6
Box End Rd MK43 . . . . 50 C6
Boxgrove Cl LU2 . . . . 117 C5
Boxgrove Priory MK41 . . . . . 39 B1
Boxted Cl LU4 . . . . 115 C5
Boyde Gdns MK40 . . . . 49 E7
Boyle Cl LU2 . . . . 123 E8
Brabazon Cl MK42 . . . . 51 A2
Braceby Cl LU3 . . . . 115 F6
Brace St ☑ MK40 . . . . 50 B8
Brache Cl LU5 . . . . 123 F6
Brache The MK45 . . . . 74 C1
Bracken Pl MK41 . . . . 39 B1
Bracklesham Gdns LU2 . . . 117 B3
Brackley Rd MK42 . . . . 50 C5
Bracknell Cl LU4 . . . . 114 F3
Bradden Cotts HP2 . . . . . . 132 F8
Bradden La HP1, HP2 . . . . 132 E7
Bradden Villas HP2 . . . . . . 132 F8
Bradford Rd LU5 . . . . 106 A5
Bradford Way LU5 . . . . 105 F5
Bradgate Rd MK40 . . . . 38 D1
Bradgers Hill Rd LU2 . . . . . 116 E4
Bradley Rd LU4 . . . . 115 D1
Bradleys Cnr SG4 . . . . 101 C1
Bradshaws Cl MK45 . . . . . . 97 C3
Braemar Ct MK40 . . . . 50 A8
Braeside MK41 . . . . 38 F4
BRAGENHAM 102 C6
Bragenham La LU7 . . . . . . 102 D5
Braggs La SG19 . . . . 57 C4
Braintree Cl LU4 . . . . 114 F3
Braithwaite Ct ☑ LU3 . . . . 116 D1
Bramble Cl
  Harpenden AL5 . . . . 130 F3
  Leighton Buzzard LU7 . . . 111 C7
  Luton LU4 . . . . 115 C4
Bramble Rd LU5 . . . . 115 C4
Brambles AL5 . . . . 64 F4
Brambles The MK45 . . . . . . 85 F4
Brambling Cl SG19 . . . . 42 C2
Bramhanger Acre LU3 . . . . 115 D7
Bramingham Bsns Pk
  LU3 . . . . 116 B8
Bramingham Prim Sch
  LU3 . . . . 116 B8
Bramingham Rd LU3 . . . . . 115 F6
Bramley Cl
  Baldock SG7 . . . . 91 F1
  Shefford SG17 . . . . 77 B2
Bramley Ct MK43 . . . . 24 F6
Brampton Cl
  Bedford MK42 . . . . 50 F5
  Harpenden AL5 . . . . 131 D1
Brampton Park Rd SG5 . . . 100 E1
Brampton Rise LU6 . . . . . . 121 C6
Brancaster Ct MK42 . . . . . . 50 F4
Brancker Ave MK42 . . . . . . 51 A2
Brandreth Ave LU5 . . . . . . 114 E1
Brandreth Pl PE19 . . . . 54 D6
Brangwyn Gdns MK41 . . . . . 38 B3
Branton Cl LU2 . . . . 117 E2
Brantwood Rd LU1 . . . . 123 C7
Braybrook Cl LU6 . . . . 54 A8
Braybrooks Dr SG19 . . . . . . 56 A7
Brayes Manor SG5 . . . . 90 F6
Brays Cl LU2 . . . . 117 B3
Brays Rd LU2 . . . . 117 B3
Brazier Cl MK45 . . . . 97 B3
Breachwell Pl LU7 . . . . 118 A1
BREACHWOOD GREEN . . . 125 D8
Breadcroft La AL5 . . . . 131 B1
Breamish Wlk MK41 . . . . . . 38 C7
Brecon Cl ☑ LU3 . . . . 123 D6
Brecon Way MK41 . . . . 38 E5
Brendon Ave
  Bedford MK41 . . . . 38 E3
  Luton LU2 . . . . 117 C1
Brentwood Cl LU5 . . . . 114 D6
Brereton Rd MK40 . . . . 50 B8
Brett Dr MK43 . . . . 36 F1
Bretts Mead LU1 . . . . 123 C5
Bretts Rd LU1 . . . . 123 C5
Brewers Hill Mid Sch
  LU6 . . . . 113 E1
Brewers Hill Rd LU6 . . . . . . 113 F1
Brewery La
  Ampthill MK45 . . . . 73 E1
  Baldock SG7 . . . . 91 E1
Brian May Gr MK45 . . . . . . 86 B3
Brian Rd LU5 . . . . 96 A2
Briar Bank Cvn Pk MK45 . . 62 F2
Briar Cl
  Ampthill MK45 . . . . 84 E8
  Luton LU2 . . . . 117 C4
Briar Patch La SG6 . . . . . . 101 D3
Briars The MK42 . . . . 49 F3
Brickfield Rd MK41 . . . . 39 B6
BRICKHILL 38 C4
Brickhill Cl
  Blunham MK44 . . . . 41 E3
  Sandy SG19 . . . . 54 D8
Brickhill Dr MK41 . . . . 38 D5
Brickhill La MK41 . . . . 129 C8
Brickhill Lower Sch MK41 . . 38 D5
Brickhill Rd
  Heath and Reach LU7 . . . 103 A7

Brickhill Rd continued
  Sandy SG19 . . . . 54 D7
Brickle Pl SG17 . . . . 78 B2
Brickly Rd LU4 . . . . 115 C5
Bridge Ct AL5 . . . . 130 F3
BRIDGE END 36 E2
Bridgeman Dr LU5 . . . . 114 D5
Bridgend MK43 . . . . 25 B4
Bridge Rd
  Bedford MK42 . . . . 50 C6
  Letchworth SG6 . . . . 101 F6
Bridge St
  Leighton Buzzard LU7 . . . 110 F7
  Luton LU1 . . . . 123 E8
  Turvey MK43 . . . . 34 D5
Bridge View MK40 . . . . 50 D8
Bridle Dr MK41 . . . . 37 C7
Brierley Cl
  Dunstable LU6 . . . . 121 D5
  Luton LU2 . . . . 117 C2
Brigginton Cotts LU7 . . . . . 111 D8
Brigham Gdns SG18 . . . . . . 67 A6
Brightman Cotts ☑ LU3 . . 116 A7
Brightmans Dr MK45 . . . . . . 74 B1
Brightwell Ave LU6 . . . . 120 C7
Brill Cl LU2 . . . . 117 D2
Brimfield Cl LU2 . . . . 117 D2
Brindley Cl SG19 . . . . 42 B1
Brinsmade Rd MK45 . . . . . . 73 F1
Bristol Rd LU3 . . . . 116 B4
Britain St LU5 . . . . 121 C8
Britannia Ave LU3 . . . . 116 B4
Britannia Ests LU3 . . . . 116 B2
Britannia Hall LU2 . . . . 124 C8
Britannia Rd MK42 . . . . 50 B6
Brittains Rise SG16 . . . . . . 88 E2
Brittany Ct LU6 . . . . 121 C8
Britten Cl MK40 . . . . 3 C8
Britten Rd LU3 . . . . 77 D3
Brittons Cl MK44 . . . . 16 E3
Brittons La MK17 . . . . 70 C3
Brive Rd LU5 . . . . 121 E6
Brixham Ct MK40 . . . . 38 E2
Broadacres LU2 . . . . 116 D6
Broad Ave MK42 . . . . 50 D8
Broadcroft SG6 . . . . 101 F2
Broadfields AL5 . . . . 130 F2
BROAD GREEN 59 B3
Broadhurst Abbey MK41 . . . 51 A8
Broadmead SG18 . . . . 67 B5
Broad Mead LU3 . . . . 116 A3
Broadmead Bsns Pk
  MK43 . . . . 61 C2
Broadmead Lower Sch
  MK43 . . . . 61 C2
Broadmead Rd MK43 . . . . . 61 C2
Broadmead Sch LU1 . . . . . 123 E5
Broad Oak Ct LU2 . . . . 117 D3
Broad Rush Gn LU7 . . . . . . 110 E8
Broad St SG17 . . . . 78 B2
Broadwater Ave SG6 . . . . . 101 E5
Broadwater Dale SG6 . . . . . 101 E5
Broadway
  Houghton Conquest MK45 . 74 B8
  Letchworth SG6 . . . . 101 F5
Broadway Ct SG6 . . . . 101 E5
Broadway The MK40 . . . . . . 38 B1
Broad Wlk
  Clifton SG17 . . . . 78 A2
  Dunstable LU5 . . . . 121 B8
Broad Wlk The PE19 . . . . . . 22 E3
Brocas Way LU7 . . . . 118 A3
Brocket Ct LU4 . . . . 115 D5
Brockwell MK43 . . . . 37 A8
Brockwood Cl SG19 . . . . . . 44 D6
BROGBOROUGH 71 D1
BROMHAM 36 F3
Bromham CE Lower Sch
  MK43 . . . . 36 F3
Bromham Mill* MK43 . . . . . 37 A2
Bromham Rd
  Biddenham MK40 . . . . 37 D1
  Bromham MK40 . . . . 37 A2
Bromley Gdns LU5 . . . . 114 D5
Brompton Cl LU3 . . . . 115 F8
Bronte Ave SG5 . . . . 100 E1
Brook Cl
  ☑ Dunstable LU6 . . . . 114 A1
  Henlow SG16 . . . . 78 D1
  Upper Caldecote SG18 . . . 66 B8
Brook Ct LU3 . . . . 116 D1
Brook Dr MK42 . . . . 49 C3
BROOK END
  MK17 . . . . 94 A6
  MK44 . . . . 50 E5
  SG19 . . . . 56 C6
Brook End
  North Crawley MK16 . . . . . 58 A6
  Potton SG19 . . . . 56 B7
Brookend Dr MK45 . . . . 97 B3
Brookes Rd MK45 . . . . 84 F3
Brookfield Cl LU5 . . . . 114 D5
Brookfield Pk LU5 . . . . 114 C5
Brookfield Pk Cvn Pk
  LU6 . . . . 120 A8
Brookfield Rd MK41 . . . . . . 38 F2
Brookfields
  Pavenham MK43 . . . . 26 C4
  Potton SG19 . . . . 56 B7
Brook La
  Flitton MK45 . . . . 85 D4
  Great Barford MK44 . . . . . 41 A5
  Harrold MK43 . . . . 22 A7
  Newton Blossomville MK43 34 B3
  Renhold MK41 . . . . 39 B6
  Upper Dean PE28 . . . . 5 B4

Ben-Bun **135**

Brooklands MK42 . . . . 49 C8
Brooklands Ave LU7 . . . . . 111 B6
Brooklands Cl LU8 . . . . 115 C6
Brooklands Dr LU7 . . . . 111 C7
Brooklands Mid Sch LU7 . . 111 C6
Brooklands Rd MK44 . . . . . . 10 F1
Brookmead SG17 . . . . 88 C6
Brook Rd
  Marston Moretaine MK43 . 72 C7
  St Neots PE19 . . . . 22 C4
Brookside
  Campton SG17 . . . . 87 F8
  Great Barford MK44 . . . . . 41 A5
  Letchworth SG6 . . . . 101 F5
  Meppershall SG17 . . . . . . 88 C6
  Renhold MK41 . . . . 39 B7
  Shillington SG5 . . . . 87 E1
Brookside Wlk LU7 . . . . . . 111 C6
Brook St
  Bedford MK42 . . . . 50 D5
  Edlesborough LU6 . . . . . . 119 F4
  Hargrave NN9 . . . . 1 E3
  Leighton Buzzard LU7 . . . 111 C7
  Luton LU3 . . . . 123 D8
  St Neots PE19 . . . . 22 E5
Brookvale SG16 . . . . 90 E6
Brook Way MK43 . . . . 36 E2
BROOM 66 C3
Brookvale LU3 . . . . 116 C5
Broom Crossroads SG18 . . 66 A1
Broom Hall LU6 . . . . 66 C2
Broomhills Rd LU2 . . . . 103 A1
Brooms Rd LU2 . . . . 124 A8
Broomstick Ind Est LU6 . . . 119 E4
Broughton Ave
  Luton LU3 . . . . 116 C5
  Toddington LU5 . . . . 105 E6
Broughton Rd MK17 . . . . . . 70 C3
Browning Cl
  Bromham MK43 . . . . 36 E2
  Rushden NN10 . . . . 8 D8
Browning Dr PE19 . . . . 22 C6
Browning Rd
  Harpenden AL5 . . . . 131 C2
  Luton LU4 . . . . 115 A2
Brownlow Ave LU6 . . . . 119 F3
Brownlow Rise LU6 . . . . . . 120 A8
Browns Cl MK43 . . . . 72 C7
Brown's Cl LU4 . . . . 115 D5
Browns Cres LU5 . . . . 95 F3
Browns Ct MK40 . . . . 50 C8
Brownshill MK45 . . . . 74 C1
Brownslea LU7 . . . . 111 C7
Brown's Sq PE19 . . . . 22 F5
Browns Way MK17 . . . . 81 E5
Broxley Mead LU4 . . . . 115 E5
Bruce Rd MK42 . . . . 49 D3
Brunel Cl LU4 . . . . 114 E3
Brunel Rd
  Bedford MK41 . . . . 51 A8
  Luton LU4 . . . . 114 E3
Brunswick Cl SG18 . . . . 67 A8
Brunswick St LU2 . . . . 123 F8
Brunt's La SG18 . . . . 66 F6
Brussels Way LU3 . . . . 116 A3
Bruthwaite Gn MK41 . . . . . . 39 C4
Bryans Cres MK16 . . . . 58 A6
Bryant Ct AL5 . . . . 131 A3
Bryants Cl SG5 . . . . 87 F2
Bryant Way LU5 . . . . 105 F5
Bryony Cl MK41 . . . . 39 B1
Bryony Way LU2 . . . . 113 E1
Buchanan Cl LU2 . . . . 124 B8
Buchanan Dr LU2 . . . . 124 B8
Buckfast Ave MK41 . . . . 38 F5
Buckingham Cl LU3 . . . . . . 115 F7
Buckingham Mews MK45 . . 84 F1
Buckle Cl LU3 . . . . 115 F7
Buckley Rd PE19 . . . . 22 E4
Bucks Cl MK43 . . . . 36 F2
Buckwood Ave LU5 . . . . . . 114 F1
Buckwood La LU6 . . . . 127 C7
Buckwood Rd AL3 . . . . 128 C6
BUDNA 53 C3
Budna Rd SG19 . . . . 53 C4
Buff La SG19 . . . . 45 F1
Bull Pond La LU6 . . . . 121 B7
Bull St SG19 . . . . 56 A7
Bungalows The
  Harpenden AL5 . . . . 131 C3
  Toddington LU5 . . . . 106 A7
Bunhill Cl LU6 . . . . 120 F8
Bunkers Dr MK45 . . . . 63 D7
Bunkers La LU7 . . . . 110 D6
Bunting Rd LU4 . . . . 115 A4
Buntings The
  Bedford MK41 . . . . 38 D4
  Sandy SG19 . . . . 42 C2
Bunyan Cl
  Clifton SG17 . . . . 78 A2
  Gamlingay SG19 . . . . 44 A8
  Houghton Conquest MK45 . 74 A8
  Pirton SG5 . . . . 99 D4
Bunyan Cnr MK42 . . . . 50 E4
Bunyan Meeting Ho & Mus*
  MK40 . . . . 50 C8
Bunyan Rd
  Bedford MK41 . . . . 50 B5
  Biggleswade SG18 . . . . . . 67 A5
  Kempston MK42 . . . . 49 E3
  Sandy SG19 . . . . 45 E5
  Westoning MK45 . . . . 95 E5
Bunyans Cl LU3 . . . . 116 A5

Bunyans Mead MK42.....50 C3
Bunyans Wlk LU5.......99 F3
Burdett's Ct SG19.......56 A7
Bure Cl MK41.........38 D6
Burfield Ct LU2......117 D3
Burford Cl LU3.......108 A1
Burford Way SG5......100 D2
Burford Wlk LU5......114 E5
BURGE END...........99 D5
Burge End La SG5......99 C5
Burges Cl LU6........121 D6
Burgess Cl
  Haynes MK45.........75 F8
  Kempston MK42......49 D6
Burgess Way SG6.......78 D3
Burghley Cl MK45......84 C1
Burgoyne Ct SG19......56 A8
Burgoyne Mid Sch SG19..53 F7
Burleigh Pl MK43......37 A8
Burley Cl.............90 F2
Burnaby Rd MK40.......38 C1
Burnell Rise SG6.....101 D5
Burnell Wlk SG6......101 E5
Burnett Ave SG16......89 B4
Burnham Rd LU2.......117 B2
Burns Ct PE19.........22 D5
Burnt Cl
  Luton LU3..........115 F7
  St Neots PE19........22 F3
Burr Cl MK45..........97 C4
Burridge Cl MK43......72 D8
Burridge's Cl MK43....36 C7
Burrows Cl
  Clifton SG17........78 A2
  Woburn Sands MK17...81 B5
Burrsholt MK44........52 A5
Burr's Pl LU1........123 E6
Burr St
  Dunstable LU6......121 B8
  Luton LU2..........123 E8
Bursdale SG6.........101 D6
Burwell Rd PE19......22 C6
Bury Cl LU5...........95 F1
Bury Ct MK41..........39 B2
BURY END
  MK43...............36 A2
  SG5................87 E3
Bury End SG5..........99 D4
Bury Farm Cl LU7.....118 C6
Bury Hill SG19........56 B7
Bury La LU3..........108 A5
Bury Mead SG15........90 A7
Bury Mead Rd SG5.....100 F1
BURY PARK............116 B1
Bury Park Rd LU1.....123 C8
Bury Rd
  Shefford SG17.......77 E3
  Shillington SG5.....87 E2
Bury Rise MK43.......112 F5
Bury The MK43.........26 C4
Bury Wlk MK41.........39 B2
BUSHMEAD.............20 D4
Bushmead Ave MK40.....50 D8
Bushmead Cross MK44...20 C5
Bushmead Ct LU2......116 E5
Bushmead Gdns PE19....22 B3
Bushmead Prim Sch
  Luton LU2..........116 E5
  St Neots PE19........22 A3
Bushmead Priory* MK44..20 D6
Bushmead Rd
  Luton LU2..........116 E5
  St Neots PE19........22 A3
Bustard Hill PE28......6 D8
Butcher's La SG19.....57 B4
Butely Rd LU4.......115 B5
Bute Sq LU1..........123 E7
Bute St LU1..........123 E7
Butler Dr MK43........72 C3
Butler St MK44........28 F1
Butlers Yd SG7........91 E1
Butler Way MK42......49 E5
Butlin Rd LU1.......123 B7
Buttercup Cl
  Bedford MK40........50 F4
  Dunstable LU6......121 A7
Buttercup Mead LU5...67 C5
Butterfield Green Rd
  LU2...............117 A6
Buttermere Ave LU6...121 C6
Buttermere Cl
  Flitwick MK45.......84 E2
  Kempston MK42......49 D3
Buttermere Path SG18..67 A4
Butterworth Path **1**
  LU2...............123 E8
Butts The
  Langford SG18.......78 F6
  Riseley MK44........10 E1
Buxton Cl SG17........88 C6
Buxton Rd LU1.......123 D7
Buxtons La SG8........69 F3
Buzzard Rd LU4......115 A4
Byards Gn SG19........55 F8
Bye Rd MK43..........72 B3
Byfield Cl
  Luton LU4..........115 B1
  Toddington LU5.....105 E6
Byford Path LU7......111 D5
Byford Way LU7......111 D5
Bygrave Rd MK44.......91 F1
Byng Cl PE19..........22 B2
Byrnes Mews SG17......77 C3

Byron Cl
  Biggleswade SG18....67 A5
  Upper Caldecote SG18..66 C8
Byron Cres
  Bedford MK40........37 F2
  Flitwick MK45.......84 D3
Byron Pl PE19.........22 C6
Byron Rd
  Harpenden AL5......131 A2
  Luton LU4..........115 B2
Byslips Rd LU6.......127 D5

C

CADDINGTON..........122 D3
Caddington Comm AL3..128 E8
Cade Cl SG6...........91 C1
Cades Cl LU3.........123 A6
Cades La LU1.........123 A6
Cadia Cl LU1.........122 E4
Cadwell Ct SG4......101 A2
Cadwell La SG4......101 A2
Caernarvon Rd PE19....22 F1
Cainhoe Rd MK45......86 C8
Caister Rd MK41.......39 B4
Calcutt Cl LU5......114 F2
CALDECOTE............80 D1
Caldecote Lower Sch
  SG18..............66 B8
Caldecote Rd
  Ickwell SG18........65 E8
  Newnham SG7........91 E8
  St Neots PE19.......22 E3
CALDECOTT............3 C6
Caldecott Rd NN9......3 C7
Calder Gdns LU3.....103 A1
Calder Rise MK41.....38 D6
Caleb Cl LU4.........115 F2
California...........120 F6
California SG7........91 F1
Calnwood Rd LU4......115 C3
Calshot Wlk MK41......39 A5
Calverton Rd LU3.....116 A6
Camberton Rd LU7....110 E5
Cambrian Way MK41.....83 E1
Cambridge Cl SG18.....78 F4
Cambridge Ct PE19.....22 F5
Cambridge Gdns
  Langford SG18.......78 F5
  St Neots PE19.......22 F5
Cambridge Rd
  Bedford MK42, MK44..51 A5
  Cardington MK44.....51 D6
  Dunton SG18........68 D6
  Hitchin SG4........101 C2
  Langford SG18.......78 F5
  Sandy SG19.........54 C7
Cambridge St
  Luton LU1..........123 F6
  St Neots PE19.......22 F5
  Wymington NN10.......3 C7
Cambridge Way SG18...78 F5
Cam Ctr SG4.........101 A3
Camestone Lower Sch
  MK42...............49 F4
Camford Ct LU3........49 D4
Camford Way LU3.....107 B1
Campania Gr LU3.....116 A8
Campbell Cl MK42.....49 D3
Campbell Rd MK40......38 D1
Camp Dr LU5.........114 B5
Campers Ave SG6.....101 E5
Campers Rd SG6......101 E5
Campers Wlk SG6.....101 D5
Campfield Way SG6...101 D5
Campian Cl LU3......113 E1
Campin Ct MK43........60 E1
Campion Cl NN10.......8 B8
Campion Rd MK45......95 F5
Campion Way MK45.....84 D3
CAMPTON..............87 D1
Campton Lower Sch SG17 76 F1
Campton Rd
  Gravenhurst MK45, SG17 87 D6
  Meppershall SG17....87 F6
  Shefford SG17.......77 A2
Cam Sq SG4..........101 A3
Canberra Gdns LU3...116 B6
Canberra Rd MK42......50 F2
Candale Cl LU6......121 C6
Canesworde Rd LU6...121 A7
Cannock Chase MK41..109 F4
Cannon La LU2.......117 B5
Cannon's Cl SG8......69 F5
Canons Cl MK43........60 F8
Canterbury Cl
  Kempston MK42......49 E6
  Luton LU3..........115 F4
Canterbury Rd MK45...84 C1
Cantilupe Cl LU6....119 D6
Canvin Way MK43......50 E5
CAPABILITY GREEN....123 F4
Capron Cl LU3.......114 A2
Capron Rd
  Dunstable LU5......114 A2
  Luton LU3..........114 E4
Capshill Ave LU6....111 C7
Captains Cl MK44.....17 C1
Capulet Cl PE19......22 C3
Cardiff Gr LU1......123 B7
Cardiff Rd LU1......123 B7
Cardigan Cl **10** LU1...123 D8
Cardigan Gdns LU1...123 D7
Cardigan St LU1.....123 D7
Cardinal Ct **3** LU2.....116 F1
Cardinal Newman RC Sec
  Sch LU2...........108 C1

CARDINGTON...........51 D4
Cardington Ct MK42....50 F5
Cardington Rd MK42,
  MK44...............50 F6
Carfax Cl LU4.......114 E3
Carina Dr LU7.......111 C7
Carisbrooke Rd
  Harpenden AL5......131 C2
  Luton LU4..........115 E1
Carisbrooke Way
  Bedford MK41........39 A4
  St Neots PE19.......22 F2
Carlisle Cl
  Dunstable LU6......121 B6
  Sandy SG18..........54 C8
Carlow Ct LU6.......121 A8
Carlton Cl
  Luton LU3..........116 C2
  Rushden NN10........8 A7
Carlton Cres LU3....116 C2
Carlton Ct LU3......131 B1
Carlton Gdns MK41....38 D4
Carlton Jun LU7.....103 A3
Carlton Lower Sch MK43..25 A4
Carlton Rd
  Felmersham MK43.....25 F7
  Harpenden AL5......131 B2
  Harrold MK43........25 B5
  Turvey MK43.........34 C7
Carmarthen Way NN10...8 C8
Carmelite Rd LU4....115 A3
Carnaby PE28..........
Carnation Cl LU7....103 A1
Carnegie Gdns LU3...116 A8
Carnell Cl MK42......49 C2
Carnoustie Dr MK40....49 B7
Carol Cl LU3.........116 B4
Carole Cl LU1.......123 E5
Carolyn Cl LU3......116 B4
Carpenders Cl AL5...130 D4
Carrick Rd MK41......25 B4
Carriers Way MK43....49 E5
Carroll Dr MK42......50 C4
Carron Cl LU7.......110 B7
Carron Rd MK41.......38 C7
Carsdale Cl LU3......116 A6
Carter Cl MK42.......50 E6
Carteret Rd LU7.....117 C1
Carters Cl SG15......90 A7
Carters La SG19.......56 A4
Carter St SG19.......54 B8
Carters Way SG15.....90 A7
Carters Wlk SG15.....90 A7
Carterweys LU5......114 E2
Carthagena Rd SG19...55 E5
Cartmel Dr LU6......121 B6
Cartmel Priory MK41...51 B8
Cartwright Cl MK43....36 F1
Cashio La SG6........91 A1
Caslon Way LU6.......90 F1
Castle Cl
  Totternhoe LU6.....120 A8
  Wilstead MK45.......62 F4
Castle Croft Rd LU1..123 A6
Castle Ct
  Hitchin SG5........100 D1
  Rushden NN10........8 A8
Castle Gdns PE28......6 F4
Castle Hill Cl PE19...22 C2
Castle Hill St MK45...75 E1
Castle Hill Rd LU6...119 F8
Castle La MK40........50 C8
Castle Lower Sch MK40..38 C1
Castle Rd
  Bedford MK40........50 D8
  Lavendon MK46.......23 F1
Castle Rise AL4......131 F2
Castles Cl SG5........90 F8
Castle St
  Luton, High Town LU1..123 E7
  Luton, New Town LU1..123 E6
Caswell La MK17.......92 F7
Catchacre LU6.......121 A7
Cater St MK41........49 E4
Catesby Gn LU3......108 B1
Catherall Rd LU3....116 B6
Catherine Rd MK45....84 E3
Catherines Cl SG19...56 A7
Catsbrook Rd LU3....116 B6
CAULCOTT............60 E1
Cauldwell Ct
  Bedford MK40........50 A6
  Sandy SG19.........54 C8
Cauldwell Lower Sch
  MK42...............50 B6
Cauldwell St MK42....50 B7
Cauldwell Wlk MK42...50 A6
Cause End Rd MK44....60 F7
Causeway
  Felmersham MK43....16 B1
  Great Staughton PE19..13 F6
Causeway Ct PE19.....13 F6
Causeway The
  Carlton MK43.......25 B3
  Shillington MK45....86 D8
Cavalier Cl LU3.....116 A5
Cavendish Ct
  Bedford MK40........37 F2
  Biggleswade SG18....67 A6
  St Neots PE19.......22 D5
Cavendish Rd
  Luton LU3..........116 B2
  Markyate AL3.......128 D6
Cavendish St MK40....38 B1

Cave's Ct SG19........56 A7
Cave's La MK40........38 E2
Cawdor Cl MK41.......39 B4
Cawdor Pl PE19.......22 F2
Caxton Cl LU3.......115 F4
Caxton Pk MK41.......39 C3
Caxton Rd MK41.......39 C3
Caxton Rd MK41.......39 D3
Cedar Ave
  Biggleswade SG18....66 F7
  Ickleford SG5......100 E4
  Wilstead MK45.......62 F2
Cedar Cl
  Ampthill MK45.......84 E7
  Irchester NN29.......7 A7
  Luton LU4..........114 E3
  Rushden NN10........8 A8
  Shefford SG17.......77 E2
Cedars Gdns SG19.....54 B7
Cedar Rd MK42.......50 D5
Cedars Ctyd MK45.....84 E7
Cedars The
  Ampthill MK45.......84 E7
  Dunstable LU6......121 C7
  13 Harpenden AL5...131 B1
  Wootton MK43.......49 A2
Cedars Upper Sch & Com
  Coll The LU7.......110 E5
Cedars Way LU7......110 E5
Cedars Wlk MK45......84 E7
Celandine Cl NN10.....8 B7
Celandine Dr LU3....116 A8
Cemetery Rd
  Houghton Regis LU5..114 B3
  Kempston MK43......49 B3
  Shefford SG17.......77 E2
Centauri Cl LU7.....111 C8
Central App SG6.....101 F6
Central Ave
  Henlow SG16........89 B3
  Shortstown MK42.....51 A2
  Wharley End MK43....58 E2
  Whipsnade LU6......126 E8
Centrus Ind Est LU5..114 B2
Centtury Cl MK45.....84 F2
Ceres Cres LU7......111 C7
Chad La AL3.........129 C4
Chadwell Cl LU2.....116 F1
CHADWELL END.........12 C7
Chadwick Cl LU4.....114 A1
Chagford Cl MK40......38 E1
Chagny Cl SG6......101 E6
Chainbridge La PE28...2 F8
Chalfont Way LU2....117 D2
Chalgrave Rd LU5, LU7..105 D3
Chalkdown LU2.......116 E6
CHALK HILL.........113 E4
Chalk Hill LU2......117 F4
Challney Boys High Sch
  LU4...............106 E1
Challney Cl LU4.....115 D2
Challney Girls High Sch
  LU4...............106 E1
CHALTON............106 E1
Chalton Hts LU4.....106 E1
Chalton Lower Sch LU4..106 E1
Chalton Rd LU4......115 C5
Chamberlains AL5....130 A5
Chamberlains Jun LU3..103 A2
Chamberlain Way PE19..22 F7
Chambers La SG5.....100 E4
Chambers Way SG18...67 C5
Chancellors SG18.....67 C5
Chandler Path MK42...49 D5
Chandler Pl LU2.....103 A5
Chandlers Cl MK43....72 C8
Chandlers Wharf PE19..22 E5
Chandos Ct **14** MK40...38 B1
Chandos Rd
  Ampthill MK45.......84 E8
  Luton LU4..........115 F1
Chandos St MK40......38 B1
CHANNEL'S END........30 C5
Channels End Rd MK44..30 C5
Chantry Ave MK42.....49 F2
Chantry Cl MK17.......81 A6
Chantry Piece SG18...53 E2
Chantry Prim Sch LU4..114 F4
Chantry Rd MK42......49 F2
Chaomans SG6.......101 F3
Chapel Cl
  Bedford MK41........39 B1
  Great Barford MK44..40 F5
  Honeydon MK44......21 B2
  Luton LU4..........116 C8
  Shefford SG17.......77 F2
  Swineshead MK44....11 D8
  Toddington LU5.....105 F6
  Wrestlingworth SG19..57 B4
Chapel Cl SG18.......78 F6
Chapel Dr SG15.......90 A4
CHAPEL END
  MK44...............20 A1
  MK45...............51 E5
  MK45...............62 C1
  MK54...............63 A4
Chapel End Rd MK45...74 D8
Chapel Field
  Gamlingay SG19......44 D4
  Great Barford MK44..40 F5
Chapelfields MK44....18 D1
Chapel Fields SG18...66 F6
Chapel Hill NN29......7 B8
Chapel La
  Ampthill MK45.......73 E1
  Cardington MK44.....51 E5

Chapel La continued
  Colmworth MK44.......20 A1
  Ivinghoe Aston LU7...119 A1
  Northall LU6........119 A5
  Souldrop MK44.......16 A8
  Totternhoe LU6......119 F8
  Willington MK44......40 C1
  Wilstead MK45........62 F4
Chapel Path
  Houghton Regis LU5..114 B4
  2 Leighton Buzzard LU7..111 A8
Chapel Pl SG5.........90 F6
Chapel Pound MK43....37 A8
Chapel Rd
  Breachwood Green SG4..125 C8
  Flamstead AL3......129 B2
  Flitwick MK45.......84 D3
  Meppershall SG17....88 D6
Chapel St
  Dunton SG18.........68 D5
  Hinxworth SG7.......80 D6
  Luton, High Town LU1..123 E7
  Luton, New Town LU1..123 E6
  Potton SG19.........56 A7
  Woburn Sands MK17...81 B4
Chapel Viaduct LU1...123 E7
Chapel Way SG16......78 D3
Chapel Yd MK44........6 E1
Chapman Cl
  Kempston MK42......49 D6
  Potton SG19.........56 A7
Chapmans Cl NN29......7 B8
Chapman Way PE19.....22 B2
Chapterhouse Rd LU4..115 A3
Chard Dr LU3........108 B1
Charlbury Ct MK40.....38 D1
Charles St LU2......123 F8
Charles' St PE19......22 F5
Charlewood Ho MK17...81 B3
Charlotte Ave LU4.....90 C2
Charlottes Ct **2** LU1...123 D7
Charlton Cl LU3......108 B1
Charnbury Rise LU2...117 A4
Charndon Cl LU3.....108 B1
Charnocks Cl SG19....44 D5
Charnwood Ave MK41...39 B3
Chartmoor Rd LU7....111 A4
Chartwell Dr LU2....116 E3
Chase Cl SG15........90 A8
Chase Rd LU8, SG15...90 A7
Chase St LU1........123 E6
Chase The MK43.......49 A2
Chasten Hill SG6....101 D7
Chatsworth Rd LU4...116 B1
Chatteris Cl LU4....115 D4
Chatton Cl LU2......117 E2
Chaucer Dr SG18......67 A5
Chaucer Pl PE19.......22 D6
Chaucer Rd
  Bedford MK40........37 F1
  Flitwick MK45.......84 D3
  Luton LU3..........116 C2
CHAUL END............122 C7
Chaul End La LU4....115 E1
Chaul End Rd
  Caddington LU4, LU6..122 D6
  Luton LU4..........115 B1
Chauntry Cl MK45.....84 E5
Chauntry Way MK45....84 E5
Chaworth Gn **1** LU4...115 C5
CHAWSTON............31 E5
Chawston Cl PE19......22 C5
Chawston La MK44......31 F5
Cheapside LU1.......123 E7
Cheapside Sq **4** LU1...123 E7
CHEDDINGTON........118 A1
Cheddington Sta LU7..118 A2
CHELLINGTON..........25 B4
Chelmer Cl MK41......38 D7
Chelsea Gdns LU5....114 D5
Chelsea Rd LU2......110 D6
Chelsworth Cl **1** LU2..117 D1
Cheltenham Cl
  Bedford MK41........39 B3
  Rushden NN10........8 C8
CHELVESTON...........3 C8
Chelveston Base Cres NN9 3 D5
Chelveston Rd NN9.....3 A7
Cheney Cl LU5.......105 F6
Cheney Rd LU4.......115 C5
Chennells Cl SG4....101 B2
Chepstow Cl LU3.....130 F2
Chepstow Gdns MK41...39 A4
Chepstow Ct LU1.....123 F6
Chequers Cl
  Marston Moretaine MK43..60 D2
  Stotfold SG5........91 A6
Chequers Cotts LU5...127 A8
Chequers Hill
  Flamstead AL3......129 C2
  Wilden MK44.........30 A4
Chequers La LU6......58 B6
Chequer St LU1......123 F6
Chequers The LU6....119 F5
Cherry Cl MK45.......74 B8
Cherrycourt Way LU7..111 D6
Cherrycourt Way Ind Est
  LU7...............111 F7
Cherrycroft SG19.....54 D7
Cherry Gr SG19.......44 C5
Cherry Tree Cl
  Arlesey SG15........90 A4
  Luton LU2..........117 A1
Cherry Trees SG16....89 B3
Cherrytree Way MK45...85 A7
Cherry Tree Wlk
  Houghton Regis LU5..114 B4
  Leighton Buzzard LU7..110 E2

Cherry Wlk MK42 . . . . 49 F3
Chertsey Cl LU2 . . . . 124 D8
Cherwell Rd MK41 . . . . 38 C5
Chesford Rd LU2 . . . . 117 C4
Cheslyn Cl LU2 . . . . 117 E2
Chessington Cl MK41 . . . . . 51 B8
Chester Ave LU4 . . . . 115 E3
Chester Cl LU4 . . . . 115 F2
Chesterfield Way PE19 . . . . 22 E2
Chester Rd MK40 . . . . 49 E7
Chesterton Ave AL5 . . . . . 131 D1
Chesterton Ct PE19 . . . . . . 22 E6
Chesterton Mews MK40 . . . 37 F1
Chestnut Ave
Bedford MK40 . . . . 49 F7
Biggleswade SG18 . . . . 67 A6
Bromham MK43 . . . . 36 D3
Henlow SG16 . . . . 89 C3
Luton LU3 . . . . 107 C1
Chestnut Cl
Ampthill MK45 . . . . 84 F8
Dagnall HP4 . . . . 126 C5
Westoning MK45 . . . . 95 D6
Wymington NN10 . . . . 8 B5
Chestnut Cres MK45 . . . . . . 85 B8
Chestnut Ct LU6 . . . . 121 C7
Chestnut Farm SG16 . . . . . . 78 D1
Chestnut Gdns MK42 . . . . . . 49 E3
Chestnut Gr PE19 . . . . 22 F4
Chestnut Hill LU7 . . . . 110 D8
Chestnut Rise LU7 . . . . . . 110 D8
Chestnuts The PE28 . . . . 6 F5
Chethams MK42 . . . . 50 C7
Cheveralls The LU6 . . . . . 121 C6
Cheverells Cl AL3 . . . . 128 D4
CHEVERELL'S GREEN . . . 127 C4
Cheviot Cl
Bedford MK41 . . . . 38 E3
Flitwick MK45 . . . . 84 D2
Leighton Buzzard LU7 . . . . 110 C8
Luton LU3 . . . . 115 D7
Cheviot Rd LU3 . . . . 115 D7
Cheyne Cl LU6 . . . . 113 F3
Cheynes Inf Sch LU3 . . . . 115 D8
Chicheley Rd MK16 . . . . 58 A7
Chichester Cl LU5 . . . . 121 E7
CHICKSANDS 76 E4
Chicksands Ave SG17 . . . . . 76 F2
Chillingham Gn MK41 . . . . . 39 B4
Chiltern Ave
Bedford MK41 . . . . 38 E3
Edlesborough LU6 . . . . 119 E3
Chiltern Cl
Ampthill MK45 . . . . 84 F8
Flitwick MK45 . . . . 84 D2
Lidlington MK43 . . . . 72 B2
Chiltern Ct 19 AL5 . . . . 131 B1
Chiltern Gdns
Leighton Buzzard LU7 . . . . 103 A3
Luton LU4 . . . . 115 F3
CHILTERN GREEN 124 B3
Chiltern Pk LU5 . . . . 114 D2
Chiltern Pl SG16 . . . . 78 C1
Chiltern Rd
Barton-le-C MK45 . . . . 97 C2
Dunstable LU6 . . . . 114 A1
Chiltern Rise LU1 . . . . 123 D6
Chilterns The
Kensworth LU6 . . . . 127 F8
Leighton Buzzard LU7 . . . . 111 D6
Chiltern Trad Est LU7 . . . . 111 A5
Chiltern View SG6 . . . . 101 D5
Chinnor Cl MK41 . . . . 39 B1
Chobham St LU1 . . . . 123 F6
Chobham Wlk 5 LU1 . . . . . 123 E6
Christchurch Ct LU6 . . . . 114 A1
Christian Cl LU5 . . . . 95 F1
Christie Rd MK42 . . . . 50 D6
Christina Ct AL3 . . . . 128 E5
Christy's Yd SG7 . . . . 80 D6
Chudleigh Cl MK40 . . . . 38 E2
Church Ave
Ampthill MK45 . . . . 73 F1
Leighton Buzzard LU7 . . . . 111 A6
Church Cl
Bedford MK41 . . . . 39 D6
Dunstable LU5 . . . . 121 C8
Houghton Conquest MK45 . . . 74 A7
Milton Ernest MK44 . . . . 27 B5
Rushden NN10 . . . . 8 B5
Studham LU6 . . . . 127 B4
Westoning MK45 . . . . 95 D6
Church Cotts HP1 . . . . 132 D3
Church Cres SG18 . . . . 78 F7
Church Croft LU6 . . . . 119 E3
CHURCH END
LU6 . . . . 120 C7
LU7 . . . . 104 D2
MK17 . . . . 94 B5
MK40 . . . . 49 B8
MK43 . . . . 36 C8
MK43 . . . . 60 E6
MK43 . . . . 82 B5
MK44 . . . . 18 C2
MK44 . . . . 20 B2
MK44 . . . . 29 C2
MK45 . . . . 97 C1
SG15 . . . . 90 B7
SG19 . . . . 42 A7
Church End
Arlesey SG15 . . . . 90 A8
Biddenham MK40 . . . . 49 B8
Edlesborough LU6 . . . . 119 E3
Elstow MK42 . . . . 50 B3
Everton SG19 . . . . 43 C3
Felmersham MK43 . . . . 26 C8
Gamlingay SG19 . . . . 44 E5
Houghton Regis LU5 . . . . . 114 B5
Church End *continued*
Kensworth LU6 . . . . 121 E2
Markyate AL3 . . . . 128 D6
Milton Bryan MK17 . . . . 93 E2
Ravensden MK44 . . . . 29 B1
Renhold MK41 . . . . 39 D6
Steppingley MK45 . . . . 84 A3
Willington MK44 . . . . 52 B8
Church End Farm LU6 . . . 120 B7
Church End Lower Sch
MK43 . . . . 72 D7
Church End Rd MK45 . . . . . 75 C7
Church Farm Ave MK45 . . . 62 E3
Church Farm Cl
Langford SG18 . . . . 78 F7
Sutton SG19 . . . . 55 F3
Churchfield Rd LU5 . . . . . 114 B5
Churchgate MK44 . . . . 41 A4
Church Gn
Harpenden AL5 . . . . 131 A1
Milton Ernest MK44 . . . . 27 B5
Totternhoe LU6 . . . . 120 B7
Church Green Row AL5 . . 131 A1
Church Hill MK17 . . . . 81 E5
Churchill Cl
Sharnbrook MK44 . . . . 16 C3
Stewartby MK43 . . . . 61 B1
Streatley LU3 . . . . 107 F6
Churchill Dr SG17 . . . . 76 F4
Churchill Pl MK44 . . . . 40 B1
Churchill Rd
Barton-le-C MK45 . . . . 97 C3
Dunstable LU6 . . . . 121 D5
Leighton Buzzard LU7 . . . . 103 B1
Luton LU4 . . . . 116 A1
Marston Moretaine MK43 . . . 72 C8
Churchills LU5 . . . . 95 F2
Churchill Way
Sandy SG19 . . . . 54 C8
Shefford SG17 . . . . 77 C1
Church La
Arlesey SG15 . . . . 90 A7
Bedford MK41 . . . . 39 B3
Bolnhurst MK44 . . . . 19 A4
Cardington MK44 . . . . 51 D4
Colmworth MK44 . . . . 19 D4
Colmworth MK44 . . . . 20 B2
Covington PE28 . . . . 2 C2
Eaton Bray LU6 . . . . 119 E6
Everton SG19 . . . . 43 C3
Flitton MK45 . . . . 85 D4
Gamlingay SG19 . . . . 44 E5
Guilden Morden SG8 . . . . . . 69 F5
Haynes Church End MK45 . . . 75 C7
Hockliffe LU7 . . . . 104 D3
Letchworth SG6 . . . . 91 C1
Lidlington MK43 . . . . 72 C2
Little Staughton MK44 . . . . . 13 B2
Newton Bromswold NN10 . . . . 9 D8
Oakley MK43 . . . . 36 F6
Odell MK43 . . . . 15 D1
Pavenham MK43 . . . . 26 C4
Riseley MK44 . . . . 10 F2
Sharnbrook MK44 . . . . 16 C4
Stagsden MK43 . . . . 48 A7
Tilbrook PE28 . . . . 6 B7
Upper Dean PE28 . . . . 5 B4
Wrestlingworth SG19 . . . . . . 57 B3
Wymington NN10 . . . . 8 B5
Yelden MK44 . . . . 4 A3
Church Mdw PE19 . . . . 22 F5
Church Mead LU6 . . . . 127 B4
Church Meadow Cotts
HP1 . . . . 132 D3
Church Path
Cheddington LU7 . . . . 118 A1
Sandy SG19 . . . . 54 B7
Church Rd
Barton-le-C MK45 . . . . 97 D1
Colmworth MK44 . . . . 20 B1
Everton SG19 . . . . 43 C3
Flamstead AL3 . . . . 129 B2
Flitwick MK45 . . . . 84 D1
Hargrave NN9 . . . . 1 F1
Harlington LU5 . . . . 95 F2
Henlow SG16 . . . . 78 D2
Kempston MK43 . . . . 49 A4
Keysoe MK44 . . . . 12 A1
Leighton Buzzard LU7 . . . . 110 E6
Maulden MK45 . . . . 85 D8
Meppershall SG17 . . . . 88 A5
Pulloxhill MK45 . . . . 96 E8
Silsoe MK45 . . . . 86 C4
Slapton LU7 . . . . 118 D6
Slip End LU1 . . . . 123 C2
Steppingley MK45 . . . . 84 A3
Stevington MK43 . . . . 36 C7
Stotfold SG5 . . . . 90 F6
Streatley LU3 . . . . 108 A6
Studham LU6 . . . . 127 B4
Sutton SG19 . . . . 55 F4
Tingrith MK17 . . . . 94 F5
Totternhoe LU6 . . . . 120 B6
Upper Sundon LU3 . . . . 107 B3
Westoning MK45 . . . . 95 E6
Willington MK44 . . . . 52 B8
Wilstead MK45 . . . . 62 E4
Woburn Sands MK17 . . . . 81 B3
Wootton MK43 . . . . 60 F7
Church Row MK43 . . . . 60 E7
Church Sq
Leighton Buzzard LU7 . . . . 110 F6
Toddington LU5 . . . . 105 F6
Church St
Ampthill MK45 . . . . 73 F1
Aspley Guise MK17 . . . . 81 E5
Baldock SG7 . . . . 91 E1
5 Bedford MK40 . . . . 50 B8
Church St *continued*
Biggleswade SG18 . . . . 67 A6
Clifton SG17 . . . . 78 B3
Dunstable LU5 . . . . 121 C8
Dunton SG18 . . . . 68 D5
Gamlingay SG19 . . . . 44 D5
Guilden Morden SG8 . . . . . . 69 F5
Hargrave NN9 . . . . 1 E2
Langford SG18 . . . . 78 F7
Langford SG18 . . . . 78 F8
Leighton Buzzard LU7 . . . . 111 A8
Lidlington MK43 . . . . 72 C3
Luton, High Town LU2 . . . . 123 F8
8 Luton LU1 . . . . 123 E7
Luton LU2 . . . . 123 E7
Ridgmont MK43 . . . . 82 F5
Shillington SG5 . . . . 98 E8
St Neots PE19 . . . . 22 F5
Tempsford SG19 . . . . 42 A6
Church Terr MK43 . . . . 34 E5
Church Turn LU7 . . . . 111 E2
Church View
Ampthill MK45 . . . . 73 F1
Clapham MK41 . . . . 37 F5
St Neots PE19 . . . . 22 F5
Church View Ave SG5 . . . . . 87 E1
Church View Ct LU7 . . . . . 110 E6
Churchville Rd MK42 . . . . . . 50 B5
Church Wlk
Cranfield MK43 . . . . 71 A8
Dunstable LU5 . . . . 121 C8
Eggington LU7 . . . . 112 B7
Harrold MK43 . . . . 25 A6
Kempston MK42 . . . . 49 C3
Marston Moretaine MK43 . . . 72 D7
Newton Bromswold NN10 . . . . 9 D8
North Crawley MK16 . . . . . . 58 B6
Shefford SG17 . . . . 77 C3
6 St Neots PE19 . . . . 22 E5
Churnet Cl MK41 . . . . 38 D7
Cicero Dr LU3 . . . . 116 A8
Cinques Rd SG19 . . . . 44 C6
Cinques The SG19 . . . . 44 B6
Circle Bsns Ctr LU5 . . . . . . 114 B3
City La MK44 . . . . 20 C3
CLAPHAM 37 D7
CLAPHAM GREEN 36 F6
Clapham Rd MK41 . . . . 37 F4
Clare Ct SG19 . . . . 44 D5
Clare Ho SG18 . . . . 67 A6
Claremont Rd LU4 . . . . 116 B1
Clarence Ct NN10 . . . . 8 A8
Clarence Rd
Harpenden AL5 . . . . 131 A3
Leighton Buzzard LU7 . . . . 111 B8
Clarendon Ct AL5 . . . . 131 B3
Clarendon Rd
Harpenden AL5 . . . . 131 B3
Luton LU2 . . . . 116 E1
Clarendon St MK41 . . . . 38 A2
Clare Rd MK41 . . . . 38 F5
Claridge Cl LU7 . . . . 111 B5
Clarkes Way LU5 . . . . 114 C4
Clark's Pightle MK45 . . . . . . 97 C2
Claverley Gn LU2 . . . . 117 E2
Claydon Cl LU3 . . . . 116 C7
Claydon Ct MK40 . . . . 38 B1
Claydown Way LU1 . . . . . . 123 B1
Clay Furlong LU7 . . . . 111 B5
Claygate Ave AL5 . . . . 130 E2
Clay Hall Rd LU6 . . . . 127 F7
Claymore Dr SG5 . . . . 100 F5
CLEAT HILL 38 E7
Cleat Hill MK41, MK44 . . . . . 38 E7
Cleavers The LU5 . . . . 105 F5
Cleavers Wlk LU5 . . . . 105 F5
Cleave The AL5 . . . . 131 D1
Cleeve Abbey MK41 . . . . 39 B1
CLEMENT'S END 127 D3
Clements End Rd LU6,
HP2 . . . . 127 E2
Clevedon Rd LU2 . . . . 117 B2
Cleveland Dr LU7 . . . . 110 C8
Cleveland Rd AL3 . . . . 128 E5
Cleveland St MK42 . . . . 49 E4
Clifford Cres LU4 . . . . 115 D5
CLIFTON 78 B3
Clifton Fields SG17 . . . . 77 F3
Clifton House Cl SG17 . . . . 78 B3
Clifton Pk SG17 . . . . 78 A1
Clifton Rd
Dunstable LU6 . . . . 114 A1
Henlow SG16 . . . . 78 C1
Luton LU1 . . . . 123 B8
Newton Blossomville MK43 . . 34 A4
Shefford SG17 . . . . 77 D2
Clinton Ave LU2 . . . . 116 F3
CLIPSTONE 103 F1
Clipstone Brook Lower Sch
LU7 . . . . 111 B7
Clipstone Cl MK41 . . . . 39 B3
Clipstone Cres LU7 . . . . . . 111 C7
Clive Ct LU2 . . . . 116 E1
Cloches The SG19 . . . . 54 B5
Cloister Lawns SG6 . . . . . . 101 F4
Cloisters Rd
Letchworth SG6 . . . . 101 F4
Luton LU4 . . . . 115 B3
Cloisters The
Ampthill MK45 . . . . 73 F1
Bedford MK41 . . . . 39 B1
Dunstable LU5 . . . . 121 C8
Houghton Regis LU5 . . . . . 114 C6
CLOPHILL 86 D8
Clophill Rd
Gravenhurst MK45 . . . . 87 B5
Maulden MK45 . . . . 85 E8
Close Rd MK43 . . . . 26 E3
Close The
Biggleswade SG18 . . . . 66 F6
Clapham MK41 . . . . 37 E5
Great Barford MK44 . . . . 41 A5
Hardmead MK16 . . . . 46 D4
Harpenden AL5 . . . . 130 D4
Hinxworth SG7 . . . . 80 D6
Luton LU3 . . . . 116 A5
Markyate AL3 . . . . 128 E5
St Neots PE19 . . . . 22 F5
Tempsford SG19 . . . . 42 C8
Thurleigh MK44 . . . . 18 C2
Woburn Sands MK17 . . . . 81 B4
Clothall Rd SG7 . . . . 91 F1
Clovelly Way MK40 . . . . 38 F1
Clover Ave MK41 . . . . 39 B1
Clover Cl
Biggleswade SG18 . . . . 67 C4
Luton LU4 . . . . 115 A3
Clover Dr NN10 . . . . 8 C8
Clover Rd
Flitwick MK45 . . . . 84 D3
St Neots PE19 . . . . 22 C3
Club Rd MK45 . . . . 62 E3
Cluny Way SG15 . . . . 90 A5
Clyde Cres MK41 . . . . 38 D5
Clydesdale Ct LU4 . . . . 115 A3
Clydesdale Rd LU4 . . . . . . 115 A3
Coach Rd SG16 . . . . 78 D1
Cobbett La MK45 . . . . 85 D4
Cobbitts Rd MK45 . . . . 74 C1
Cobblers La MK17 . . . . 83 C3
Cobden Sq 11 MK40 . . . . 38 B1
Cobden St LU2 . . . . 116 F1
COCKERNHOE 117 F3
Cockernhoe CE Prim Sch
LU2 . . . . 117 E3
COCKHAYNE HATLEY 57 C8
Codrington Ct PE19 . . . . 22 B3
Cody Rd MK41 . . . . 37 D6
Colchester Way MK41 . . . . . 39 A5
COLD BRAYFIELD 34 B5
Coldharbour La AL5 . . . . 131 C4
Colebrook Ave LU3 . . . . . 115 C7
Colemans Cl SG5 . . . . 99 D4
Colemoreham Ct SG18 . . . . 65 E7
Coleridge Ct
9 Harpenden AL5 . . . . 131 B1
St Neots PE19 . . . . 22 C7
Coles Cl MK41 . . . . 39 A1
COLESDEN 30 E4
Colesden Rd
Chawston MK44 . . . . 31 D5
Wilden MK44 . . . . 30 C4
Colin Rd LU2 . . . . 116 F2
College Cl AL3 . . . . 129 B1
College Dr MK44 . . . . 10 F2
College Ho LU1 . . . . 123 F7
College Rd
Bedford MK42 . . . . 50 B5
Sandy SG19 . . . . 42 C1
Wharley End MK43 . . . . 58 E2
College St Ind Est MK42 . . . 50 A5
College St MK42 . . . . 50 A5
Colley Cl MK44 . . . . 20 A1
Collie Rd MK42 . . . . 50 E6
Collingdon Ct 9 LU1 . . . 123 D8
Collingdon St LU1 . . . . 123 D8
Collings Wells Cl LU1 . . . . 122 E4
Collingtree LU2 . . . . 117 B4
Collingwood Cl LU4 . . . . . 115 D3
Collingwood Rd PE19 . . . . . 22 B2
Collins Pl MK42 . . . . 50 F5
Collison Cl SG4 . . . . 101 C2
COLMWORTH 20 B2
Colmworth Bsns Pk PE19 . 22 C1
Colmworth Gdns PE19 . . . . 22 C2
Colmworth Rd MK44 . . . . . . 13 B1
Coltsfoot SG18 . . . . 67 C4
Coltsfoot Gn LU4 . . . . 115 A5
Coltsfoot Rd NN10 . . . . 8 C7
Columba Dr LU7 . . . . 111 C8
Columbine Cl MK41 . . . . 39 C4
Colwell Rise LU2 . . . . 117 E2
Colworth Rd MK44 . . . . 16 B4
Comet Dr MK42 . . . . 51 A2
Comfrey Cl NN10 . . . . 8 C7
Commerce Way
Flitwick MK45 . . . . 85 A4
Leighton Buzzard LU7 . . . . 111 E6
Letchworth SG6 . . . . 101 F6
Commerce Way Ind Est
LU7 . . . . 111 E6
Commercial Rd MK40 . . . . . 50 B8
Common Farm La MK45 . . . 84 D4
Common La
Harpenden AL5 . . . . 131 D5
Upper Sundon LU3 . . . . 107 A4
Common Rd
Kensworth LU6 . . . . 121 D1
Langford SG18 . . . . 78 E4
Potton SG19 . . . . 56 A8
Stotfold SG5 . . . . 90 F7
Studham LU6 . . . . 127 B3
Common Rise SG4 . . . . 101 A1
Common The AL5 . . . . 130 C4
Compass Dr MK42 . . . . 51 A3
Comp Gate LU6 . . . . 119 E6
Comp The LU6 . . . . 119 E6
Compton Ave LU4 . . . . 115 D4
Compton Cl
Flitwick MK45 . . . . 84 D1
St Neots PE19 . . . . 22 E2
Concorde Cl MK42 . . . . 51 A2
Concorde St LU2 . . . . 123 F8
Concord Way LU7 . . . . 111 E5
Concra Pk MK17 . . . . 81 C4
Conduit Rd MK40 . . . . 50 A8
Coneygate SG17 . . . . 88 B5
Conger La LU5 . . . . 106 A6
Coniston Cl MK42 . . . . 49 E4
Coniston Rd
Flitwick MK45 . . . . 84 E2
Leighton Buzzard LU7 . . . . 110 C7
Luton LU3 . . . . 115 F5
Connaught Rd
Harpenden AL5 . . . . 131 B2
Luton LU4 . . . . 115 F1
Connaught Way MK41 . . . . . 38 D6
Connor's Cl SG8 . . . . 69 F4
Conquest Rd
Bedford MK42 . . . . 50 C5
Houghton Regis LU5 . . . . . 114 E5
Constable Ave PE19 . . . . . . 22 D5
Constable Cl LU5 . . . . 114 D5
Constable Ct LU4 . . . . 116 A1
Constable Hill MK41 . . . . . . 38 A2
Constables Leys PE28 . . . . . . 6 F5
Conway Cl
Houghton Regis LU5 . . . . . 114 E5
Rushden NN10 . . . . 8 A8
Conway Cres MK41 . . . . 38 C5
Conway Dr MK45 . . . . 84 D1
Conway Pl PE19 . . . . 22 F2
Conway Rd LU4 . . . . 116 B1
Cookfield Cl LU6 . . . . 120 E8
Cook's Mdw LU6 . . . . 119 E4
Cooks Way
Biggleswade SG18 . . . . 67 B6
Hitchin SG4 . . . . 101 A1
Coombe Dr LU6 . . . . 120 E7
Coombs Cl MK42 . . . . 50 D6
Cooper Cl SG16 . . . . 88 E2
Cooper Dr LU7 . . . . 111 C5
Coopers Cl
Biddenham MK40 . . . . 49 C8
Biggleswade SG18 . . . . 67 B4
Great Barford MK44 . . . . 40 F5
Sandy SG19 . . . . 54 B6
Coopers Field SG6 . . . . . . 101 D7
Coopers Way LU5 . . . . 114 A4
Cooters End La AL5 . . . . . . 130 F5
Copeland Wlk MK41 . . . . . . 39 B3
Copenhagen Cl LU3 . . . . . 115 D8
COPLE 52 A6
Cople Lower Sch MK44 . . . . 52 A6
Cople Rd MK44 . . . . 51 E5
Coplowe La MK44 . . . . 17 D1
Coppens The SG5 . . . . 91 A5
Copper Beeches 11 AL5 . . 131 B1
Copper Beech Way LU7 . 103 A3
Copperfields LU4 . . . . 115 C3
Copperfields Cl LU5 . . . . 114 D4
Coppice Mead
Biggleswade SG18 . . . . 67 B5
Stotfold SG5 . . . . 90 E5
Coppice The AL5 . . . . 130 F2
Coppins The
Ampthill MK45 . . . . 84 F8
Markyate AL3 . . . . 128 D5
Copse The MK41 . . . . 39 B2
Copse Way LU3 . . . . 115 D8
Copthorne LU2 . . . . 117 D3
Copthorne Cl MK43 . . . . 37 A8
Coral Cl LU6 . . . . 119 E6
Corbet Ride LU7 . . . . 110 D8
Corbet Sq LU7 . . . . 110 D8
Corbridge Dr LU2 . . . . 117 E1
Corby Cl MK42 . . . . 50 D4
Cordwainer Hts NN29 . . . . . . 7 B8
Corfe Pl PE19 . . . . 22 F2
Corfe Rd MK41 . . . . 39 A4
Corinium Gdns LU3 . . . . . . 116 A8
Cormorant Way LU7 . . . . . 111 C5
Corncastle Rd LU1 . . . . . . 123 D6
Corncrake Cl LU2 . . . . 117 C5
Cornel Cl LU1 . . . . 123 A7
Cornel Ct LU1 . . . . 123 A7
Cornelia Ct 3 AL5 . . . . 131 A2
Corner Cl
Letchworth SG6 . . . . 101 E6
Podington NN29 . . . . 7 E1
Corner Wood AL3 . . . . 128 D5
Cornish Cl SG17 . . . . 77 C3
Cornland MK41 . . . . 39 A3
Cornwall Ct PE19 . . . . 22 C4
Cornwallis Cl MK43 . . . . 36 E3
Cornwallis Dr PE19 . . . . 22 A3
Cornwall Rd
Ampthill MK45 . . . . 84 F8
Bedford MK40 . . . . 38 D2
Harpenden AL5 . . . . 131 B2
Coronation Bsns Pk MK43 61 E5
Coronation Rd MK43 . . . . . . 59 B1
Corunna Cl PE19 . . . . 22 C5
Cosgrove Way LU1 . . . . . . 115 D1
Cosmic Ave MK42 . . . . 50 A4
Costin St MK40 . . . . 50 B8
Cotefield LU4 . . . . 115 C3
Cotefield Dr LU7 . . . . 103 B3
Cotman Cl MK41 . . . . 38 B3
Cotswold Bsns Pk LU1 . . . 122 D2
Cotswold Cl MK41 . . . . 38 F2
Cotswold Dr LU7 . . . . 110 C8
Cotswold Gdns LU3 . . . . . . 115 C7
Cotswold Pl MK45 . . . . 84 D2
Cottage Rd SG19 . . . . 42 B1
COTTON END 63 D7
Cotton End Lower Sch
MK45 . . . . 63 D8
Cotton End Rd MK45 . . . . . . 63 B5
Cottril Way MK42 . . . . 50 E6
Coulon Cl NN29 . . . . 7 A7

Coulson Ct LU1 ....122 F8
Council Cotts
  Radwell SG7 ....91 C4
  Sharnbrook MK44 ....16 F4
Council Hos
  Ivinghoe Aston LU6 ......119 A1
  Podington NN29 ....7 E1
Countess Ct PE19 ....22 B3
Countess Ct **4** LU2 ......116 D1
Countess Gdns MK42 .....49 D3
Court Dr LU5 ....114 B1
Courtfields AL5 ....131 D1
Court La MK43 ....36 B7
Courtlands LU7 ....110 E6
Courtlands Dr SG18 ......67 C3
Court Rd MK43 ....71 B8
Court The MK17 ....70 C3
Covent Garden Cl LU4 ...115 F3
Coventry Rd MK40 ....49 F8
Coverdale LU4 ....115 B6
COVINGTON 2 D2
Cow Cl SG18 ....67 A3
Cowdray Cl LU2 ....117 C3
Cow La LU6 ....119 E4
Cowper Ct AL3 ....128 D5
Cowper Rd
  Bedford MK40 ....37 F2
  Harpenden AL5 ....131 C1
  Markyate AL3 ....128 D5
Cowper Rise AL3 ....128 D5
Cowpers Ct PE19 ....22 D6
Cowper St LU1 ....123 E5
Cowridge Cres LU2 ......124 A8
Cowslip Cl NN10 ....8 C8
Cowslip Hill SG5 ....101 E2
Cox's Cl
  Bedford MK40 ....49 F7
  Sharnbrook MK44 ....16 B4
Cox's Way SG15 ....90 A6
Coyney Gn LU3 ....116 C1
Crab Apple Way SG19 ....44 C5
Crab La SG18 ....67 A6
Crabtree Inf Sch AL5 ....131 C1
Crabtree La
  Harpenden AL5 ....131 C1
  Harpenden AL5 ....131 D2
Crab Tree La SG5 ....99 D4
Crabtree Way LU6 ....114 B2
Crackle Hill Rd SG17 ...88 C6
Craddock Ct NN29 ....7 B8
Craddocks Dr LU3 ....103 A3
Cradock Rd LU4 ....115 B1
Cranborne Cl MK41 ....39 B4
Cranbrook MK17 ....81 B5
Cranbrook Dr LU3 ....115 D8
Crancott Cl MK45 ....74 B8
Cranes Cl MK43 ....34 E5
CRANFIELD 59 C2
CRANFIELD 59 B1
Cranfield Lower Sch
  MK43 ....59 B1
Cranfield Rd
  Astwood MK16 ....47 B2
  Salford MK17 ....70 D5
  Woburn Sands MK17 .....81 B7
  Wootton MK43 ....60 E5
Cranfield Technology Pk
  MK43 ....59 C1
Cranfield Univ MK43 .....58 E2
Cranfield Univ Silsoe Coll
  MK45 ....86 C3
Cranford Ct AL5 ....131 C1
Cranleigh Gdns LU3 .....116 D3
Crawley Cl LU1 ....116 B6
Crawley Green Inf Sch
  LU2 ....124 B8
Crawley Green Rd
  Luton LU2 ....124 A8
  Luton, Wigmore LU2 ....117 D1
Crawley Rd
  Cranfield MK43 ....59 C3
  Luton LU1 ....123 D8
  Woburn MK17 ....82 A1
Crayton Rd MK45 ....84 E8
Crecy Ct PE19 ....22 C5
Crediton Cl MK40 ....38 E2
Creran Wlk LU7 ....110 C7
Crescent Cl LU5 ....105 F5
Crescent Ct
  Lidlington MK43 ....72 B3
  Toddington LU5 ....105 F5
Crescent Rd LU2 ....123 F8
Crescent Rise LU2 ....123 F8
Crescent The
  Ampthill MK45 ....84 E7
  Bedford MK40 ....38 B1
  Beeston SG19 ....54 B5
  Caddington LU1 ....122 E3
  Cotton End MK45 ....63 D7
  Henlow SG16 ....89 C4
  Hitchin SG5 ....100 D1
  Moggerhanger MK44 .....53 C8
  Shortstown MK42 ....51 A3
  Stanford SG18 ....78 A7
  Stewartby MK43 ....61 C1
  St Neots, Eaton Socon PE19 .22 C3
  St Neots, PE19 ....22 F6
  Toddington LU5 ....105 F5
  Wharley End MK43 ....58 E2
Cressener Terr **5** PE19 ..22 F5
Cresta Ct LU5 ....121 C4
Cresta Ho **3** LU1 ....123 D7
Crest The
  Dunstable LU5 ....114 E1
  Luton LU3 ....116 B7

Criccieth Way PE19 ....22 F1
Cricket Cl MK41 ....39 A2
Cricketer's Rd SG15 ......90 A4
Cricket La MK41 ....39 A2
Crocus Way NN10 ....8 B7
Croft Ct **4** AL5 ....131 B1
Croft Gn LU6 ....120 F8
Croft La SG6 ....71 C1
Crofton Cl MK41 ....38 D4
Croft Rd LU2 ....117 B3
Croft Stewart SG19 ......56 C6
Crofts The
  Sharnbrook MK44 ....16 E4
  Stotfold SG5 ....90 F6
Croft The
  Bedford MK41 ....39 A2
  Flitwick MK45 ....84 E3
  Luton LU3 ....115 D8
Cromer Way
  Luton, Stopsley Common
   LU2 ....116 C6
  Luton, Warden Hill LU2 .116 D7
Cromwell Ct
  Kempston MK42 ....49 E4
  St Neots PE19 ....22 F3
Cromwell Hill LU2 ....116 D1
Cromwell Rd
  Barton-le-C MK45 ....97 C3
  Bedford MK40 ....49 F7
  Luton LU3 ....116 D1
  St Neots PE19 ....22 F3
Cromwell Way SG5 ....99 D4
CROOK CORNER 11 A3
Crosby Cl
  Dunstable LU6 ....121 C6
  Luton LU4 ....116 A2
CROSS END 18 E1
Cross End MK44 ....18 E1
Cross End La MK44 ....18 E2
CROSSHALL 22 D7
Crosshall Inf Sch PE19 ..22 C6
Crosshall Jun Sch PE19 ..22 C6
Cross Hall Rd PE19 ......22 D6
Cross Keys Mall **8** PE19 ..22 E5
Crosslands LU1 ....122 E3
Crossleys SG6 ....90 F2
Crosspaths AL5 ....130 C4
Cross St N **2** LU6 ....114 A1
Cross St
  Bedford MK40 ....38 B1
  Covington PE28 ....1 C7
  Letchworth SG6 ....101 F7
  Luton LU2 ....123 E8
Cross The SG19 ....44 D5
Crossway LU7 ....111 D7
Cross Way AL5 ....131 C3
Crossways LU1 ....115 C5
Crossways Cl SG16 ....78 C1
Crossways Pk SG15 ....89 F2
Cross Way The LU1 ......123 C5
Crowe Rd MK40 ....49 D3
Crow La
  Husborne Crawley MK43 ..82 B4
  Woburn Sands MK17 .....81 B8
Crowland Rd LU2 ....117 C5
Crown La SG18 ....78 F6
Crown Lodge SG15 ....90 A4
Crown Pl MK42 ....50 B7
Crown Quay MK40 ....50 B8
Crown Wlk PE19 ....22 B4
Crowther Ct SG18 ....66 F7
Croxden Way MK42 ....50 D3
Croxley Ct LU7 ....110 F7
Croxton Cl **3** LU3 ....116 A7
Croyland Dr MK40 ....50 D3
Cryselco Cl MK42 ....49 D2
Cubbington Cl LU3 ....116 A7
Cuckoo Cl SG18 ....90 A4
Cuckoo's Nest LU2 ......124 A7
Cuffley Cl LU3 ....115 F4
Culloden Cl PE19 ....22 C5
Culver Ho MK40 ....38 A2
Culverhouse Cl LU3 ......116 C3
Culworth Cl LU1 ....122 E3
Cumberland St
  Houghton Regis LU5 ....114 B4
  Luton LU1 ....123 E6
Cumberland Way PE19 ....22 F1
Cumbria Cl LU5 ....114 E5
Cunningham Way PE19 ....22 F2
Curlew Cl SG6 ....90 E1
Curlew Cres MK41 ....38 B4
Curlew Rd LU2 ....117 C5
Curzon Rd LU5 ....114 E6
Cusworth Way LU6 ....113 E1
Cusworth Wlk LU6 ....113 E1
Cutcliffe Gdns MK40 .....49 F8
Cutcliffe Gr MK40 ....49 F8
Cutcliffe Pl MK40 ....49 F8
Cutenhoe Rd LU1 ....123 E4
Cutlers Gn LU2 ....117 F2
Cutlers Way LU7 ....111 B6
Cut Throat Ave HP4, LU6 .126 E7
Cut Throat La MK41 ......37 F2
Cygnus Dr LU2 ....123 F8
Cymbeline Ct **6** MK40 ....38 A1
Cynthia Ct MK43 ....61 A6

D

Daffodil Dr NN10 ....8 B7
Dag La MK44 ....10 F2
DAGNALL 126 C6
Dagnall Rd
  Dunstable LU6 ....120 D2
  Great Gaddesden HP1 ...132 C5
Dagnalls SG6 ....101 F2

Dagnall Sch HP4 ....126 C5
Dahl Cl MK42 ....50 C4
Dahlia Cl LU2 ....117 B4
Dairy Cotts SG5 ....98 B2
Dairy Ct PE19 ....22 F6
Daisy Croft NN10 ....8 C8
Dalby Cl LU4 ....115 B3
Dale Cl
  Bedford MK41 ....39 A3
  Dunstable LU5 ....114 F1
  Toddington LU5 ....105 F5
Dale Rd
  Dunstable LU5 ....114 F1
  Luton LU1 ....123 C7
Dale The SG6 ....101 E5
Dalewood AL5 ....131 D1
Dalkeith Rd AL5 ....131 C1
Dallas Rd MK42 ....50 A6
Dalling Dr LU5 ....114 C5
Dallow Prim Sch LU1 ....123 C8
Dallow Rd LU1 ....123 B8
Dalroad Ind Est LU1 ....123 B8
Dalton Cl LU3 ....108 B1
Dame Alice Harpur Sch
  MK40 ....50 C7
Dame Alice St MK40 ......38 B1
Dammersey Cl AL3 ....128 F4
Dane Cl
  Harpenden AL5 ....131 C4
  Stotfold SG5 ....90 F8
Danefield Rd SG5 ....99 C4
Dane La MK45 ....62 C5
Dane Rd
  Barton-le-C MK45 ....99 D3
  Luton LU3 ....116 C2
Danesborough Dr MK17 ...81 A2
Danescroft SG5 ....91 A1
Dane St MK40 ....50 B8
Danes Way LU7 ....111 D7
Daneswood MK17 ....81 A1
Danvers Dr LU3 ....108 C1
Dapifer Dr SG19 ....54 C8
Dark La SG18 ....66 F6
Darlington Cl SG19 ......42 D1
Darlow Dr MK40 ....37 D1
Darrington Ct PE19 ......22 B3
Dartmouth Mews LU4 ....115 D3
Dart Rd MK41 ....38 C5
Darwin Rd MK42 ....50 C5
Daubeney Cl LU5 ....95 F2
Daubeney Mid Sch MK42 ..49 F3
Dauphin Cl **9** LU6 ....116 D1
David Evans Ct SG6 ......101 D7
Davis Cl MK42 ....50 B5
Davis Cres SG5 ....99 D4
Davis' Row SG15 ....90 A4
Dawlish Dr MK40 ....38 E1
Dawlish Rd LU4 ....115 F3
Dawson Cl SG16 ....78 B1
Daysfield MK45 ....74 B8
Day's La MK40 ....37 D1
Deacon Ave MK42 ....49 C3
Deacon Mews MK43 ....72 C8
Deacons Ct **6** LU2 ....123 D8
Deacons Way SG5 ....100 D1
DEADMAN'S CROSS 76 C8
Deadman's Hill MK45 ....75 B2
Dean Cl NN10 ....8 C8
Deans Mdw HP4 ....126 C5
Dean St MK41 ....38 F1
Dearmans Cl MK45 ....75 C1
Dearne Villas MK40 ......50 A8
Dearne Wlk MK41 ....38 C5
Deepdale LU4 ....115 D3
Deepdale SG19 ....55 D7
Deepdale Water Gardens*
  SG19 ....55 D7
Deep Denes LU2 ....117 A2
Deep Spinney MK40 ....37 C1
Deeside MK41 ....38 D5
Deethe MK17 ....81 B5
Degray Manor SG5 ....81 B5
De Grey Mausoleum*
  MK45 ....85 D4
De Havilland Ave MK42 ..51 B2
Delamere Cl SG19 ....42 B1
Delamere Gdns LU7 ......110 C7
Delamere Wlk MK41 ......39 B3
Delco Way LU1 ....124 A5
Delfield Gdns MK41 ......39 B3
Dell Cl AL5 ....131 B3
Dellcot Cl LU2 ....117 B4
Dellfield Ct LU2 ....117 B4
Dellmont Rd LU5 ....114 B5
Dell Rd LU5 ....114 B5
Dells La AL5 ....67 A5
Dells The SG18 ....67 A5
Dell The
  Caddington LU1 ....122 E3
  Heath and Reach LU7 ...103 B5
  Kempston MK42 ....49 B2
  Luton LU1 ....123 C7
Delmead La AL3 ....129 C1
Delphine Cl LU1 ....123 B6
De Montfort Ct LU5 ......105 F4
Denbigh Cl MK43 ....72 D8
Denbigh High Sch LU3 ...116 C2
Denbigh Inf Sch LU3 ....116 B2
Denbigh Jun Sch LU3 ....116 B2
Denbigh Rd
  Luton LU3 ....116 B2
  Milton Ernest MK44 .....39 A4
Dencora Way LU3 ....115 B8
Dene Cl MK17 ....81 C4
Denel Cl LU5 ....84 E4
Dene Way SG18 ....66 B8
Denham LU3 ....115 E8
Denham Cl LU3 ....107 E1
Denmark Cl LU3 ....107 E1

Denmark St MK40 ....50 E8
Dennis Ct MK42 ....49 D2
DENNIS GREEN 44 C4
Dennis Rd MK42 ....49 D2
Denny Cres SG18 ....78 F8
Denton Cl
  Irchester NN29 ....7 B8
  Kempston MK42 ....49 E4
Denton Dr MK43 ....72 C7
Dents Rd MK42 ....50 D5
De Parys Ave MK40 ....38 B1
Derby Pl MK40 ....38 B1
Derby Rd LU4 ....115 C2
Derwent Ave
  Biggleswade SG18 ....67 B4
  Luton LU3 ....116 B7
Derwent Cotts MK43 ......26 B3
Derwent Dr LU6 ....121 C6
Derwent Lower Sch SG16 ..89 B5
Derwent Pl MK42 ....50 B6
Derwent Rd
  Harpenden AL5 ....130 C4
  Henlow SG16 ....89 B4
  Leighton Buzzard LU7 ...110 B7
  Luton LU3 ....124 A8
Derwent Rise MK43 ....84 E2
Des Fuller Ct **3** LU1 ....123 E6
Deverell Way LU7 ....111 C5
Devizes Ave MK41 ....39 A5
Devon Rd
  Bedford MK41 ....38 D2
  Luton LU1 ....116 A2
Devonshire Rd **5** AL5 ...131 B1
Dewlands MK43 ....36 F7
Dew Pond Rd MK45 ....84 D1
Dewsbury Rd LU3 ....116 C6
Dexter Cl LU3 ....108 B1
DIAMOND END 124 C6
Dickens Bvd SG5 ....90 C2
Dickens Cl MK43 ....24 F6
Dickens Ct SG18 ....67 A5
Dickens La LU7 ....113 A5
Dickens Rd MK45 ....84 C3
Dickerson Cl SG19 ....54 D6
Digby Ct PE19 ....22 B3
Digby Rd LU2 ....111 A8
Dillock La MK43 ....48 C1
Dimmock Cl LU7 ....111 C4
Dimmock Rd MK43 ....66 F7
Dines Cl MK45 ....62 E4
Dingle Dell LU7 ....102 F2
Disbrowe Ct NN9 ....3 C7
Ditchling Cl LU2 ....117 C3
Ditmas Ave MK42 ....49 C2
Ditton Gn LU2 ....117 C3
Docklands SG5 ....99 D4
Dodds Cl MK41 ....11 B3
Doggett St LU1 ....123 F5
Dog Kennel Path LU6 ....114 B1
Dolce Way MK42 ....16 B3
Dolmans Pl **12** LU6 ......121 C6
Dolphin Cl LU6 ....114 E6
Dolphins Way SG19 ......44 D6
Don Butler Cl MK45 ......86 B3
Donlee Furlong LU7 .....111 C7
Donnelly Dr MK41 ....39 B1
Dony Field Centre LU2 ..116 E6
Doolittle Mill MK45 .....84 D5
Dorchester Cl LU5 ....114 E5
Dorchester Way MK42 ....50 C3
Dordans Rd LU4 ....115 F4
Dorel Cl LU2 ....115 D8
Dornan Ct LU1 ....123 E5
Dorrington Cl LU3 ......116 A7
Dorset Ct **8** LU1 ....123 F6
Dorsey Dr MK42 ....50 B5
Dothans Cl MK44 ....40 F5
Doug Harris Way MK45 ...86 B3
Douglas Cres LU5 ....114 B2
Douglas Rd
  Bedford MK41 ....38 D6
  Harpenden AL5 ....130 C4
  Luton LU4 ....116 A2
Dove Cl SG19 ....42 C2
Dovedale LU2 ....116 C6
Dovehouse Cl
  Bromham MK43 ....36 F2
  St Neots PE19 ....22 B3
Dove House Cl LU6 ......119 F3
Dove House Dr SG16 .....78 D1
Dovehouse Hill LU2 .....117 B1
Dove House La LU5 ......105 F5
Dove La MK43 ....25 A6
Dover Cl LU3 ....116 A3
Dover Cres MK41 ....39 A4
Dove Rd MK41 ....38 D4
Dovery Down Lower Sch
  LU7 ....103 A2
Dove Tree Rd LU7 ....111 C8
Dove Wlk MK45 ....84 E1
Downfield Way MK43 ......84 E4
Downham Rd MK17 ....81 C4
Downlands LU3 ....115 C7
DOWNSIDE 39 A3
Downside Gdns LU5 ......56 A8
Downside Inf Sch LU4 ...115 D3
Downside Jun Sch LU4 ...115 D3
Downside Lower Sch
  LU5 ....121 E7
Downs Rd
  Dunstable LU5 ....121 D8
  Luton LU5 ....121 D8
Downs View LU4 ....115 D4
Downton Ct **2** LU3 ....116 A7
Downview LU3 ....115 B2
Drakeloe Cl MK17 ....92 F8

Drake Rd PE19 ....22 B2
Drakes Cl LU5 ....121 D8
Drapers Mews LU3 ....116 C1
Draper Way LU7 ....111 C5
Drayton Cl NN10 ....8 A8
Drayton Rd
  Kempston MK42 ....49 D2
  Luton LU1 ....115 A3
Drewells La PE19 ....33 E4
Drivers Ct LU7 ....111 D7
Drive The
  Harpenden AL5 ....131 A1
  Ivinghoe Aston LU6 ....119 A1
  Oakley MK43 ....36 F7
  Sharnbrook MK44 ....16 C4
  Wharley End MK43 ....58 D2
Drove Rd
  Biggleswade SG18 ....67 B6
  Gamlingay SG19 ....44 B7
Drovers Way LU6 ....120 F8
Drummonds The LU4 .....115 C2
Drury Cl LU3 ....114 C5
Drury La LU3 ....114 C5
Dryden Ct PE19 ....22 F5
Dubbs Knoll Rd SG8 ......69 F5
Duchess Cl PE19 ....22 A3
Duchess Ct LU5 ....114 C1
Duchess Rd MK42 ....50 F4
Duchy Cl NN9 ....3 B3
DUCK END
  MK43 ....36 B6
  MK45 ....62 A1
  MK45 ....62 C5
  MK45 ....85 B8
Duck End Cl MK45 ....62 A1
Duck End La
  Biddenham MK40 ....37 B1
  Maulden MK45 ....85 B8
  Wilstead MK45 ....62 C5
Duck La
  Shefford SG17 ....77 C3
  St Neots PE19 ....22 F7
  Woburn MK17 ....92 F7
Duckmill Cres MK42 ......50 C7
Duck Mill La MK42 ....50 C7
DUCK'S CROSS 30 C5
Dudley Cl MK42 ....49 E3
Dudley St
  Bedford MK40 ....50 E8
  Leighton Buzzard LU7 ...111 A6
  Luton LU2 ....123 E8
Dugdale Ct SG5 ....100 C1
Duke Dr MK41 ....37 D7
Dukeminster Trad Est
  LU5 ....114 C1
Dukes Ave LU6 ....126 E8
Dukes Ct
  Flitwick MK45 ....85 A2
  Luton LU2 ....123 D6
Dukes Rd
  Ampthill MK45 ....84 E8
  St Neots PE19 ....22 B4
Dukes Ride
  Leighton Buzzard LU7 ...102 F3
  13 Luton LU2 ....116 D1
Dukes Row PE28 ....6 F5
Duke St
  Aspley Guise MK17 ......81 D4
  Bedford MK40 ....50 C8
  Luton LU2 ....123 D8
DULOE 21 F6
Duloe Brook PE19 ....22 B5
Duloe Rd PE19 ....22 B5
Dulverton Ct LU7 ....110 C8
Dumble Cl **8** LU1 ....123 D6
Dumfries St LU1 ....123 D6
Duncan Rd MK43 ....58 E2
Duncombe Cl LU3 ....116 C6
Duncombe Ct LU3 ....114 E2
Duncombe Dr
  Dunstable LU5 ....114 E2
  Leighton Buzzard LU7 ...111 A6
Duncots Cl SG5 ....100 E3
Dundee Rd NN29, MK11 ...14 C4
Dunham Cl MK42 ....50 A5
Dunkirk Cl LU2 ....116 A2
Dunlin SG6 ....90 E1
Dunmow Ct LU3 ....116 D2
Dunraven Ave LU1 ....123 A8
Dunsby Rd LU3 ....116 A6
Dunsmore Rd LU1 ....123 C6
DUNSTABLE 121 D8
Dunstable Cl
  Flitwick MK45 ....84 E2
  Luton LU4 ....116 A1
Dunstable Coll LU5 .....114 C1
Dunstable Ct LU4 ....115 F2
Dunstable Downs Cntry Pk*
  LU6 ....120 E7
Dunstable Icknield Lower
  Sch LU6 ....121 B8
Dunstable Pl **1** LU1 .....123 D7
Dunstable Rd
  Caddington LU1 ....122 C3
  Dagnall HP4, LU6 ....126 C7
  Eaton Bray LU6 ....120 A5
  Flamstead AL3 ....129 F1
  Flitwick MK45 ....114 B3
  Luton LU4 ....114 B3
  Studham LU6 ....127 B6
  Tilsworth LU7 ....113 A6
  Toddington LU5 ....105 F3
  Totternhoe LU6 ....113 C8
Dunstable St MK45 ....84 E8
Dunstall Rd MK45 ....97 C2

Dunster Gdns MK41 ....39 B5
Dunster Way PE19 ....22 F2
DUNTON 68 D5
Dunton La
  Biggleswade SG18 ....67 C4
  Biggleswade SG18 ....67 E4
Dunton Lower Sch SG18 ..68 D5
Dunnegan Way MK41 ....38 F5
Dunville Rd MK40 ....49 F8
Durbar Rd LU4 ....116 B1
Durham Cl
  Biggleswade SG18 ....67 A4
  Flitwick MK45 ....84 E4
Durham Rd LU2 ....124 A7
Durler Ave MK42 ....49 C3
Durler Gdns LU1 ....123 D5
Durrell Cl LU7 ....110 E7
DUTTER END 44 E6
Dutter End SG19 ....44 E5
Duxford Cl LU3 ....116 B7
Dyers Rd LU6 ....119 E7
Dylan Ct LU5 ....114 C5
Dynes PI MK41 ....53 C7
Dynevor Cl MK43 ....36 E2
Dynevor Rd MK40 ....38 A1

E

Eagle Centre Way LU4 ...115 B7
Eagle Cl LU4 ....115 A4
Eagle Ct SG7 ....91 E1
Eagle Dr MK45 ....84 D2
Eagle Farm Rd SG18 ....67 B5
Eagle Gdns MK41 ....38 B3
Eagle Way MK43 ....24 F6
Earl Cl PE19 ....22 B4
Earls Ct LU5 ....114 C1
Earls Holme MK42 ....49 D6
Earlsmead SG6 ....101 F3
Earls Meade LU2 ....116 D1
Easby Abbey MK41 ....51 B8
Easedale Cl LU6 ....121 C6
Easingwold Gdns LU1 ..122 F8
Eastcheap SG6 ....101 F6
East Cl SG4 ....101 B1
Eastcote Cl LU2 ....117 D1
EASTCOTTS 51 A4
Eastcotts Rd MK42 ....50 F5
East Ct
  Bedford MK41 ....39 A2
  St Neots PE19 ....22 F5
Eastdale Cl MK44 ....50 A4
EAST END
  MK43 ....59 C2
  MK44 ....30 B3
East End
  Houghton Regis LU5 ...114 C5
  Pavenham MK43 ....26 F3
East End La MK44 ....30 B3
Eastern Ave
  Dunstable LU5 ....121 D8
  Henlow SG16 ....89 C3
Eastern Way
  Heath and Reach LU7 ..103 D5
  Letchworth SG6 ....91 A1
Eastfield Cl LU2 ....117 C4
East Hill LU3 ....116 B6
Easthill Rd LU4 ....114 C5
East Hills MK43 ....59 B1
EAST HYDE 130 F8
East La LU2 ....44 C6
East Lodge Sch SG17 ...77 A2
Eastnor Gdns MK41 ....39 A4
Easton Cl MK45 ....84 F3
Easton Rd MK45 ....84 F3
East Rd
  Langford SG18 ....78 F8
  Sandy SG19 ....54 B8
  Wharley End MK43 ....58 D2
East Side SG19 ....54 C5
East Sq MK42 ....51 A3
East St
  Irchester NN29 ....7 B8
  Kimbolton PE28 ....6 F4
  Leighton Buzzard LU7 ..111 B8
  Lilley LU2 ....109 D2
  St Neots PE19 ....22 F5
Eastville Rd MK42 ....50 B5
East Wlk SG18 ....67 B7
EATON BRAY 119 F6
Eaton Bray Lower Sch
  LU6 ....119 F6
Eaton Bray Rd
  Northall LU6 ....119 C5
  Totternhoe LU6 ....119 E8
EATON FORD 22 D6
Eaton Ford Gn PE19 ...22 D5
Eatongate Cl LU6 ....119 F4
Eaton Green Rd LU2 ...124 D8
Eaton Pk LU6 ....119 F6
Eaton PI LU7 ....117 D1
Eaton Rd MK42 ....49 E2
EATON SOCON 22 C3
Eaton Valley Rd LU2 ...124 B8
Ebble Mead MK41 ....38 D6
Ebenezer St [6] LU1 ...123 D6
Eddiwick Ave LU5 ....114 D7
Edens La MK43 ....25 B2
Eden Way
  Bedford MK41 ....38 D5
  Leighton Buzzard LU7 ..111 B5
Edgcott Cl LU3 ....108 B1
Edgcumbe Ct SG19 ....54 C7
Edgecote Cl LU1 ....122 E3
Edgehill Gdns LU3 ....115 C8
Edgewood Dr LU2 ....117 C6

Edinburgh Cl MK42 ....50 D5
Edinburgh Dr PE19 ....22 C4
Edison Rd MK41 ....39 C3
Edith Cavell Lower Sch
  MK41 ....38 A2
Edkins Cl LU2 ....116 E5
EDLESBOROUGH 119 E4
Edlesborough Sch LU6..119 E3
Edward Arnold Ct MK42..49 D5
Edward Cl SG19 ....54 D7
Edward Peake Mid Sch
  SG18 ....67 C8
Edward Rd
  Bedford MK42 ....50 A6
  Biggleswade SG18 ....67 B7
  Irchester NN29 ....7 B7
  St Neots PE19 ....22 F2
Edward St
  Dunstable LU5 ....114 B1
  Leighton Buzzard LU7 ..111 A8
  Luton LU2 ....116 F1
EDWORTH 80 A6
Edworth Rd SG18 ....79 C5
Egdon Dr LU2 ....116 C6
EGGINGTON 112 B7
Egglestone Cl MK42 ...49 D4
Eighth Ave LU3 ....115 D7
Eileen Wade Lower Sch
  PE28 ....5 B4
Eisenhower PI SG17 ....76 E2
Eisenhower Rd SG17 ...77 C1
Elaine Gdns LU1 ....123 A1
Eldefield SG6 ....101 D2
Elderberry Cl LU2 ....117 B4
Elder Cl SG19 ....54 B6
Eldon Rd LU4 ....115 C1
Eldon Way SG18 ....67 A4
Eleanor Cl MK17 ....92 F7
Eleanor Ct [4] LU6 ....121 B8
Eleanor's Cross [5] LU6..121 B8
Eleanor Wlk MK17 ....92 F7
Elgar Dr SG17 ....77 D3
Elgar Path LU2 ....123 E8
Elger Cl MK40 ....37 D1
Eliot Way SG5 ....90 D3
Elizabeth Ct
  Dunstable LU5 ....121 C8
  Henlow SG16 ....78 D1
  [9] Luton LU1 ....123 D6
  St Neots PE19 ....22 F5
Elizabeth St LU1 ....123 D6
Elizabeth Way SG19 ...44 C6
Ella Ct LU2 ....116 F1
Ellenhall Cl LU3 ....116 C1
Ellenshaw Ct MK45 ....84 F4
Ellerdine Cl LU3 ....116 B4
Ellesmere Cl LU6 ....120 C6
Ellington Rd MK42 ....50 B5
Elliot Cres MK41 ....39 B3
Ellis Rd MK41 ....38 D3
Elliswick Rd AL5 ....131 B2
Elm Ave LU1 ....122 E3
Elm Cl
  Bedford MK41 ....38 E4
  Campton SG17 ....76 F1
  Hargrave NN9 ....1 F2
  Henlow SG16 ....78 D1
Elm Dr MK45 ....86 B5
Elm Farm Cl SG17 ....78 B2
Elmfield Ct LU2 ....117 A1
Elm Gr
  Toddington LU5 ....105 F6
  Woburn Sands MK17 ...81 B4
Elm Ho PE19 ....22 F3
Elmhurst Gdns SG5 ....87 F1
Elm Lodge PE19 ....22 F2
Elmore Rd LU2 ....117 A1
Elm Park Cl LU5 ....114 D6
Elm Rd
  Biggleswade SG18 ....67 B5
  Shefford SG17 ....77 D2
Elms Cl MK45 ....84 F7
Elmsdale Rd MK43 ....61 A8
ELMS FARM 39 C3
Elmside LU6 ....127 E8
Elms Ind Est
  Bedford, Elms Farm MK41..39 D3
  Bedford, Goldington MK41..39 B3
Elms La MK45 ....63 C4
Elms The
  Kempston MK42 ....49 E3
  Leighton Buzzard LU7 ..110 E7
Elm Tree Ct LU2 ....117 E3
Elm Tree Gr MK41 ....19 C7
Elmtree Rd SG19 ....54 B8
Elmwood MK43 ....34 E6
Elmwood Cres
  Flitwick MK45 ....84 E2
  Luton LU2 ....116 E3
Elphick Cl SG18 ....66 F6
ELSTOW 50 C2
Elstow Lower Sch MK42..50 B4
Elstow Moot Hall Mus*
  MK42 ....50 C2
Elstow Rd
  Bedford MK42 ....50 C5
  Kempston MK42 ....49 F4
Elstow Storage Depot
  MK45 ....62 A4
Elveden Cl LU2 ....116 E6
Elvington Gdns LU3 ...108 B1
Ely Cl MK45 ....84 E4
Ely Croft SG18 ....67 A4
Ely Way
  Kempston MK42 ....49 E6
  Luton LU1 ....115 D4
Embankment The MK40..50 D8
Embla Cl MK41 ....39 E3

Emerald Rd LU4 ....115 A3
Emerton Way MK43 ...60 F8
Emery PI PE19 ....22 F7
Emmer Gn LU2 ....117 F2
Emmerton Rd MK43 ...49 D5
Empire St SG18 ....66 F5
Empress Rd LU3 ....115 E4
Emu Cl LU7 ....123 A5
Enderby Rd LU3 ....116 C6
Endsleigh Rd MK42 ...50 B6
Enfield Cl LU3 ....114 D6
Engayne Ave SG19 ....42 B1
England Ave LU6 ....113 F3
Englands La LU1 ....121 C8
Englefield LU2 ....123 A1
Englehurst AL5 ....131 D1
Ennerdale Ave LU6 ...121 B7
Ennerdale Cl MK42 ...49 D3
Ennismore Gn LU2 ....117 F1
Enslow Cl LU1 ....122 E3
Enterprise Ctr [1] LU2..123 F8
Enterprise Way
  Flitwick MK45 ....84 F3
  Leighton Buzzard LU7 ..111 A1
  Luton LU3 ....116 B8
Epping Way LU3 ....107 C1
Epping Wlk MK41 ....39 B3
Epsom Cl
  Leighton Buzzard LU7 ..110 D3
  Rushden NN10 ....4 B8
Ereswell Rd LU3 ....116 A7
Eriboll Cl LU7 ....110 B6
Erin Cl LU4 ....116 A2
Erin Ct LU4 ....116 A2
Ermine PI [8] LU2 ....116 D1
Escarpment Ave HP4,
  LU6 ....120 A1
Eskdale LU4 ....115 C5
Esmonde Cl LU7 ....111 D5
Essex Cl LU1 ....123 F6
Essex Ct [7] LU1 ....123 F6
Essex Gdns MK42 ....50 D5
Etonbury Mid Sch SG15..90 C7
Eton Cl MK40 ....38 D2
Ettrick Dr MK41 ....39 C4
Eugster Ave MK42 ....49 C3
Evans Cl LU5 ....114 E4
Evans Yd LU7 ....103 B4
Evedon Cl LU3 ....115 F6
Evelyn Cl LU4 ....116 A8
Evelyn Way MK29 ....7 C7
Everard Rd MK41 ....38 F2
Everest Cl SG15 ....90 B5
Evergreen Way LU3 ...116 A8
EVERSHOLT 94 B7
Eversholt Ho LU7 ....111 A6
Eversholt Lower Sch
  MK17 ....94 A8
Eversholt Rd
  Ridgmont MK43 ....82 F4
  Steppingley MK45 ....83 F3
EVERTON 43 C3
Everton Hill SG19 ....43 B3
Everton Lower Sch SG19..43 C3
Everton Rd
  Gamlingay Great Heath
    SG19 ....43 E3
  Potton SG19 ....43 C5
  Sandy SG19 ....43 B3
Eves Field MK45 ....85 D3
Evesham Abbey MK41 ..51 A8
Evesham Ct MK41 ....38 C5
Exeter Cl SG18 ....66 F5
Exeter Wlk MK41 ....39 A5
Exton Cl MK44 ....117 A1
Exton Ct MK45 ....85 A8
EYEWORTH 68 F8
Eyeworth Rd SG19 ....57 B2
Eyncourt Rd LU5 ....114 D2
Eynesbury CE Prim Sch
  PE19 ....22 F4
Eynesbury Gn PE19 ...22 F4
Eynsford Rd LU4 ....115 D3

F

Fairfax Ave LU3 ....115 D7
Fairfax Cl SG17 ....78 A3
Fairfax Ct PE19 ....22 D3
Fairfax Rd MK40 ....49 F7
Fairfield LU3 ....44 D5
Fairfield Cl
  Dunstable LU5 ....114 F1
  Harpenden AL5 ....131 D1
Fairfield Rd
  Biggleswade SG18 ....66 F1
  Dunstable LU5 ....114 E1
Fairford Ave LU2 ....116 E4
Fairgreen Rd LU1 ....122 F3
Fairground Way SG17 ..78 B2
Fairholme
  Bedford MK41 ....38 F3
  Biggleswade SG18 ....66 F7
Fairlands SG18 ....66 F7
Fairmead Cres NN10 ...7 F8
Fair Oak Ct LU2 ....116 F3
Fair Oak Dr LU2 ....116 F3
Fair Way MK44 ....40 F5
Fairways The MK45 ...86 C4
Fairway The MK41 ....39 A5
Fakeswell La SG16 ....88 E2
Falcon Ave MK41 ....38 C5
Falcon Cl
  Dunstable LU5 ....114 A1
  Sandy SG19 ....42 B1
Falcon Cres MK45 ....84 E1

Falconers Field AL5 ...130 E3
Falconers Rd LU2 ....117 B1
Faldo Rd
  Barton-le-C MK45 ....97 B4
  Bedford MK42 ....50 D6
Fallow Dr PE19 ....22 B5
Fallowfield
  Ampthill MK45 ....84 E7
  Leighton Buzzard LU7 ..111 C7
  Luton LU3 ....116 C4
Fallows Gn AL5 ....131 B3
Falstaff Rd PE19 ....22 C3
Falstone Gn LU2 ....117 E1
FANCOTT 106 B4
Faraday Cl LU4 ....115 C1
Faraday Gdns SG5 ....90 C2
Faraday Rd MK42 ....50 C5
Faraday Sq MK42 ....50 C5
Farcet Ct PE19 ....22 C6
Fareham Way LU5 ....114 E5
Faringdon Rd LU4 ....115 C3
Farley Ct LU2 ....123 C8
Farley Farm Rd LU1 ...123 B5
FARLEY HILL 123 C5
Farley Hill LU1 ....123 C5
Farley Jun Sch LU1 ...123 C6
Farley Lodge LU1 ....123 D5
Farley Way MK43 ....36 C7
Farm Ave AL5 ....130 D4
Farmbrook LU2 ....116 D7
Farm Cl
  Ampthill MK45 ....84 D7
  Houghton Regis LU5 ..114 C5
  Letchworth SG6 ....91 A1
  Wyboston MK44 ....31 F6
Farm Gn LU1 ....123 C5
Farm Rd LU1 ....130 B7
FARNDISH 7 B4
Farndish Rd NN29 ....7 B8
Farnham Dr NN10 ....7 F8
Farnham Way MK41 ...39 A5
Farley Gr LU2 ....124 A7
Farrell Rd MK43 ....60 F7
Farrer St MK42 ....49 E4
Farrer Top AL3 ....128 E5
Farriers Cl SG7 ....91 E1
Farrow Cl LU3 ....108 C1
Farrowby Ct MK43 ....27 A1
Farr's La LU2 ....125 B1
Farsands MK43 ....36 F8
Faulkner's Way LU7 ...110 E7
Faynes Ct SG19 ....54 C7
Fearnhill Sch SG6 ....101 C5
Fearnley Cres MK42 ...50 A4
Feeden Ho MK43 ....58 D3
Felbrigg Cl LU2 ....117 F2
Felix Ave LU2 ....117 A2
FELMERSHAM 26 C7
Felmersham Ct LU1 ...123 D7
Felmersham Gravel Pits
  Nature Reserve* MK43..16 C1
Felmersham Rd
  Carlton MK43 ....25 C5
  Luton LU3 ....123 A7
  Radwell MK43 ....26 E7
Felstead Cl LU2 ....116 F3
Felstead Way LU2 ....116 F3
Fen Cl LU2 ....117 D1
Fen End SG5 ....90 E6
FENLAKE 50 E5
Fenlake Rd MK42 ....50 D6
Fensome Dr LU5 ....114 E5
Fenwick Cl LU3 ....116 B5
Fenwick Rd LU3 ....114 C5
Feoffee Almshouses
  MK45 ....73 F1
Fermor Cres LU2 ....117 C1
Ferndale [7] AL5 ....131 A2
Ferndale Rd LU1 ....123 B7
Fern Gdns MK45 ....84 E3
Fernheath LU3 ....108 A1
Fernlea Cl MK40 ....49 E7
Fernwood Sch MK17 ...81 B2
Ferrars Ave PE19 ....22 E4
Ferrars Cl LU4 ....115 B1
Ferrars Inf Sch LU4 ...115 B3
Ferrars Jun Sch LU4 ...115 B3
Festival Rd SG19 ....55 F7
Fetlock Cl MK41 ....37 D7
Field Cottage Rd PE19..22 D3
Field End Cl LU2 ....117 C4
Fieldfare
  Letchworth SG6 ....90 E1
  Sandy SG19 ....42 C2
Field Fare La LU4 ....115 A5
Fieldgate Rd LU4 ....115 D2
Fielding Ct PE19 ....22 C7
Field La SG6 ....101 F4
Fieldside MK41 ....39 B3
Fieldside Rd MK45 ....85 E1
Fields Rd MK43 ....61 A6
Fields The SG18 ....67 A8
Fieldyke Cl SG17 ....88 C5
Fildyke Rd SG17 ....88 C5
Filbert Cl SG19 ....54 B6
Filland Ct SG19 ....54 B6
Filmer Rd LU4 ....115 E4
Finchale Priory MK41 ..51 B8
Finch Cl LU4 ....115 A4
Finch Cres LU7 ....110 C5
Finches The
  Bedford MK40 ....38 A1
  Sandy SG19 ....42 C2
Finch Wlk MK45 ....84 E1
Finley Rd AL5 ....131 D3
Finsbury Rd LU3 ....115 D5
Finway LU2 ....123 A8
Firbank Cl LU3 ....107 C1

Firbank Ct LU7 ....111 B5
Firbank Ind Est LU1 ...123 A8
Firbank Rd MK42 ....50 C6
Firbank Way LU7 ....111 C7
Firecrest SG6 ....90 E1
Firs Lower Sch The MK45..84 E8
Firs Path LU7 ....103 A1
First Ave LU6 ....121 B7
Firs The
  Harpenden AL5 ....131 D2
  Kempston MK42 ....49 F3
Fir Tree Cl MK45 ....84 E1
Fir Tree Rd MK45 ....86 B4
Fisher Cl MK45 ....97 B3
Fishers Cl
  Gravenhurst MK45 ....87 C4
  Great Barford MK44 ...40 E6
Fishers Yd PE19 ....22 E5
Fitzgerald Cl MK42 ...50 C6
Fitzroy Ave LU3 ....116 B3
Fitzwarin Cl LU3 ....115 C8
Five Oaks LU1 ....122 F4
Five Oaks Mid Sch LU1..122 F3
Five Springs LU3 ....115 E6
Five Springs Ct LU3 ...115 E6
Five Springs Sch LU3 ..115 F7
FLAMSTEAD 129 B1
Flamstead Sch AL3 ...129 B1
Flanders Cl MK41 ....50 A5
Flawn Way PE19 ....22 B3
Flax Mews AL3 ....128 E5
Fleming Cl MK40 ....37 C1
Fleming Dr SG5 ....90 C2
FLEWTON END 27 C5
Flexmore Way SG18 ...78 F5
Flight Path SG16 ....89 B3
Flint Cl LU3 ....115 E7
Flint Ct
  Dunstable LU6 ....114 A1
  Luton LU1 ....123 D5
Flintings The HP2 ....132 F8
Flint Way
  Bedford MK41 ....39 B5
  Bedford, Woodside MK41..39 A4
  St Neots PE19 ....22 E2
Flintwick Rd MK45 ....84 A3
FLITTON 85 E4
Flitton Hill MK45 ....85 E5
Flitton Rd
  Greenfield MK45 ....85 D3
  Pulloxhill MK45 ....85 E1
FLITWICK 84 D2
Flitwick Lower Sch MK45..84 E2
Flitwick Rd
  Ampthill MK45 ....84 E6
  Flitwick MK45 ....95 E7
  Maulden MK45 ....85 B7
  Steppingley MK45 ....84 B3
  Westoning MK45 ....95 E6
Flitwick Sta MK45 ....84 E2
Florence Ave LU3 ....115 D6
Flowerdale Wlk MK41 ..39 B4
Flowers Ind Est [1] LU1..123 E6
Flowers Way LU1 ....123 E7
Folly Farm MK43 ....71 A8
Folly La
  Caddington LU1 ....122 E4
  North Crawley MK16 ...58 B5
Fontwell Cl MK40 ....38 D1
Football Cl SG7 ....91 E1
Foot La NN9 ....3 C8
Ford Cl PE19 ....22 D5
Ford End Rd MK40 ....49 F7
Fordfield Rd MK45 ....84 B6
Ford La MK44 ....31 E1
Ford The MK41 ....37 E5
Forest Ctr The* MK43 ..72 E8
Foresters Cl MK41 ....64 A1
Forge Cl
  Chalton LU4 ....106 E2
  St Neots PE19 ....22 B2
Forge Gdns MK44 ....4 A3
Forrest Cres LU2 ....117 A3
Forty Foot La MK44 ...9 A1
Foster Cl LU4 ....114 C3
Foster Gr SG19 ....54 C6
Foster Hill Rd MK40 ...38 B1
Foster PI MK42 ....49 E4
Foster Rd
  Harlington LU5 ....95 F2
  Kempston MK42 ....49 E5
  Wootton MK43 ....60 F8
Foster St MK40 ....38 B1
Foster Way MK41 ....60 F8
Foston Cl LU3 ....115 F6
Foundry La SG18 ....67 A5
Foundry Way PE19 ....22 B1
Fountaine Ct MK45 ...73 D1
Fountain Gr MK42 ....49 D5
Fountains Rd
  Bedford MK41 ....38 F5
  Luton LU3 ....116 D3
Fourth Ave LU3 ....115 D7
Fowler Cl MK42 ....49 D5
Fowlers Dr SG17 ....88 B6
Foxbrook MK43 ....36 C7
Fox Brook Ct PE19 ....22 F5
Foxbury Cl LU2 ....116 D6
Fox Cl
  Clapham MK41 ....37 C7
  Dunton SG18 ....68 C5
Fox Cnr SG8 ....69 F5
FOX CORNER 103 A7
Foxdell Inf Sch LU1 ...123 A8
Foxdell Jun Sch LU1 ..122 E8

Fox Dells LU6........... 121 C5
Foxglove Cl
  Rushden NN10...........8 C8
  St Neots PE19.........22 C5
Foxglove Dr SG18......67 C4
Foxglove Way MK42.....50 E4
Fox Hedge Way MK44...16 B3
Foxhill LU2.............116 E5
Fox Hill SG8...........69 F5
Fox Hill Rd SG8.......69 F5
Foxlease MK41.........38 C5
Frampton Ct MK41.....38 C5
Frances Ashton Ho **11**
  LU6...................121 B8
Frances Ct LU7........110 E7
Franciscan Cl NN10...7 F8
Francis Cl SG5.........90 E6
Francis Groves Cl MK41..38 D4
Francis Rd SG7.........80 C6
Francis St LU1.........123 D8
Frank Hamel Ct MK45..97 C2
Franklin Ave MK45.....97 B3
Franklin Cl
  Marston Moretaine MK43..60 D2
  Pirton SG5............99 D4
Franklin Gdns SG4....101 B1
Franklin Rd
  Biggleswade SG18.....66 F5
  Dunstable LU6........120 F8
Franklyn Gdns MK40...37 C1
Franks Cl SG16........89 B5
Fraser Rd MK44........51 C6
Frederick St LU2......116 E1
Frederick Street Pas
  LU2...................116 E1
Freeman Ave LU3......116 B8
Freemans Cl
  Hitchin SG5..........100 D1
  Houghton Regis LU5..114 A4
Freemantle Ct PE19...22 B3
Freewaters Cl SG5....100 E4
Frenchmans Cl LU5....105 E5
French's Ave LU6......113 E2
French's Gate LU6....113 F2
Frensham Dr SG4......101 C2
Freshwater Cl LU5....115 F7
Friars Cl LU1..........123 B5
Friars Ct LU1..........123 B5
Friars Way LU1........123 B5
Friars Wlk
  Dunstable LU6........121 B8
  Sandy SG19...........54 D8
Friary Field LU6......121 B8
Friday St LU7.........110 F7
Friendless La Al3.....128 F2
Friesian Cl LU4.......115 A3
Frinton Cl NN10.......7 F8
Friston Gn LU2........117 D1
Froghall Rd MK45......84 C5
Frome Cl
  Bedford MK41.........38 C5
  Luton LU4............115 E4
Front St LU1..........123 C1
FROXFIELD.............93 E7
Fuchsia Way NN10.....8 B7
Fulbourne Cl LU4.....115 E4
Fulbrook Mid Sch MK17..81 B5
Fullers Ct SG6........101 E7
Fulmar Rd MK41.......38 D4
Fulmore Cl AL5........131 D4
Furlay Cl SG6.........101 D7
Furlong La LU6........120 C7
Furlong The MK41.....38 E4
Furness Ave LU6......121 C7
Furness Cl MK41......38 F5
Furrows The LU3......116 B7
Furze Cl LU2..........116 D7
Furzedown Ct **18** MK45..131 B1
Furzefield MK41......38 F3
Furzen Cl LU6.........121 C5
Furzenhall Rd SG18...55 A1
Fyne Dr LU7...........110 C8

G

Gables The LU7........110 E6
Gable Way LU5........114 C6
Gadsden Turn LU7....111 E2
Gade Valley Cotts HP1..132 E4
Gadsby St MK40.......50 C8
Gadsden Cl MK43......59 D2
Gainsborough Ave PE19..22 D5
Gainsborough Dr LU5..114 D5
Gainsborough Rise MK41..38 B3
Gainsford Cres SG4...101 C2
Gale Ct MK45..........97 C2
Gales Pl MK45.........63 D7
Gallery The
  Letchworth SG6......101 F6
  7 Luton LU1.......123 E7
Galleywood SG5.......100 D4
Galliard Cl LU3........116 A4
Galloway Cl MK42......49 C3
Galston Rd LU3........115 D8
Gamblingay Village Coll
  SG19................44 D5
Gamligay Fst Sch SG19..44 D5
GAMLINGAY.............44 C4
GAMLINGAY CINQUES...44 C6
GAMLINGAY GREAT
  HEATH...............43 E3
Gamlingay Rd
  Gamlingay SG19......44 D8
  Potton SG19.........44 C1

Garden Cl MK42........49 D5
Gardener Pl MK40......37 C1
Gardeners Cl
  Flitwick MK45.........85 A3
  Maulden MK45.........85 C8
Gardeners La SG16....78 D2
Garden Fields SG19...55 F8
Garden Fields Ct NN29..7 C8
Garden Hedge LU7....111 A8
Gardenia Ave LU3.....116 A4
Garden Leys LU7......111 C6
Gardens Rd LU6.......121 C7
Gardens The
  Henlow SG16.........89 D8
  Stotfold SG5.........90 E6
Gardner Ct LU1........123 E4
Garden's Cl LU6.......120 E7
Garfield Ct LU1.......117 D3
Garfield St MK41......38 B2
Garland Way LU1......111 D5
Garner Cl SG18.......53 E2
Garnith Cl MK42......49 F4
Garnes Groves Cl MK41..38 D4
Garretts Mead LU1....117 B3
Garter Ct **10** LU2....116 D1
Gas House La MK45....73 F2
Gatehill Gdns LU3....108 B1
Gateshead Cl SG19....42 C1
Gaunts Way SG6.......91 A2
Gayland Ave LU1......124 B8
Gayton Cl LU3.........116 A4
Gazelle Cl LU4........22 B5
Gelding Cl LU4........114 F5
Geldonia Ave MK40...38 D2
Gelt The MK41.........38 C7
Gemini Cl LU7.........111 D8
Gentian Cl NN10......8 C8
George Ct
  Biggleswade SG18....67 A5
  Leighton Buzzard LU7..111 B7
George Pi PE19.......22 F2
George St W LU1.......123 E7
George St
  Bedford MK40.........50 E8
  Clapham MK41........37 D6
  Dunstable LU6........114 B1
  Leighton Buzzard LU7..111 A7
  Luton LU1............123 E7
  Markyate AL3.........128 E5
  Maulden MK45........74 C1
  Shefford SG17.......77 C2
  Woburn MK17.........92 F6
Georgetown SG19.....42 A1
Georgetown Rd SG19..42 A1
Georgina Ct SG15.....90 A3
Gerald Ct MK40.......37 F1
Gerard Ct **2** AL5.....131 A2
Gernon Rd SG6........101 D5
Gernon Wlk SG6.......101 F5
Gery Ct PE19..........22 C5
Gibbards Ct MK44.....16 B3
Gibbons Rd MK40.....50 A8
Gibraltar Lodge AL5..131 D3
Gibson Dr LU1.........111 D5
Gifford Rd MK40......50 A8
Gig La LU7............103 B5
Gilbert Cl MK42.......49 D6
Gilbert Ct AL5.........131 B4
Gilbert Inglefield Mid Sch
  LU7..................103 C1
Gilbert Mews **6** LU7..111 A8
Gilded Acre LU6.......121 C5
Gilder Cl LU3..........116 A8
Gilderdale LU4........115 A8
Gillam St LU2.........123 E8
Gillan Way LU1........114 E5
Gillespie Cl MK42.....50 C6
Gilpin Cl
  Houghton Regis LU5..114 D5
  Stanford SG18........78 A7
Gilpin Cl AL5..........131 C1
Gilpin St LU1.........114 A2
Gilwell Cl MK41.......38 E5
Gipping Cl MK41......38 D7
Gipsy La
  Luton LU1............124 A6
  Slapton LU7.........118 D8
Girdle Rd SG4.........101 A2
GIRTFORD..............54 A8
Girtford Cres SG19....54 B7
Glade The
  Bromham MK43........36 C3
  Letchworth SG6......101 F3
Gladstone Ave LU1....123 C7
Gladstone Cl SG18....67 A6
Gladstone St MK41....38 B2
Glaisdale LU4.........115 C5
Glamis Ct PE19........22 E2
Glamis Wlk MK41......39 A4
Glastonbury Abbey MK41..51 B8
Glebe Ave
  Arlesey SG15.........90 A7
  Flitwick MK45........84 E2
Glebe Cl
  Sandy SG19...........54 B8
  Thurleigh MK44......18 C2
Glebe Gdns LU5.......95 F2
Glebe Ho MK40........38 C2
Glebe Rd
  Ampthill MK45.......84 E7
  Bedford MK40........38 C1
  Biggleswade SG18....67 B7
  Sandy SG19..........54 C8
Glebe Rise MK44......16 C4
Glebe The
  Campton SG17........76 F1
  Clapham MK41........37 C7

Glebe The continued
  Gravenhurst MK45.......87 C5
  Lavendon MK46.........34 A8
Glebe Way MK45........74 A7
Glemsford Cl LU4......115 B6
Glemsford Dr AL5......131 D2
Glenariff PE19.........22 E4
Glenavon Rd MK41.....39 C4
Gleneagles Dr LU2....116 E6
Glenfield Rd LU3......116 A4
Glen Miller Mus* MK41..27 F2
Glenrose Ave MK41....38 B4
Glen The
  Caddington LU1......122 E3
  Kempston MK42......49 D3
Glenwood Sch LU6....121 E5
Globe Cl AL5..........131 B1
Globe La LU1..........102 E1
Glossop Way SG15.....90 B7
Gloucester Cl MK45...84 E8
Gloucester Rd
  Bedford MK42.........50 C5
  1 Luton LU1........123 F6
Glovers Ct SG5........100 F1
Godfrey La MK44......16 E4
Godfreys Cl LU1.......123 B6
Godfreys Ct LU1.......123 B6
Godso Cl MK41........38 F2
Godwin MK43..........36 F2
Godwin Way MK43.....36 F2
Gold Crest Cl LU4.....115 A5
Goldcrest Way MK41...38 B4
Golden Riddy LU7....110 E8
GOLDINGTON...........39 B2
Goldington Ave MK40..38 D1
Goldington Gn MK41...39 A2
Goldington Green Lower Sch
  MK41...............39 B1
Goldington Mid Sch MK41..38 F2
Goldington Rd MK41...39 A1
Gold La MK40..........37 B1
Gold St
  Podington NN29......7 E2
  Riseley MK44.........10 F2
Goldstone Cres LU4...114 E2
Goodhall Cres MK45...86 C8
Good Intent LU6.......119 E4
Goodman Dr LU2......111 B5
Goodman Rd MK42....50 B5
Goodmayes Cl MK42...50 F6
Goodrich Ave MK41...39 B4
Goodwins Yd MK44....41 A5
Goodwood Cl MK45...86 C8
Gooseberry Hill LU3..116 B7
Goose Gn LU7.........104 D2
Gordon St LU1........123 D7
Gorham Pl PE19.......22 D4
Gorham Way LU5......114 F2
Gorst Cl SG6..........101 E5
Gosforth Cl MK41.....42 C2
Goshawk Cl LU4......115 A4
GOSSARD'S GREEN......59 C4
Gostwick Pl MK41.....52 C8
Gostwick Rd MK42....50 F6
GOSWELL END..........95 F3
Gothic Mede Lower Sch
  SG15...............90 A5
Gothic Way AL5.......90 B5
Goulsbra Rd NN10....8 D8
Gower Dr MK40.......37 C1
Graces La MK43.......59 C3
Grafton Rd MK40.....50 A8
Graham Gdns LU3....115 C8
Graham Rd LU5.......121 E7
Grampian Way LU3....115 C8
Granary La AL5.......131 C1
Granby Ave AL5.......131 D2
Granby Rd LU4........115 B6
Granet Cl MK41.......37 F1
Grange Ave LU4.......115 A4
Grange Cl
  Houghton Conquest MK45..74 A7
  Irchester NN29......7 B7
  Leighton Buzzard LU7..110 D6
  Markyate AL3........128 D6
  Oakley MK43.........37 A8
Grange Ct
  Bromham MK43........36 F3
  Heath and Reach LU7..103 A6
  Letchworth SG6......91 A1
Grange Dr SG5.........90 F5
Grange Farm Cl MK45..97 B3
Grange Gdns
  Beeston SG19........54 B5
  Campton SG17.......76 F1
  Heath and Reach LU7..103 B6
  Sharnbrook MK44....16 C4
  Toddington LU5......95 B8
Grange Jun Sch SG6...91 A2
Grange La
  Bromham MK43........36 F3
  Cople MK44..........52 A5
Grange Rd
  Ampthill MK45.......84 E7
  Barton-le-C MK45....77 A7
  Bedford MK41........39 A1
  Blunham MK44.......41 E5
  Felmersham MK43....16 A5
  Letchworth SG6......101 F8
  Toddington LU5......95 B8
Grange Specl Sch MK42..49 E5
Grange St SG17........78 A3
Grange The
  Lower Caldecote SG18..54 D2
  Toddington LU5......105 F5

Grangeway
  Houghton Regis LU5..114 E6
  Rushden NN10.........8 A8
Grange Way
  Irchester NN29.......7 B7
  Willington MK44......52 C8
Grange Wlk LU5.......105 F6
Gransden Cl LU3......116 A7
Grant Gdns AL5.......131 B2
Grantham Rd LU4.....116 B1
Granville Rd
  Hitchin SG4..........101 C1
  Luton LU1............123 B8
Granville St MK42.....50 A6
Graphic Cl LU6........121 D6
Grasmere Ave
  Harpenden AL5.......131 C1
  Luton LU3............116 B7
Grasmere Cl
  Dunstable LU6.......121 B7
  Flitwick MK45.........84 E2
  Kempston MK42......49 E3
Grasmere Rd
  Biggleswade SG18....67 A4
  Luton LU6............116 C7
Grasmere Way LU7...110 D7
Grasmere Wlk LU6...114 C6
Grass Yd PE28.........6 F4
Gratton Rd MK40.....49 F8
Gravel Pit Rd MK42...49 E3
Gravenhurst Lower Sch
  MK45...............87 C4
Gravenhurst Rd
  Campton SG17.......87 F8
  Shillington SG5.....87 E4
Graylings The MK41...38 F4
Grays Cl MK45.........97 C3
Grays Gr MK44........13 B2
Gray's Rd SG19.......44 D6
Grazebrook MK41.....38 F4
Graze Hill MK44......22 B8
Great Aldens MK41...38 F4
GREAT BARFORD.......40 F4
Great Barford Lower Sch
  MK44...............40 F5
Great Bramingham La
  LU3................108 B2
GREAT BRICKHILL.....102 C8
GREAT DENHAM........49 C8
Great Farm Cl MK43..79 C2
GREAT GADDESDEN.....132 D3
Great Gaddesden CE Prim
  Sch HP1............132 D3
Great Gn SG5..........99 D4
Great Hill SG17.......77 C4
Great La MK45........75 D4
Great Marlings LU2...117 C2
Great Northern Rd LU5..121 D8
Great North Rd
  St Neots PE19.......22 B3
  Wyboston MK44......32 A6
Great Portway MK40..49 B6
GREAT STAUGHTON....13 F6
Great Staughton Prim Sch
  PE19...............13 F6
Greaves Way LU7....111 D6
Grebe Cl MK45........84 D2
Greenacre Dr
  Rushden NN10........8 B7
  Rushden NN10........8 B7
Greenacres MK41....38 E4
Green Acres
  Gamlingay SG19......44 C5
  Lilley LU2...........109 D2
Green Bushes LU4....115 D6
Green Cl
  Luton LU4...........115 C5
  Stanbridge LU7......112 D5
Green Ct **6** LU4......115 C5
Green Dragon Ct **8** LU1..123 F6
GREEN END
  MK44...............13 A3
  MK44...............40 E6
  MK44...............49 A3
Green End
  Gamlingay SG19......44 C5
  Little Staughton MK44..13 A3
  Workhouse End MK41..40 A5
Green End Rd
  Great Barford MK44..40 E6
  Kempston MK43......49 A4
GREENFIELD...........85 D2
Greenfield CE Lower Sch
  MK45...............85 D2
Greenfield Cl LU6....113 E1
Greenfield La SG5....100 E4
Greenfield Rd
  Flitton MK45.........85 A3
  Flitwick MK45........85 D1
  Pulloxhill MK45......85 D1
  Westoning MK45.....95 F6
Greenfields SG5......87 E1
Greenfields Way LU6..68 D5
Green Gables PE19....22 D4
Greengate LU3........115 C8
Greenhill LU7........103 A1
Greenhill Ave LU6....116 E3
Greenhill St **12** MK40..50 B8
Green La
  Aspley Guise MK17...81 E4
  Clapham MK41........37 C6
  Dunstable LU6.......120 E8
  Eaton Bray LU6......119 D7
  Everton SG19........43 C3
  Great Staughton PE19..13 F6
  Hitchin SG4.........101 B1

Green La continued
  Kensworth LU6.......127 E8
  Letchworth SG6......91 B1
  Luton LU2...........117 C4
  Markyate AL3........128 E8
  Renhold MK41........39 B6
  Swineshead MK44....11 C8
  Westoning MK45.....111 C8
Greenlands LU7.......110 C7
Greenleas Lower Sch
  LU7................110 C7
Green Milverton LU3..116 A7
Green Oaks LU2.......116 F3
Greenriggs LU2........117 F2
Greensand Ridge MK43..72 B7
Greens Cl SG19........54 C7
Greenshields Rd MK40..50 E8
Greenside Pk LU2.....116 E3
Green The
  Bromham MK43........36 F3
  Cardington MK44....51 D4
  Chelveston NN9......3 C8
  Edlesborough LU6....119 F4
  Great Staughton PE19..13 F7
  Harrold MK43.........25 A6
  Houghton Regis LU5..114 C4
  Luton LU4...........115 C5
  Marston Moretaine MK43..72 D7
  Newnham SG7........91 E7
  Peters Green LU2....125 C3
  Stotfold SG5.........90 F7
  Turvey MK43.........58 E2
  Wharley End MK43...58 E2
Greenview Cl MK44...49 C3
Greenway SG17........77 A1
Greenways
  Eaton Bray LU6......119 D7
  Flitwick MK45........84 F3
  Luton LU2...........117 B5
Gregories Cl LU3......116 D1
Gregory Cl SG17.......88 B5
Greig Cl SG17.........77 D3
Grenadier Cl MK41....38 C7
Grenidge Way MK43...36 F8
Grenville Way PE19...22 B2
Gresham Cl LU2.......124 D8
Gresham Ct MK40.....38 D2
Gresham Way SG17...77 C4
Greskine Cl MK41.....39 C4
Greycote MK42........51 A2
Greyfriars MK40......50 B8
Greys Education Ctr
  MK42...............49 D4
Greystoke Wlk MK41..38 F4
Grimaldi Ave LU3.....116 A3
Grisedale Ct MK42....49 E2
Groat La SG19........44 D8
Grosvenor Gdns
  Biggleswade SG18....67 B6
  St Neots PE19.......22 E6
Grosvenor Rd
  Baldock SG7.........91 F1
  Luton LU3...........116 B5
Grosvenor Rd W SG7..91 F1
Grosvenor St MK42...50 C6
GROVE..............111 A1
Grovebury Cl LU6....121 D6
Grovebury Ct MK43...60 F7
Grovebury Place Est
  LU7................111 A6
Grovebury Rd
  Leighton Buzzard LU7..111 A4
  Leighton Buzzard LU7..111 A5
Grovebury Road Ind Est
  LU7................111 A5
Grovebury Turn LU7...111 C1
Grove Ct
  Arlesey SG15.........90 A8
  Turvey MK43..........34 E6
Grove End LU1.........123 B5
Grove Ho SG4.........101 A2
Grovelands Ave SG4...101 C2
Groveland Way SG5...91 A5
Grove Park Rd LU1....123 B3
Grove Pl
  2 Bedford MK40.....50 C8
  Leighton Buzzard LU7..111 A6
Grove Rd
  Dunstable LU5.......121 D7
  Hitchin SG4.........100 F1
  Houghton Regis LU5..114 C7
  Leighton Buzzard LU7..111 A6
  Luton LU1............123 D7
  Slip End LU1.........123 B2
  Turvey MK43.........34 E6
Groveside SG16.......78 D2
Grove The
  Bedford MK40........38 C1
  Biggleswade SG18....67 B5
  Houghton Conquest MK45..74 A7
  Lidlington MK43......73 C2
  Luton LU1...........123 B5
  Silsoe MK45..........86 B5
  St Neots PE19.......22 E6
  Westoning MK45.....95 D6
  Woburn Sands MK17..81 B5
Guardian Ind Est LU1..123 C8
Guernsey Cl LU4......115 A3
GUILDEN MORDEN......69 F4
Guilden Morden CE Prim Sch
  SG8.................69 F5
Guildford St LU1.....123 E7
Guinness Pl MK41.....51 A8
Guise Ct MK17........81 F4
Gulliver Cl MK42......49 D5
Gunnersbury Pk MK41..39 B1
Gurney Ct LU6.........119 F6
Gurney's La SG5......100 B7
Guru Ravidass La MK40..50 A8

Gwyn Ct 2 MK40 50 B8
Gwyn St 5 MK40 38 B1
Gypsy La
Aspley Guise MK17 81 F3
Biggleswade SG18 66 D5

H

Hackett Pl MK16 58 A6
Haddon Cl NN10 8 A8
Haddon Ct 20 AL5 131 B1
Haddon Rd LU2 123 F8
Haden Cl MK41 38 A3
Hadfield Ct MK42 50 B6
Hadleigh Cl MK41 39 A4
Hadley Ct LU3 116 D1
Hadlow Down Cl LU3 116 A5
Hadrian Ave LU5 114 E2
Hadrian Lower Sch LU5 114 E2
Hagdell Rd LU1 123 C5
Hailes Cl MK41 38 E5
Halegate MK43 60 F8
Hale Lodge MK40 38 C2
Hales Mdw AL5 131 A2
Halesowen Dr MK42 50 D3
Half Moon La
Dunstable LU5 121 D7
Pepperstock LU1 129 C8
Half Moon Pl LU6 121 D7
Halfway Ave LU4 115 D1
Halifax Rd MK42 51 A2
Hallards The PE19 22 C6
Hall Ave NN10 8 A8
Hall Cl
Harrold MK43 25 A6
Sharnbrook MK44 16 C4
HALL END
MK43 60 D8
MK45 86 A8
Hall End Cl MK45 86 B8
Hall End Rd MK43 60 E7
Halley's Way LU5 114 D4
Hall La PE28 6 C8
Hall Mead SG6 101 D6
Hall Rd PE19 22 E3
Hallside SG18 68 C5
Hall Way MK45 63 D7
Hallwicks Rd LU2 117 B3
Hallworth Dr SG5 90 E6
Hallworth Ho SG5 90 E6
Halsey Rd MK42 49 E5
Halyard Cl LU3 116 B6
Halyard High Sch LU4 114 F3
Hamble Rd MK41 38 D7
Hambling Pl LU6 120 F8
Hambridge Way SG5 99 D4
Hambro Cl LU2 130 F7
Hamer Ct LU2 116 D8
Hamilton Cl HP4 126 C5
Hamilton Ct 4 LU7 111 A7
Hammerdell SG6 101 D7
Hammersmith Cl LU5 114 C5
Hammersmith Gdns LU5 114 C5
Hammond Ct LU1 123 C1
Hammond Rd MK41 39 D4
Hampden Cl MK45 84 E1
Hampden Ct MK40 37 B1
Hampden Rd
Flitwick MK45 84 E1
Hitchin SG4 101 C1
Hampshire Way LU3 107 E1
Hampton Cl MK45 62 F4
Hampton Rd LU4 123 B8
Hamsterley Cl MK41 39 B4
Hancock Dr LU2 116 E5
Handcross Rd LU2 117 D2
Handley Page Cl MK43 58 E2
Hanover Cl PE19 22 D5
Hanover Ct
Leighton Buzzard LU7 110 D7
Luton LU4 115 D5
Wootton MK43 60 F8
Hanover Pl MK45 97 C4
HANSCOMBE END 98 D8
Hanscombe End Rd SG5 98 D7
Hanswick Cl LU2 117 B2
Hanworth Cl LU2 116 D7
Harbrook La SG17 78 A2
Harbury Dell LU3 116 B7
Harcourt Cl LU7 110 E7
Harcourt St LU1 123 E5
Hardenwick Ct 4 AL5 131 A2
Harding Cl
Bedford MK42 50 E6
Luton LU3 115 E7
Harding Ct AL5 131 B4
Harding Par 8 AL5 131 B1
HARDMEAD 46 D4
Hardmead Rd MK43 34 A3
Hardwick Cl SG17 77 C3
Hardwick Gn LU3 116 B7
Hardwick Hill MK45 61 F7
Hardwick Mews MK17 81 B3
Hardwick Pl MK17 81 B4
Hardwick Rd
Bedford MK42 50 C6
St Neots PE19 22 E3
Woburn Sands MK17 81 B4
Hardy Pl PE19 22 D6
Harefield Ave MK42 50 A4
Harefield Ct LU1 122 F8
Harefield Rd LU1 122 F8
Harepark Terr SG16 88 E3
Harewelle Way MK43 25 A7
Harewood Rd MK42 50 C4
Hargood Ct PE19 22 B3
HARGRAVE 1 E2
Hargreaves Ct MK42 50 C4
Harkness Ct SG4 101 B1
Harkness Way SG4 101 C2
Harland Rd PE19 22 F6
Harlech Ct PE19 22 F2
Harlech Rd MK41 38 F4
Harlestone Cl LU3 108 A1
Harling Rd LU6 120 B4
HARLINGTON 95 F1
Harlington Lower Sch LU5 95 F2
Harlington Rd
Sharpenhoe MK45 96 C3
Toddington LU5 106 B7
Upper Sundon LU3 107 B5
Harlington Sta LU5 95 E1
Harlington Upper Sch LU5 95 F3
HARLINGTON WOOD END 95 B3
Harmill Ind Est LU7 111 A5
Harmony Row LU7 111 E5
Harold Rd MK45 97 C3
HARPENDEN 130 D2
Harpenden Cl MK41 39 A1
Harpenden Memorial Hospl AL5 131 B2
Harpenden Prep Sch AL5 130 F2
Harpenden Rise AL5 130 F3
Harpenden Sta AL5 131 B1
Harps Hill AL3 128 E5
Harpur Ctr 8 MK40 50 B8
Harpur Sq 15 MK40 50 B8
Harpur St MK40 50 B8
Harrier Cl SG18 66 F4
Harriers The SG19 42 B1
Harrier Way MK42 49 E2
Harrington Dr MK41 38 E4
Harrington Hts LU5 114 A5
Harris Cl MK42 49 E4
Harris Ct MK45 97 B4
HARROLD 24 F6
Harrold Lower Sch MK43 24 F6
Harrold Odell Country Park* MK43 25 B7
Harrold-Odell Visitor Ctr* MK43 25 B6
Harrold Priory MK41 39 B1
Harrold Priory Mid Sch MK43 24 F6
Harrold Rd MK46 24 C1
HARROWDEN 51 A3
Harrowden Ct LU2 124 C8
Harrowden La
Bedford MK42 50 E4
Harrowden MK42, MK44 51 B4
Harrowden Mid Sch MK42 50 E5
Harrowden Rd
Bedford MK42 50 F4
Luton LU2 124 C8
Harrow Piece MK45 85 C8
Harrow Rd LU7 111 B5
Harry Scott Ct LU4 115 C6
Harter Ave MK43 71 B7
Harter Rd MK42 49 D2
HART HILL 117 A1
Hart Hill Dr LU2 123 F8
Hart Hill La LU2 123 F8
Hart Hill Prim Sch LU2 123 F8
Hartington St MK41 38 B2
Hart La LU2 124 A8
Hartland Ave MK40 38 E1
Hartley Rd LU2 123 F8
Hartop Cl MK41 38 F4
Hartsfield JMI Sch SG7 91 F1
Hartsfield Rd LU2 117 B2
Hartshill MK41 38 E3
Hartwell Cres LU7 111 B7
Hartwell Dr MK42 49 E6
Hartwell Gdns AL5 130 E1
Hartwell Gr LU7 111 A7
Hart Wlk LU2 117 A1
Hartwood 3 LU2 123 F8
Harvest Cl LU4 115 A3
Harvester Ct LU7 111 D7
Harvey Cl SG18 66 C8
Harvey Rd
Bedford MK41 39 A2
Dunstable LU6 120 D7
Rushden NN10 8 B7
Harvey's Hill LU2 116 F5
Harvey St PE19 22 E4
Haselfoot SG6 101 E6
Hasketon Dr LU4 115 B6
Haslingden Cl AL5 130 D3
Hassett St MK40 50 B8
Hastingbury Upper Sch & Com Coll MK42 49 C2
Hastings Rd
Barton-le-C MK45 97 C3
Kempston MK42 49 D2
Hastings St LU1 123 D6
HATCH 53 F4
Hatch Comm SG19 53 F4
HATCH END 19 A7
Hatch La MK44 19 A6
Hat Factory The LU1 123 E7
Hatfield Ave MK43 71 B7
Hatfield Cl MK45 84 F3
Hatfield Cres
Bedford MK41 38 F1
Flitwick MK45 84 F3
Hatfield Rd MK45 84 F3
Hathaway Cl
Luton LU4 115 B2
St Neots PE19 22 C3
HATLEY END 57 B5
Hatley Rd
Gamlingay SG19 45 B4
Potton SG19 56 E7
HATLEY ST GEORGE 45 F3
Hatters Way LU1 123 B8
Havelock Cl
Gamlingay SG19 44 C5
Sandy SG19 42 B1
Havelock Rd
Biggleswade SG18 67 A7
Luton LU2 116 E1
Havelock Rise LU2 116 E1
Havelock St MK40 50 A7
Haven The SG5 90 F6
Haverdale LU4 115 C4
Hawes Cl MK45 84 E3
Hawesmere Cl SG18 67 A4
Hawk Cl MK45 84 D2
Hawk Dr
Bedford MK41 38 B6
Sandy SG19 42 B2
Hawker Cl LU7 111 D5
Hawkesford Way PE19 22 F7
Hawkfield SG6 101 E8
Hawkfields LU2 116 E6
Hawkins Rd MK42 50 C5
Hawthorn Ave LU2 117 B4
Hawthorn Cl
Ampthill MK45 84 F7
Biggleswade SG18 66 F8
Dunstable LU6 121 C7
Turvey MK43 34 E6
Hawthorn Cres LU1 122 E3
Hawthorne Ave MK40 49 F7
Hawthorne Cl LU7 110 E8
Hawthorne Ct MK45 75 E1
Hawthorn End SG19 44 C5
Hawthorn Hill SG6 101 F7
Hawthorn Park Lower Sch LU5 114 D6
Hawthorn Rd PE19 22 E6
Hawthorns The
Cranfield MK43 59 B1
Henlow SG16 78 D3
Hawthorn Way
Lower Stondon SG16 88 F2
Silsoe MK45 86 B4
Hay Cl NN10 8 B8
Haycroft
Luton LU2 116 E6
Wootton MK43 61 A6
Hayes Cl LU2 117 C5
Hayhurst Rd LU4 115 B1
Hay La AL5 131 A1
Haylands Way MK41 38 F2
Hayley Ct LU5 114 C6
Hayling Dr LU2 117 D3
Haylock Cl MK42 49 D2
Haymarket Rd LU4 114 E4
Haymoor SG6 101 E7
HAYNES 64 A1
HAYNES CHURCH END 75 C7
Haynes Lower Sch MK45 64 A1
Haynes Rd MK42 50 C5
HAYNES WEST END 74 F5
Hayton Cl LU3 108 B2
Hazelbury Cres LU1 123 C8
Hazelbury Ct LU1 123 C8
Hazel Cl SG17 77 B2
Hazeldene Lower Sch MK41 38 E3
Hazel Gr SG5 90 E5
Hazel Wlk SG18 66 F8
Hazelwood Cl LU2 117 B4
Hazelwood La MK45 73 E3
Hazelwood Rd MK42 50 D5
Heacham Cl LU4 115 B4
HEATH AND REACH 103 B5
Heath Cl
Luton LU1 123 B6
Woburn Sands MK17 81 C3
Heathcliff Ave SG5 90 B2
Heath Ct LU7 102 F3
Heather Dr SG18 67 C4
Heather Gdns MK41 39 B1
Heather Mead LU6 119 E4
Heathermere SG6 90 F1
Heathfield MK41 39 A3
Heathfield Cl LU1 122 F4
Heathfield Lower Sch LU1 122 E4
Heathfield Rd
Hitchin SG5 100 F1
Luton LU3 116 C4
Heath Gn LU7 103 A5
Heath La MK17 81 A2
Heath Park Dr LU7 103 A2
Heath Park Rd LU7 103 A3
Heath Rd
Gamlingay SG19 44 B4
Leighton Buzzard LU7 103 A2
Heath The LU7 102 E4
Heathwood Cl LU7 103 A3
Heathwood Lower Sch LU7 103 B3
Heaton Dell LU2 117 E1
Hebden Cl LU4 115 B4
Hedgerow The LU4 115 D6
Hedley Rise LU2 117 F2
Hedley Way MK45 86 B8
Heights The LU3 115 E5
Helen Ho MK42 50 B6
Helford Cl MK41 38 D6
Helmsley Ave MK41 39 A5
Helmsley Cl LU4 115 C5
Hemel Hempstead Rd HP4 126 F1
Hemingford Dr LU2 116 D6
Hempsals PE19 22 C6
Hen Brook PE19 22 F4
Henderson Way MK42 49 F4
Henge Way LU3 115 E7
Henley Cl LU5 114 E5
Henley Rd MK40 50 A8
HENLOW 78 D1
HENLOW CAMP 89 A3
Henlow Ind Est SG16 89 B4
Henlow Mid Sch SG16 78 D1
Henry Ct LU6 121 A8
Henson Cl MK43 58 E2
Henstead Pl LU2 117 D1
Herbrand Rd MK42 51 A4
Hercules Cl LU7 111 C8
Hereford Gr SG18 67 A4
Hereford Rd
Bedford MK42 50 E4
Luton LU4 115 A3
Hermitage Gdns MK45 63 D7
Hermitage The SG15 90 B8
Herne Cl LU5 105 F7
Heron Cl
Biggleswade SG18 66 F4
Sandy SG19 54 B6
Shefford SG17 77 C2
Heron Dr LU2 116 E6
Heron Hts MK41 39 A2
Heron Quay MK40 50 B8
Heron Rd MK45 84 E1
Heronscroft MK41 38 F2
Herons Mead MK43 36 F2
Heron Trad Est LU3 115 C7
Heron Way SG5 90 E6
HERRING'S GREEN 63 D6
Heswall Ct 5 LU1 123 F6
Hever Cl NN10 8 C8
Hewlett Rd LU3 115 E5
HEXTON 98 B2
Hexton JMI Sch SG5 98 A1
Hexton Rd
Barton-le-C, Church End MK45 97 D2
Barton-le-C MK45 97 C2
Lilley LU2 109 C4
Heywood Dr LU2 116 F2
Hibberts Ct SG6 101 E7
Hibbert St LU1 123 E6
Hibbert Street Almshouses 13 LU1 123 E6
Hickling Cl
Bedford MK40 49 E7
Luton LU2 117 D1
Hickling Way AL5 131 C3
Hickman Ct LU3 115 D8
Hicks Rd AL3 128 F6
Higham Dr LU2 117 D1
HIGHAM GOBION 98 A6
Higham Park Rd NN10 9 A5
Higham Rd
Barton-le-C MK45 97 D4
Chelveston NN9 3 B7
High Ave SG6 101 E4
High Banks LU7 112 C5
High Beeches Prim Sch AL5 131 D1
High Beech Rd LU3 115 D7
Highbury Gr MK41 37 E6
Highbury Rd LU3 116 C1
Highbush Rd SG5 90 E5
Highcroft LU7 111 C6
High Dane SG4 101 A2
High Elms MK43 25 A1
HIGHER BERRY END 83 A1
HIGHER RADS END 94 C6
Highfield
Bedford MK41 38 C5
Letchworth SG6 101 E4
Highfield Cres MK43 71 C1
Highfield Oval AL5 131 A4
Highfield Parc MK43 27 B1
Highfield Rd
Flitton MK45 85 E4
Kempston MK42 49 E3
Leighton Buzzard LU7 111 C6
Luton LU4 116 B1
Oakley MK43 27 B1
Highfields MK45 95 E6
Highfield Sch The SG6 101 D4
Highfields Cl LU5 115 A2
Highfields Ct MK45 95 E6
Highlands MK45 84 E3
Highlands Lodge Art Ctr SG17 87 D7
High Mead LU3 116 A3
Highmoor AL5 131 A4
Highover Cl LU2 117 B1
Highover JMI Sch SG4 101 C1
Highover Rd SG6 101 D5
Highover Way SG4 101 B1
High Point 14 LU1 123 D6
High Rd
Beeston SG19 54 B5
Broom SG18 66 D3
Cotton End MK45 63 D5
Shillington SG5 98 E8
High Rd The
Felmersham MK43 26 C8
Harrowden MK42 51 A4
High Ridge
Harpenden AL5 130 E3
Luton LU2 117 C1
High St N LU6 114 A1
High St S LU6 121 C7
High St
Arlesey SG15 90 A5
Bedford MK40 50 C8
Biggleswade SG15 67 A6
High St *continued*
Blunham MK44 41 E3
Broom SG18 66 C3
Carlton MK43 25 A3
Chelveston NN9 3 C8
Clophill MK45 75 D1
Cranfield MK43 59 B2
Dunton SG18 68 D5
Eaton Bray LU6 119 E6
Edlesborough LU6 119 E3
Eggington LU7 112 B7
Elstow MK42 50 B4
Eyeworth SG19 68 F8
Flamstead AL3 129 B2
Flitton MK45 85 D4
Flitwick MK45 84 E3
Gravenhurst MK45 87 C4
Great Barford MK44 41 A4
Greenfield MK45 85 C2
Guilden Morden, Eyeworth SG19 69 A8
Guilden Morden SG8 69 F4
Harpenden AL5 131 A1
Harrold MK43 24 F6
Henlow SG16 78 D2
Hinxworth SG7 80 D6
Houghton Conquest MK45 74 B8
Houghton Regis LU5 114 B4
Irchester NN29 7 B8
Kempston MK42 49 C3
Kimbolton PE28 6 F4
Langford SG18 78 F6
Leighton Buzzard LU7 111 A7
Lidlington MK43 72 C2
Lower Dean PE28 5 C7
Luton LU4 115 C4
Markyate AL3 128 E5
Meppershall SG17 88 B5
North Crawley MK16 58 B6
Oakley MK43 36 F8
Odell MK43 25 C8
Pavenham MK43 26 B3
Pirton SG5 99 D4
Podington NN29 7 E2
Pulloxhill MK45 85 E1
Ridgmont MK43 82 F5
Riseley MK44 11 A2
Roxton MK44 31 E2
Sandy SG19 54 C7
Sharnbrook MK44 16 D4
Shefford SG17 77 C3
Silsoe MK45 86 C4
Souldrop MK44 16 B8
Stagsden MK43 48 A6
St Neots, Eynesbury PE19 22 E5
St Neots PE19 22 B8
Stotfold SG5 90 F6
Sutton SG19 56 A3
Swineshead MK44 11 D8
Thurleigh MK44 18 C2
Tilbrook PE28 6 B6
Tingrith MK17 94 F5
Toddington LU5 105 F6
Turvey MK43 34 E5
Upper Dean PE28 5 B4
Westoning MK45 95 E6
Wilden MK44 29 F3
Woburn Sands MK17 81 B4
Wrestlingworth SG19 57 B3
Wymington NN10 8 B5
Yelden MK44 4 A2
High Street Mews LU7 111 A6
High Top Barns MK44 4 A2
HIGH TOWN 122 E8
High Town Rd LU2 116 F1
High View
Bedford MK41 39 A3
Markyate AL3 128 E5
Highway The MK42 51 A3
High Wood Cl LU1 122 F7
Hillary Cl LU3 115 D7
Hillary Cres LU1 123 C6
Hillary Rise SG15 90 B5
Hillborough Cres LU5 114 C7
Hillborough Inf Sch LU1 123 C6
Hillborough Jun Sch LU1 123 C6
Hillborough Rd LU1 123 D6
Hillbrow SG6 101 D5
Hill Cl
Harpenden AL5 131 C4
Luton LU3 116 C7
Wingfield LU7 105 E1
Hill Cres MK43 71 C1
Hillcrest MK43 59 C2
Hillcrest Ave LU2 116 C8
Hillcrest Sch (Regis Education Ctr) LU5 114 E6
Hillcroft LU6 113 E1
Hill Croft Cl LU4 115 C6
Hilldene Cl MK45 84 E3
Hill End House La MK43 72 B2
Hillesden Ave MK42 50 B4
Hillfield Ave SG4 101 A2
HILLFOOT END 87 E1
Hillfoot Rd SG5 87 E1
Hillgate SG4 101 A3
Hillgrounds Rd MK42 49 D6
Hill La
Biggleswade SG18 66 F7
Ickwell SG18 65 F6
Upper Caldecote SG18 66 C7
Hill Milford AL5 131 D3
Hill Pickford AL5 131 D4

Hill Rise
Bedford MK41 . . . . .38 B2
Kempston MK42 . . . . .49 B2
Luton LU3 . . . . .115 D7
Hills Cl MK44 . . . . .31 E1
Hillside
Chelveston NN9 . . . . .3 B8
Houghton Regis LU5 . . . . .114 B5
Hillside Cl SG5 . . . . .87 E1
Hillside Rd
Dunstable LU5 . . . . .121 D7
Harpenden AL5 . . . . .130 F3
Leighton Buzzard LU7 . . . .103 A2
Luton LU3 . . . . .116 D1
Shillington SG5 . . . . .87 E1
Upper Stondon SG16 . . . . .88 E3
Hills Lower Sch The
MK41 . . . . .38 E3
Hillson Cl MK43 . . . . .72 D8
Hills View LU3 . . . . .107 B4
Hill The MK44 . . . . .41 E3
Hilltop Cl LU1 . . . . .123 C7
Hilltop View SG17 . . . . . . .88 B6
Hill View SG19 . . . . .54 C5
Hillview Cres LU2 . . . . . . .116 C8
Hill View La LU7 . . . . .111 D2
Hillway MK17 . . . . .81 A6
Hillyfields LU6 . . . . .121 C6
Hilton Ave LU6 . . . . .121 B6
Himley Gn LU7 . . . . .110 D6
Hindburn Cl MK41 . . . . .38 D5
Hine Way SG5 . . . . .100 C1
Hinksley Rd MK45 . . . . . . .84 F3
Hinton Cl LU7 . . . . .111 D7
Hinton Wlk LU5 . . . . .114 E6
HINWICK 14 D7
Hinwick Cl SG5 . . . . .90 B7
Hinwick Hall Coll of F Ed
NN29 . . . . .7 C1
Hinwick Rd NN29 . . . . .7 A2
HINXWORTH 80 C5
Hinxworth Rd
Hinxworth SG7 . . . . .80 C3
Hinxworth SG7 . . . . .80 F4
HITCHIN 101 B2
Hitchin Bsns Ctr The
SG4 . . . . .101 A3
Hitchin La SG17 . . . . .78 B2
Hitchin Rd
Arlesey SG15 . . . . .90 A2
Henlow SG16 . . . . .89 C6
Hexton SG5 . . . . .98 E1
Letchworth SG6 . . . . .101 E3
Luton LU2 . . . . .117 A4
Pirton SG5 . . . . .99 E2
Shefford SG17 . . . . .77 C1
Stotfold SG5 . . . . .90 E5
Upper Caldecote SG18 . . . .66 B7
Hitchin Road Ind & Bsns Ctr
SG15 . . . . .90 A3
Hitchin Road Ind Est
LU2 . . . . .116 F1
Hitchin St SG18 . . . . .66 F5
Hitchmead Rd SG18 . . . . . .67 B6
Hitchmead Spec Sch
SG18 . . . . .67 C6
Hitherfield La AL3 . . . . . .131 A2
Hives The PE19 . . . . .22 D4
Hockley Ct
Hockliffe LU7 . . . . .104 E2
Marston Moretaine MK43 . .72 D8
HOCKLIFFE 104 F2
Hockliffe Bsns Pk LU7 . . .104 F1
Hockliffe Ho LU7 . . . . . . .111 B7
Hockliffe Lower Sch
LU7 . . . . .104 E3
Hockliffe Rd
Bedford MK40 . . . . .50 D6
Hockliffe LU7, MK17 . . . . .104 F6
Leighton Buzzard LU7 . . . .111 C7
Tebworth LU7 . . . . .105 B1
Hockliffe St LU7 . . . . .111 A7
Hockwell Ring LU4 . . . . . .115 C4
Hodder Rd MK41 . . . . .38 C7
Hogarth Cl MK41 . . . . .38 B2
Hogarth Pl PE19 . . . . .22 D5
Hog Hall La HP4 . . . . . . .126 A5
Holcroft Rd AL5 . . . . .131 D3
Holden Cl MK40 . . . . .37 C1
Holford Way LU3 . . . . . . .108 A8
Holgate Dr LU4 . . . . .115 B3
Holkham Cl LU4 . . . . .115 A4
Holland Ct LU3 . . . . .116 C2
Holland Rd
Ampthill MK45 . . . . .84 E7
Luton LU3 . . . . .116 B2
Hollick's La LU6 . . . . .121 D2
Hollies Ct LU7 . . . . .110 E7
Hollies The
Kempston MK42 . . . . .49 F3
Shefford SG17 . . . . .77 C3
Hollies Wlk MK43 . . . . .60 F8
HOLLINGTON 85 E6
Hollis La MK44 . . . . .29 F2
Holliwick Rd LU5 . . . . . . .114 E2
Hollowell Ct NN10 . . . . .8 D3
Hollybush Hill SG5 . . . . . .109 F1
Hollybush La
Harpenden AL3 . . . . .129 B3
Harpenden AL5 . . . . .131 A3
Hollybush Rd
Flitwick MK45 . . . . .84 F2
Luton LU2 . . . . .117 C1
Holly Cl SG18 . . . . .67 A8
Holly Farm Cl LU1 . . . . . .122 E3

Holly La AL5 . . . . .131 E6
Holly St LU1 . . . . .123 E6
Holly Street Trad Est [12]
LU1 . . . . .123 E6
Holly Wlk
Harpenden AL5 . . . . .131 D1
Silsoe MK45 . . . . .86 B4
Woburn Sands MK17 . . . . .81 B2
Holmbrook Ave LU3 . . . . .116 C5
HOLME 65 C3
Holme Cl MK43 . . . . .72 D8
Holme Court Ave SG18 . . . .67 B3
Holme Cres SG18 . . . . .67 A5
HOLME GREEN 66 B2
Holmemead Mid Sch
SG18 . . . . .67 B4
Holme St MK42 . . . . .50 B7
Holmewood Rd MK45 . . . . .85 D2
Holmfield Cl
Luton LU1 . . . . .123 D5
Toddington LU5 . . . . .105 E5
Holm Oak Gn MK44 . . . . . .51 D4
Holmscroft Rd LU3 . . . . . .115 F6
Holmwood Cl LU5 . . . . . . .114 D2
Holt Row MK42 . . . . .50 B7
Holts Cl LU6 . . . . .114 B1
Holtsmere Cl LU2 . . . . . . .117 D1
HOLWELL 100 B7
Holwell Rd
Holwell SG5 . . . . .100 C7
Pirton SG5 . . . . .99 E6
HOLYWELL 127 B6
Holywell CE Mid Sch
MK43 . . . . .59 B1
Holywell Cl LU6 . . . . .127 C6
Holywell Ct LU3 . . . . .116 B4
Holywell Rd LU6 . . . . .127 B6
Homebrook Ho MK42 . . . . .50 C7
Home Cl
Houghton Conquest MK43 . .74 A8
Luton LU4 . . . . .115 C4
Renhold MK41 . . . . .39 B6
Sharnbrook MK44 . . . . . . .16 D3
Stotfold SG5 . . . . .90 F7
Wilstead MK45 . . . . .62 E3
Homedale Dr LU4 . . . . . . .115 D2
Homedell Ho AL5 . . . . . . .130 E3
Home Farm Cl SG19 . . . . . .42 B8
Home Farm Ct LU7 . . . . . .117 D5
Home Farm Way MK45 . . . .95 E5
Homefield SG7 . . . . .30 B6
Homefield Rd MK44 . . . . . .31 E5
Home Rd MK43 . . . . .48 F3
Homerton Rd LU3 . . . . . . .116 A6
Homestead Way LU1 . . . . .123 C5
HONEYDON 21 B2
Honeydon Ave PE19 . . . . . .22 C5
Honeydon Rd MK44 . . . . . .20 C2
Honeygate LU2 . . . . .116 E4
Honey Hill SG19 . . . . .44 A8
Honey Hill Gdns MK40 . . . .49 E7
Honey Hill Rd MK40 . . . . . .49 E7
Honeysuckle Ave MK45 . . . .62 F2
Honeysuckle Cl SG18 . . . . .67 C4
Honeysuckle Way MK41 . . . .39 B1
HONEYWICK 119 E8
Honeywick La LU6 . . . . . . .119 E8
Honiton Mews LU3 . . . . . .115 A6
Honiton Way MK40 . . . . . . .38 E2
Hoo Cl MK43 . . . . .60 F8
Hooked La MK45 . . . . .63 A5
Hookhams La MK41 . . . . . .39 B6
Hoo La MK43 . . . . .60 E3
Hooper Cl MK42 . . . . .49 C2
Hoo Rd SG17 . . . . .88 D6
Hoo St LU1 . . . . .123 E5
Hoo The MK42 . . . . .49 F4
Hoover Pl SG17 . . . . .76 E2
Hope Rd MK42 . . . . .50 B4
Horace Brightman Cl
LU3 . . . . .116 A7
Horace Gay Gdns SG6 . . . .101 E6
Hornbeam Cl
Leighton Buzzard LU7 . . . .111 C8
Podington NN29 . . . . .7 E2
Hornbeams The MK42 . . . . .49 F4
Horne La
Bedford MK40 . . . . .50 B8
Potton SG19 . . . . .56 A7
Hornes End Rd MK45 . . . . .84 E1
Hornsby Cl LU2 . . . . .117 C1
Horsefair La MK43 . . . . . . .25 C8
Horsepool La MK43 . . . . . . .82 A3
Horseshoe Cl
Dunton SG18 . . . . .68 D5
Marston Moretaine MK43 . .60 E1
Horseshoe Ct MK42 . . . . . .49 D3
Horseshoe The MK42 . . . . .50 B7
Horsham Cl LU2 . . . . .117 D2
Horsler Cl MK45 . . . . .97 C2
Horslow St SG19 . . . . .56 A7
HORTON 118 B3
Horton Rd
Horton LU7 . . . . .118 A2
Slapton LU7 . . . . .118 C6
Hospital Rd SG15 . . . . .90 A4
Hotch Croft MK43 . . . . . . .59 C3
Houghton Cl MK45 . . . . . . .84 E7
HOUGHTON CONQUEST . .74 B7
Houghton Conquest Lower
Sch MK45 . . . . .74 B7
Houghton House (rems of)*
MK45 . . . . .73 F7
Houghton Mews [11] LU3 . .123 D6
Houghton Par LU6 . . . . . . .114 A2
HOUGHTON PARK 114 E6
Houghton Park Rd LU5 . . .114 E6

Houghton Rd
Bedford MK42 . . . . .50 B6
Houghton Regis LU5 . . . . .114 A3
HOUGHTON REGIS 114 B6
Houghton Regis Lower Sch
LU5 . . . . .114 A4
House La SG15 . . . . .90 A7
Howard Ave MK40 . . . . . . .49 F8
Howard Cl
Cardington MK44 . . . . .51 E4
Haynes MK45 . . . . .63 F1
Luton LU3 . . . . .116 A4
Stotfold SG5 . . . . .90 E5
Wilstead MK45 . . . . .62 E3
Howard Crt MK45 . . . . .84 E1
Howard Cur [7] MK40 . . . . .50 B8
Howard Pl
Bedford MK40 . . . . .49 F8
Dunstable LU5 . . . . .121 D7
Howard Rd PE19 . . . . .22 C1
Howard Road Ind Est
PE19 . . . . .22 C2
Howard's Cl SG18 . . . . .65 F1
Howards Mews MK45 . . . . .86 C8
Howard St
Bedford MK40 . . . . .50 C8
Kempston MK42 . . . . .49 F4
Howberry Gn SG15 . . . . . . .90 A3
Howbury St MK40 . . . . .50 D8
Howden Gdns MK40 . . . . . .37 C1
HOWELLBURY 89 B1
HOW END 73 E6
How End Rd MK45 . . . . . . .73 E6
Howes Dr MK43 . . . . .72 C7
Howes La MK45 . . . . .95 E6
How Field AL5 . . . . .130 E3
Howitt's Gdns PE19 . . . . . .22 F2
Howitt's La PE19 . . . . .22 F2
Howkin Cl MK43 . . . . .36 E2
Howland Pl MK17 . . . . .92 F7
Hoylake Ct LU1 . . . . .123 F5
Hubbard Cl MK45 . . . . .84 E1
Huckleberry Cl LU3 . . . . .116 A8
Hucklesby Way LU2 . . . . .123 D8
Huddleston Way MK41 . . . .51 A8
HUDNALL CORNER 132 B7
Hudnall Rd HP4 . . . . .132 A7
Hudson Cl MK43 . . . . .72 B3
Hudson Rd MK41 . . . . .39 C3
HULCOTE 70 E2
Hulme Cl
Clapham MK41 . . . . .37 C7
Kempston MK42 . . . . .49 C2
Humber Ave MK41 . . . . . . .38 D5
Humberley Cl PE19 . . . . . .22 F3
Humberstone Cl LU4 . . . . .115 E2
Humberstone Rd LU4 . . . .115 E2
Humphrey Talbot Ave
LU6 . . . . .126 F7
Humphrys Rd LU3 . . . . . . .116 D4
Hunston Cl LU4 . . . . .116 A8
Hunter Cl MK42 . . . . .51 A2
Hunters Cl SG5 . . . . .90 E6
Hunter's Cl MK41 . . . . .37 C6
Hunters Way PE28 . . . . .4 F5
Hunters Wlk MK44 . . . . . . .11 B3
Huntingdon Rd
Kempston MK42 . . . . .49 D3
St Neots PE19 . . . . .22 F7
Huntingdonshire Regional
Coll (St Neots Ctr) PE19 . .22 F6
Huntingdon St PE19 . . . . . .22 F6
Hunting Gate SG4 . . . . . . .101 A3
Hunting Hall LU2 . . . . . . .124 C8
Hunts Cl LU1 . . . . .123 C6
Hunts Field MK40 . . . . .49 F5
Hunts La MK43 . . . . .26 B8
Huntsmans Cl HP4 . . . . . .126 C5
Huntsmans Way MK44 . . . .27 B5
Hunts Path MK43 . . . . .37 A8
Hurlock Cl LU4 . . . . .121 A6
Hurlock Way LU4 . . . . . . .115 C5
Hurst Gr
Bedford MK40 . . . . .49 F8
Bedford MK43 . . . . .72 B3
Hurst Way LU3 . . . . .115 F5
HUSBORNE CRAWLEY . . .82 B4
Husborne Crawley Lower Sch
MK43 . . . . .82 B4
Hutton Way MK17 . . . . . . .81 B5
Hyacinth Way NN10 . . . . . . .8 B7
Hyde Ave SG5 . . . . .90 E5
Hyde Cl AL5 . . . . .131 B4
Hyde Ho [5] LU2 . . . . .123 F8
Hyde La LU2 . . . . .123 C2
Hyde Rd MK41 . . . . .122 F4
Hyde The LU1 . . . . .114 C6
Hyde View Rd AL5 . . . . . .131 B4
Hylus Dr LU7 . . . . .111 D8

I

Ibbet La SG19 . . . . .55 F7
Ibbett Cl MK43 . . . . .49 A2
Ibbetts Yd [4] PE19 . . . . . .22 E5
ICKLEFORD 100 E4
Ickleford Bury SG5 . . . . . .100 D4
Ickleford Gate SG5 . . . . . .100 D3
Ickleford Prim Sch SG5 . . .100 E4
Ickleford Rd SG5 . . . . . . .100 F1
Ickley Cl LU4 . . . . .115 B5
Icknield Cl SG5 . . . . .100 E4
Icknield Gn SG6 . . . . .101 E6
Icknield High Sch LU3 . . .116 C5
Icknield Ho LU7 . . . . .111 A4
Icknield Inf Sch SG6 . . . . .101 D6
Icknield Prim Sch LU3 . . .116 B5

Icknield Rd LU3 . . . . .115 F4
Icknield St LU6 . . . . .121 B8
Icknield Villas [10] LU6 . . .121 B8
Icknield Way
Baldock SG7 . . . . .91 E1
Dunstable LU5 . . . . .120 B1
Dunstable, Well Head LU5 .120 D5
Letchworth SG6 . . . . .101 E6
Luton LU3 . . . . .116 B7
Icknield Way E SG7 . . . . . .91 F1
Icknield Way Farm Cotts
LU6 . . . . .120 D3
ICKWELL 65 E7
ICKWELL GREEN 65 E8
Ickwell Rd
Northill SG18 . . . . .53 D1
Upper Caldecote SG18 . . . .66 A8
Iddesleigh Rd MK40 . . . . . .49 F7
Idenbury Ct LU1 . . . . .123 C7
Ilford Cl LU2 . . . . .117 D3
Imberfield LU4 . . . . .115 C3
Index Cl LU6 . . . . .121 D7
Index Dr LU6 . . . . .121 D7
Ingles Cl PE19 . . . . .22 F6
Ingram Cl MK43 . . . . .72 C8
Ingram Gdns LU2 . . . . . . .116 D7
Inkerman Rise PE19 . . . . . .22 C5
Inkerman St LU1 . . . . .123 D7
Inns La MK45 . . . . .86 B3
Instow Cl MK40 . . . . .38 E2
Interchange Ret Pk MK42 . .49 F2
IRCHESTER 7 B6
Irchester Prim Sch NN29 . . .7 A8
Irchester Rd NN29 . . . . .7 B4
IRELAND 77 A7
Ireton Cl PE19 . . . . .22 F3
Irthing Cl MK41 . . . . .38 D6
Irvine Cl MK41 . . . . .38 D5
Irwin Rd MK40 . . . . .38 E1
Isis Rd MK41 . . . . .38 C5
Isis Wlk LU7 . . . . .103 B3
Isle of Wight La LU6 . . . . .121 A3
Ison Cl MK40 . . . . .49 D8
Itchen Cl MK41 . . . . .38 C5
Ivel Bury SG18 . . . . .66 F7
Ivel Ct
Barton-le-C MK45 . . . . . . .97 D3
Bedford MK41 . . . . .38 D6
Langford SG18 . . . . .78 E5
Ivel Dr SG17 . . . . .77 D2
Ivel Cl SG5 . . . . .100 F1
Ivel Cotts SG18 . . . . .66 F1
Iveldale Dr SG17 . . . . .77 D3
Ivel Gdns SG18 . . . . .66 F6
Ivel Rd
Sandy SG19 . . . . .54 C6
Shefford SG17 . . . . .77 D2
Ivel View SG19 . . . . .54 D6
Ivel Way
Flitwick MK45 . . . . .85 A3
Stotfold SG5 . . . . .90 F8
Ivester Ct LU7 . . . . .110 E6
IVINGHOE ASTON 119 E1
Ivinghoe Bsns Ctr LU5 . . . .114 B3
Ivinghoe Way LU6 . . . . . . .119 E1
Ivy Cl
Dunstable LU6 . . . . .113 C1
Tempsford SG19 . . . . .42 B8
Ivy Ct LU1 . . . . .123 B8
Ivy La
Heath and Reach MK17 . . .102 C8
Wilstead MK45 . . . . .63 A4

J

Jacey Ct MK42 . . . . .49 D6
Jackman Cl MK43 . . . . .36 F1
Jack's La MK43 . . . . .34 F5
Jackson Pl SG17 . . . . .76 E2
Jacksons Cl LU1 . . . . .119 E4
Jackson St SG7 . . . . .91 E1
Jacobs Cl SG19 . . . . .56 A8
Jacques La MK45 . . . . .75 E1
James Ct
Luton LU4 . . . . .115 B2
[14] Luton, New Town LU1 . .123 E6
St Neots PE19 . . . . .22 F2
James Foster Ho SG18 . . . .67 A5
James Marshall Commercial
Ctr AL5 . . . . .131 A1
Jameson Rd AL5 . . . . .131 B3
James St
[9] Bedford MK40 . . . . . . .50 B8
Irchester NN29 . . . . .7 B7
Jansel Ho LU2 . . . . .117 A4
Jardine Way LU5 . . . . .121 E7
Jasmine Cl
Bedford MK41 . . . . .39 C4
Biggleswade SG18 . . . . . . .67 C4
Jasmine Ct SG5 . . . . .90 F7
Jasmine Gdns NN10 . . . . . . .8 B7
Jay Cl SG6 . . . . .101 E8
Jays The SG19 . . . . .42 C2
Jaywood LU2 . . . . .117 C6
Jeans Way LU1 . . . . .114 F1
Jelicoe Pl PE19 . . . . .22 A2
Jenkins Cl PE19 . . . . .22 D5
Jenkyn Rd MK43 . . . . .60 E6
Jennings Ave PE19 . . . . . . .22 A3
Jennings Cl SG19 . . . . .55 F8
Jeremiah Cl MK45 . . . . . . .97 C3
Jerrard Cl LU3 . . . . .111 C6
Jersey Rd LU4 . . . . .115 A3
J F Kennedy Dr SG17 . . . . .76 E2

Jilliter Rd LU4 . . . . .115 A2
JOCKEY END 132 F8
Joes Cl MK45 . . . . .85 C2
John Barker Pl SG5 . . . . . .100 C1
John Bunyan Dr MK45 . . . . .85 B8
John Bunyan Upper Sch &
Com Coll MK42 . . . . .50 E4
John Donne CE Lower Sch
MK44 . . . . .41 E3
John Howland Cl SG16 . . . .78 D1
Johnson Cl
Biddenham MK40 . . . . .37 C1
Marston Moretaine MK43 . .72 C8
Johnson Dr LU7 . . . . .111 C4
John St LU1 . . . . .123 E7
Joint The SG17 . . . . .78 B2
Jordan Cl SG16 . . . . .78 D2
Jowitt Ave MK42 . . . . .49 F4
Jubilee Cl
Clifton SG17 . . . . .78 B2
Lower Stondon SG16 . . . . .89 B3
St Neots PE19 . . . . .22 E4
Stanbridge LU6 . . . . .43 D6
Stubble Cres SG15 . . . . . . .90 A2
Jubilee Ct
[3] Dunstable LU6 . . . . . . .114 A1
Harpenden AL5 . . . . .131 C3
Jubilee Gdns
Biggleswade SG18 . . . . . . .67 B3
Rushden NN10 . . . . .8 C8
Jubilee La SG18 . . . . .72 E1
Jubilee St LU2 . . . . .77 C4
Jubilee St LU1 . . . . .116 F1
Judges La LU7 . . . . .110 F6
Judith Gdns
Kempston MK42 . . . . .49 D3
Potton SG19 . . . . .56 B8
Julia Ct LU3 . . . . .116 A4
Julius Gdns LU3 . . . . .115 F7
Juniper Cl
Luton LU4 . . . . .115 C2
Silsoe MK45 . . . . .86 C4
Juniper Wlk MK42 . . . . . . .49 F2
Jupiter Dr LU7 . . . . .111 D8
Jutland Rise PE19 . . . . . . .22 C5

K

Karen Ho SG16 . . . . .89 A4
Katherine Dr LU5 . . . . . . .114 F2
Katherine's Ct MK45 . . . . .84 E8
Katherine's Gdn MK45 . . . .84 E8
Kathie Rd MK42 . . . . .50 D5
Kayser Ct SG18 . . . . .66 F4
Keaton Cl LU5 . . . . .114 D6
Keats Cl MK40 . . . . .37 F2
Keats Ct PE19 . . . . .22 C6
Keats Ho [15] MK45 . . . . . .131 E1
Keats Rd MK45 . . . . .84 D3
Keeble Cl LU4 . . . . .117 E1
Keeley Farm Ct MK43 . . . . .48 F1
KEELEY GREEN 48 E1
Keeley La MK43 . . . . .48 E1
Keepers Cl LU2 . . . . .117 C2
Kelling Cl LU2 . . . . .116 F4
Kelvin Ave MK42 . . . . .50 C5
Kelvin Cl LU1 . . . . .123 E6
Kempsey Cl LU2 . . . . .117 D2
Kempster Cl MK40 . . . . . . .50 A8
KEMPSTON 49 C4
KEMPSTON CHURCH
END 49 B4
Kempston Ct MK45 . . . . . . .61 E5
KEMPSTON HARDWICK . .61 D5
Kempston Hardwick Gypsy
Site MK45 . . . . .61 F5
Kempston Hardwick Sta
MK43 . . . . .61 D6
Kempston Rd MK42 . . . . . . .50 A6
Kempston Rural Lower Sch
MK43 . . . . .48 C4
KEMPSTON WEST END . . .48 C4
Kendal Cl LU3 . . . . .115 D7
Kendal Dr MK45 . . . . .84 E2
Kendale Rd LU4 . . . . .115 B2
Kendal Gdns LU7 . . . . . . .110 C7
Kendall Dr SG17 . . . . .76 F3
Kendall Rd MK42 . . . . .49 D3
Kenilworth Cl PE19 . . . . . . .22 C3
Kenilworth Rd LU1 . . . . . .123 C8
Kenilworth Wlk MK41 . . . . .39 A4
Kennedy Ct LU7 . . . . .110 F7
Kennedy Rd MK42 . . . . . . .50 C5
Kennel La AL5 . . . . .130 A5
Kennell Hill MK44 . . . . . . .16 D3
Kennesbourne Ct AL5 . . . .130 D4
Kenneth Rd LU2 . . . . .117 A1
Kenneth Way MK45 . . . . . . .62 B6
Kennington Rd LU3 . . . . . .116 B3
Kensington Ct LU5 . . . . . . .114 E4
KENSWORTH 127 E8
KENSWORTH COMMON . .121 D1
Kensworth Ct LU4 . . . . . . .115 B3
Kensworth Gate LU6 . . . . .121 C7
Kensworth Lower Sch
LU6 . . . . .127 F8
KENSWORTH LYNCH 121 A1
Kensworth Rd MK40 . . . . . .127 D4
Kent Ave MK42 . . . . .50 C5
Kent Cl MK45 . . . . .95 E5
Kentmere Cl MK42 . . . . . . .49 D3
Kent Rd
Houghton Regis LU5 . . . . .114 D7
Luton LU1 . . . . .122 F8
Kentwick Sq LU5 . . . . .114 D7

Kenworth Ct MK41 . . . . 38 B2
Kenwyn Cl MK41 . . . . 39 C5
Kernow Ct LU2 . . . . 117 A1
Kerrison Cl MK43 . . . . 72 C3
Kershaw Cl LU3 . . . . 116 A8
Kershope Cl MK41 . . . . 39 C3
Kestrel Rd
  Bedford MK40 . . . . 38 C4
  Flitwick MK45 . . . . 84 D1
Kestrel Way
  Luton LU4 . . . . 115 A5
  Sandy SG19 . . . . 42 B2
Keswick Cl LU2 . . . . 121 B7
Ketton Cl LU2 . . . . 124 A7
Ketton Ct LU2 . . . . 124 A7
Keymer Cl LU7 . . . . 117 C3
KEYSOE 12 B2
Keysoe Rd
  Riseley MK44 . . . . 11 B1
  Thurleigh MK44 . . . . 18 D3
KEYSOE ROW 19 C7
Keysoe Row E MK44 . . . . 19 D8
Keysoe Row W MK44 . . . . 19 B7
Keyston Rd PE28 . . . . 2 D2
Kidner Cl LU2 . . . . 116 E5
Kielder Path 2 MK41 . . . . . . 39 B4
Kilby Rd LU7 . . . . 104 F2
Kilmarnock Dr LU2 . . . . 116 E5
Kiln La MK45 . . . . 75 D2
Kiln Rd MK45 . . . . 61 E4
Kiln Way LU5 . . . . 115 A1
Kilpin Cl MK42 . . . . 50 D6
Kilpin Gn MK16 . . . . 58 B6
Kimberley SG6 . . . . 90 F2
Kimberley Cl LU4 . . . . 114 E3
Kimberwell Ct LU5 . . . . 105 F4
Kimble Dr MK41 . . . . 38 A8
KIMBOLTON 6 F6
Kimbolton Ave MK40 . . . . 38 D2
Kimbolton Cl MK41 . . . . 38 E3
Kimbolton Ct MK40 . . . . 38 D2
Kimbolton Prep Sch PE28 . . 6 E5
Kimbolton Rd
  Bedford MK40, MK41 . . . . . . 38 D4
  Chelveston NN9 . . . . 3 D8
  Pertenhall MK44 . . . . 12 D7
  St Neots PE19 . . . . 22 A8
  Wilden MK44 . . . . 19 D4
Kimbolton Sch PE28 . . . . 6 F4
Kimpton Bottom AL5,
  SG4 . . . . 131 E2
Kimpton Rd
  Luton LU1, LU2 . . . . 124 A6
  Peters Green LU2, SG4 . . . . . 125 E2
King Cup Cl NN10 . . . . 8 C7
King Edward Rd MK41 . . . . . . 39 A1
Kingfisher Bsns Pk MK42 . . 50 C6
Kingfisher Cl
  Bedford MK41 . . . . 38 D3
  Biggleswade SG18 . . . . 66 F5
  Sandy SG19 . . . . 42 C2
Kingfisher Rd
  Flitwick MK45 . . . . 84 D1
  Shefford SG17 . . . . 77 C2
King George Cl SG18 . . . . . . 78 F7
King Georges Cl SG5 . . . . . . 100 D1
Kinghamway LU2 . . . . 116 E1
King Henry Ct LU3 . . . . 116 B2
Kingsbrook Rd MK42 . . . . 50 C7
Kingsbury Ave LU5 . . . . 114 E1
Kingsbury Ct LU5 . . . . 121 C8
Kingsbury Gdns LU4 . . . . . . 114 F1
Kings Cl MK44 . . . . 10 F2
Kingscroft Ave LU5 . . . . 114 C1
Kings Ct
  Dunstable LU5 . . . . 114 C1
  Flitwick MK45 . . . . 84 F2
Kingsdown Ave LU2 . . . . 116 D5
Kings Hedges SG5 . . . . 100 C1
Kings Houghton Mid Sch
  LU5 . . . . 114 D7
Kingsland Cl LU4 . . . . 114 E4
Kingsland Rd 7 LU1 . . . . . . 123 F6
Kingsland Rd LU1 . . . . 123 F6
Kingsley Ave SG5 . . . . 90 C3
Kingsley Ct SG19 . . . . 54 B8
Kingsley Rd
  Bedford MK40 . . . . 50 E8
  Luton LU3 . . . . 116 A5
Kings Mead LU6 . . . . 119 E3
Kingsmead Pk Mobile Home
  Pk NN10 . . . . 8 C7
Kingsmede SG17 . . . . 77 C3
Kingsmoor Cl MK45 . . . . 84 F3
Kingsmoor Lower Sch
  MK45 . . . . 84 F3
King's Pl MK42 . . . . 50 B6
Kings Pond Cl SG18 . . . . 68 D5
Kings Rd
  Maulden MK45 . . . . 74 C1
  St Neots PE19 . . . . 22 B3
King's Rd
  Broom SG18 . . . . 66 C3
  Flitwick MK45 . . . . 84 F2
  Sandy SG19 . . . . 54 C7
  St Neots PE19 . . . . 22 F6
King St
  Clapham MK41 . . . . 37 D6
  Dunstable LU5 . . . . 121 C8
  Houghton Regis LU5 . . . . . . 114 B4
  Kempston MK42 . . . . 49 E4
  Leighton Buzzard LU7 . . . . . 111 A8
  Luton LU1 . . . . 123 E7
  Markyate AL3 . . . . 128 E5
  Potton SG19 . . . . 56 A7
Kingston Cl MK41 . . . . 49 E6
Kingston Ct MK42 . . . . 50 A6
Kingston Rd LU2 . . . . 116 F1

Kingsway
  Bedford MK42 . . . . 50 C7
  Dunstable LU5 . . . . 114 C1
  Luton LU4 . . . . 116 A1
  Stotfold SG5 . . . . 90 F7
Kings Way LU7 . . . . 112 D5
Kingsway Gdns SG5 . . . . 90 F7
Kingsway Ind Est LU1 . . . . 123 A8
Kingswood Ave SG4 . . . . . . 101 D1
Kingswood Cl MK45 . . . . 74 B7
King's Wood National Nature
  Reserve* LU7 . . . . 103 A8
Kingswood Way MK40 . . . . . . 49 B6
King William Cl
  Barton-le-C MK45 . . . . 97 D4
  Kempston MK42 . . . . 49 D4
King William Rd MK42 . . . . . . 49 C4
Kinloch Ct 6 AL5 . . . . 131 A8
Kinmoor Cl LU3 . . . . 107 D1
Kinross Cres LU3 . . . . 115 D8
Kinsbourne Cl AL5 . . . . 130 C4
Kinsbourne Cres AL5 . . . . . . 130 C4
Kinsbourne Ct AL5 . . . . 130 F3
KINSBOURNE GREEN MK27 . . 125 C5
Kinsbourne Green La
  AL5 . . . . 130 B3
Kipling Pl PE19 . . . . 22 D5
Kipling Rd LU3 . . . . 116 B6
Kipling Way AL5 . . . . 131 B1
Kirby Dr LU3 . . . . 116 A8
Kirby Rd LU6 . . . . 121 A8
Kirkdale Ct 8 LU1 . . . . 123 E6
Kirkdale Rd LU1 . . . . 131 A2
Kirkman Cl MK42 . . . . 50 C6
Kirkstall Ct MK42 . . . . 50 C3
Kirkstone Dr LU6 . . . . 121 B6
Kirkwick Ave AL5 . . . . 131 A1
Kirkwood Ct LU4 . . . . 114 F3
Kirton Way LU5 . . . . 114 E6
Kitchener Pl MK43 . . . . 61 D1
Kitelands Rd SG18 . . . . 67 C4
Kiteleys Gn LU7 . . . . 111 C8
Kite Way SG6 . . . . 101 E8
Kittiwake Cl SG18 . . . . 66 F4
Klondyke AL5 . . . . 130 D4
Knaresborough Ct PE19 . . . . 22 F1
Knarsdale Wlk 5 MK41 . . . . 39 B4
Knaves Hill LU7 . . . . 110 D8
Kneller Cl MK41 . . . . 38 A2
Knights Ave MK41 . . . . 37 D7
Knights Cl
  Eaton Bray LU6 . . . . 119 F5
  St Neots PE19 . . . . 22 B4
Knights Ct LU6 . . . . 119 E5
Knights Field LU2 . . . . 116 D1
Knoll Rise LU2 . . . . 116 E4
Knolls The SG19 . . . . 54 B5
Knolls View
  Northall LU6 . . . . 119 B5
  Totternhoe LU6 . . . . 112 F1
Knolls Way SG17 . . . . 77 F2
Knoll The
  Maulden MK45 . . . . 85 D8
  Woburn Sands MK17 . . . . . . 81 A1
KNOTTING 9 E3
KNOTTING GREEN 9 F1
Knotting La MK44 . . . . 10 C1
Knotting Rd MK44 . . . . 10 C7
Knotts Cl LU6 . . . . 121 C5
Knowl Piece SG4 . . . . 101 A3
Kymbrook Lower Sch
  MK44 . . . . 19 C7
Kym Rd PE19 . . . . 22 C4
Kynance Cl LU2 . . . . 117 A2

L

Laburnam Rd SG18 . . . . 67 B7
Laburnham Ave MK45 . . . . . . 62 E2
Laburnum Cl MK40 . . . . 49 F7
Laburnum Cl LU3 . . . . 116 C7
Laburnum Gr LU3 . . . . 116 B7
Laburnum Lower Sch
  SG19 . . . . 54 B7
Laburnum Rd SG19 . . . . 54 B7
Lachbury Cl LU3 . . . . 123 A6
Ladybridge Terr MK43 . . . . . 34 E5
Ladyhill LU4 . . . . 115 B6
Lady Way PE19 . . . . 22 B4
Lady Zia Wernher Special
  Sch LU2 . . . . 117 B3
Lakefield Ave LU5 . . . . 105 F5
Lakes Cl SG18 . . . . 78 E5
Lake St LU7 . . . . 110 E7
Lakeview MK43 . . . . 60 E1
Lalleford Rd LU2 . . . . 117 D1
Lamb Mdw SG15 . . . . 90 A3
Lambourn Cl LU2 . . . . 116 E6
Lambourn Gdns AL5 . . . . . . 130 F3
Lambourn Way MK41 . . . . . . 38 D6
Lambs Cl LU5 . . . . 114 F1
Lamers Rd LU2 . . . . 117 B2
Lammas Mead SG5 . . . . 100 E2
Lammas Way
  Ampthill MK45 . . . . 84 E6
  Letchworth SG6 . . . . 101 F8
  St Neots PE19 . . . . 22 E6
Lammas Wlk LU7 . . . . 111 A7
Lammerside MK41 . . . . 39 C5
Lamorna Cl LU3 . . . . 115 F6
Lamsey Ct 1 MK41 . . . . . . 111 A8
Lancaster Ave
  Bedford MK40 . . . . 50 C5
  Luton LU2 . . . . 116 C8
Lancaster Cl MK45 . . . . 97 D4
Lancaster Pl SG17 . . . . 77 C1

Lancaster Rd MK42 . . . . 51 A2
Lanchester Cl MK41 . . . . 37 E6
Lanchester Rd MK43 . . . . . . 58 D2
Lancing Rd LU2 . . . . 117 D3
Lancot Ave LU6 . . . . 120 F8
Lancotbury Cl LU6 . . . . 120 C7
Lancot Dr LU6 . . . . 120 F8
Lancot Lower Sch LU6 . . . . 120 E8
Lancot Pl LU6 . . . . 120 E8
Landrace Rd LU4 . . . . 114 C1
Landseer Wlk MK41 . . . . 38 A2
Lane's Cl LU7 . . . . 103 A4
Lane The
  Chalton LU4 . . . . 106 E1
  Tebworth LU7 . . . . 105 B3
  Wyboston MK44 . . . . 31 F6
Langdale MK41 . . . . 38 E3
Langdale Ave AL5 . . . . 131 D2
Langdale Cl LU6 . . . . 121 C7
Langdale Rd LU6 . . . . 121 B6
LANGFORD 78 E6
Langford Dr LU2 . . . . 117 A3
LANGFORD END 32 E1
Langford Lower Sch SG18 78 F7
Langford Mill SG18 . . . . 78 F7
Langford Rd
  Biggleswade SG18 . . . . 66 F2
  Henlow SG16 . . . . 78 D4
Langham Cl LU2 . . . . 116 D7
Langham Ho 8 LU1 . . . . . . 123 D8
Langlands Rd MK41 . . . . 39 A4
Langleigh SG6 . . . . 90 F1
Langley Gdns SG19 . . . . 55 E7
Langley St LU1 . . . . 123 E6
Langley Terrace Ind Pk 10
  LU1 . . . . 123 F1
Langridge Ct LU6 . . . . 113 F1
Langwood Cl PE19 . . . . 22 C6
Lansbury Cl PE19 . . . . 22 E4
Lansdowne Rd
  Bedford MK40 . . . . 38 A1
  Luton LU3 . . . . 116 D1
Lansdowne Terr 7 MK40 . . 38 A1
Lanthony Ct SG5 . . . . 90 A4
Lapwater Way LU4 . . . . 115 F1
Lapwing Rd LU4 . . . . 115 A4
Larch Cl NN29 . . . . 7 A7
Larches The
  Kempston MK42 . . . . 49 F3
  Luton LU2 . . . . 116 D7
Larkins Cl SG7 . . . . 91 F1
Lark Rise Lower Sch
  LU6 . . . . 121 B6
Larkspur Gdns LU4 . . . . 115 F2
Larks Rise SG19 . . . . 42 C2
Larkway
  Bedford MK41 . . . . 38 D4
  Flitwick MK45 . . . . 84 D2
Latimer Rd LU1 . . . . 123 E6
Launton Cl LU3 . . . . 108 B1
Laurel Cl PE19 . . . . 22 F4
Laurel Mews SG7 . . . . 91 F1
Laurelside Wlk LU5 . . . . . . 115 A2
Laurel View 2 SG8 . . . . 67 A6
Laurel Way MK42 . . . . 100 E3
Laurel Wlk MK42 . . . . 50 A3
Lavender Cl LU2 . . . . 116 E7
Lavender Ct
  Ampthill MK45 . . . . 84 E7
  Baldock SG7 . . . . 91 E1
Lavender Way
  Biggleswade SG18 . . . . 67 C5
  Rushden NN10 . . . . 8 C8
LAVENDON 34 A8
Lavenham Dr MK40 . . . . 37 C1
Lawford Cl MK41 . . . . 123 C7
Lawn Gdns LU1 . . . . 123 D6
Lawnside Rd LU3 . . . . 67 B6
Lawns Lower Sch
  SG18 . . . . 67 B6
Lawns The SG19 . . . . 43 C3
Lawrence End Rd LU2 . . . . . 125 D4
Lawrence Rd
  Biggleswade SG18 . . . . 67 A6
  St Neots PE19 . . . . 22 C5
Lawrence St MK40 . . . . 49 F7
Lawrence Way LU6 . . . . 113 F2
Laxton Cl MK43 . . . . 34 E6
Laxton Ct
  Luton LU2 . . . . 117 C1
  St Neots PE19 . . . . 22 D1
Laycock Abbey MK41 . . . . . . 51 B8
Layham Dr LU2 . . . . 116 F2
Lea Bank Cl LU3 . . . . 115 E6
Lea Bank Ct LU3 . . . . 115 E6
Leacroft AL5 . . . . 131 A3
Lea Cl AL5 . . . . 131 A3
Leafield LU3 . . . . 115 F4
Leafield Ct MK45 . . . . 84 E8
Leafields LU3 . . . . 115 F4
Leaf Rd LU5 . . . . 114 B6
LEAGRAVE 115 A5
Leagrave High St LU4 . . . . 115 B3
Leagrave Prim Sch LU4 . . . 115 C4
Leagrave Rd LU4 . . . . 115 E5
Leagrave Sta LU4 . . . . 115 C5
Lealands High Sch LU3 115 C8
Lea Manor High Sch LU3 115 F8
Lea Manor Recn Ctr LU3 115 F8
Leamington Rd LU3 . . . . . . 116 A1
Lea Prim Sch The AL5 . . . . 131 A2
Lea Rd
  Ampthill MK45 . . . . 84 F8
  Harpenden AL5 . . . . 131 B3
  Luton LU1 . . . . 123 F7
Learoyd Way LU7 . . . . 111 D6
Leasey Bridge La AL4,
  AL5 . . . . 131 F1

Leaside LU5 . . . . 114 E6
Leaside Ct AL5 . . . . 131 C3
Leasway MK41 . . . . 38 F3
Leathwaite Cl LU3 . . . . 116 A6
LEA VALLEY 131 F2
Lea Wlk AL5 . . . . 131 C4
Leck Ho 10 LU7 . . . . 111 A7
LEDBURN 110 C1
Ledburn Gr LU7 . . . . 110 E6
Ledgemore La HP2 . . . . 132 F5
Ledwell Rd LU1 . . . . 122 F3
Lee Bridge Cnr LU2 . . . . . . 130 F7
Lee Cl MK40 . . . . 37 C1
Lee Ct PE19 . . . . 22 E5
LEEDON 111 D7
Leedon Lower Sch LU7 . . . . 111 C6
Lee Farm Cotts MK44 . . . . . 15 C6
Lees Cl SG18 . . . . 68 D5
Leghorn Cres LU4 . . . . 115 A1
Leigh Cl LU5 . . . . 105 F6
Leigh Ct MK40 . . . . 38 B1
Leighfield Cl MK41 . . . . 39 C3
LEIGHTON BUZZARD 111 A7
Leighton Buzzard Narrow
  Gauge Railway* LU7 . . . . 103 C1
Leighton Buzzard Rd
  HP1 . . . . 132 E2
Leighton Buzzard Sta
  LU7 . . . . 110 E6
Leighton Ct
  Bedford MK41 . . . . 38 C5
  Dunstable LU5 . . . . 121 A8
Leighton Mid Sch LU7 . . . . 110 F6
Leighton Rd
  Ascott LU7 . . . . 110 A3
  Eggington LU7 . . . . 112 A7
  Heath and Reach LU7 . . . . . 103 B4
  Leighton Buzzard, Eggington
  LU7 . . . . 112 B8
  Leighton Buzzard LU7 . . . . 102 B1
  Leighton Buzzard LU7 . . . . 102 A2
  Northall LU6 . . . . 119 C4
  Stanbridge LU7 . . . . 112 B5
  Toddington LU5 . . . . 105 E5
Leighton St MK17 . . . . 92 C6
Leith Rd MK42 . . . . 50 F5
Lely Cl MK41 . . . . 38 A3
Lennon Ct LU1 . . . . 123 D7
Lennox Gn LU2 . . . . 117 F2
Leopold Rd LU2 . . . . 117 D7
Lesbury Cl LU2 . . . . 117 E1
Leston Cl LU4 . . . . 114 E8
LETCHWORTH 101 C5
Letchworth La SG6 . . . . 101 F3
Letchworth Mus & Art Gall*
  SG6 . . . . 101 D4
Letchworth Rd LU3 . . . . . . 116 A4
Letchworth Sta SG6 . . . . . . 101 F6
Levellers La PE19 . . . . 22 F3
Levendale LU4 . . . . 114 D4
Leven Wlk MK41 . . . . 38 C7
Lewens Croft MK16 . . . . 47 A3
Lewes Gdns MK41 . . . . 39 A5
Lewis La SG15 . . . . 90 A6
LEWSEY FARM 114 E4
Lewsey Park Ct LU4 . . . . . . 115 A4
Lewsey Rd LU4 . . . . 115 B2
Leyburne Rd LU3 . . . . 116 B6
Leydene Pl SG17 . . . . 76 F3
Leygreen Cl LU2 . . . . 124 A8
Leyhill Dr LU1 . . . . 123 B4
Leys Ave SG6 . . . . 101 F6
Ley Side MK43 . . . . 36 F2
Leys Rd PE19 . . . . 22 E6
Leys The
  Ampthill MK45 . . . . 84 F7
  Biggleswade SG18 . . . . 78 F6
  Woburn Sands MK17 . . . . . . 81 A4
Leyton Gn AL5 . . . . 131 A1
Leyton Rd AL5 . . . . 131 A1
Library Rd LU1 . . . . 123 E7
Library Wlk MK41 . . . . 38 F4
Lichfield LU5 . . . . 114 A4
Lichfield Cl MK42 . . . . 49 E5
Liddel Cl LU3 . . . . 116 A2
Liddel Way LU3 . . . . 116 A2
Liddiard Dr LU3 . . . . 111 D5
Lidgate Cl LU4 . . . . 115 B6
LIDLINGTON 72 B2
Lidlington Sta MK43 . . . . . . 72 B3
Life Cl LU4 . . . . 114 F4
Lighthorne Rise LU3 . . . . . . 116 A7
Lilac Ave MK45 . . . . 62 F2
Lilac Gr
  Biggleswade SG18 . . . . 67 C5
  Luton LU3 . . . . 107 C1
  Rushden NN10 . . . . 8 B7
Lilac Wlk MK42 . . . . 49 F3
Lilleshall Dr MK42 . . . . 50 C3
LILLEY 109 D2
Lilley Bottom LU2 . . . . 117 F8
Lilleyhoo La LU2, SG5, ... 109 F2
Lily Cl MK42 . . . . 50 A3
Limbersey La MK45 . . . . 74 D3
LIMBURY 115 E5
Limbury Rd LU3 . . . . 115 F4
Lime Ave
  Beeston SG19 . . . . 54 B6
  Luton LU3 . . . . 115 C3
Lime Cl
  Barton-le-C MK45 . . . . 97 C3
  Bromham MK43 . . . . 36 E1
  Flitwick MK45 . . . . 85 C1
Lime Gr
  Leighton Buzzard LU7 . . . . 110 E8
  St Neots PE19 . . . . 22 F6

Lime Gr continued
  Woburn Sands MK17 . . . . . 81 B4
Lime St MK40 . . . . 50 B8
Limes The
  Arlesey SG15 . . . . 90 A8
  Luton LU1 . . . . 123 C6
Limetree Ave LU4 . . . . 130 A7
Lime Tree Cl LU3 . . . . 107 C1
Lime Tree Dr SG18 . . . . 68 C5
Lime Tree Rd SG17 . . . . 78 A3
Lime Tree Wlk SG18 . . . . . . 67 A7
Lime Wlk
  Dunstable LU5 . . . . 121 D8
  Henlow SG16 . . . . 78 D2
Linacres LU4 . . . . 115 D4
Linbridge Way LU2 . . . . . . 117 C2
Linclare Pl PE19 . . . . 22 C3
Lincoln Cl
  Dunstable LU5 . . . . 121 F6
  Flitwick MK45 . . . . 84 E4
Lincoln Cres SG18 . . . . 67 A4
Lincoln Ct MK40 . . . . 50 E8
Lincoln Rd
  Kempston MK42 . . . . 49 D2
  Luton LU4 . . . . 116 B1
  Shortstown MK42 . . . . 51 A2
Lincoln Way LU5 . . . . 96 A2
Lincombe Slade LU7 . . . . . . 110 C8
Lincroft
  Cranfield MK43 . . . . 59 B1
  Oakley MK43 . . . . 37 A7
Lincroft Mid Sch MK43 . . . . 37 A7
Lincroft Cl LU4 . . . . 114 F1
Lindencroft SG6 . . . . 91 A1
Linden Cl
  Bedford MK40 . . . . 38 A2
  4 Luton LU2 . . . . 123 F8
Linden Rd
  Bedford MK40 . . . . 38 A1
  Dunstable LU5 . . . . 114 F2
  Luton LU4 . . . . 115 E4
Lindens The LU5 . . . . 114 B4
Lindisfarne Gr
  Sandy SG19 . . . . 54 C2
  St Neots PE19 . . . . 22 F1
Lindisfarne Priory MK41 . . 51 B8
Lindler Ct LU7 . . . . 111 A6
Lindley Cl AL5 . . . . 131 A4
Lindsell Cres SG18 . . . . 67 A7
Lindsey Rd LU2 . . . . 117 B2
Link Rd NN10 . . . . 8 B7
Links The MK42 . . . . 49 E3
Links Way LU3 . . . . 116 D8
Link The
  Houghton Regis LU5 . . . . . 114 B5
  Letchworth SG6 . . . . 91 A1
Linkway MK41 . . . . 39 A2
Link Way SG17 . . . . 77 C2
Linley Dell LU2 . . . . 117 D2
Linley Rd PE19 . . . . 22 E3
Linmere Wlk LU5 . . . . 114 E6
Linnet Cl
  Letchworth SG6 . . . . 101 E8
  Luton LU4 . . . . 115 A4
  Sandy SG19 . . . . 42 C2
Linnet Way MK41 . . . . 38 C4
Linnins Pond AL3 . . . . 128 F7
LINSLADE 110 D7
Linslade Lower Sch LU7 . . 110 D7
Linslade Mid Sch LU7 . . . . 110 C6
Linslade Rd LU7 . . . . 102 F4
Linton Cl PE19 . . . . 22 A3
Linwood Gr LU7 . . . . 111 B6
Lippitts Hill LU2 . . . . 116 E5
Lipscombe Dr MK45 . . . . . . 84 E1
Liscombe Rd LU5 . . . . 121 D8
Liston Cl LU4 . . . . 115 B5
Litchfield MK44 . . . . 11 A2
LITTLE BARFORD 32 E6
Little Beeches SG18 . . . . . . 66 F7
Little Berries LU3 . . . . 115 E7
Little Bridge Rd LU2 . . . . . 111 D1
Littlebury Cl SG5 . . . . 91 A5
Little Church Rd LU7 . . . . . 117 B3
Little Comm AL5 . . . . 58 A7
LITTLE CRAWLEY 58 A7
Littledale St MK42 . . . . 49 F5
LITTLE END 22 B1
Little End Rd PE19 . . . . 22 B2
Little End Road Ind Est
  PE19 . . . . 22 B2
Littlefield Rd LU2 . . . . 117 B2
Littlegreen La LU1 . . . . . . 122 E3
Little Grove Pl MK40 . . . . . . 50 C8
Little Headlands MK41 . . . . 38 F4
LITTLE HEATH 44 C3
Little Heath LU3 . . . . 44 C4
Little Hill LU7 . . . . 111 E2
Little La
  Clophill MK45 . . . . 75 D1
  Hockliffe LU7 . . . . 104 F1
  Pirton SG5 . . . . 99 D5
LITTLE ODELL 34 B1
Little Portway MK40 . . . . . . 49 B6
Little Spinney MK45 . . . . . . 59 C3
LITTLE STAUGHTON 13 A2
Little Staughton Airfield
  MK44 . . . . 20 D8
Little Staughton Rd MK44 . . 20 C3
Little Townsend Cl MK44 . . 50 D4
Little Wood Croft LU5 . . . . 115 C7
LITTLEWORTH 63 A4
LITTLE WYMINGTON 4 A7
Liverpool Rd LU1 . . . . 123 D7
Livingstone Lower Sch
  MK41 . . . . 38 A2

Loake Cl MK41..........37 C7
Locarno Ave LU4......115 C6
Lochy Dr LU7..........110 C7
Lockhart Cl LU6......121 E6
Lockington Cres LU5..114 F2
Lodge Ave MK42........49 C3
Lodge Cl MK44.........16 C4
Lodge Ct SG5.........100 E3
Lodge Gdns AL5.......131 A2
Lodge Rd
 Cranfield MK43.......71 A7
 Rushden NN10..........8 A8
 Sharnbrook MK44......16 C4
Lodge The MK44........37 D6
Lodge The Nature Reserve*
 SG19.................54 F4
Loftus Cl LU4........115 B3
Lollard Cl LU4.......114 E3
Lombard St MK43.......72 C3
Lombardy Cl MK41......38 E4
Lomond Dr LU7........110 C7
London End
 Irchester NN29........7 B8
 Milton Ernest MK44..27 F6
 Woburn MK17..........92 F6
London La MK45........74 D6
London Luton Airport
 LU2.................124 D7
London Rd
 Astwick SG18.........79 C4
 Bedford MK42.........50 D6
 Biggleswade SG18.....67 C4
 Dunstable LU6.......121 D6
 Luton LU1...........129 F7
 Luton, New Town LU1.123 E4
 Markyate AL3........128 F5
 Sandy SG19...........54 B7
 Woburn MK17..........93 B3
London Road Ind Est
 SG19.................42 A1
London Road Trad Est
 SG18.................67 C3
London Row SG15.......90 A3
Long Acre SG17........88 B5
Longborns MK44........59 C2
Longbrooke LU5.......114 D4
Long Cl
 Lower Stondon SG16..88 E2
 Luton LU2...........117 C3
Longcroft Ave AL1....130 F1
Longcroft La MK43.....72 D8
Longcroft Rd MK45.....97 B2
Long Croft Rd LU1....123 A7
Longden Cl MK45.......64 A1
Long Dr MK45..........76 A5
Longfellow Ave PE19...22 D5
Longfield Ct SG6.....101 D7
Longfield Dr LU4.....115 D1
Longfield Rd SG19.....54 B8
Long Hedge LU5.......121 D8
Longholme Way MK40, MK41,
 MK42................50 E7
Long La
 Gamlingay SG19.......45 B6
 Tingrith LU5.........95 A2
Longleat MK41.........39 B1
Longleat Cl MK45......84 D1
Long Mdw
 Dunstable LU6.......121 A8
 Markyate AL3........128 F5
Longmead SG6.........101 E7
Long Mead LU5........114 B6
Longmeadow LU5......114 C5
Longmeadow Dr
 Ickleford SG5.......100 F5
 Wilstead MK45........62 E2
Long Twitchell SG18...66 F6
Long Wlk SG17........76 D3
Lonsdale Cl LU3......116 B5
Lords Cl LU7.........112 E5
Lord's Hill LU5......105 F1
Lordsmead MK43.......59 C2
Lords Mead LU6......116 E6
Lords Terr LU6.......119 E6
Loring Rd
 Dunstable LU6.......113 F1
 Sharnbrook MK44......16 B4
Lorraine Ct MK41......39 A1
Lorraine Rd MK43......16 A5
Lorrimer Cl LU2......116 E6
Loseby Cl NN10.........8 A8
Lothair Rd LU2.......117 A4
Lottings Way PE19.....22 C6
Loval Wlk MK42........49 E3
Lovell Memorial Homes
 MK45................37 B6
Lovell Rd
 Bedford MK42.........50 F5
 Oakley MK43..........37 B6
Lovent Dr LU7........111 B7
Loveridge Ave MK42....49 D6
Lovers' Wlk LU5......121 C8
Lovet Rd MK45.........84 E1
Lovett Gn MK45........96 C3
Lovett Way LU5.......114 D3
LOWER BERRY END......94 A8
LOWER CALDECOTE......54 D2
LOWER DEAN............5 C7
LOWER END
 LU6.................112 E1
 MK17................81 C8
Lower End Rd MK17.....81 C8
Lower Farm Cotts SG18.80 B7
Lower Farm Rd MK43....37 C4

LOWER GRAVENHURST...87 C3
LOWER GREEN.........100 E5
Lower Harpenden Rd LU1,
 LU2.................124 C3
Lower Luton Rd AL5...131 C3
LOWER RADS END.......94 D6
LOWER SHELTON........60 C2
Lower Shelton Rd MK43.60 D2
LOWER STONDON........88 F2
LOWER SUNDON.......107 C3
Lowry Dr LU5.........114 D5
Lowry Rd PE19.........22 C6
Lowsdon La MK44......10 F1
Lowther Rd
 Bedford MK41.........38 E5
 Dunstable LU6.......121 D5
Loyne Cl LU7.........110 C8
Lucas Ct MK40.........37 C1
Lucas Gdns LU3.......116 B8
Lucas Way SG17........77 C4
Lucerne Way LU3......116 C4
Ludlow Ave LU4......123 E4
Ludlow Wlk MK41......39 A4
Ludun Cl LU5.........121 E8
Luffenham Pl SG17....76 D3
Luke Pl MK42..........50 C4
Luke St PE19..........22 C2
Lullington Cl LU7....117 C3
Lunedale Cl MK42......49 E3
Lune Wlk MK41........38 C5
Lurke St MK40.........50 C8
LUTON..............123 D4
Luton Airport Parkway Sta
 LU2.................124 B5
Luton Dr The LU1....124 B3
Luton & Dunstable Hospl
 (Faringdon Wing) LU4.115 C3
Luton Ent Pk LU3....115 B8
Luton Int Ret LU1...123 E7
Luton La AL3.........130 B1
Luton Maternity Hospl
 LU4.................115 C2
Luton Mus & Art Gall*
 LU1.................116 D2
Luton Rd
 Barton-le-C MK45....97 B1
 Caddington LU1......123 A4
 Chalton LU4.........106 C3
 Cockernhoe LU2......117 E3
 Dunstable LU5.......114 E1
 Harpenden AL5.......130 D4
 Luton LU1...........115 A7
 Markyate AL3........128 F7
 Peters Green SG4....125 F2
 Streatley LU3.......108 A6
 Wilstead MK45........62 E3
Luton Regional Sports Ctr
 LU2.................117 A5
Luton Ret Pk LU1....124 B6
Luton Sixth Form Coll
 LU2.................116 E4
Luton Sta LU2.......123 E8
Luton Town FC LU1...123 C8
Luton White Hill LU2.117 F8
Luxembourg Cl LU3...115 D8
Lyall Cl MK45.........84 F2
Lyall Ct MK45.........85 A4
Lychmead SG17........78 B3
Lydds Hill MK43.......82 E5
Lydekker Mews 1 AL5.131 A2
Lydford Cl MK40.......38 E1
Lye Hill SG4.........125 D7
Lymans Rd SG15.......90 A6
Lyme Rd MK45.........84 E8
Lymington Gdns MK41..39 C4
Lynch Hill LU6.......123 A8
Lynchhurst Cl AL5...131 C2
Lyndhurst Dr AL5....131 C2
Lyndhurst Rd LU1....123 C7
Lyneford Way NN10.....7 F8
Lyneham Rd LU7......117 C1
Lynn Cl MK42..........50 C2
Lynton Ave SG15.......90 A5
Lynton Gr MK42........50 B4
Lynwood Ave LU2.....114 A1
Lynwood Lodge 6 LU6.114 A1
Lyon Cl MK42..........49 E2
Lypsitt Comm SG17....88 C6
Lyra Gdns LU7........111 D8
Lytham Rd MK40.......49 B6
Lytton Ave SG6......101 F5
Lywood Rd LU7.......111 C6

M

Mabel Rd MK42.........50 B5
MacAulay Rd LU4.....115 A2
MACKERYE END.......131 F4
Maddison Ho PE19.....22 E6
Magdalene Cl SG18....68 D5
Magnolia Ave MK42....49 F2
Magnolia Cl LU3.....116 A2
Magnolia Dr NN10......8 B7
Magnolia Pl SG18.....67 C4
Magpie Ave MK43......61 C1
Magpies The
 Luton LU2...........116 E6
 Maulden MK45........74 C1
Mags La MK17.........93 E1
Mahew Ct MK42........49 D5
Maia Cl MK41..........50 C3
Maidenbower Ave LU6.113 F1
Maidenhall Inf Sch LU4.116 A2
Maidenhall Jun Sch LU4.116 A2
Maidenhall Rd LU4...116 A2

Main Rd
 Astwood MK16.........47 A3
 Biddenham MK40......49 C8
Main Rd N HP4.......126 A6
Main Rd S HP4.......126 D4
Main St SG19.........45 F3
Maitland St MK40.....50 B8
Malakand Rd MK42.....50 A5
Malaunay Pl SG19.....54 C7
Malcote Cl MK40.......37 C1
Malden Ho PE19........22 E6
Maldon Ct AL5.......131 B2
Malham Cl
 Flitwick MK45........84 E2
 Luton LU4...........115 F2
Mallard Cl SG17......77 C2
Mallard Dr LU7........22 F4
Mallard Gdns LU3....116 A5
Mallard Hill MK41....38 C4
Mallard La PE19.......22 F4
Mallow The LU3......115 F3
Mall The LU5........114 C1
Malmesbury Abbey MK41..51 A8
Malms Cl LU3........121 D1
Malthouse Gn LU2....117 F1
Malthouse La SG5.....91 A7
Malting La HP4......126 C5
Maltings Cl MK43.....59 A1
Maltings Orch SG5....99 D3
Maltings Pl SG19.....44 D5
Maltings The
 Ampthill MK45........73 E1
 Dunstable LU6.......114 A1
 Henlow SG16.........78 D1
 Leighton Buzzard LU7.111 B6
 Letchworth SG6.......91 C1
 Shefford SG17........77 C3
 St Neots PE19........22 C5
Maltings Way MK44....41 A5
Malvern Ave MK41.....38 F2
Malvern Cl MK45......84 D2
Malvern Dr LU7......110 C8
Malvern Rd LU3......123 B7
Malzeard Ct 17 LU3..116 D1
Malzeard Rd LU3.....116 D1
Manchester Pl LU1...114 B1
Manchester St LU1...123 E7
Mancroft Rd LU2.....122 E2
Mander Cl LU5.......105 F6
Mandrell Cl LU5.....114 A2
MANGROVE GREEN.....117 E4
Mangrove Rd
 Cockernhoe LU2......117 E4
 Luton LU2...........117 C2
Manland Ave AL5.....131 C2
Manland Prim Sch AL5.131 B3
Manland Way AL5.....131 C3
Manning Cl LU5......114 C5
Manning Pl LU7......117 C2
Mannock Way LU1.....111 D5
Manor Ave LU7.......104 C2
Manorbier Rd MK41....38 F5
Manor Cl
 Bromham MK43........37 A4
 Carlton MK43.........25 A3
 Clifton SG17.........78 A3
 Great Staughton PE19.13 F6
 Harlington LU5.......95 F2
 Ickleford SG5.......100 E3
 Irchester NN29........7 B8
 Langford SG18........78 F6
 Letchworth SG6......101 F3
 Salford MK17.........70 D3
 Westoning MK45.......95 E5
 Wilden MK44..........29 F3
Manor Ct
 Caddington LU1......122 F4
 Leighton Buzzard LU7.102 E2
 Marston Moretaine MK43.72 C7
 Rushden NN10.........8 C8
Manor Farm Bsns Pk SG5.98 A6
Manor Farm Ct
 Barton-le-C MK45....97 C3
 Luton LU1...........115 C3
Manor Farm Way MK44..16 C3
Manor Gdns MK45......49 B8
Manor Hospl MK40.....49 B8
Manor House Cl PE19..22 C2
Manor La NN10.........8 A5
Manor Lodge MK42.....49 D4
Manor Park Dr MK45...95 D6
Manor Pk LU5........114 C4
Manor Pl SG18........66 B8
Manor Rd
 Barton-le-C MK45....97 D3
 Bedford MK42.........39 A2
 Biddenham MK40......49 B8
 Caddington LU1......122 F2
 Gamlingay SG19......44 D6
 Henlow SG16.........78 C1
 Kempston Hardwick MK43.61 D6
 Lea valley AL4......131 F2
 Luton LU1...........107 C3
 Luton LU4...........115 D8
 Marston Moretaine MK43.72 C7
 Rushden NN10.........8 B8
 Sandy SG19..........54 B8
 Toddington LU5......105 F6
 Wootton MK43........61 A7
Manor The SG5.......100 D3
Manor Way
 Cotton End MK45......63 D7
 Flitwick MK45........84 D2
 Letchworth SG6......101 F3
 Potton SG19.........56 B8
Manse Ct AL3........128 F5
Mansfield Rd LU4....116 B1

Manshead CE Upper Sch
 LU1.................121 F5
Manshead Ct LU5.....121 D6
Mansion La MK43......24 F6
Manton Cl MK45.......84 F8
Manton Ctr The MK41..38 A3
Manton Dr LU2.......116 D3
Manton La MK41.......38 A3
Manton Rd LU6.......120 D5
Manx Cl LU4.........116 A2
Maple Cl
 Biggleswade SG18....67 A7
 Clifton SG17.........77 F2
 Greenfield MK45......85 D2
 Lower Stondon SG16..88 E2
Maple Ct
 Gamlingay SG19......44 C5
 18 Luton LU1.......123 D6
Maple Dr SG17........77 E2
Maple Flats AL5.....131 A3
Maple Gdns MK44......11 A3
Maple Gr MK17........81 B4
Maple Rd
 Harpenden AL5.......130 F1
 Sandy SG19..........42 C1
Maple Rd E LU4......123 D8
Maple Rd W LU4......123 D8
Maples The
 Kempston MK42.......49 E3
 Silsoe MK45.........86 B4
Maple Tree Lower Sch
 SG19................42 B2
Maple Way
 Cranfield MK43.......71 A8
 Kensworth LU6......127 E8
Maple Wood NN10......8 B7
Marbury Pl LU3......116 A2
Marchioness Way PE19..22 B4
Mardale Ave LU6.....121 C6
Mardale Cl MK42......49 E4
Mardle Cl LU1.......122 E2
Mardle Rd LU7.......110 E6
Maree Cl LU7........110 C7
Maresfield Ave SG17..76 F2
Mareth Rd MK42.......50 A5
Margaret Beaufort Mid Sch
 MK44................11 B3
Margetts Rd MK42.....49 F4
Margrett La MK45.....96 F6
Marigold Way MK45....84 E1
Marina Ct MK42.......50 A6
Marina Dr LU6.......120 E7
Market Mews 8 LU7...111 A7
Market Rd
 Ampthill MK45........73 E1
 Woburn MK17.........92 F7
Market Sq
 Bedford MK40.........50 B8
 Biggleswade SG18....67 A6
 Leighton Buzzard LU7.111 A7
 Luton LU1...........123 B6
 Potton SG19.........56 A7
 Sandy SG19..........54 C7
 St Neots PE19........22 E4
 Toddington LU5......105 F6
Markfield Cl LU2....116 C7
Markham Cres LU5....114 F2
Markham Rd LU3......116 C6
Mark Rutherford Rd
 MK41................50 D6
Mark Rutherford Upper Sch
 & Com Coll MK41.....39 A5
MARKYATE...........128 E6
Markyate Village Sch
 AL3................128 D6
Marlborough Ct LU2..122 F4
Marlborough Lower Sch
 MK40................49 F8
Marlborough Pk MK42..49 F6
Marlborough Pl LU5..105 F6
Marlborough Rd
 Bedford MK40.........49 F8
 Luton LU3...........116 D1
Marley Fields LU7...111 D6
Marlin Cl LU4.......114 E4
Marlin Rd LU4.......114 E4
Marlow Ct MK42.......49 F6
Marlowe Ct PE19......22 C6
Marlow Way MK41......38 C6
Marmet Ave SG6.....101 E6
Marne St MK42........50 A5
Marquis Cl
 Harpenden AL5.......131 D2
 St Neots PE19........22 B4
Marquis Ct
 12 Luton LU3.......116 D1
 Woburn MK17.........92 F7
Marquis Hill SG5......88 A1
Marquis La AL5......131 D2
Marriott Rd LU3.....116 B6
Marriotts Ct MK43....26 B8
Marschefield SG5......90 E6
Marshall Cl MK42.....49 F4
Marshall Ct MK41.....39 A1
Marshall Rd
 Luton LU2...........117 C2
 St Neots PE19........22 F5
Marshalls Ave SG5....87 F1
Marshalls Way AL4...131 F2
MARSH FARM.........115 E2
Marsh Ho LU3........115 F4
Marsh La MK44........27 F8
Marsh Leys Ind Est MK43..61 D8
Marsh Rd LU3........115 F4
Marsh The MK42.......49 E2
Marsom Gr LU3......116 B8
Marston Gdns LU2....116 D4

Marston Hill MK43.....59 F2
MARSTON MORETAINE...72 D8
Marston Rd MK43......72 C3
Marston Thrift (Nature
 Reserve)* MK43......71 E8
Marston Vale Mid Sch
 MK43................61 C1
Marston Vale Millennium
 Country Pk* MK43...72 E7
Marston Vale Millennium
 Ctry Pk* MK43.......60 F1
Martham Cl MK40......49 D7
Martham Ct AL5......131 C3
Martin Cl MK41.......38 D4
Martindales The LU2.123 F7
Martin Rd MK45.......84 D1
Martins Dr The LU7..102 F1
Martin Way SG6......101 D5
Mary Bassett Lower Sch
 LU7................110 F7
Mary Brash Ct LU2...117 C3
Maryland Coll MK17....92 E6
Maryport Rd LU4.....116 A2
Maryville Rd MK42....50 B5
Marywells SG17.......88 B5
Masefield Ave PE19...22 C6
Masefield Cl AL5....131 B4
Masefield Ct AL5....131 B4
Maskell Dr MK41......39 C5
Massey Cl MK42.......49 E4
Masters Cl LU1......123 B5
Matlock Cres LU4....115 C1
Matthew St LU6......121 B8
Mattocks Rd SG5.....100 C1
MAULDEN............74 C1
Maulden Cl LU2......117 C1
Maulden Lower Sch
 MK45................85 D8
Maulden Rd MK45......85 A4
Maulden Road Ind Est
 MK45................85 A4
Maule Cl PE19........22 E1
Maundsey Cl LU6.....121 D5
Maurice Cl PE28.......6 F5
May Cl
 Eaton Bray LU6......119 C6
 Rushden NN10.........8 C7
Maycroft SG6.........91 A1
Maye Dicks Rd NN10....8 C8
Mayer Way LU5.......114 A3
Mayes Cl MK44........29 F2
Mayfield Cl
 Harpenden AL5.......130 E3
 Kempston MK42.......49 E5
Mayfield Cres SG19...88 E2
Mayfield Cts SG19....54 B7
Mayfield Rd
 Dunstable LU5.......121 D7
 Luton LU4...........117 B4
Mayfields SG17.......77 D3
Mayhew Cl MK43......36 E1
Maynards The SG18....66 C3
Maytree Ave LU4.....115 C4
May Rd MK43.........34 C6
May St LU1..........123 E5
Mead End SG18........67 B5
Meadhook Dr MK45....97 B3
Mead Open Farm & Rare
 Breeds* LU7........112 A2
Meadowbank SG4.....101 B1
Meadow Cl
 Beeston SG19........54 B5
 St Neots PE19........22 F5
Meadow Croft LU2....122 F4
Meadow Farm Rd MK43..48 B2
Meadow La
 Bedford MK44.........51 D7
 Gamlingay SG19......44 D3
 Houghton Regis LU5..114 B5
Meadow Piece MK45....76 A8
Meadow Rd
 Luton LU3...........116 B4
 Toddington LU5......105 F5
Meadows The
 Flitwick MK45........84 D5
 Stewartby MK43......61 C1
 Wingfield LU7.......105 E1
Meadowsweet
 Lower Stondon SG16..88 F2
 St Neots PE19........22 B6
Meadow Sweet Rd NN10..8 C7
Meadow View MK17....81 D6
Meadowview Rd MK43...49 C3
Meadow Way
 Ampthill MK45........84 D7
 Dunstable LU6.......122 C4
 Leighton Buzzard LU7.111 D7
 Letchworth SG6......101 F5
 Stotfold SG5.........90 F6
Meadow Wlk SG16.....78 D1
Meads Cl LU6........114 C5
Mead's Cl MK17.......93 E2
Mead Prim Sch The
 LU6................116 A6
Meads The
 Eaton Bray LU6......119 E5
 Letchworth SG6......101 E6
 Luton LU3...........116 A3
Mead The SG5........100 F2
Meadway
 Bedford MK41.........39 A2
 Dunstable LU6.......121 A7
 Harpenden AL5.......131 C3
 Leighton Buzzard LU7.111 C8
Meadway Ct LU6......120 F7
Medallion Ct 4 PE19..22 F5
Medbury La MK42......50 C2

Medina Rd LU4 . . . 116 A1
Medley Cl LU6 . . . 119 F5
Medlows A5 . . . 130 E2
Mednenham Ave SG17 . . 76 F2
Medusa Way SG19 . . . 42 B1
Medway Cl MK45 . . . 84 D2
Medway Ct MK41 . . . 38 D5
Mees Cl LU3 . . . 107 F1
Meeting Cl MK45 . . . 63 D7
Meeting La SG19 . . . 56 A7
Meeting House La SG7 . . 91 E1
Melbourn Ct SG5 . . . 90 F6
Melbourne St MK42 . . 50 E7
MELCHBOURNE . . . 10 D8
Melchbourne Rd MK44 . . 9 F4
Melford Cl 3 LU2 . . . 117 D1
Melfort Dr LU7 . . . 110 B6
Melrose Dr MK42 . . . 50 C3
Melson Sq 9 LU1 . . . 123 E7
Melson St LU1 . . . 123 E7
Melton Ct LU6 . . . 120 F7
Melton Wlk LU5 . . . 114 E6
Memorial La
  Bletsoe MK44 . . . 17 C1
  Felmersham MK43 . . 26 C8
Memorial Rd LU3 . . . 115 F4
Mendham Way MK45 . . 86 C8
Mendip Cl MK45 . . . 84 D2
Mendip Cres MK41 . . . 38 F3
Mendip Way LU3 . . . 107 C1
Mentmore Cl MK40 . . . 49 B6
Mentmore Cres LU6 . . 121 C5
Mentmore Gdns LU7 . . 110 C5
Mentmore Rd LU7 . . . 110 C5
Mentone Ave MK17 . . . 81 C4
Mepham Rd MK43 . . . 60 F8
MEPPERSHALL . . . 88 B5
Meppershall CE Lower Sch
  SG17 . . . 88 B5
Meppershall Rd
  Meppershall SG17, SG5 . 88 A3
  Upper Stondon SG16 . . 88 D4
Merchant La
  Cranfield MK43 . . . 59 A1
  Wharley End MK43 . . 58 F2
Mercury Pl SG17 . . . 76 D3
Mercury Way LU7 . . . 111 D8
Merlin Dr SG19 . . . 42 B2
Merlin Gdns MK41 . . . 38 C4
Merlins Ct LU1 . . . 111 A4
Mersey Cl MK45 . . . 84 D2
Mersey Pl 1 LU1 . . . 123 D7
Mersey Way MK45 . . . 38 C5
Merton Ho MK40 . . . 38 B1
Merton Rd MK40 . . . 38 D2
Mews The
  3 Harpenden AL5 . . . 131 B1
  Letchworth SG6 . . . 91 C1
Meyrick Ave LU1 . . . 123 C6
Meyrick Ct LU1 . . . 123 D6
Mickle Hill PE28 . . . 2 D7
MIDDLE END . . . 120 A8
Middlefield Com Prim Sch
  PE19 . . . 22 C7
Middlefield Ind Est SG19 . 54 D8
Middlefield La SG19 . . 89 C7
Middlefields SG6 . . . 90 F1
Middlefields Ct SG6 . . 90 F1
Middle Gn LU7 . . . 111 C8
Middleham Cl SG19 . . 54 C8
Middlemarch SG5 . . . 90 C3
Middlesex Univ (Bedford)
  MK40 . . . 38 A6
Middleton Cl LU7 . . . 117 D4
Middleton Way LU7 . . 111 D5
Midhurst SG6 . . . 101 F8
Midhurst Gdns LU3 . . 116 C4
Midland Cl SG17 . . . 77 C2
Midland Cotts SG4 . . 101 A1
Midland Rd
  Bedford MK40 . . . 50 B8
  Luton LU2 . . . 123 E8
  Sandy SG19 . . . 54 B8
Midland Way SG16 . . 89 B3
Midway LU7 . . . 111 C7
Milburn Cl LU3 . . . 108 B1
Milburn Rd MK41 . . . 39 B4
Milebush LU7 . . . 110 C8
Mile Rd MK42 . . . 50 D4
Miles Ave LU2 . . . 111 B7
Miles Dr SG17 . . . 78 B2
Milestone Rd SG5 . . . 100 D2
Miletree Cres LU6 . . . 121 D6
Miletree Ct LU6 . . . 111 B8
Mile Tree Rd LU7 . . . 103 E4
Milford Hill AL5 . . . 131 D4
Milford Park Hospl MK44 . 31 E6
Millards Ct
  Cranfield MK43 . . . 59 C2
  Flitwick MK45 . . . 84 D3
Millard Way SG4 . . . 101 C1
Millbank
  Bedford MK40 . . . 50 D8
  Leighton Buzzard LU7 . 110 F8
MILLBROOK . . . 73 A2
Millbrook Rd MK42 . . 50 B6
Millbrook Sta MK45 . . 72 F6
Mill Cl
  Biggleswade SG18 . . 66 F5
  Henlow SG16 . . . 78 D3
  Stotfold SG5 . . . 91 A6
Mill End Cl LU6 . . . 119 F4
Miller Cl MK41 . . . 37 C6
Miller Rd MK42 . . . 50 B5
Millers Cl LU7 . . . 111 D5
Millers Ct SG18 . . . 66 F6
Millers Lay LU5 . . . 114 F2
Millers Way LU5 . . . 114 A4

Mill Est NN10 . . . 8 B7
Millfield MK43 . . . 36 F2
Millfield Cl
  Cranfield MK43 . . . 59 B2
  Flitwick MK45 . . . 85 A2
Millfield La AL3, LU1 . . 122 D2
Millfield Mews LU1 . . 122 D2
Millfield Rd LU3 . . . 116 B3
Millfield Way LU1 . . . 122 D3
Mill Hill
  Keysoe MK44 . . . 12 B2
  Thurleigh MK44 . . . 18 B1
Mill Hill Rd PE19 . . . 22 C5
Milliners Way LU3 . . . 116 C1
Mill La
  Arlesey SG15 . . . 89 F4
  Astwick SG5 . . . 79 F1
  Barton-le-C MK45 . . 97 C3
  Biggleswade SG18 . . 66 F5
  Campton SG17 . . . 88 A8
  Clophill MK45 . . . 75 C1
  Everton SG19 . . . 43 D1
  Flamstead AL3 . . . 129 A1
  Greenfield MK45 . . 85 C3
  Hexton SG5 . . . 98 C3
  Houghton Conquest MK45 . 62 B1
  Hulcote MK17 . . . 70 E1
  Kempston MK42 . . 49 C4
  Keysoe MK44 . . . 12 B2
  Langford SG18 . . . 78 E7
  Odell MK43 . . . 25 D8
  Pavenham MK43 . . 26 B3
  Potton SG43 . . . 55 F8
  Salford MK17 . . . 70 C3
  Sandy SG19 . . . 54 B6
  St Neots PE19 . . . 22 F8
  Stotfold SG5 . . . 91 A6
  Tempsford SG19 . . 44 D5
  Turvey MK43 . . . 34 D5
  Woburn Sands MK17 . 81 C5
Mill Mdw SG18 . . . 78 E7
MILLOW . . . 68 C4
Mill Rd
  Colmworth MK44 . . 30 C7
  Cranfield MK43 . . . 59 C2
  Houghton Regis LU5 . 114 A4
  Husborne Crawley MK43 . 82 D5
  Leighton Buzzard LU7 . 111 A8
  Sharnbrook MK44 . . 16 F3
  Slapton LU7 . . . 118 D7
  Stanbridge LU7 . . . 112 C6
  Stanford SG18 . . . 78 B7
  Thurleigh MK44 . . . 28 B7
Mill Rise MK43 . . . 36 F2
Mill St
  Bedford MK40 . . . 50 C8
  Gamlingay SG19 . . 44 D5
  Luton LU1 . . . 123 D8
Millstream Cl SG4 . . . 101 A1
Millstream Ct SG17 . . 77 D3
Millstream Way LU7 . . 110 F7
Mills Wlk SG19 . . . 54 C8
Mill Tower LU7 . . . 119 E6
Mill Vale Mid Sch LU5 . 114 E2
Mill View Ct PE19 . . . 22 C2
Mill Way MK17 . . . 81 D5
Millwood Ct SG5 . . . 90 F6
Millwright Way MK45 . . 84 D4
Milner Ct LU1 . . . 123 E8
Milne Row MK41 . . . 37 F1
Milton Ave PE19 . . . 22 D6
MILTON BRYAN . . . 93 E1
Milton Ct 12 MK41 . . . 131 B1
MILTON ERNEST . . . 27 A5
Milton Ernest Lower Sch
  MK44 . . . 27 B5
Milton Rd
  Bedford MK40 . . . 37 F1
  Clapham MK41 . . . 37 C7
  Flitwick MK45 . . . 84 D3
  Harpenden AL5 . . . 131 B1
  Luton LU1 . . . 123 D6
Milton Way LU5 . . . 114 D4
Milton Wlk LU5 . . . 114 D4
Milverton Gn LU3 . . . 116 A7
Minden Cl MK45 . . . 84 E4
Minden Ct PE19 . . . 22 C5
Minorca Way LU3 . . . 115 A3
Miss Joans Ride HP4,
  LU6 . . . 126 E7
Mistletoe Ct LU2 . . . 124 C8
Mistletoe Hill LU2 . . . 124 C8
Mitchell Cl MK42 . . . 51 A3
Mitchell Rd MK43 . . . 58 E2
Mitford Cl MK41 . . . 39 B1
Mitre Cl MK43 . . . 39 B1
Mixes Hill Ct LU2 . . . 117 A4
Mixes Hill Rd LU2 . . . 117 A4
Mixies The SG5 . . . 90 E6
Moakes The LU3 . . . 115 E7
Moat Farm Cl
  Greenfield MK45 . . 85 B2
  Marston Moretaine MK43 . 72 C7
Moat La LU3 . . . 116 D4
Mobbs Cl MK42 . . . 49 D5
Mobley Gn LU2 . . . 117 B3
MOGGERHANGER . . . 53 C6
Moggerhanger Lower Sch
  MK44 . . . 53 C7
Moira Cl LU3 . . . 115 D7
Molescroft AL5 . . . 130 D4
Molivers La MK43 . . . 36 F3
Molly Moore Ave MK42 . 49 D3
Monarch Cl MK42 . . . 124 C8
Monarch Rd PE19 . . . 22 C8
Monklands SG6 . . . 101 D6
Monks Cl
  Dunstable LU5 . . . 114 E1

Monks Cl continued
  Letchworth SG6 . . . 101 C6
  Monkshill MK41 . . . 39 A3
Monks Row MK43 . . . 26 B3
Monmouth Cl
  Bedford MK40 . . . 50 D5
  Toddington LU5 . . . 105 E6
Monmouth Rd LU5 . . 95 F3
Monoux Pl SG17 . . . 54 C7
Monoux Rd MK43 . . . 61 A6
Montagu Cl PE19 . . . 22 E4
Montagu La 3 LU4 . . 115 C6
Montagu Gdns PE28 . . 6 F5
Montagu Ho PE19 . . . 22 E4
Montagu Sq PE19 . . . 22 E4
Montagu St PE19 . . . 22 E4
Montgomery Ave SG17 . 77 C1
Montgomery Cl
  Leighton Buzzard LU7 . 103 B1
  Stewartby MK43 . . . 61 C1
Montgomery Ct MK42 . 50 A5
Montgomery Rd LU3 . . 67 D3
Monton Cl LU3 . . . 115 F6
Montrose Ave LU3 . . . 116 C3
Moore Cres LU6 . . . 114 C4
Moor End LU6 . . . 119 F5
Moor End Cl LU6 . . . 119 F4
Moor End La
  Eaton Bray LU6 . . . 119 F5
  Felmersham MK43 . . 26 F8
Moor End Rd MK43 . . 26 F8
Moore's Cl MK45 . . . 85 C3
Moores Wlk 7 PE19 . . 22 E5
Moorhouse Path LU7 . . 111 D5
Moorhouse Way LU7 . . 111 D5
Moor La
  Bedford MK42 . . . 50 D4
  Flitwick MK45 . . . 85 A2
  Maulden MK45 . . . 85 D3
Moorland Cl MK45 . . 85 D3
Moorland Gdns LU2 . . 123 D8
Moorland Rd AL5 . . . 131 B4
Moorlands Sch LU2 . . 116 C2
Moor Pond Piece MK45 . 73 D1
Moor Rd PE19 . . . 13 E1
Moor St LU1 . . . 123 D8
Moors View MK43 . . . 85 B2
Moore The MK45 . . . 85 A2
Morar Cl LU7 . . . 110 C7
Morcambe Cl LU4 . . . 115 B3
Morcom Rd LU6 . . . 121 E6
Mordaunt Cl MK43 . . 34 E6
Moreteyne Rd MK43 . . 72 D8
Moreton Ave AL5 . . . 130 F2
Moreton End Cl AL5 . . 130 F2
Moreton End La AL5 . . 130 F2
Moreton Pk LU2 . . . 130 F3
Moreton Pl AL5 . . . 130 F3
Moreton Rd N LU2 . . . 117 A2
Moreton Rd S LU2 . . . 117 A2
Morgan Cl LU2 . . . 115 E3
Morgans Cl MK45 . . . 62 F3
Morland Cl MK43 . . . 38 C6
Morland Way MK43 . . 38 B3
Morrell Cl LU3 . . . 116 A7
Morris Cl
  Henlow SG16 . . . 89 C5
  Luton LU3 . . . 115 E8
Morris Gdns MK43 . . 84 D7
Morris Wlk MK44 . . . 31 F6
Mortimer Cl LU1 . . . 123 A7
Mortimer Rd MK42 . . 49 D6
Mossbank Ave LU2 . . 124 C8
Mossdale Ct 3 LU4 . . 115 C3
Moss La MK7 . . . 50 C1
Mossman Dr LU1 . . . 122 E4
Moss Way SG5 . . . 100 C1
Mostyn Rd LU3 . . . 115 F6
Moulton Ave MK42 . . 50 A6
Moulton Rise LU2 . . . 123 F8
Mountbatten Ct PE19 . . 22 C4
Mountbatten Dr SG18 . 67 A7
Mountbatten Gdns LU7 . 103 B1
Mountbatten Pl MK41 . 39 B1
Mountbatten Way SG17 . 76 E4
Mount Dr MK41 . . . 39 A3
Mountfield Rd LU2 . . 116 E2
Mountfort Cl PE19 . . . 22 F3
Mount Grace Rd LU2 . . 117 C6
Mountjoy SG4 . . . 101 C1
MOUNT PLEASANT . . 61 A8
Mount Pleasant
  Aspley Guise MK17 . . 81 F4
  Ridgmont MK43 . . . 82 C6
Mount Pleasant Ave LU5 . 105 F4
Mount Pleasant Rd
  Clapham MK41 . . . 37 D6
  Luton LU1 . . . 115 C6
Mount The
  Aspley Guise MK17 . . 81 D4
  4 Luton LU2 . . . 123 D8
Mountview AL5 . . . 121 E6
Mowbray Cl MK43 . . 36 E3
Mowbray Cres SG5 . . 90 F7
Mowbray Dr LU7 . . . 110 D7
Mowbray Pl MK44 . . . 40 C1
Mowbray Rd MK42 . . 50 C8
Mowhills MK43 . . . 24 F6
Moxes Wood LU3 . . . 115 E7
Muddy La SG6 . . . 101 F3
Muirfield
  Biddenham MK40 . . 49 B6
  Luton LU2 . . . 116 E6
Mulberry Cl
  Biggleswade SG18 . . 66 F8
  Luton LU1 . . . 123 B7

Mulberry Cl continued
  Stotfold SG5 . . . 90 F5
Mulberry Way SG5 . . 100 D2
Mulberry Wlk MK42 . . 49 F3
Mullen Cl PE19 . . . 22 C5
Mullion Cl LU2 . . . 117 B5
Mullway SG6 . . . 101 C6
Muntjac Cl PE19 . . . 22 B5
Murdock Rd MK41 . . 38 A4
Murfitt Way SG19 . . . 44 D6
Murrell Cl PE19 . . . 22 F7
Murrell Ct PE19 . . . 22 F7
Murrells Cl SG5 . . . 90 F7
Murrells La SG5 . . . 91 A5
Musgrave Way 6 PE19 . 22 F5
Mussons Path LU2 . . . 116 E1
Muswell Cl LU3 . . . 116 B6
Muswell Rd MK42 . . . 50 B5
Mutford Croft 2 LU2 . . 117 D1
Myers Rd SG19 . . . 56 A8
Myrtle Rd MK42 . . . 50 D5

N

Nagshead La MK44 . . . 32 A5
Nags Head La NN9 . . . 1 F2
Napier Cl LU2 . . . 123 D7
Napier Hall LU2 . . . 124 C8
Napier Rd
  Luton MK41 . . . 39 D3
  Luton LU1 . . . 123 D7
Nappsbury Rd LU4 . . 115 D5
Narrow Path MK17 . . 81 B3
Naseby Pl MK45 . . . 84 E4
Naseby Rd LU1 . . . 123 B7
Nash Cl LU5 . . . 114 D5
Nash Rd MK42 . . . 50 E6
Navigation Wharf PE19 . 22 E5
Nayland Cl LU2 . . . 117 E1
Naylor Ave MK42 . . . 49 E2
Neale Rd MK43 . . . 60 F8
Neale Way MK43 . . . 60 F8
Neath Abbey MK41 . . 51 B8
Nebular Ct LU7 . . . 111 C8
Needham Rd LU4 . . . 115 B6
Needwood Rd MK41 . . 39 C3
Nelson Rd
  Chicksands SG17 . . 76 E4
  Dagnall HP4 . . . 126 C5
  Leighton Buzzard LU7 . 103 B1
  St Neots PE19 . . . 22 B2
Nelson St MK40 . . . 49 F7
Nene Rd
  Flitwick MK45 . . . 84 D2
  Henlow SG16 . . . 89 B4
  St Neots PE19 . . . 22 B2
Neotsbury Ct MK45 . . 84 F8
Neotsbury Rd MK45 . . 84 F8
Neptune Cl LU3 . . . 114 E6
Neptune Gdns LU7 . . 111 D8
Neptune Sq LU3 . . . 114 E6
Nethercott Cl LU2 . . . 117 C1
Netherstones SG5 . . . 90 F7
Nettle Cl LU4 . . . 114 C3
NETTLEDEN . . . 132 B1
Nettleden Rd HP1 . . . 132 C1
Nettleton Cl LU2 . . . 111 C6
Nevells Gn SG6 . . . 101 F6
Nevells Rd SG6 . . . 101 F6
Nevern Gdns MK40 . . 37 C1
Neville Cl MK43 . . . 36 E2
Neville Ct MK43 . . . 36 F2
Neville Rd LU3 . . . 116 B4
Neville Road Pas LU3 . . 116 A5
Nevis Cl LU7 . . . 110 C7
Newark Ave LU4 . . . 39 A5
Newark Rd LU4 . . . 114 D6
New Barn Farm La LU5 . 106 D3
New Bedford Rd
  Luton LU1 . . . 123 D8
  Luton LU3 . . . 116 D3
Newbold Rd LU3 . . . 116 B7
Newbury Cl
  Kempston MK42 . . 49 D4
  Luton LU4 . . . 115 C2
  Silsoe MK45 . . . 86 B5
Newbury Ct MK45 . . 86 B5
Newbury Ho MK40 . . 38 D2
Newbury La MK45 . . 86 B5
New Cl MK44 . . . 28 F1
Newcombe Rd LU1 . . 123 C7
New Cotts AL3 . . . 128 E6
New Inn Rd SG7 . . . 80 D5
Newis Cres SG17 . . . 78 B2
Newlands Rd
  Luton LU3 . . . 123 C3
  Westoning MK45 . . 95 C6
Newman Way LU7 . . 111 B7
NEW MILL END . . . 124 D1
NEWNHAM . . . 91 E8
Newnham Ave MK41 . . 50 F8
Newnham Cl LU2 . . . 117 D1
Newnham Mid Sch MK41 . 38 C2
Newnham Rd
  Bedford MK40 . . . 50 C8
  Henlow SG16 . . . 91 E6
Newnham St MK40 . . 50 C8
Newport Pagnell Rd
  Hardmead MK16 . . 47 D5
Newport Rd
  Hardmead MK16 . . 47 D5
  Woburn MK17 . . . 92 F8
  Woburn Sands MK17 . 81 A6
New Rd
  Bromham MK43 . . . 36 E1
  Clifton SG17 . . . 78 A1

New Rd continued
  Colmworth MK44 . . . 29 F8
  Great Barford MK44 . . 41 B5
  Harrold MK43 . . . 24 E6
  Leighton Buzzard LU7 . 110 F2
  Maulden MK45 . . . 85 C6
  Sandy SG19 . . . 54 D5
New St
  Irchester NN29 . . . 7 B8
  Luton LU1 . . . 123 E6
  Shefford SG17 . . . 77 C2
  Slip End LU1 . . . 123 C1
  St Neots PE19 . . . 22 E5
Newstead Way MK41 . . 38 F5
New Street Ct NN29 . . 7 B8
NEWTON . . . 68 B5
NEWTON
  BLOSSOMVILLE . . . 34 A4
Newton Blossomville CE First
  Sch MK43 . . . 34 B4
NEWTON BROMSWOLD . 9 D8
Newtondale LU4 . . . 115 C5
Newton Rd
  Bedford MK42 . . . 50 C5
  Chelveston NN10 . . 3 B3
  Rushden NN10 . . . 8 F8
  Turvey MK43 . . . 34 E5
Newton Way
  Leighton Buzzard LU7 . 111 D6
  Sandy SG19 . . . 54 C8
NEW TOWN . . . 123 C5
Newtown
  Henlow SG16 . . . 78 D3
  Kimbolton PE28 . . . 6 F5
  Potton SG19 . . . 55 D7
  St Neots PE19 . . . 22 B8
Newtown Ct SG18 . . . 67 B7
Newtown La PE28 . . . 6 F5
New Town Rd 9 LU1 . . 123 E6
New Town St LU1 . . . 123 E6
NEW WATER END . . . 94 B8
New Wlk
  Shillington SG5 . . . 87 E1
  Shillington SG5 . . . 87 F1
New Woodfield Gn LU5 . 121 E6
Nicholas Way 6 LU5 . . 121 B8
Nicholls Cl
  Barton-le-C MK45 . . 97 C3
  Marston Moretaine MK43 . 72 C8
Nicholls Cl LU2 . . . 117 C2
Nichols Cl LU2 . . . 117 C2
Nicholson Dr LU7 . . . 111 D5
Nickleby Way LU5 . . . 90 C2
Nightingale Ave MK41 . 38 C5
Nightingale Cl LU3 . . . 117 C6
Nightingale Cl LU2 . . 123 C8
Nightingale Mews SG17 . 77 C2
Nightingale Terr SG15 . 90 A3
Nightingale Way MK43 . 16 B4
Nimbus Pk LU5 . . . 114 C3
Nimrod Dr SG17 . . . 76 F4
Ninelands LU7 . . . 104 F2
Ninfield Ct LU2 . . . 117 C3
Ninth Ave LU3 . . . 115 D7
Nith Wlk MK41 . . . 38 C7
Nodders Way MK40 . . 37 C1
Noke Shot AL5 . . . 131 C4
Norcott Cl LU3 . . . 121 D7
Norfolk Cl MK41 . . . 38 D6
Norfolk Rd
  Dunstable LU5 . . . 121 F6
  Luton LU2 . . . 124 A7
  Turvey MK43 . . . 34 E6
Norman Cl MK44 . . . 40 F5
Normandy Cl MK42 . . 50 A5
Normandy La SG18 . . 67 D3
Norman Rd
  Barton-le-C MK45 . . 97 C4
  Luton LU3 . . . 116 B2
  Sharnbrook MK44 . . 16 D3
Normans Cl SG6 . . . 90 F1
Norman Way
  Dunstable LU6 . . . 120 E8
  Irchester NN29 . . . 7 C8
Norse Rd MK41 . . . 39 C3
NORTHALL . . . 119 B6
Northall Cl LU6 . . . 119 B6
Northall Rd LU6 . . . 119 B6
Northampton Rd
  Bromham MK43 . . . 36 B3
  Bromham MK43 . . . 36 E3
North Area Pupil Referral
  Unit SG5 . . . 101 D3
Northbridge St SG17 . . 77 C3
Northbridge Wharf SG17 . 77 C3
Northcliffe LU6 . . . 119 F6
Northcote MK41 . . . 39 A3
Northcourt LU3 . . . 103 A1
NORTH CRAWLEY . . . 58 A6
Northcroft SG19 . . . 54 C7
North Ct AL3 . . . 128 E5
Northdale Cl MK42 . . 50 A4
North Dr MK42 . . . 51 A3
North Dell Way LU3 . . 123 B6
NORTH END
  MK43 . . . 47 D8
  MK44 . . . 17 D3
North End MK42 . . . 50 C4
Northern Ave SG16 . . 89 C3
Northfield Cl
  Gamlingay SG19 . . 44 D6
  Henlow SG16 . . . 78 D2

Northfield Rd
Guilden Morden SG7 . . . . **69** C2
Harpenden AL5 . . . . **131** C4
Wyboston MK44. . . . . **21** F1
Northfields
Biggleswade SG18. . . . . **67** A7
Dunstable LU5. . . . . **114** A3
Letchworth SG6 . . . . **90** F1
Northfields Inf Sch SG6 . . . . **90** F1
Northfields Tech Coll
LU5. **114** A3
North Hertfordshire Coll
SG6 . . . . **101** F5
NORTHILL. **53** E2
Northill CE Lower Sch
SG18 . . . . **53** D2
North La
Gamlingay SG19 . . . . **44** B6
Haynes MK45 . . . . **85** A6
North Luton Ind Est LU4 . . **115** B7
North Par 2 MK40. . . . . **38** B1
North Rd SG7. . . . . **91** E2
North St
Leighton Buzzard LU7 . . . . . . **111** A7
Luton, High Town LU2 . . . . . **123** E8
Luton LU2. . . . . **116** E1
North Star Dr LU7 . . . . **111** C8
North Station Way LU4. . . **114** A2
Northview Rd
Houghton Regis LU5 . . . . **114** A2
Luton LU2. . . . . **116** F2
Northway St MK42. . . . . **50** D6
Northwell Dr LU3. . . . . **115** F7
Northwood End Rd MK45. . **76** B7
Northwood La MK45 . . . . . . **63** A4
NORTON. **91** C1
NORTON BURY. **91** C2
Norton Bury La SG6 . . . . . . **91** C2
Norton Ct LU4. . . . . **121** B8
Norton Mill La SG6 . . . . . . **91** C3
Norton Rd
Letchworth SG6. . . . . **91** C2
Luton LU3. . . . . **115** F4
Stotfold SG5 . . . . **91** A4
Norton Road Prim Sch
LU3. **115** F4
Nunnery La LU3 . . . . **116** B5
Nurseries The LU6 . . . . **119** E6
Nursery Cl
Biggleswade SG18. . . . . **67** B8
Clophill MK45. . . . . **86** B8
Dunstable LU6 . . . . **121** A8
Potton SG19. . . . . **55** E7
Nursery Dr SG19. . . . . **54** A8
Nursery Gdns MK41. . . . . . . **38** D4
Nursery Par LU3 . . . . **115** E5
Nursery Rd
Luton LU3. . . . . **115** F5
St Neots PE19 . . . . **22** F4
Nutleigh Gr SG5 . . . . **100** D1
Nutwood Cl MK41. . . . . **39** C3
Nymans Cl LU2 . . . . **117** D3

O

Oak Ave MK45 . . . . **62** F2
Oak Bank Dr LU2 . . . . **103** A3
Oak Bank Special Sch
LU7. **103** A3
Oak Cl
Dunstable LU5. . . . . **121** D8
Harlington LU5 . . . . **95** F1
Irchester NN29 . . . . **7** A7
Sandy SG19 . . . . **54** B8
Westoning MK45 . . . . **95** E6
Wootton MK43. . . . . **61** A8
Oak Cres
Biggleswade SG18. . . . . **67** B4
Potton SG19. . . . . **55** F7
Upper Caldecote SG18 . . . . . . **66** B8
Oakcroft MK43. . . . . **48** A6
Oak Dr
Greenfield MK45 . . . . **85** D2
Henlow SG16. . . . . **78** D1
Oaken Pin Cl MK43 . . . . **71** B8
Oak Gdns MK43. . . . . **72** C2
Oakham Cl NN10. . . . . **8** A8
Oaklands Rd MK40. . . . . **38** D2
OAKLEY. **37** A7
Oakley Cl LU4 . . . . **115** D5
Oakley Gn LU7 . . . . **103** B1
Oakley Lower Sch MK43. . . **37** A7
Oakley Rd
Bromham MK43 . . . . **37** A4
Clapham MK41. . . . . **37** C6
Luton LU4 . . . . **115** E3
Oak Rd
Bedford MK42 . . . . **50** E5
Flitwick MK45 . . . . **84** F2
Luton LU4 . . . . **123** C8
Oakridge Pk LU7 . . . . **111** B5
Oaks The
Heath and Reach LU7 . . . . . **103** A5
Silsoe MK45. . . . . **86** C4
Slip End LU1 . . . . **123** C1
Oak Tree Cl SG6 . . . . **101** E4
Oak Tree Row LU2 . . . . . . **117** A2
Oakway LU6 . . . . **127** B7
Oakwell Cl LU6 . . . . **120** F7

Oakwood Ave LU5 . . . . **121** E7
Oakwood Dr LU3 . . . . **115** C8
Oakwood Rd SG17 . . . . **77** D2
Oasis Pool MK42. . . . . **50** E7
Oatfield Cl LU4 . . . . **114** F4
Oatfield Gdns LU7 . . . . **111** D7
Oban Terr LU1 . . . . **123** B8
Oberon Ct MK40 . . . . **38** A1
Ockendon Cl PE19 . . . . **22** B3
ODELL. **25** C8
Odell Cl MK42 . . . . **49** D6
Odell Rd
Odell MK43 . . . . **25** A8
Sharnbrook MK44 . . . . **16** B2
Odin Cl MK41. . . . . **39** D4
Offa Rd MK42. . . . . **50** B6
Old Allotments The MK44 . **13** A2
Old Bakery Yd SG18. . . . . . . **68** D5
Old Barn Cl SG16. . . . . **78** D2
Old Barns The MK40. . . . . . . **49** B8
Old Bedford Rd
Luton LU2 . . . . **116** D6
Luton LU2 . . . . **116** E4
Potton SG19. . . . . **55** F7
Old Brewery Cl SG5 . . . . . . **90** F7
Old Bridge Ct SG17 . . . . **77** C2
Old Bridge Way SG17 . . . . . **77** C2
Old Chapel Mews LU7 . . . . **111** A6
Old Chapel The PE19 . . . . . . **22** B2
Old Church Path MK45 . . . . **75** E1
Old Dairy Cl LU5. . . . . **114** F2
Old Farm Cl LU7 . . . . **118** A3
Oldfield Farm Rd
Henlow SG16 . . . . **89** B4
Henlow SG16 . . . . **89** C4
Oldfield Rd MK40 . . . . **49** E8
Old Ford End Rd MK40 . . . . **49** E7
Old Hale Way SG5 . . . . **100** C2
Old Harrowden Rd MK42 . . **51** A3
Old Hat Factory The 1
LU2. **116** D1
Oldhill LU6 . . . . **121** D6
OLDHILL WOOD. **127** D6
Oldhill Wood LU6 . . . . **127** D6
Old Kiln La MK45 . . . . **75** C2
OLD LINSLADE. **102** D3
Old Linslade Rd LU7 . . . . . **102** D3
Old Main Rd MK45. . . . . **75** A6
Old Market Ct PE19 . . . . **22** E5
Old Mews MK41 . . . . **38** A2
Old Mill Cl SG18 . . . . **78** E7
Old Mill La MK45 . . . . **87** D4
Old Milton Rd MK44 . . . . **28** A8
Old Oak Cl SG15. . . . . **90** A8
Old Orch LU1 . . . . **123** D5
Old Orchard The SG18. . . . . **67** B6
Old Rd
Barton-le-C MK45 . . . . **97** C1
Leighton Buzzard LU7 . . . . . . **110** E7
Old Rd The MK43. . . . . **16** D1
Old Rectory Cl AL5 . . . . **131** A2
Old School Ct
Clifton SG17 . . . . **78** B2
Eaton Bray LU6 . . . . **119** E6
Hockliffe LU7 . . . . **104** E2
2 Leighton Buzzard LU7 . . **111** A7
Old School Gdns
Barton-le-C MK45 . . . . **97** C3
St Neots PE19 . . . . **22** C2
Wootton MK43. . . . . **60** F7
Old School La SG18. . . . . **78** A7
Old School Wlk
Arlesey SG15. . . . . **90** A4
Slip End LU1 . . . . **123** C1
Old School Yd PE19 . . . . **22** F4
Old Silsoe Rd MK45. . . . . **86** C8
Old Station Ct MK44 . . . . . . **41** D2
Old Station Way SG17. . . . . **77** C3
Old Vicarage Gdns
Henlow SG16. . . . . **78** D2
Markyate AL3 . . . . **128** D6
OLD WARDEN. **65** B4
Old Watling St AL3 . . . . **129** B3
Old Way MK44 . . . . **17** C1
Oldways Rd MK44. . . . . **28** F1
Oliver Cl MK40 . . . . **38** B1
Oliver's La SG5 . . . . **90** F7
Oliver St MK45. . . . . **84** F7
Olivier Way SG17 . . . . **78** B2
Olyand Ct LU1 . . . . **123** B6
Olympic Cl LU3 . . . . **107** E1
Olympus Rd LU6. . . . . **89** B4
Ombersley Rd MK42 . . . . **50** B6
Omega Ct LU7 . . . . **111** C8
Omega Ctr The SG18 . . . . . . **67** D3
Onley Ct SG19 . . . . **54** D6
Onslow Rd LU4 . . . . **115** D5
Openshaw Way SG6. . . . . . . **101** F6
Orchard Ave AL5. . . . . **130** F1
Orchard Cl
Barton-le-C MK45 . . . . **97** C1
Bedford MK41 . . . . **38** E3
Biggleswade SG18. . . . . **67** B6
Bromham MK43 . . . . **37** A4
Caddington LU1 . . . . **122** E4
Cranfield MK43 . . . . **59** A1
Gravenhurst MK45 . . . . **72** C7
Houghton Regis LU5 . . . . **114** B3
Letchworth SG6 . . . . **101** F8
Meppershall SG17 . . . . **88** C6
Potton SG19. . . . . **56** A7
St Neots PE19 . . . . **22** C4
Toddington LU5 . . . . **105** F6
Orchard Dr
Chicksands SG17 . . . . **76** F2
Leighton Buzzard LU7 . . . . . **110** D6
Wilstead MK45 . . . . **62** E3

Orchard End LU6 . . . . **119** E4
Orchard Est LU7 . . . . **112** A7
Orchard Ho LU5 . . . . **95** F2
Orchard La MK43 . . . . **24** F7
Orchard Pl MK29. . . . . **7** A8
Orchard Rd
Baldock SG7 . . . . **91** E1
Beeston SG19 . . . . **54** C5
Hitchin SG4 . . . . **101** B1
Pulloxhill MK45 . . . . **96** E8
Totternhoe LU6 . . . . **120** B8
Orchard St MK42. . . . . **49** F3
Orchards The
Eaton Bray LU6 . . . . **119** E7
Silsoe MK45. . . . . **86** C4
Slip End LU1 . . . . **123** C2
Orchard The MK44. . . . . **10** F2
Orchard Way
Cranfield MK43 . . . . **59** A1
Eaton Bray LU6 . . . . **119** F5
Flitwick MK45 . . . . **84** F2
Great Barford MK44 . . . . **41** A4
Letchworth SG6 . . . . **101** F8
Lower Stondon SG16. . . . . **89** B3
North Crawley MK16. . . . . **58** A6
Stanbridge LU7 . . . . **112** D5
Orchid Cl
Dunstable LU6 . . . . **113** E1
St Neots PE19 . . . . **22** C6
Ordelmere SG6 . . . . **90** F1
Oregon Way LU3 . . . . **116** A8
Orion Way LU7 . . . . **111** D8
Ormesby Way MK40. . . . . **49** E7
Ormsby Cl LU1 . . . . **123** E5
Osborn Cres SG17 . . . . **77** C2
Osborne Ave SG17 . . . . **76** E2
Osborne Ct 3 SG17 . . . . . . **123** F6
Osborne Rd
Dunstable LU6 . . . . **121** B7
Luton LU1 . . . . **123** F6
Osborn Ho 1 LU6 . . . . **121** B8
Osborn Rd MK45 . . . . **97** C2
Osier Cl PE19 . . . . **22** C6
Osier Link MK45 . . . . **84** F7
Osprey Cl
Kempston MK42 . . . . **49** E2
Sandy SG19 . . . . **42** B2
Osprey Rd
Biggleswade SG18. . . . . **66** F5
Flitwick MK45 . . . . **84** E2
Osprey Wlk LU4 . . . . **115** A5
Ossory Pl MK44 . . . . **28** A8
Ossory Way MK42 . . . . **50** B6
Othello Ct MK40 . . . . **37** F2
Otterton Cl AL5. . . . . **130** F3
Otter Way PE19 . . . . **22** B5
Otter Wlk MK41. . . . . **38** C5
Oulton Rise AL3 . . . . **131** C3
Our Lady RC Prim Sch
SG5 . . . . **100** C2
Ouseland Rd MK40. . . . . **49** E7
Ouseley Cl LU4 . . . . **115** D3
Ouse Rd
Bedford MK41 . . . . **39** A2
St Neots PE19 . . . . **22** C4
Oval The SG16 . . . . **89** C3
Overdale MK41 . . . . **39** A3
Overend Green La LU7 . . . **103** C6
Overfield Rd LU2 . . . . **117** C1
Overhills Prim Sch PE28 . . . **6** F5
Overlord Cl SG17 . . . . **77** C1
Overstone Rd
Harpenden AL5 . . . . **131** C1
Luton LU4 . . . . **115** D1
Overtrees AL5 . . . . **130** F3
Oving Cl LU2 . . . . **117** D2
Owen Cl
Kempston MK42 . . . . **49** D3
Marston Moretaine MK43 . . . **72** C8
Owen Jones Cl SG16. . . . . . . **89** C5
Owlswood SG19 . . . . **42** B2
Oxendon Ct LU7 . . . . **102** F2
Oxen Rd LU2 . . . . **116** F1
Oxford Rd 2 LU1 . . . . **123** E6
Oxford St NN10 . . . . **4** A3
Ox La AL5 . . . . **131** B3

P

Padbury Ho 4 MK40 . . . . **38** A1
Paddlers Ct MK40. . . . . **49** E7
Paddock Cl
Clapham MK41. . . . . **37** C6
Letchworth SG6 . . . . **101** F5
Luton LU4 . . . . **114** F5
Paddocks The
Bromham MK43 . . . . **36** F1
Flitwick MK45 . . . . **84** D5
Leighton Buzzard LU7 . . . . . **110** F8
Potton SG19. . . . . **55** F7
Toddington LU5 . . . . **106** A5
Paddock The
Biddenham MK40 . . . . **49** D8
Lidlington MK43 . . . . **72** C2
St Neots PE19 . . . . **22** D5
Page's Almshouses 5
LU7. **111** A8
Page's Ind Pk LU7 . . . . **111** B5
Paignton Cl LU4 . . . . **115** D4
Paines Mill PE19. . . . . **22** E6
Paisley Cl LU4 . . . . **115** A5
Palace St SG18 . . . . **67** A5
Palgrave Rd MK42 . . . . **50** B7
Palma Cl LU6 . . . . **113** F3

Palmer Cl SG17. . . . . **77** C3
Palmerston St MK41. . . . . . . **38** B2
Palmerston Way SG5. . . . . . . **90** C2
Parade The
1 Dunstable LU6 . . . . **114** A1
Letchworth SG6. . . . . **90** F1
Luton LU3 . . . . **115** C7
Paradine Rd MK42 . . . . **50** D6
Parish Cl MK41. . . . . **39** B4
Park Ave
Bedford MK40 . . . . **38** C2
Houghton Regis LU5 . . . . **114** C5
Luton LU2 . . . . **115** C7
Totternhoe LU6 . . . . **120** B8
Park Ave N AL5. . . . . **130** F1
Park Ave S AL5. . . . . **130** F1
Park Cl
Markyate AL3 . . . . **128** D5
Moggerhanger MK44. . . . . **53** B6
Park Cres MK41. . . . . **61** C1
Park Ct
Luton LU2 . . . . **116** D1
Sandy SG19 . . . . **54** C3
PARK END. **36** D7
Parker Cl
Letchworth SG6. . . . . **101** E4
St Neots PE19 . . . . **22** E2
Parkers La SG17. . . . . **77** C2
Park Farm LU7 . . . . **105** B2
Park Farm Cl SG16. . . . . **78** D2
Park Farm Ct MK41 . . . . **37** F6
Parkfield AL3 . . . . **128** D5
Parkfields Mid Sch LU5 . . **105** F7
Park Hill
Ampthill MK45. . . . . **73** E1
Harpenden AL5 . . . . **130** F2
Toddington LU5 . . . . **105** F7
Park La
Blunham MK44 . . . . **41** E3
Eaton Bray LU6 . . . . **119** D6
Gamlingay SG19 . . . . **44** C5
Henlow SG16. . . . . **78** D1
Kimbolton MK44, PE19 . . . . . . **6** F7
Sharnbrook MK44 . . . . **16** E5
Parkland MK43 . . . . **26** D3
Parkland Dr LU1 . . . . **123** D5
Parklands MK41 . . . . **38** F2
Park Lane Cres SG16. . . . . . . **78** D2
Park Leys LU5 . . . . **95** F1
Parkmead SG17 . . . . **77** C2
Park Meadow Cl MK45 . . . . . **97** B3
Park Mews
Leighton Buzzard LU7 . . . . . **111** A6
Sandy SG19 . . . . **54** C7
Park Mount AL5 . . . . **130** F3
Park Palings Wlk MK43 . . . . **75** F8
Park Rd
Dunstable LU5 . . . . **121** C7
Kempston MK42 . . . . **49** F5
Melchbourne MK44 . . . . **10** D3
Moggerhanger MK44. . . . . **53** B6
Roxton MK44 . . . . **31** E2
Sandy SG19 . . . . **54** C7
Stevenston MK43 . . . . **22** F7
St Neots PE19 . . . . **22** F7
Toddington LU5 . . . . **105** F7
Westoning MK45 . . . . **95** E5
Wilstead MK45 . . . . **62** E2
Park Rd N
Bedford MK41 . . . . **38** B2
Houghton Regis LU5 . . . . **114** D4
Park Rd W MK41. . . . . **38** B2
Park Rise AL5 . . . . **130** E3
Park Rise Cl AL5 . . . . **130** E3
Park St W LU1. . . . . **123** E7
PARKSIDE. **114** D5
Parkside
Gravenhurst MK45 . . . . **87** B4
Milton Ernest MK44. . . . . **27** B5
Parkside Cl LU5 . . . . **114** D6
Parkside Dr LU5 . . . . **114** D6
Parkside Flats LU6. . . . . . . **121** C8
Park Sq LU1 . . . . **123** E7
Park St
Ampthill MK45. . . . . **73** E1
Dunstable LU6 . . . . **114** A1
Luton LU1 . . . . **123** E7
Woburn MK17 . . . . **93** A7
Parkstone Ct MK41. . . . . **38** E6
Park Terr 2 LU1 . . . . **123** F6
PARK TOWN. **123** F6
Park Viaduct LU1 . . . . **123** F6
Park View MK44 . . . . **41** D3
Park View Cl LU3 . . . . **115** D6
Park View Ct
Leighton Buzzard LU7 . . . . . **110** E7
St Neots PE19 . . . . **22** D5
Park View Dr AL3 . . . . **128** D6
Parkview La LU7 . . . . **105** C2
Parkway
Houghton Regis LU5 . . . . **114** E6
Woburn Sands MK17 . . . . **81** A6
Park Way PE19 . . . . **22** F7
Parkway Rd LU1 . . . . **116** B5
Parmiter Way MK45 . . . . **84** D7
Parrish Cl MK42 . . . . **72** D8
Parrot Cl LU1. . . . . **123** D5
Parsonage Cl MK43 . . . . **37** A7
Parson's Cl AL3. . . . . **129** B1
Parsons Rd NN29 . . . . **7** B8
Partridge Cl LU4 . . . . **115** A5
Partridge La MK43 . . . . **36** D1
Partridge Piece
Cranfield MK43 . . . . **59** C3
Sandy SG19 . . . . **42** B2
Parys Rd LU3 . . . . **116** B6

Pascomb Rd LU6 . . . . **120** F8
Pashley Cl PE19 . . . . **22** E2
Pasture La SG4 . . . . **125** E8
Pasture Rd SG6. . . . . **101** C3
Pastures Ct LU4 . . . . **115** A3
Pastures The
Edlesborough LU6 . . . . **119** F3
Lower Stondon SG16. . . . . **88** E3
Stewartby MK43 . . . . **61** C1
Upper Caldecote SG18 . . . . . . **66** C8
Pastures Way LU4 . . . . **115** A3
Pathway The MK45 . . . . **74** B1
Patterdale LU6 . . . . **121** B7
Patteshull Ct MK40. . . . . **50** B8
Paula Radcliffe Way MK41,
MK43 . . . . **37** C5
Paulsons Cl MK44. . . . . **11** C3
Paul Waller Ave MK42. . . . . **51** B3
PAVENHAM. **26** B4
Pavenham Rd
Felmersham MK43 . . . . **26** C7
Pavenham MK43 . . . . **26** F3
Sharnbrook MK43 . . . . **25** D4
Pax Hill MK41 . . . . **38** E4
Payne Rd MK43 . . . . **60** F7
Paynes Ct SG6 . . . . **91** A1
Peach Cl LU1. . . . . **123** F6
Peach's Cl MK43. . . . . **25** A6
Peacock Mews 6 LU7 . . . . **111** A7
Peacock Rd MK42 . . . . **36** E2
Peakes End MK45 . . . . **84** A3
Pearcey Rd MK42 . . . . **50** C5
Pearmain Cl MK41 . . . . **38** F1
Pearson Cl PE19 . . . . **22** E2
Peartree Cl
Shefford SG17 . . . . **77** C2
Stevenage SG1 . . . . **105** E5
Pear Tree Cl
Bromham MK43 . . . . **36** D1
Lower Stondon SG16. . . . . **89** B3
Peartree Rd LU7 . . . . **111** A8
Pear Tree Rd MK44 . . . . **117** C4
Pear Tree View MK45 . . . . . . **50** C2
Peashill La MK44 . . . . **40** F6
Pebblemoor LU6 . . . . **119** F3
Pebbles The SG7. . . . . **91** C4
Peck Ct MK43 . . . . **97** B4
Peckworth Ind Est SG16. . . **89** A4
Peddars La LU2 . . . . **112** D4
Pedley Hill HP4, LU6 . . . . . **127** C1
Pedley La SG17. . . . . **77** F3
Peel Pl 7 LU1 . . . . **123** D7
Peel's Pl SG19 . . . . **54** D7
Peel St
7 Bedford MK40 . . . . **38** B1
Houghton Regis LU5 . . . . **114** B5
Luton LU1 . . . . **123** D7
Peer Rd PE19 . . . . **22** B4
Peers Dr MK17 . . . . **81** E3
Pegasus Ct SG18. . . . . **66** F7
Pegasus Dr SG18 . . . . **67** D3
Pegasus Mews SG18 . . . . **67** D3
PEGSDON. **99** D1
Pegsdon Cl LU3 . . . . **116** B7
Pegsdon Way SG5 . . . . **98** E1
Pelican Way SG6 . . . . **90** F1
Pemberley Ave MK40. . . . . . . **38** C2
Pemberley La MK40. . . . . **38** C1
Pembroke Ave
Luton LU4 . . . . **115** F3
St Neots PE19 . . . . **22** F2
Pembroke Cl MK43. . . . . **72** D8
Pembroke Rd MK45 . . . . **74** B7
Pembroke St MK40 . . . . **50** D8
Penda Cl LU3. . . . . **115** F7
Pendennis Rd MK41. . . . . **39** A4
Penfold Cl SG17 . . . . **77** A2
Penhill LU3 . . . . **115** E6
Penhill Cl LU3 . . . . **115** E6
Penley Cl MK41 . . . . **38** F1
Penley Way LU7 . . . . **111** A5
Pennine Rd MK41. . . . . **38** E3
Pennine Rise MK45 . . . . **84** D2
Pennivale Cl LU7 . . . . **111** A8
Pennyfarthers Cl MK45 . . . . **86** B8
Penrith Ave LU6 . . . . **121** B7
Penrwyn Ct PE19 . . . . **22** F1
Penshurst Cl AL5 . . . . **130** D4
Pentelowes The PE28 . . . . . . **2** D2
Pentland Cl LU3 . . . . **54** B8
Pentland Rise MK45 . . . . **38** E3
Penwright Cl MK42 . . . . **49** D5
Peppercorns La PE19 . . . . . . **22** C2
PEPPERSTOCK. **123** C1
Pepys End LU6 . . . . **127** C7
Percheron Dr LU4 . . . . **115** A3
Percival Way LU2 . . . . **124** C7
Peregrine Rd LU4. . . . . **115** A4
Periwinkle La
Dunstable LU5. . . . . **121** C7
Hitchin SG5 . . . . **100** F1
Periwinkle Rd LU6 . . . . **121** C7
Perkins Rd MK41. . . . . **39** C2
Perring Cl MK44 . . . . **14** A1
PERRY GREEN. **124** C3
Perrymead LU2 . . . . **117** F2
Perry Mead LU6 . . . . **119** E6
Pershore Rd MK41. . . . . **38** E3
PERTENHALL. **12** C8
Pertenhall Rd MK44. . . . . **12** B4
Petersfield Gdns LU3 . . . . . **107** E1
PETERS GREEN. **125** C3
Petley Cl MK45 . . . . **84** E1

Petteril Wlk MK41 . . . . .38 C7
Petunia Ct LU3 . . . . 116 C1
Pevensey Cl LU2 . . . . .117 D4
Pevensey Gr MK45 . . . . .84 C1
Pevensey Rd MK41 . . . . .39 A3
Pheasant Wlk MK45 . . . . .84 D2
Philip Gdns PE19 . . . . .22 F2
Philip Larkin Ho MK40 . . . . . . .50 A8
Phillips Mdws MK44 . . . . .4 A3
Phillpotts Ave MK40 . . . . .38 E1
Phipps Cl MK45 . . . . .62 F3
Phoenix Cl LU7 . . . . 111 D8
Phoenix Sq PE19 . . . . .22 E6
Pickering Cl SG19 . . . . .54 C8
Pickford Hill AL3 . . . . 131 C3
Pickford Rd AL3 . . . . 128 C3
Pie Cnr AL3 . . . . 129 B1
Pie Gdn AL3 . . . . 129 C1
Pietley Hill AL3 . . . . 129 A1
Pigeonwick AL3 . . . . 131 B3
Piggottshill La AL5 . . . . 131 E1
Piggotts La LU4 . . . . 115 D4
Pilcroft St MK42 . . . . .50 C7
Pilgrim Ctr MK41 . . . . .38 D3
Pilgrims Cl
  Bedford MK45 . . . . .50 C4
  Flitwick MK45 . . . . .84 E3
  Harlington LU5 . . . . .95 F1
Pilgrims Pre-Prep Sch
  MK41 . . . . .38 C3
Pilgrims Way MK42 . . . . .50 C4
Pillinge Rd MK43 . . . . .61 C1
Pinchmill Cl MK44 . . . . .16 C3
Pinchmill Lower Sch
  MK43 . . . . .26 C8
Pinchmill Way MK44 . . . . .16 C3
Pine Cl
  Biggleswade SG18 . . . . .67 A7
  Irchester NN29 . . . . .7 A7
  Leighton Buzzard LU7 . . . . . 103 A2
  Rushden NN10 . . . . .8 A8
Pine Crest Mews LU7 . . . . 110 E6
Pine Gr MK17 . . . . .81 A4
Pinemead SG17 . . . . .77 E2
Pines The
  Ampthill MK45 . . . . .84 E8
  Kempston MK42 . . . . .49 F3
Pine View Pk MK45 . . . . .86 B7
Pinewood Cl LU3 . . . . 107 C1
PINFOLDPOND 92 E6
Pinford Dell **4** LU2 . . . . .117 D1
Pinkle Hill Rd LU7 . . . . 103 A5
Pinsent Ave MK43 . . . . .36 E1
Pioneer Pk MK42 . . . . .50 B5
Pipers Croft LU6 . . . . .120 F7
Pipers Hill LU2 . . . . .52 A8
Pipers La AL3, LU1 . . . . .122 F1
Pipit Cl MK45 . . . . .84 E2
Pipit Gr SG19 . . . . .42 B2
Pipit Rise MK41 . . . . .38 D4
PIRTON 99 E4
Pirton Hill Inf Sch LU4 . . . . . . .115 B6
Pirton Hill Jun Sch LU4 . . . . . .115 B6
Pirton Rd
  Holwell SG5 . . . . 100 A7
  Luton LU4 . . . . 115 D5
Pirton Sch SG5 . . . . .99 D4
Pitsdean Rd PE19 . . . . .33 F3
Pitsford Terr LU2 . . . . 117 A1
Pix Ct SG15 . . . . .90 A8
Pixmore Way SG6 . . . . 101 F5
Pix Rd SG5 . . . . .90 C5
Place Theatre The MK40 . . . . . .38 E1
Plaiters Cl MK43 . . . . .26 B3
Plaiters Way LU5 . . . . 114 A5
Planes The MK42 . . . . .49 E3
Plane Tree Cl SG19 . . . . .44 C6
Plantation Rd
  Leighton Buzzard LU7 . . . . . 102 F3
  Luton LU3 . . . . 115 D7
Platt Cl LU4 . . . . 115 D4
Platz Ho LU5 . . . . 114 D5
Playfield Cl SG18 . . . . .67 B5
Playford Sq LU4 . . . . 115 D5
Pleasance The AL5 . . . . 130 D4
Pleasant Pl SG19 . . . . .54 C7
Plewes Cl LU6 . . . . 127 E8
Plough Cl
  Cranfield MK43 . . . . .71 A8
  Luton LU4 . . . . 114 E4
Plough Ct LU4 . . . . 114 E4
Ploversfield SG19 . . . . .42 B2
Plover Way MK41 . . . . .38 B4
Plummer Haven LU7 . . . . 103 A1
Plummers La
  Haynes MK45 . . . . .75 F8
  Peters Green LU2 . . . . 125 C2
Plumpton Cl LU2 . . . . 117 A8
Plum Tree La LU7 . . . . 111 A8
Plum Tree Rd SG16 . . . . .89 B2
Plymouth Cl LU2 . . . . 117 B1
PODINGTON 7 E1
Podington Prim Sch NN29 . . . . .7 E1
Podington Rd NN10 . . . . .8 A4
Poets Ct AL5 . . . . 131 B1
Poets Gn LU4 . . . . 115 A2
Pokas Cotts NN9 . . . . .3 C8
Polam Sch MK40 . . . . .38 A1
Polegate LU7 . . . . 117 D2
Polhill Ave MK40, MK41 . . . . . .38 E2
Pollards Cl MK45 . . . . .62 E3
Pollards Way
  Lower Stondon SG16 . . . . . . .89 A3
  Pirton SG5 . . . . .99 D4
Polo Field Way MK42 . . . . .50 A2
Polzeath Cl LU2 . . . . 124 C8
Pomeroy Gr LU2 . . . . .116 E6
Pomfret Ave LU2 . . . . 116 F1

Pond Cl LU4 . . . . .115 B5
Pondwick Rd MK45 . . . . .130 E2
Pondwicks Rd LU1 . . . . .123 F7
Pope Cl MK45 . . . . .84 E1
Pope Rd PE19 . . . . .22 E4
Popes Ct LU2 . . . . 116 D1
Popes Way MK45 . . . . .60 E7
Popham Cl PE19 . . . . .22 A3
Poplar Ave
  Bedford MK41 . . . . .38 E4
  Luton LU3 . . . . 116 C8
  Wilstead MK45 . . . . .62 F2
Poplar Cl
  Biggleswade SG18 . . . . .67 A8
  Irchester NN29 . . . . .7 A7
  Leighton Buzzard LU7 . . . . . 103 A2
  Roxton MK44 . . . . .31 E1
  Rushden NN10 . . . . .8 A8
  Silsoe MK45 . . . . .86 C4
Poplar Dr SG5 . . . . .90 F7
Poplar Gr SG19 . . . . .54 B7
Poplar Rd MK45 . . . . .127 E8
Poplars Cl LU6 . . . . .117 B3
Poplars The
  Ampthill MK45 . . . . .84 F8
  Arlesey SG15 . . . . .90 A8
  Ickleford SG5 . . . . 100 F5
Poppy Cl NN10 . . . . .8 C4
Poppy Field SG18 . . . . .67 C5
Poppyfields MK41 . . . . .39 C4
Porlock Dr LU2 . . . . .117 C1
Porters Hill AL5 . . . . 131 C4
Portland Cl
  Bedford MK41 . . . . .39 A2
  Houghton Regis LU5 . . . . . . 114 B4
Portland Ct LU4 . . . . 116 A1
Portland Ind Est SG15 . . . . . . .90 A3
Portland Rd LU4 . . . . 116 A1
Portland Ride LU5 . . . . 114 B2
Portman Cl SG5 . . . . 100 D2
Portnall Pl MK43 . . . . .59 B1
Portobello Cl MK45 . . . . .97 C2
Porz Ave LU5 . . . . 114 D3
Postley Rd MK42 . . . . .49 E2
POTSGROVE 81 B8
Potten End Hill HP1 . . . . 132 F1
Potters Cross MK43 . . . . .61 A8
POTTER'S END 94 A5
Potter Way MK42 . . . . .50 C4
Pottery Cl LU3 . . . . .115 F7
POTTON 56 B7
Potton Lower Sch SG19 . . . . . .55 F7
Potton Rd
  Biggleswade SG18 . . . . .67 A7
  Biggleswade SG18 . . . . .67 B8
  Everton SG19 . . . . .43 D7
  Gamlingay Great Heath
    SG19 . . . . .43 F3
  Gamlingay SG19 . . . . .44 D3
  Guilden Morden SG8 . . . . . . .69 F6
  Sandy SG19 . . . . .55 B6
  St Neots PE19 . . . . .22 F2
  Wrestlingworth SG19 . . . . . . .57 B8
Poulter Cl **6** MK40 . . . . .50 B8
Pound Cl
  Blunham MK44 . . . . .41 E4
  Langford SG18 . . . . .78 F7
  Upper Caldecote SG18 . . . . . .54 B8
Pound Gn SG18 . . . . .69 F5
Pound La
  Kimbolton PE28 . . . . .6 F4
  North Crawley MK16 . . . . . . .58 B7
Pounds Cl MK43 . . . . .59 B1
Pound The MK45 . . . . .95 E6
Powells Rd LU7 . . . . .77 C3
Power Ct LU1 . . . . .123 F7
Powers Cl SG19 . . . . .42 B1
Powis Mews MK45 . . . . .84 D1
Powis Pl LU4 . . . . 116 A2
Powis Rd MK41 . . . . .39 B4
Poynters Rd LU4 . . . . 114 E3
Prebendal Dr LU2 . . . . 123 B2
Prebend St MK40 . . . . .50 B7
Prentice Gdns MK42 . . . . .49 F6
Prentice Way LU2 . . . . 124 D7
Presentation Cl LU5 . . . . 114 B4
Preserview Wlk MK41 . . . . .37 E5
President Way LU2 . . . . 124 D8
Preslent Cl SG5 . . . . .87 F1
Preston Cl MK45 . . . . .84 E8
Preston Gdns LU2 . . . . 116 F2
Preston Path LU2 . . . . 116 F2
Preston Rd
  Bedford MK40 . . . . .49 B8
  Toddington LU5 . . . . 106 A5
Prestwick Cl LU2 . . . . 116 E5
Prestwick Rd MK40 . . . . .49 B8
Priestleys LU2 . . . . 123 A7
Primary Way SG15 . . . . .90 A4
Primrose Cl
  Arlesey SG15 . . . . .90 A4
  Biggleswade SG18 . . . . .67 C4
  Flitwick MK45 . . . . .84 D2
  Marston Moretaine MK43 . . .72 C7
Primrose Ct LU6 . . . . .121 A8
Primrose La LU5 . . . . 114 B4
Prince Andrew Dr SG5 . . . . . . .91 A6
Prince Charles Ave SG5 . . . . . .91 A6
Prince Ct PE19 . . . . .22 B5
Prince Edward Way SG5 . . . . . .91 A6
Prince Harry Cl SG5 . . . . .91 A6
Prince Philip Ave MK43 . . . . . . .58 C2
Princes Cl
  Dunstable LU5 . . . . 114 C1
  Leighton Buzzard LU7 . . . . . 110 F4
Princes Pl **16** LU2 . . . . 116 D1
Princes Rd MK45 . . . . .36 E1
Princess Cl MK43 . . . . .84 F2

Princess St
  Clapham MK41 . . . . .37 D6
  Luton LU1 . . . . 123 D7
Princes St
  8 Bedford MK40 . . . . .38 B1
  Dunstable LU6 . . . . 121 A8
  Toddington LU5 . . . . 106 A5
Prince's St SG5 . . . . .90 F7
Prince Way LU2 . . . . .124 D8
Prinknash Rd MK41 . . . . .38 E5
Printers Ct MK45 . . . . .73 F1
Printers Way LU6 . . . . 114 B1
Prior Ct MK41 . . . . .37 C6
Priors Cl NN10 . . . . .7 F8
Priors Hill SG5 . . . . .99 C4
Priory Bsns Pk MK44 . . . . .51 C6
Priory Cl
  Harrold MK43 . . . . .25 A6
  Turvey MK43 . . . . .35 B5
Priory Ct
  1 Bedford MK40 . . . . .38 B1
  Dunstable LU5 . . . . 121 C8
Priory Ctry Pk * MK41 . . . . . . .51 A7
Priory Gate SG17 . . . . .77 A2
Priory Gdns LU2 . . . . 116 D4
Priory Lower Sch MK40 . . . . . .50 A8
Priory Mall **2** PE19 . . . . .22 C6
Priory Mews PE19 . . . . .22 C6
Priory Mid Sch LU3 . . . . 116 C6
Priory Orch AL3 . . . . .129 B2
Priory Park Inf Sch PE19 . . . . .22 F6
Priory Rd
  Campton SG17 . . . . .76 F1
  Dunstable LU5 . . . . 121 C8
  St Neots PE19 . . . . .22 F6
Priory Sch The SG5 . . . . 100 C2
Priory The MK42 . . . . .22 E5
Priory Terr **4** MK40 . . . . .50 B8
Proctor Cl MK40 . . . . .49 D5
Proctor Way LU2 . . . . 124 C7
Progress Pk MK42 . . . . .50 A2
Progress Way
  Elstow MK42 . . . . .50 B4
  Luton LU4 . . . . 115 B7
Prospect Ave LU2 . . . . .7 A7
Prospect Rd SG18 . . . . .78 F6
Prospect Row **3** MK42 . . . . . .50 B7
Prospect Way LU2 . . . . 124 C7
Provost Way LU2 . . . . 124 C8
Prudden Cl MK40 . . . . .49 C8
Prudence Cl LU5 . . . . .95 F1
Puddephat's La AL3 . . . . 128 C1
Pulford Rd LU7 . . . . 110 F6
Pulford's CE Lower Sch
  LU7 . . . . .111 A6
Pulloxhill Rd MK45 . . . . .85 D2
Pulloxhill Lower Sch
  MK45 . . . . .96 B8
Pulloxhill Rd MK45 . . . . .85 D2
Purbeck Cl MK45 . . . . .39 A2
Purcell Rd LU4 . . . . 114 F3
Purcell Way LU7 . . . . .77 C3
Purley Ctr LU3 . . . . .116 E7
Purway Cl LU3 . . . . 115 E7
Purwell Wlk LU7 . . . . 103 B3
PUTNOE 38 E5
Putnoe Hts MK41 . . . . .38 F4
Putnoe La MK41 . . . . .38 E4
Putnoe Lower Sch MK41 . . . . . .39 A4
Putnoe St MK41 . . . . .39 A4
Putteridge High Sch
  LU2 . . . . .117 C5
Putteridge Jun & Inf Sch
  LU2 . . . . .117 C5
Putteridge Par LU2 . . . . .117 B4
Putteridge Rd LU2 . . . . 117 C5
Putteridge Recn Ctr LU2 . . . . .117 C5
Putterills The AL5 . . . . 131 A1
Pyghtle Cl LU1 . . . . .123 A7
Pyghtle The
  Luton LU1 . . . . 123 A7
  Turvey MK43 . . . . .34 D1
  Westoning MK45 . . . . .95 E5
Pyms Cl MK44 . . . . .40 F5
Pym's Way SG19 . . . . .42 B1
Pynders La LU2 . . . . 114 E2
Pytchley Ct LU2 . . . . 116 E5

Q

Quadrant The
  Houghton Regis LU5 . . . . . . 114 C5
  Letchworth SG6 . . . . 101 F6
Quantock Cl
  Bedford MK41 . . . . .38 E2
  Luton LU3 . . . . 116 B8
Quantock Rise LU3 . . . . .108 B1
Quantocks The MK45 . . . . .84 D2
Quantrelle Cl MK42 . . . . .51 A3
Quarry Wlk LU6 . . . . 121 A7
Queen Alexandra Rd
  MK41 . . . . .39 A1
Queen Anne's Cl SG5 . . . . .90 F5
Queen Elizabeth Cl SG17 . . . . .77 D2
Queensbury Cl MK40 . . . . .49 F8
Queensbury Upper Sch
  LU6 . . . . .121 B7
Queens Cl
  Flitwick MK45 . . . . .84 F2
  4 Luton LU1 . . . . .123 E6
  Northill SG18 . . . . .53 E1
  Oakley MK43 . . . . .36 F8
Queen's Cl MK41 . . . . .37 D1
Queens Cres MK41 . . . . .37 D7

Queen's Cres MK41 . . . . .38 F3
Queens Ct
  Dunstable LU5 . . . . 114 C1
  14 Luton LU2 . . . . 116 D1
  Shefford SG17 . . . . .77 D2
  St Neots PE19 . . . . .22 B3
Queen's Ct MK41 . . . . .38 B1
Queen's Dr MK43 . . . . .38 F3
Queens Gdns PE19 . . . . .22 B4
QUEEN'S PARK 49 F8
Queens Park Lower Sch
  MK40 . . . . .49 F8
Queensmead
  Dunstable LU5 . . . . 114 B1
  St Neots PE19 . . . . .22 F7
Queensway
Queen's Way SG18 . . . . .78 F8
Quenby Way MK43 . . . . .36 F1
Queenswood Dr SG4 . . . . 101 C1
Quickswood LU3 . . . . 116 A7
Quilter Cl LU3 . . . . .115 F4

R

Raban Ct SG7 . . . . .91 F1
Race Meadows Way MK42 . . . .49 F2
Rackman Dr LU3 . . . . 116 C5
Radburn Ct LU6 . . . . 114 A1
Radnor Rd LU4 . . . . 114 F4
Radnor Wlk MK41 . . . . .39 B3
Radstone Pl LU2 . . . . 117 E1
RADWELL 26 E8
SG7 .91 C4
Radwell La SG7 . . . . .91 C4
Radwell Rd
  Felmersham MK43 . . . . .26 D8
  Milton Ernest MK43, MK44 . .26 F6
Raglan Ct LU4 . . . . .114 F3
Raglan Gn MK42 . . . . .39 A4
Railton Rd MK42 . . . . .49 D1
Railway Cotts
  Kempston Hardwick MK43 . . .61 F4
  Oakley MK43 . . . . .37 A8
Railway View **1** SG18 . . . . . .67 A6
Rainbow Special Sch
  MK43 . . . . .36 D3
Raleigh Cl PE19 . . . . .22 A2
Raleigh Gr LU4 . . . . 115 D1
Raleigh St MK40 . . . . .49 F7
Rally The SG15 . . . . .90 A7
Ramerick Gdns SG15 . . . . .90 A2
Ramillies Cl MK42 . . . . .49 F5
Ramridge Prim Sch LU2 . . . . .117 B2
Ramridge Rd LU2 . . . . .117 A2
Ramsay Cl MK41 . . . . .38 B3
Ramsey Cl
  Kempston MK42 . . . . .49 D2
  Luton LU4 . . . . 114 F3
Ramsey Ct LU4 . . . . 114 F3
Ramsey Manor Lower Sch
  MK43 . . . . .97 D2
Ramsey Rd MK45 . . . . .97 C3
Ram Yd MK40 . . . . .50 C8
Randall Dr LU5 . . . . 105 F5
Randalls Cl MK43 . . . . .36 F2
Rand's Cl SG5 . . . . 100 B7
Rand's Cotts SG5 . . . . 100 B7
Rand's Mdw SG5 . . . . 100 B7
Rannock Gdns LU7 . . . . 110 C7
Ranock Cl LU5 . . . . 115 D8
Ranworth Wlk MK40 . . . . .49 D7
Rapper Ct LU3 . . . . .16 C8
Raunds Rd NN9 . . . . .3 C8
Ravenbank Rd LU2 . . . . 117 C5
Ravenhill Way LU4 . . . . 115 B4
Ravensburgh Cl MK45 . . . . . . .97 B3
Ravenscourt LU6 . . . . 113 F3
RAVENSDEN 29 B1
Ravensden CE Lower Sch
  MK44 . . . . .29 B1
Ravensden Rd
  Renhold MK41 . . . . .39 B7
  Wilden MK44 . . . . .29 D3
Ravensthorpe LU2 . . . . 117 B4
Raven Wlk MK45 . . . . .84 E2
Raymond Cotts SG5 . . . . 100 E4
Raynham Way LU2 . . . . 117 D1
Raynsford Lower Sch
  SG16 . . . . .78 D1
Ray's Cl MK43 . . . . .50 C7
Reach Gn LU7 . . . . 103 A6
Reach La LU7 . . . . 103 B5
Readers Cl LU6 . . . . 114 B2
Readshill MK45 . . . . .86 C8
Ream Cl PE19 . . . . .22 E2
Reaper Cl LU4 . . . . 114 E4
Recreation Rd LU5 . . . . 114 C6
Recreation Rise MK45 . . . . . . .87 C4
Rectory Cl
  Carlton MK43 . . . . .25 A4
  Clifton SG17 . . . . .78 B3
  Slapton LU7 . . . . 118 D6
Rectory Ct SG19 . . . . .54 D7
Rectory Farm Bsns Pk
  SG16 . . . . .88 D4
Rectory La
  Ampthill MK45 . . . . .73 F1
  Cranfield MK43 . . . . .71 B8

Rectory La continued
  Houghton Conquest MK45 . . .74 A7
  Lilley LU2 . . . . 109 D2
Rectory Rd
  Campton SG17 . . . . .76 F1
  Meppershall SG17 . . . . .88 B5
  Steppingley MK45 . . . . .83 F3
Redbourne Upper Sch & Com
  Coll MK45 . . . . .84 E6
Red Cedar Rd MK43 . . . . .36 C4
Reddall Cl MK42 . . . . .50 F5
Redding Cl NN10 . . . . .8 A7
Reddings La AL3 . . . . 129 F1
Rede Cl MK41 . . . . .38 C6
Redferns Cl LU1 . . . . 123 A6
Redferns Ct LU1 . . . . 123 A6
Redfield Cl LU4 . . . . 116 A1
Redgrave Gdns LU3 . . . . 115 F7
Redhill Rd SG5 . . . . 100 D1
Redhoods Way E SG6 . . . . . . 101 E7
Redhoods Way W SG6 . . . . . . 101 E7
Red Lion Ct MK43 . . . . .59 B1
Redman Gdns SG18 . . . . .67 A7
Redmire Cl LU4 . . . . 115 A6
Red Oak Cl MK43 . . . . .36 C4
Redoubt Cl SG4 . . . . 101 A1
Red Rails LU1 . . . . 123 C5
Red Rails Ct LU1 . . . . 123 C5
Redwald Cl MK42 . . . . .49 E4
Redwing Cl MK41 . . . . .38 C4
Redwood Cl NN29 . . . . .7 A7
Redwood Dr LU3 . . . . 115 A3
Redwood Glade LU7 . . . . 103 A3
Redwood Gr MK42 . . . . .50 C6
Reed Pl AL5 . . . . .130 F3
Reedsdale LU2 . . . . .117 F2
Reeve Cl LU7 . . . . .111 A8
Reeves Ave LU3 . . . . 116 B4
Regency Court Park Homes
  SG16 . . . . .88 E2
Regency Ct LU6 . . . . 121 C7
Regent Cl
  Bedford MK41 . . . . .38 F4
  St Neots PE19 . . . . .22 B4
Regent Ct
  1 Bedford MK40 . . . . .38 A1
  Stotfold SG5 . . . . .90 F3
Regents Mews MK40 . . . . .49 C8
Regent St
  Dunstable LU5 . . . . 114 B1
  Leighton Buzzard LU7 . . . . . 111 B1
  Luton LU1 . . . . 123 F8
  Stotfold SG5 . . . . .90 F7
Reginald St LU2 . . . . 116 A1
Regis Rd LU4 . . . . 114 F4
Rendlesham Wlk MK41 . . . . . . .39 C3
RENHOLD 39 E6
Renhold Lower Sch MK41 . . . . .39 D6
Renhold Rd MK44 . . . . .29 E1
Renshaw Cl LU2 . . . . 117 E2
Repton Cl
  Bedford MK41 . . . . .38 F4
  Luton LU3 . . . . 115 F6
Repton Rd SG17 . . . . .78 B2
Reston Path LU2 . . . . 117 E2
Restormel MK41 . . . . .38 F5
Retreat The LU5 . . . . 114 F1
Reynes Cl MK43 . . . . .72 C7
Reynes Dr MK43 . . . . .37 A8
Reynolds Cl
  Bedford MK41 . . . . .38 A2
  Biggleswade SG18 . . . . .67 A7
  Wharley End MK43 . . . . .58 D1
Reynolds Ct PE19 . . . . .22 B6
Rhineland Way MK41 . . . . .38 D6
Ribble Way MK41 . . . . .38 C6
Ribocon Way LU4 . . . . 115 B7
Richards Cl LU1 . . . . 123 B6
Richard's Cres SG18 . . . . .65 A4
Richards Ct LU1 . . . . 123 B5
Richard St LU5 . . . . 121 C8
Richbell Ct MK40 . . . . .38 B1
Richmond Ct PE19 . . . . .22 F1
Richmond Ct LU2 . . . . 116 F1
Richmond Ct LU2 . . . . 116 F1
Richmond Hill Sch LU2 . . . . . . 116 E2
Richmond Rd
  Bedford MK41 . . . . .38 D1
  Leighton Buzzard LU7 . . . . . 111 C6
  Westoning MK45 . . . . .95 E6
Rickyard Cl LU2 . . . . 117 D1
Rickyard The SG6 . . . . .91 C1
Riddy La LU3 . . . . 116 C5
Ride The LU6 . . . . 120 B6
Ridge Ave AL5 . . . . 130 E4
Ridgebridge Way LU7 . . . . . . .110 F6
Ridge Cl LU2 . . . . 117 D1
Ridgeley Dr LU7 . . . . 111 C5
Ridge Rd MK42 . . . . .49 B2
Ridgeway
  Harpenden AL5 . . . . 130 E4
  Kensworth LU6 . . . . 127 E8
  St Neots PE19 . . . . .22 F3
Ridgeway Ave LU3 . . . . 108 B2
Ridge Way SG19 . . . . .53 E8
Ridgeway Bsns Pk The
  SG16 . . . . .88 E2
Ridgeway Sch MK42 . . . . .49 C2
Ridgeway The
  Bedford MK41 . . . . .39 A4
  Blunham MK44 . . . . .53 E8
  Flitwick MK45 . . . . .84 E4
  Potton SG19 . . . . .56 A7
Ridgewood Dr AL5 . . . . 130 E4
Ridgewood Gdns AL5 . . . . 130 E4
RIDGMONT 82 E5

Ridgmont Lower Sch
MK43 . . . . .82 F4
Ridgmont Rd MK43 . . . . .82 D4
Ridgmont Sta MK43 . . . . .82 C7
Ridgmount St MK42 . . . . .50 B6
Ridgway MK17 . . . . .81 B6
Ridgway Rd
Brogborough MK43 . . . . . . .71 C1
Luton LU2 . . . . .116 F1
Ridings The
Luton LU3 . . . . 116 C1
Markyate AL3 . . . . .128 E6
Riglen Cl MK40 . . . . .72 C3
Ringmer Ct LU2 . . . . .117 C3
RINGSHALL 126 B1
Ringshall Rd HP4 . . . . .126 B3
Ringwood Cl MK42 . . . . .49 F4
Ringwood Rd LU2 . . . . .116 D7
Ripley Rd LU4 . . . . .115 C1
Ripon Cl MK42 . . . . .49 E6
Ripon Ct SG18 . . . . .67 A4
Risborough Ct MK41 . . . . . . .38 F1
Risborough Rd MK41 . . . . . . .38 F1
RISELEY 11 A2
Riseley CE Lower Sch
MK44 . . . . .10 F2
Riseley Rd MK44 . . . . .12 A3
Risings The MK41 . . . . .39 A3
Rival Houses MK45 . . . . .97 C4
Riverbanks Cl AL5 . . . . .131 C4
River Ct SG5 . . . . .100 F4
Riverford Dr MK41 . . . . .39 B1
Riverford Cl AL5 . . . . .131 B4
Riverhead Gdns SG19 . . . . . .54 B6
River Hill AL3 . . . . .129 B2
River La MK44 . . . . .27 B4
River Mead SG5 . . . . .100 C2
Rivermead Ct SG18 . . . . .78 E5
River Rd PE19 . . . . .22 C4
River Row MK43 . . . . .26 B3
Riverside
Leighton Buzzard LU7 . . . . 111 A8
Shefford SG17 . . . . .77 C3
Riverside Cl MK42 . . . . .50 A6
Riverside Est AL5 . . . . .131 C4
Riverside Gdns SG18 . . . . . . .78 E5
Riverside Rd LU3 . . . . .116 A5
Riverside View MK44 . . . . . . .27 A5
Riversmead PE19 . . . . .22 E6
River St MK40 . . . . .50 B8
River Terr
St Neots, Eynesbury PE19 . . .22 E4
St Neots PE19 . . . . .22 E5
Riverview Way MK42 . . . . . . .49 C4
River Way LU3 . . . . .115 E5
Robert Allen Ct LU1 . . . . . . .123 E6
Robert Bloomfield Mid Sch
SG17 . . . . .77 B2
Robert Bruce Mid Sch
MK42 . . . . .49 D4
Robert Hunt Gdns SG19 . . . .54 B7
Robert Peel Lower Sch
SG19 . . . . .54 C8
Robert Saunders Ct SG6 . . . .101 E4
Roberts Cl PE19 . . . . .22 B2
Roberts Dr MK43 . . . . .60 E2
Robertson Cnr LU6 . . . . . . .120 F4
Robin Cl
Flitwick MK45 . . . . .84 E2
Sandy SG19 . . . . .42 B1
Robin Ct AL5 . . . . .131 B4
Robin Hill MK41 . . . . .38 C4
Robins Folly MK44 . . . . .28 E7
Robinson Cres LU5 . . . . .95 F2
Robinson Ct SG19 . . . . .44 D6
Robinson Pool* MK40 . . . . . .38 B2
Robinswood LU2 . . . . .116 E5
Robinswood Cl LU7 . . . . .102 F2
Rochdale Ct 8 LU3 . . . . . . .123 E6
Rochester Ct MK42 . . . . .50 C6
Rochester Mews LU7 . . . . . .110 E7
Rochford Dr LU2 . . . . .117 E2
Rockbeck Cl MK42 . . . . .49 E4
Rock Cl LU7 . . . . .110 D6
Rockingham Ct NN10 . . . . . . .8 A8
Rockingham Wlk MK41 . . . . . .39 B3
Rock La LU7 . . . . .110 D7
Rockley Ct LU7 . . . . .110 E7
Rockley Rd LU1 . . . . .123 A7
Rodean Ct MK40 . . . . .38 D2
Rodeheath LU4 . . . . .115 D3
Rodney Cl LU4 . . . . .114 F3
Roebuck Cl LU1 . . . . .123 B6
Roe Cl SG5 . . . . .90 E5
Roecroft Lower Sch SG19 . . . .90 F6
Roedean Cl LU2 . . . . .117 D3
Roe End La AL3 . . . . .128 A4
Roe Gn PE19 . . . . .22 B5
Roff Ave MK41 . . . . .38 B2
Rogate Rd LU2 . . . . .117 C5
Roise St 8 MK40 . . . . .38 B1
Roise St MK40 . . . . .38 B1
Roman Ct 2 LU5 . . . . .114 B4
Roman Gdns LU5 . . . . .114 B4
Roman Paddock MK43 . . . . . .25 A6
Roman Rd
Barton-le-C MK45 . . . . .97 D3
Luton LU4 . . . . .115 E3
Roman View SG19 . . . . .54 D6
Roman Way
Flitwick MK45 . . . . .84 F4
Irchester NN29 . . . . .7 B7
Markyate AL3 . . . . .128 E6
Romany Cl SG6 . . . . .101 C6
Romney Ct PE19 . . . . .22 C5

Romney Wlk MK41 . . . . .38 B3
Romsey Way MK42 . . . . .50 C3
Ronald Cl MK42 . . . . .49 E2
Rondini Ave LU3 . . . . .116 B3
Rookery Dr LU2 . . . . .116 E6
Rookery Rd MK44 . . . . .31 F8
Rookery The SG19 . . . . .42 C2
Rookery Wlk SG17 . . . . .78 B2
Rooksmead MK41 . . . . .91 A6
Rook Tree Cl SG5 . . . . .91 A6
Rook Tree La SG5 . . . . .91 A6
Rooktree Way MK45 . . . . .64 A1
Roosevelt Ave
Leighton Buzzard LU7 . . . . 111 B8
Shefford SG17 . . . . .77 C1
ROOTHAM'S GREEN 30 A7
Ropa Ct LU7 . . . . .110 F7
Rope Wlk MK42 . . . . .50 C7
Ropkins Cl MK45 . . . . .95 F6
Rosamond Rd MK40 . . . . .38 E1
Rosata La SG17 . . . . .76 E4
Rosebay Cl MK45 . . . . .84 D3
Rosebery Ave
Harpenden AL5 . . . . .130 F1
Leighton Buzzard LU7 . . . .110 E7
Rosebery Ct LU7 . . . . .110 E7
Roseby Way MK41 . . . . .51 A8
Rose Cotts SG15 . . . . .90 A6
Rose Ct
Eaton Bray LU6 . . . . .119 D6
Irchester NN29 . . . . .7 B8
St Neots PE19 . . . . .22 C4
Rosedale LU5 . . . . .114 E5
Rosedale Cl LU3 . . . . .115 C7
Rosedale Way MK42 . . . . .49 E4
Rose La SG6 . . . . .67 A6
Rosemary Dr MK43 . . . . .36 F2
Rosemont Cl SG6 . . . . .101 E6
Rose Wlk
Ampthill MK45 . . . . .73 E1
Houghton Regis LU5 . . . . .114 E6
Toddington LU5 . . . . .105 F5
Rose Wood Cl LU2 . . . . .116 F1
Roslyn Way LU5 . . . . .114 A5
Ross Cl LU1 . . . . .123 B6
Rossendale Wlk 1 MK41 . . . .39 B4
Rossfold Rd LU3 . . . . .115 D8
Rosslyn Cres LU3 . . . . .116 C5
Rossway LU1 . . . . .123 B1
Rothamsted Ave AL5 . . . . . .131 A1
Rothamsted Ct AL5 . . . . . . .131 A1
Rothbury Cl SG19 . . . . .42 C2
Rothbury Ct 3 MK41 . . . . . . .39 B4
Rotheram Ave LU1 . . . . .123 B5
Rother Cl MK41 . . . . .38 D5
Rother Field LU2 . . . . .117 D3
Rotherwood Cl LU6 . . . . .113 E1
Rothesay Rd LU1 . . . . .123 D7
Rothsay Gdns MK40 . . . . .38 D1
Rothsay Pl MK40 . . . . .50 D8
Rothsay Rd MK40 . . . . .38 D1
Rothschild Rd LU7 . . . . .110 E8
Rotten Row MK44 . . . . .10 F2
Roundel Dr LU7 . . . . .111 D5
Roundfield Ave AL5 . . . . . . .131 D3
ROUND GREEN 116 F2
Roundmead MK41 . . . . .39 A2
Roundwood Cl SG4 . . . . .101 C2
Roundwood Ct LU5 . . . . .130 F3
Roundwood Gdns AL5 . . . . . .130 F2
Roundwood La AL5 . . . . .130 D3
Roundwood Park Sch
AL5 . . . . .130 E2
Roundwood Pk AL5 . . . . . . .130 E3
Roundwood Prim Sch
AL5 . . . . .130 E2
Rousbury Rd MK43 . . . . .61 C1
Rowallan Dr MK41 . . . . .38 E5
Rowan Cl LU1 . . . . .123 B7
Rowan Cres
Biggleswade SG18 . . . . . . .67 B2
Letchworth SG6 . . . . .101 E7
Rowan Ct LU6 . . . . .54 B8
Rowan Gdns SG19 . . . . .44 C5
Rowans The
Kempston MK42 . . . . .49 F3
Silsoe MK45 . . . . .86 C4
Rowan Way MK43 . . . . .71 A8
Rowelfield LU2 . . . . .117 C1
Rowington Cl LU2 . . . . .117 E2
Rowlandson Way MK41 . . . . .38 C4
Rowlands The SG18 . . . . .67 C4
Rowland Way SG6 . . . . .101 F6
Rowley Furrows LU7 . . . . . .110 E8
Rowney Forest Walk*
SG17 . . . . .76 F5
Roxhill Rd MK43 . . . . .59 F3
ROXTON 31 F1
Roxton CE Lower Sch
MK44 . . . . .31 E2
Roxton Rd
Great Barford MK44 . . . . . .41 B7
Roxton MK44 . . . . .31 E4
Royal Ct PE19 . . . . .22 B4
Royal Oak Cl SG18 . . . . .67 B3
Royal Oak La SG5 . . . . .99 D4
Royal Wlk LU6 . . . . .121 C7
Royce Cl LU6 . . . . .120 F7
Royce Ct PE19 . . . . .22 D5
Royce Rd MK43 . . . . .58 D3
Roydon Cl LU4 . . . . .115 A4
Royle Gdns MK42 . . . . .50 C5
Royston Cl SG19 . . . . .56 A7
Royston Rd SG7 . . . . .91 F1
Royston St SG19 . . . . .56 A7
Rudyard Cl LU4 . . . . .115 D3
Rueley Dell Rd LU2 . . . . . . .109 D2
Ruffs Furze MK43 . . . . .36 F7

Runfold Ave LU3 . . . . .116 A5
Runham Cl LU4 . . . . .115 A4
Runley Rd LU1 . . . . .122 F7
Runnalow SG6 . . . . .101 E7
Rushall Gn LU2 . . . . .117 E2
Rushbrook Cl MK45 . . . . .73 F1
Rush Ct MK40 . . . . .38 C1
RUSHDEN 8 D8
Rushden Hospl NN10 . . . . .8 B8
Rushden Rd
Milton Ernest MK44 . . . . . .27 B5
Newton Bromswold NN10 . . . .9 C7
Wymington NN10 . . . . .8 A6
RUSHMERE 102 F4
Rushmoor Sch MK40 . . . . . . .37 F2
Rushmore Cl LU1 . . . . .122 E4
Rusper Gn LU2 . . . . .117 D3
Russel Ctr MK45 . . . . .84 E2
Russell Ave MK40 . . . . .50 E8
Russell Cl LU6 . . . . .127 E8
Russell Cres MK45 . . . . .85 D8
Russell Ct PE19 . . . . .22 F6
Russell Dr
Ampthill MK45 . . . . .84 F7
Willington MK44 . . . . .40 C1
Russell Gr AL5 . . . . .73 B2
Russell Lower Sch MK45 . . . .84 F8
Russell Rd LU5 . . . . .105 F5
Russell Rise LU1 . . . . .123 D6
Russell St
Luton LU1 . . . . .123 D6
St Neots PE19 . . . . .22 F5
Woburn Sands MK17 . . . . . .81 C4
Russell Way
Leighton Buzzard LU7 . . . . 111 D7
Wootton MK43 . . . . .60 F6
Russell Wlk SG5 . . . . .90 D3
Russet Cl
Bedford MK41 . . . . .38 C7
Stewartby MK43 . . . . .61 B1
Russett Cl MK45 . . . . .73 E1
Ruthin Cl LU1 . . . . .123 D5
Rutland Cres LU2 . . . . .124 A7
Rutland Ct LU2 . . . . .124 A7
Rutland Gdns SG19 . . . . .54 D7
Rutland Hall LU2 . . . . .124 A7
Rutland Rd MK40 . . . . .50 A8
Ryans Cl LU2 . . . . .116 C5
Rycroft Ave PE19 . . . . .22 F6
Rydal Cres SG18 . . . . .67 A4
Rydal Way LU3 . . . . .115 F5
Ryder Ave SG5 . . . . .100 D3
Ryder Way SG5 . . . . .100 D3
Rye Cl
Harpenden AL5 . . . . .131 A5
Leighton Buzzard LU7 . . . .111 D7
St Neots PE19 . . . . .8 C8
St Neots PE19 . . . . .22 F1
Rye Cres MK44 . . . . .52 A6
Ryecroft Way LU2 . . . . .117 A4
Ryefield LU3 . . . . .108 A1
Rye Hill
Harpenden AL5 . . . . .131 A4
2 Luton LU2 . . . . .116 D1
Rye The LU6 . . . . .119 C8
Rylands Heath LU2 . . . . . . .117 D2
Rylands Mews LU7 . . . . .111 A6
Rylands Rd LU7 . . . . .111 A6
Ryswick Rd MK42 . . . . .50 A5
Ryton Cl
Bedford MK41 . . . . .38 C6
Luton LU2 . . . . .123 B6

S

Sabel Cl SG18 . . . . .67 C3
Sacombe Gn LU3 . . . . .108 B1
Sacred Heart Jun & Inf Schs
LU2 . . . . .117 A3
Saddle Cl MK41 . . . . .37 C7
Saddlers Mews AL3 . . . . . . .128 E5
Sadleirs Gn MK17 . . . . .81 B5
Saffron Cl
Arlesey SG15 . . . . .90 A7
2 Luton LU2 . . . . .116 D7
Saffron Ct SG8 . . . . .67 A5
Saffron Hill SG6 . . . . .101 E6
Saffron Rd SG18 . . . . .67 A5
Saffron Rise LU6 . . . . .119 E6
St Albans Rd MK40 . . . . .38 C3
St Albans Ct MK45 . . . . .84 E4
St Albans Rd AL5 . . . . .131 B1
St Aldates Ct LU3 . . . . .108 A1
St Andrew's Ave AL5 . . . . . .130 F1
St Andrews CE Lower Sch
SG18 . . . . .66 F6
St Andrews Cl
Biggleswade SG18 . . . . . . .66 F6
Flitwick MK45 . . . . .84 E4
Leighton Buzzard LU7 . . . .111 A7
St Andrew's Cl
Ampthill MK45 . . . . .73 F1
Slip End LU1 . . . . .123 B1
St Andrews Ct SG18 . . . . .66 F6
St Andrews La
Houghton Regis LU5 . . . . .114 C5
Kimbolton PE28 . . . . .6 F4
St Andrews Mews LU1 . . . . .123 B1
St Andrews Rd MK40 . . . . . . .38 C2
St Andrew's Sch MK40 . . . . . .38 C2
St Andrew's St
Biggleswade SG18 . . . . . . .66 F6
Leighton Buzzard LU7 . . . .111 A7
St Andrew's Way SG18 . . . . . .78 F8
St Andrews Wlk LU1 . . . . . .123 B1
St Ann's Rd LU1 . . . . .123 F7

St Anselm Pl PE19 . . . . .22 E6
St Augustine Ave LU3 . . . . .116 B3
St Augustine's Rd MK40 . . . .38 D2
St Bede's RC Mid Sch
MK40 . . . . .38 A1
St Bernard's Ct LU3 . . . . . . .116 C3
St Catherines Ave LU3 . . . . .116 B3
St Christopher Sch SG6 . . . .101 F3
St Christopher's Ct LU5 . . . .114 F1
St Christopher's Lower Sch
LU5 . . . . .114 F2
St Cuthberts Ct 3 MK40 . . . .50 C8
St Cuthbert's St 1 MK40 . . . .50 C8
St David's Way LU5 . . . . . . .114 D4
St Dominics Sq LU4 . . . . . . .114 F4
St Edmond Rd MK40 . . . . . . .38 D2
St Ethelbert Ave LU3 . . . . . .116 C4
St Faiths Cl SG4 . . . . .101 B1
St Francis Coll SG6 . . . . .101 E4
St Francis Ct SG17 . . . . .77 C3
St Francis Way SG17 . . . . . . .77 C2
St George's Cl
Leighton Buzzard LU7 . . . .111 B8
Toddington LU5 . . . . .105 F6
St George's Lower Sch
LU7 . . . . .111 B8
St George's Rd MK40 . . . . . . .38 C2
St George's Sch AL5 . . . . . .131 B2
St Georges Sq 10 LU1 . . . . .123 E7
St Georges Tower SG19 . . . . .45 F3
St Gregory's RC Mid Sch
MK40 . . . . .37 E1
St Helena Rd MK42 . . . . .50 D5
St Helenas Gdn MK42 . . . . . .50 B4
St Hilda's Sch AL5 . . . . .130 F2
St Ives Cl LU3 . . . . .116 B3
St James CE Lower Sch
MK40 . . . . .37 C1
St James Cl
Houghton Regis LU5 . . . . .114 E4
Pulloxhill MK45 . . . . .96 E8
St James Rd AL5 . . . . .131 B4
St James' Rd LU3 . . . . .116 B3
St James's Ct AL5 . . . . .131 B3
St John Cl LU1 . . . . .123 B5
St John Rigby RC Lower Sch
MK41 . . . . .38 E2
St John's Cl MK42 . . . . .49 D3
St Johns Cl LU7 . . . . .112 C5
St Johns Ct LU1 . . . . .123 B5
St Johns Ctr MK42 . . . . .50 C7
St John's Homes MK42 . . . . .49 D4
St John's Rd
Arlesey SG15 . . . . .90 A4
Moggerhanger MK44 . . . . . .53 C7
St Neots PE19 . . . . .22 A4
St Johns St MK42 . . . . .49 F6
St John's
Bedford MK42 . . . . .50 C7
Biggleswade SG18 . . . . . . .67 A7
Kempston MK42 . . . . .49 D3
St John's Terr LU1 . . . . .123 D7
St John's Wlk MK41 . . . . .38 C3
St Joseph's Cl LU3 . . . . .116 A4
St Joseph's RC Inf Sch
LU3 . . . . .116 A4
St Joseph's RC Lower Sch
MK40 . . . . .49 E8
St Katharines Cl SG5 . . . . . .100 D3
St Kilda Rd LU4 . . . . .114 F4
St Lawrence Lower Sch
NN10 . . . . .8 A5
St Lawrences Ave LU3 . . . . .116 A4
St Lawrence Wlk NN10 . . . . . .8 B5
St Leonard's Ave MK42 . . . . .50 C6
St Leonard's Cl LU7 . . . . . . .103 B3
St Leonard's Way LU6 . . . . .118 D7
St Loyes St 11 MK40 . . . . . . .50 B8
St Luke's Cl LU4 . . . . .115 E2
St Margaret of Scotland RC
Jun Sch LU1 . . . . .123 B5
St Margaret of Scotland RC
Inf Sch LU1 . . . . .123 B5
St MARGARET'S 132 C3
St Margarets Cl
Lidlington MK43 . . . . .72 C3
Streatley LU3 . . . . .108 A6
St Margarets Gdns SG18 . . . .67 C4
St Marks Cl MK45 . . . . .84 F4
St Mark's Cl SG5 . . . . .100 D3
St Martin de Porres RC Prim
Sch LU3 . . . . .116 A4
St Martin's Ave LU2 . . . . . . .116 F2
St Martins Cl MK45 . . . . .84 F4
St Martins Cl AL5 . . . . .131 C4
St Martins Way MK42 . . . . . .51 A5
St Mary's Ave SG5 . . . . .90 F6
St Marys Cl
Bletsoe MK44 . . . . .17 C1
Elstow MK42 . . . . .50 B4
Marston Moretaine MK43 . . .72 D7
St Mary's Cl
Felmersham MK43 . . . . . . .26 C8
Letchworth SG6 . . . . .101 F7
Pirton SG5 . . . . .99 D4
Tebworth LU7 . . . . .105 C2
St Mary's (Clophill) Lower
Sch MK45 . . . . .75 D1
St Marys Ct PE19 . . . . .22 C3

St Mary's Ct
8 Dunstable LU6 . . . . . . .121 B8
Leighton Buzzard LU7 . . . .110 D8
St Neots PE19 . . . . .22 E4
St Mary's Gate LU6 . . . . . . .121 B8
St Mary's Glebe LU6 . . . . . . .119 C4
St Mary's Nursing Ctr
LU1 . . . . .123 D7
St Mary's Pl MK42 . . . . .88 B5
St Mary's RC Lower Sch
LU1 . . . . .121 F6
St Marys Rd MK43 . . . . .60 F7
St Mary's Rd LU1 . . . . .123 F7
St Mary's St
Bedford MK42 . . . . .50 C7
St Neots PE19 . . . . .22 E4
St Mary's (Stotfold) Lower
Sch SG5 . . . . .91 A6
St Mary's Way LU7 . . . . .110 E8
St Mary's Wlk SG19 . . . . .54 B7
St Mathews Cl MK42 . . . . . . .49 D3
St Matthews Cl LU2 . . . . . . .116 C1
St Matthew's Inf Sch
LU2 . . . . .116 E1
St Mellion Dr MK40 . . . . .49 B7
St Michaels Ave LU5 . . . . . .114 B4
St Michael's Cres LU3 . . . . .116 D3
St Michael's Ct MK40 . . . . . .38 D2
St Michael's Rd MK40 . . . . . .38 D2
St Mildreds Ave LU3 . . . . . .116 C3
St Monica's Ave LU3 . . . . . .116 B3
ST NEOTS 22 B6
St Neots Com Coll PE19 . . . . .22 E2
St Neots L Ctr PE19 . . . . .22 E2
St Neots Mus* PE19 . . . . . . .22 E1
St Neots Rd
Bedford MK41 . . . . .40 B3
Bolnhurst MK44 . . . . .19 E4
Little Barford PE19 . . . . . . .33 F7
Sandy SG19 . . . . .54 B8
St Neots PE19 . . . . .22 D4
St Nicholas CE Prim Sch
Harpenden AL5 . . . . .131 A1
Letchworth SG6 . . . . .91 C1
St Nicholas Cl MK17 . . . . . . .94 F5
St Nicholas Ct AL5 . . . . .130 F3
St Ninian's Sch 7 LU2 . . . . .123 D8
St Olam's Cl LU3 . . . . .116 B3
St Olives SG5 . . . . .90 E6
St Pauls Cl MK45 . . . . .84 F3
Saint Paul's Gdns LU1 . . . . .123 E5
St Paul's Rd
Bedford MK40 . . . . .38 C3
Luton LU1 . . . . .123 E5
St Paul's Sq MK40 . . . . .50 B8
St Peter's Ave SG15 . . . . .90 A7
St Peter's Cl MK45 . . . . .84 F4
St Peters Cl MK45 . . . . .16 C4
St Peters Ct SG19 . . . . .56 A8
St Peter's Rd LU7 . . . . .123 B7
St Peter's Rd LU5 . . . . .121 C8
St Peter's St MK40 . . . . .38 C3
St Saviours's Cres LU1 . . . . .123 D6
St Swithuns Lower Sch
LU1 . . . . .54 C7
St Swithun's Way SG19 . . . . .54 D7
St Thomas More RC Prim
Sch SG6 . . . . .101 D4
St Thomas More RC Sch
MK41 . . . . .38 C6
St Thomas's Ct LU2 . . . . . . .117 A4
St Thomas's Rd LU2 . . . . . . .117 A4
St Vincent Gdns LU4 . . . . . .115 D3
St Vincents MK17 . . . . .81 C4
St Vincent's RC Lower Sch
LU5 . . . . .114 C5
St Winifreds Ave LU3 . . . . . .116 C3
Salcombe Cl MK40 . . . . .38 E1
Sale Dr SG7 . . . . .91 F1
SALFORD 70 C3
Salford Rd
Aspley Guise MK17 . . . . . . .81 D7
Brogborough MK43 . . . . . . .82 B8
Salisbury Ave AL5 . . . . .131 A1
Salisbury Cl SG5 . . . . .90 D2
Salisbury Ho 8 MK40 . . . . . .38 A1
Salisbury Rd
Baldock SG7 . . . . .91 F1
Flitwick MK45 . . . . .84 E4
Harpenden AL5 . . . . .131 D3
Luton LU1 . . . . .123 D6
Salisbury St MK41 . . . . .38 B2
Sallowsprings LU6 . . . . .120 F2
SALPH END 39 B6
Saltash Cl MK40 . . . . .49 C6
Saltdean Cl LU2 . . . . .117 D4
Salters Way LU6 . . . . .113 F3
Saltfield Cres LU4 . . . . .115 C4
Sambar Cl PE19 . . . . .22 B5
Sampshill Rd MK45 . . . . .95 E5
Samuel Whitbread Com Coll
SG17 . . . . .77 E2
Sandalwood Cl LU3 . . . . . . .116 B7
Sandell Cl LU2 . . . . .116 F2
Sanderling Cl SG6 . . . . .101 E8
Sanders Cl MK42 . . . . .49 D6
Sanderson Ct MK45 . . . . .84 E4
Sanders Rd MK43 . . . . .95 E6
Sanders Way MK43 . . . . .60 F8
Sandfields Rd PE19 . . . . .22 F5
Sandford Rise SG19 . . . . .54 A7
Sandgate Rd LU4 . . . . .115 D2
Sandhill Cl MK45 . . . . .73 A1
Sandhills LU7 . . . . .111 D7
Sandhouse Cotts LU7 . . . . . .103 D8
Sandhurst Pl MK42 . . . . .50 B6
Sandhurst Rd MK42 . . . . .50 B6

Barton-le-C MK45 . . . . .97 B8
Biggleswade SG18 . . . . .67 A6
Northill SG18 . . . . .53 E1
Sandy SG19 . . . . .54 E7
Sandland Cl LU6 . . . . .114 A1
Sandleford Dr MK42 . . . . . . .50 E3
Sandon Cl SG19 . . . . .54 C8
Sandpiper Ct SG18 . . . . .66 F5
Sandpiper Way LU7 . . . . . . .111 C5
Sand Rd MK45 . . . . .85 E3
Sandringham Dr LU5 . . . . . .114 E4
Sandringham Rd MK45 . . . . .84 D1
SANDY 54 C6
Sandy Acres MK45 . . . . .74 B1
Sandy Bsns Pk SG19 . . . . . .42 C2
Sandye La MK44 . . . . .11 D8
Sandye Place Mid Sch
SG19 . . . . .54 C6
Sandy La
Chicksands SG17 . . . . .76 E5
Husborne Crawley MK17 . . . .82 D3
Leighton Buzzard LU7 . . . . .103 A3
Tilbrook PE28 . . . . .6 C6
Woburn Sands MK17 . . . . . . .81 B2
Sandy Rd
Bedford MK41 . . . . .39 A1
Everton SG19 . . . . .43 B2
Potton SG19 . . . . .55 E7
Willington MK44 . . . . .52 E8
Sandy Sta SG19 . . . . .54 D6
Sandy Upper Sch & Com Coll
SG19 . . . . .42 A1
Sandy View SG18 . . . . .67 B8
Sanfoin Rd LU4 . . . . .115 A4
San Remo Rd MK17 . . . . . . .81 F4
Santa Pod Raceway NN29 . .15 C6
Santingfield N LU1 . . . . . . .123 B6
Santingfield S LU1 . . . . . . .123 B6
Sarum Rd LU3 . . . . .115 F4
Saturn Cl LU7 . . . . .111 D8
Saucey Ave
Harpenden AL5 . . . . .131 B3
Harpenden AL5 . . . . .131 C2
Saucey Wood AL5 . . . . .131 E4
Saucey Wood La AL5 . . . . . .131 E4
Saucey Wood Prim Sch
AL5 . . . . .131 D4
Saunders Gdns MK40 . . . . . .49 E7
Saunders Piece MK45 . . . . . .84 C3
Savannah Cl MK42 . . . . .49 F5
Savernake Wlk MK41 . . . . . .39 B3
Savile's Cl PE19 . . . . .22 D7
Saville Ct MK41 . . . . .41 A5
Sawtry Cl LU3 . . . . .116 A6
Sawyers Cres NN9 . . . . .3 B8
Sax Ho SG6 . . . . .90 E1
Saxon Ave SG5 . . . . .90 F8
Saxon Cl
Dunstable LU6 . . . . .120 E8
Flitwick MK45 . . . . .84 F4
Harpenden AL5 . . . . .131 C4
Letchworth SG6 . . . . .90 F1
Roxton MK44 . . . . .31 E1
Saxon Cres MK45 . . . . .97 C4
Saxon Ctrk MK42 . . . . .49 E4
Saxon H PE19 . . . . .22 F4
Saxon Pool & L Ctr SG18 . . .67 C5
Saxon Rd LU3 . . . . .116 C2
Saxon Rise NN29 . . . . .7 C8
Saxons Cl LU7 . . . . .111 C7
Saxtead Cl LU2 . . . . .117 D1
Saywell Rd LU2 . . . . .117 B1
SCALD END 28 C3
Scawsby Cl LU6 . . . . .113 E1
Sceptre Sch LU5 . . . . .114 F1
School Cl SG19 . . . . .44 D5
School Hill NN10 . . . . .7 B8
School House Mews
MK45 . . . . .86 C4
School La
Bolnhurst MK44 . . . . .19 D4
Carlton MK43 . . . . .25 A2
Colmworth MK44 . . . . .20 A2
Eaton Bray LU6 . . . . .119 F6
Great Barford MK44 . . . . . . .41 A5
Greenfield MK45 . . . . .85 F2
Husborne Crawley MK43 . . .82 B4
Irchester NN29 . . . . .7 A8
Luton LU4 . . . . .115 D4
Podington NN29 . . . . .7 F2
Roxton MK44 . . . . .31 F2
Shefford SG17 . . . . .77 B2
Southill SG18 . . . . .65 D1
Stewartby MK43 . . . . .61 C1
St Neots, Eynesbury PE19 . .22 E4
Wootton MK43 . . . . .60 F7
School Rd NN29 . . . . .7 A8
Scotchbrook Rd MK43 . . . . .72 D7
Scothfield Cl LU2 . . . . .117 D3
Scott Ave MK42 . . . . .51 A2
Scott Ct LU5 . . . . .114 C1
Scott Lower Sch MK45 . . . . .38 C5
Scott Rd LU3 . . . . .116 B3
Seabrook LU4 . . . . .115 B3
Seaford Cl LU2 . . . . .117 C3
Seal Cl LU4 . . . . .115 D3
Seamons Cl LU6 . . . . .121 D6
Sears Ct SG17 . . . . .76 F8
Sears The LU6 . . . . .119 B5
Seaton Dr MK40 . . . . .38 E2
Seaton Rd LU4 . . . . .115 F3
Sebright Rd Al3 . . . . .128 E5
Sedbury Cl LU3 . . . . .116 A6
SEDDINGTON 54 C3
Sedgwick Rd LU4 . . . . .115 B7
Seebohm Cl SG5 . . . . .100 C1

Segenhoe Cl MK43 . . . . .82 F5
Selbourne Rd LU4 . . . . .116 A2
Selina Cl LU3 . . . . .115 C7
Selsey Dr LU2 . . . . .117 D4
Selsey Way MK41 . . . . .38 C2
Sergeants Way MK41 . . . . . .39 C2
Servite Ho LU4 . . . . .115 C3
Setchel PE19 . . . . .22 D7
Severalls The LU2 . . . . .117 B3
Severn Cl MK45 . . . . .84 D2
Severn Way MK41 . . . . .38 C5
Severn Wlk LU7 . . . . .103 B3
SEVICK END 29 E1
Sewell Ct LU3 . . . . .113 D2
Sewell La LU6 . . . . .113 D3
Sexton Ave MK42 . . . . .50 A8
Seymour Ave LU1 . . . . .123 F5
Seymour Rd LU1 . . . . .123 F5
Shackleton Lower Sch
MK42 . . . . .50 C5
Shady Wlk PE19 . . . . .22 F5
Shaftesbury Ave
Bedford MK40 . . . . .50 A8
St Neots PE19 . . . . .22 F5
Shaftesbury Dr SG5 . . . . . . .90 C3
Shaftesbury Rd LU4 . . . . . .116 B1
Shakespeare Dr SG18 . . . . . .66 C8
Shakespeare Rd
Bedford MK40 . . . . .38 A1
Harpenden AL5 . . . . .131 C1
Luton LU4 . . . . .115 B2
St Neots PE19 . . . . .22 C3
Shaldon Ct MK40 . . . . .38 E2
Shanklin Cl LU3 . . . . .116 A7
Shannon Cl
Lower Stondon SG16 . . . . . .88 F2
Sandy SG19 . . . . .42 B1
Shannon Ct SG19 . . . . .54 C7
Shannon Sq SG19 . . . . .55 F7
SHARNBROOK 16 B4
Sharnbrook Cl MK44 . . . . . . .16 D4
Sharnbrook John Gibbard
Lower Sch MK44 . . . . .16 D4
Sharnbrook Rd MK44 . . . . . .16 B7
Sharnbrook Upper Sch &
Com Coll MK44 . . . . .16 B3
Sharnside MK44 . . . . .16 D4
Sharose Ct Al3 . . . . .128 E5
Sharp Cl MK45 . . . . .86 B7
SHARPENHOE 87 C2
Sharpenhoe Clappers*
LU3 . . . . .107 F7
Sharpenhoe Rd
Barton-le-C MK45 . . . . .97 B2
Streatley LU3 . . . . .107 F7
Sharples Gn LU3 . . . . .116 B8
Sharps Way SG4 . . . . .101 A1
Shay La PE28 . . . . .5 B4
Shearley Cl MK42 . . . . .50 C4
Sheepcote Cres LU7 . . . . . .103 A5
Sheepfold Hill MK45 . . . . . . .84 F3
Sheeplands MK43 . . . . .39 B3
SHEEPLANE 92 C2
Sheeplane MK17 . . . . .92 C2
SHEEPTICK END 72 A3
Sheeptick End MK43 . . . . . .72 B3
Sheepwalk Cl SG19 . . . . . . .56 B6
Sheep Wlk SG18 . . . . .67 D7
Sheffield Cl SG19 . . . . .56 A7
SHEFFORD 77 D3
Shefford Bsns Pk SG17 . . . .77 C3
Shefford Ind Pk SG17 . . . . . .77 C2
Shefford Lower Sch SG17 . .77 B2
Shefford Rd
Clifton SG17 . . . . .77 F2
Clophill MK45 . . . . .76 A2
Meppershall SG17 . . . . .88 C7
Sheldon Ct MK17 . . . . .81 B4
Shelford La MK44 . . . . .20 B3
Shelley Ct [16] AL5 . . . . .131 B1
Shelley Pl PE19 . . . . .22 D6
Shelley Rd LU4 . . . . .115 B2
Shelton Ave LU5 . . . . .105 F4
Shelton Cl LU5 . . . . .105 F4
Shelton Ct MK44 . . . . .40 F5
Shelton Lower Sch MK43 . . .60 C3
Shelton Rd
Hargrave NN9 . . . . .1 A4
Upper Dean PE28 . . . . .5 A5
Shenley Way LU7 . . . . .117 A3
Shenley Cl LU7 . . . . .103 B3
Shenley Hill Rd LU7 . . . . . .103 C3
Shenley Rd MK42 . . . . .74 B1
Shepherds Cl LU5 . . . . .95 F1
Shepherds Mead
Hitchin SG5 . . . . .100 F2
Leighton Buzzard LU7 . . . . .103 A1
Shepherds Way AL5 . . . . . .130 D4
Sherborne Ave LU4 . . . . . . .116 D6
Sherbourne Way MK41 . . . . .38 F5
Sherd Cl LU3 . . . . .115 F7
Sheridan Rd LU3 . . . . .115 A4
Sheriden Cl LU4 . . . . .114 B1
Sheringham Cl LU2 . . . . . . .116 C7
Sherwood SG6 . . . . .101 F8
Sherwood Rd LU4 . . . . .116 A2
Sherwood Terr NN9 . . . . .7 B8
Sherwood Wlk MK41 . . . . . .39 B3
SHILLINGTON 87 F1
Shillington Lower Sch
SG5 . . . . .87 E1
Shillington Rd
Gravenhurst MK45 . . . . .87 D4
Lower Stondon SG5 . . . . . . .88 C2
Meppershall SG17 . . . . .88 B4
Pirton SG5 . . . . .99 B5
Shingle Cl LU3 . . . . .116 A8
Ship Rd LU7 . . . . .110 E6

Shirdley Rd PE19 . . . . .22 F4
Shire La MK16 . . . . .58 E4
Shires The LU2 . . . . .116 D1
Shirley Rd LU1 . . . . .123 C8
Shortcroft Ct MK45 . . . . .97 B2
Shortmead St SG18 . . . . . . .66 F6
Short Path LU5 . . . . .114 C6
Shorts Ave MK42 . . . . .51 A2
Short St MK40 . . . . .49 F7
SHORTSTOWN 51 A2
Shortstown Lower Sch
MK42 . . . . .50 F2
Shrubbery La MK44 . . . . .29 C4
Shuttleworth Collection Mus
The* SG18 . . . . .65 E3
Shuttleworth College
SG18 . . . . .65 D5
Shuttleworth Ct SG18 . . . . . .67 A6
Shuttleworth Ct Bsns Pk
MK43 . . . . .39 C3
Shuttleworth Rd MK41 . . . . .39 C2
Sibley Cl LU2 . . . . .117 B3
Sibton Abbey MK41 . . . . . . .51 B8
Sidings The MK42 . . . . .50 C6
Sidmouth Cl MK40 . . . . .38 E2
Sidney Rd
Ampthill MK45 . . . . .84 E7
Bedford MK40 . . . . .37 F1
Signal Cl SG16 . . . . .89 B3
Silbury Ct MK45 . . . . .86 B5
Silecroft Rd LU2 . . . . .124 B8
SILSOE 86 B4
Silsoe CE Lower Sch
MK45 . . . . .86 C4
Silsoe Rd
Flitton MK45 . . . . .85 E3
Maulden MK45 . . . . .85 E7
Silverbirch Ave SG5 . . . . . . .90 F8
Silverbirches La MK17 . . . . .81 B2
Silver Birches The MK42 . . .49 F2
Silverburn Cl MK41 . . . . .39 C5
Silverdale St MK42 . . . . .49 F4
Silver End Rd MK45 . . . . . . .63 F1
Silver St
Bedford MK40 . . . . .50 B8
Great Barford MK44 . . . . . . .40 F5
Guilden Morden SG8 . . . . . . .69 F4
Luton LU1 . . . . .123 E7
Steventon MK43 . . . . .36 B7
St Neots PE19 . . . . .22 F4
Silverweed PE19 . . . . .22 C4
Simdims MK43 . . . . .35 A1
Simkin Cl LU2 . . . . .117 D2
Simkins Dr MK45 . . . . .97 C4
Simpson Cl LU2 . . . . .115 D2
Singer Way MK42 . . . . .49 D2
Singer Way MK42 . . . . .49 D2
Singlets La AL3 . . . . .129 C2
Sir Herbert Janes Village
The LU4 . . . . .115 D4
Sir John Lawes Sch AL5 . .131 C3
Sir Malcolm Stewart Homes
MK43 . . . . .73 C8
Sir Peter's Way HP4 . . . . . .126 E6
Skegsbury La SG4 . . . . .125 F1
Skelton Cl LU3 . . . . .108 B1
Skerne Pas MK41 . . . . .38 C7
Skimpot Rd LU4 . . . . .115 A1
Skipton Cl SG19 . . . . .54 C8
Skua Cl LU4 . . . . .115 A5
Slade The
Clapham MK41 . . . . .37 E6
Clophill MK45 . . . . .75 C1
Wrestlingworth SG19 . . . . . .57 B3
SLAPTON 118 D6
Slapton La LU6 . . . . .118 F6
Slate Hall LU3 . . . . .107 A4
Slater Ct MK42 . . . . .49 D5
Slate Row MK44 . . . . .16 A8
Slickett's La LU6 . . . . .119 F3
SLIP END 123 C2
Slip End Lower Sch LU1 . . .123 B1
Slip The MK43 . . . . .26 C7
Slype The SG15 . . . . .131 F6
Smithcombe Cl MK45 . . . . . .97 C3
Smiths Lane Mall [5] LU1 . . .123 E7
Smiths Sq [4] LU1 . . . . .123 E7
Snagge Ct MK43 . . . . .60 E1
SNAILSWELL 100 E5
Snailswell La SG5 . . . . .100 E5
Snowdrop Wlk SG18 . . . . . . .67 C5
Snowford Cl [1] LU3 . . . . . . .116 A7
Snow Hill MK45 . . . . .74 B1
Sollersott Hall SG6 . . . . . . .101 F4
Sollershott E SG6 . . . . .101 E4
Sollershott W SG6 . . . . .101 E4
Solway Rd N LU3 . . . . .116 A3
Solway Rd S LU3 . . . . .116 A3
Someries Jun & Inf Sch
LU2 . . . . .117 C3
Someries Rd AL5 . . . . .131 C3
Somersby Cl LU3 . . . . .123 E5
Somerset Ave LU2 . . . . .117 A1
Somerton Cl MK41 . . . . .39 A5
Sopwith Way MK42 . . . . .51 A2
Sorrel Cl LU3 . . . . .116 B8
Souberie Ave SG6 . . . . .101 F5
Soulbury Rd LU7 . . . . .110 D7
SOULDROP 16 B8
Souldrop Rd MK44 . . . . .16 C5
Southampton Gdns LU3 . . .107 A4
South Ave MK42 . . . . .50 C1
Southbridge St SG17 . . . . . .77 C3
Southcott Village LU7 . . . . .110 D7
Southcott Ave LU7 . . . . .110 D6
Southcott Rd LU7 . . . . .110 D7

Southcroft Ho LU7 . . . . .110 D7
Southdown Rd AL5 . . . . .131 B1
South Dr MK42 . . . . .50 C1
South Drift Way LU1 . . . . . .123 B5
SOUTH END 50 B5
South End Jun & Inf Scts
NN10 . . . . .8 B8
South End La LU6 . . . . .119 B4
South End Rd MK16 . . . . . . .89 C3
Southern Rise LU2 . . . . .130 F7
Southern Way
Letchworth SG6 . . . . .101 E8
Studham SG6 . . . . .127 C4
Southfield Jun & Inf Schs
LU4 . . . . .114 F4
Southfields
Dunstable LU6 . . . . .121 D6
Kempston MK43 . . . . .50 A3
Southgate Ct [5] AL5 . . . . . .131 A2
South Gr NN10 . . . . .8 B8
SOUTHILL 77 E8
Southill Lower Sch SG18 . . .65 D1
Southill Rd
Broom SG18 . . . . .66 B2
Cardington MK44 . . . . .51 E4
Southland Rise SG18 . . . . . .78 F5
Southlands Lower Sch
SG18 . . . . .67 B4
South Luton High Sch
LU1 . . . . .123 F5
Southlynn Ho [2] LU2 . . . . .123 F8
South Rd
Luton LU1 . . . . .123 D6
Sandy SG19 . . . . .54 B7
South St
Leighton Buzzard LU7 . . . . .111 B7
St Neots PE19 . . . . .22 E5
Stevenage SG6 . . . . .40 F5
South View
Biggleswade SG18 . . . . .67 A5
Letchworth SG6 . . . . .90 F1
Southview Gdns LU7 . . . . . .111 B6
Southview Rd AL5 . . . . .130 D3
Southville Rd MK42 . . . . . . .50 B3
Southway MK42 . . . . .50 B3
South Wlk SG18 . . . . .67 B7
Southwood Rd LU5 . . . . .114 B1
Sovereign Pk LU4 . . . . .115 F1
Sovereigns Quay MK40 . . . .50 B8
Sowerby Ave LU2 . . . . .117 C3
Spa Ho PE19 . . . . .22 F5
Sparhawke SG16 . . . . .91 A1
Sparksfield SG16 . . . . .78 D2
Sparrow Cl LU4 . . . . .115 A4
Sparrow Hall Bsns Pk
LU6 . . . . .119 D3
Spayne Cl LU3 . . . . .116 A6
Spear Cl LU3 . . . . .115 E6
SPEEDWELL 93 A5
Speedwell Cl LU3 . . . . .116 A8
Spencer Cl
Potton SG19 . . . . .56 A8
St Neots PE19 . . . . .22 D6
Spencer Ct LU7 . . . . .103 B1
Spencer Ho SG5 . . . . .90 F6
Spencer Rd
Luton LU3 . . . . .116 C2
Sandy SG19 . . . . .54 B7
Spencers The MK44 . . . . . . .41 A5
Spenser Ct MK40 . . . . .37 F1
Spenser Rd
Bedford MK40 . . . . .37 F1
Harpenden AL5 . . . . .130 E3
Spensley Rd MK45 . . . . .95 E5
Spinney Bglws LU7 . . . . . . .118 C6
Spinney Cres LU5 . . . . .120 F8
Spinney La MK17 . . . . .81 F4
Spinney Rd
Chawston MK44 . . . . .39 B3
Luton LU3 . . . . .115 D7
Spinney The
Bedford MK41 . . . . .39 B3
Harpenden AL5 . . . . .130 E3
Spire Harpenden Hospl
(private) AL5 . . . . .131 A4
Spitfire Rd SG17 . . . . .77 C1
Spittlesea Rd LU2 . . . . .124 C7
Spoondell LU6 . . . . .121 A6
Spratts La LU6 . . . . .121 F1
Spreckley Cl SG16 . . . . .89 B5
Spriggs Cl MK41 . . . . .37 C7
Springbrook PE19 . . . . .22 C4
Spring Cl
Ampthill MK45 . . . . .84 F7
Biggleswade SG18 . . . . .67 B6
Springfield SG18 . . . . .68 C5
Springfield Ave MK42 . . . . . .49 E4
Springfield Cres AL5 . . . . . .131 C4
Springfield Ct LU7 . . . . .110 F2
Springfield Dr MK43 . . . . . . .36 E3
Springfield Lower Sch
MK42 . . . . .49 F3
Springfield Rd
Dunstable LU6 . . . . .120 D5
Leighton Buzzard LU7 . . . . .110 F2
Luton LU3 . . . . .116 C6
Rushden NN10 . . . . .8 D8
Springfield Way MK42 . . . . .59 C2
Spring Gdns MK42 . . . . .50 A4
Spring Gr
Sandy SG19 . . . . .54 B7
Woburn Sands MK17 . . . . . .81 B5

Spring Hill MK44 . . . . .13 A3
Spring La
Stagsden MK43 . . . . .48 C6
Yelden MK44 . . . . .4 A3
Spring Pl [5] LU1 . . . . .123 D6
Spring Rd
Clifton SG17 . . . . .78 A2
Harpenden AL5 . . . . .130 A4
Kempston MK42 . . . . .50 A4
Letchworth SG6 . . . . .101 E4
Letchworth SG6 . . . . .101 E6
Springshott SG6 . . . . .101 E5
Springside LU7 . . . . .110 F2
Spruce Wlk MK42 . . . . .49 F3
Spurcroft LU3 . . . . .108 C1
Square The
Aspley Guise MK17 . . . . . . .81 A4
Dunstable LU6 . . . . .121 B8
Wilstead MK45 . . . . .62 E4
Squires Cl SG17 . . . . .77 E2
Squires Ct SG17 . . . . .22 C4
Squires Pl LU5 . . . . .105 F6
Squires Rd
Marston Moretaine MK43 . . .72 D7
Wootton MK43 . . . . .60 F6
Stables The
Ampthill MK45 . . . . .84 F7
Leighton Buzzard LU7 . . . . .110 A6
Stadium Est The LU4 . . . . . .115 B1
Stafford Rd MK42 . . . . .50 A6
STAGSDEN 48 A7
Stagsden Rd MK43 . . . . .36 E2
Staines Sq LU6 . . . . .121 E7
Stainmore Rd MK41 . . . . . . .39 C4
Stakers Cl AL5 . . . . .131 B1
STANBRIDGE 112 C5
Stanbridge Crossing
LU7 . . . . .112 B3
STANBRIDGEFORD 112 C5
Stanbridge Lower Sch
LU7 . . . . .112 D5
Stanbridge Rd
Billington LU7 . . . . .111 F1
Leighton Buzzard LU7 . . . . .111 C6
Tilsworth LU7 . . . . .112 F2
Totternhoe, Lower End
LU6 . . . . .112 C2
Totternhoe, Stanbridgeford
LU7 . . . . .112 E2
Stanbridge Road Terr
LU7 . . . . .111 B6
Stanbridge View MK45 . . . . .97 C2
Stanbridge Way MK45 . . . . .74 B8
Stanbrook Way MK44 . . . . . .4 A3
Stancliffe Rd MK41 . . . . .38 C5
Standalone Farm* SG6 . . . .101 D7
Standalone Warren MK76 . . .76 C7
STANFORD 78 A7
Stanford La SG17 . . . . .78 A3
Stanford Rd
Clifton SG17, SG18 . . . . . . .78 A5
Luton LU2 . . . . .117 A1
Shefford SG17 . . . . .77 D3
Southill SG18 . . . . .77 F8
Stanhope Rd MK41 . . . . .38 B4
Stanley Cl MK45 . . . . .96 E1
Stanley Livingstone Ct [2]
LU3 . . . . .123 D6
Stanley Rd LU3 . . . . .108 A5
Stanley St
Bedford MK41 . . . . .38 B2
Kempston MK42 . . . . .49 F4
Luton LU1 . . . . .123 E6
Stanmore Cres LU3 . . . . . . .115 F4
Stannard Way MK44 . . . . . . .51 C6
Stanton Rd
Kempston MK42 . . . . .49 D5
Luton LU3 . . . . .115 C1
Stapleford Rd LU2 . . . . .117 C4
Stapleton Rd MK42 . . . . .50 D4
STAPLOE 21 D6
Staploe Rd MK44 . . . . .21 D2
Starey Cl MK44 . . . . .27 B5
Starling Cl SG19 . . . . .42 B1
Starling Way MK41 . . . . .38 D5
Startpoint LU1 . . . . .123 C7
Stately Ct LU3 . . . . .116 D1
Statham Cl LU3 . . . . .108 B1
Station App AL5 . . . . .131 B1
Station Cres SG19 . . . . .55 F7
Station Par SG6 . . . . .101 F6
Station Rd
Ampthill MK45 . . . . .84 C7
Bedford MK45 . . . . .84 C7
Arlesey SG15 . . . . .90 A4
Baldock SG7 . . . . .91 F1
Bedford MK42 . . . . .50 C7
Biggleswade SG18 . . . . .67 A5
Blunham MK44 . . . . .42 A1
Cheddington LU7 . . . . .118 A1
Dunstable LU5 . . . . .121 D8
Flitwick MK45 . . . . .84 F2
Gamlingay SG19 . . . . .44 F4
Hargrave NN9 . . . . .1 D7
Harlington LU5 . . . . .95 F1
Harpenden AL5 . . . . .131 C2
Irchester NN29 . . . . .7 C8
Langford SG18 . . . . .67 E6
Leighton Buzzard LU7 . . . . .110 F7
Letchworth SG6 . . . . .101 F6
Lidlington MK43 . . . . .72 B3
Lower Stondon SG16 . . . . . .88 D3
Luton, High Town LU1 . . . . .123 E8

Station Rd continued
Luton, Leagrave LU4 . . . . .115 E5
Marston Moretaine MK43 . . .72 D6
Oakley MK43 . . . . .37 A8
Potton SG19 . . . . .55 F7
Ridgmont MK43 . . . . .82 E6
Sandy SG19 . . . . .54 D6
Sharnbrook MK44 . . . . .16 E4
Stanbridge LU7 . . . . .112 D4
Tempsford SG19 . . . . .42 C8
Tilbrook PE28 . . . . .6 F2
Toddington LU5 . . . . .106 A7
Turvey MK43 . . . . .35 B5
Willington MK44 . . . . .52 C8
Woburn Sands MK17 . . . . . . .81 B5
Station Sq MK45 . . . . .84 E2
Station Way SG6 . . . . .101 E6
Staughton Pl PE19 . . . . .22 C4
Staughton Rd MK44 . . . . .12 D5
Staunton Ho MK17 . . . . .92 F7
Staveley Rd
Dunstable LU6 . . . . .121 B6
Luton LU4 . . . . .115 C1
Stephens Gdns LU2 . . . . . . .117 A3
Stephenson Cl LU7 . . . . .110 E6
Stephenson Lower Sch
MK42 .50 E5
STEPPINGLEY 84 A3
Steppingley Hospl MK44 . . . .84 C4
Steppingley Rd MK45 . . . . . .84 D3
Steppingley Road Trad Est
MK45 .84 E3
Steppingstone Pl LU7 . . . .111 B6
Stepping Stones The
LU3 . . . . .115 E5
Stevenson Ct PE19 . . . . .22 D6
STEVINGTON 36 B7
Stevington Windmill★
MK43 .36 C6
STEWARTBY 61 C1
Stewartby Sta MK43 . . . . . . .61 B1
Stewartby Way MK43 . . . . . . .61 C1
Stewart Cl MK43 . . . . .37 A4
Stewart Clark Ct 4 LU4 . . . .114 A1
Stewart Ct MK43 . . . . .61 A6
Stewart Rd AL5 . . . . .131 B2
Stileman Way MK44 . . . . . . .16 C4
Stile The LU7 . . . . .103 A5
Stillitters Farm Rd MK43 . . .70 E8
Stipers Cl LU6 . . . . .121 C6
STIPERS HILL 121 D5
Stirling Cl SG19 . . . . .42 B1
Stirling Rd MK42 . . . . .51 A2
Stivers Way LU5 . . . . .95 F3
Stockbridge Rd SG17 . . . . . .78 C3
Stockdale LU5 . . . . .105 F5
Stocker Way PE19 . . . . .22 E2
Stockgrove Ctry Pk★
LU7 . . . . .102 F7
Stockgrove Park Ho LU7 .102 F8
Stockholm Way LU3 . . . . . .115 E8
Stockingstone Rd LU2 . . . .116 E3
Stocks La SG19 . . . . .44 D5
Stockwell Farm Rd LU5 . .106 C4
Stockwood Craft Mus &
Gdns★ LU1 . . . . .123 D4
Stockwood Cres LU1 . . . . . .123 D6
Stockwood Ct 16 LU1 . . . . .123 D6
Stockwood Pk★ LU1 . . . . . .123 D3
Stoke Albany Mews 3
MK40 .38 A1
Stoke Rd LU7 . . . . .102 D1
Stokesay Cl MK41 . . . . .38 E4
Stondon Lower Sch SG16 . .88 E3
Stondon Rd SG17 . . . . .88 C4
Stondon Transport
Museum★ SG16 . . . . .88 F3
Stone Cl MK40 . . . . .49 B6
Stonecroft SG19 . . . . .54 D7
Stonedale Rd MK42 . . . . .50 A4
Stonehenge Works★
LU7 . . . . .103 E3
Stonehill JMI Sch SG6 . . . . .90 E1
Stoneland Ave SG18 . . . . . . .67 A7
Stoneleigh Cl LU3 . . . . .116 B7
Stoneley SG6 . . . . .90 F1
Stonemason Cl AL3 . . . . . . .131 A3
Stone Pine Rd MK43 . . . . . . .36 D3
Stonesdale LU4 . . . . .115 C4
Stoneways Cl LU4 . . . . .115 C6
Stoneygate Rd LU4 . . . . . . .115 D3
Stonnells Cl SG6 . . . . .101 F6
STOPSLEY 117 B4
STOPSLEY COMMON 116 F6
Stopsley Com Prim Sch
LU2 . . . . .117 A4
Stopsley High Sch LU2 . . .116 F4
Stopsley Way LU2 . . . . .117 A3
Stormont Rd SG5 . . . . .100 F1
STOTFOLD 90 G7
STOTFOLD COMMON 79 E1
Stotfold Ho SG17 . . . . .90 F6
Stotfold Rd
Arlesey SG15 . . . . .90 C7
Hinxworth SG7 . . . . .80 C1
Letchworth SG4, SG6 . . . . . .101 C4
Letchworth SG6 . . . . .90 D1
Stour Way MK41 . . . . .38 C5
Stow Rd PE28 . . . . .6 F5
Stratford Cl LU5 . . . . .95 F1
Strand The MK45 . . . . .75 C1
Strangers Way LU4 . . . . . . .115 C4
STRATFORD 54 E4
Stratford Cl LU5 . . . . .105 E6

Stratford Ct MK40 . . . . .38 A2
Stratford Pl PE19 . . . . .22 C3
Stratford Rd
Luton LU4 . . . . .116 B1
Sandy SG19 . . . . .54 E5
Stratford Way MK43 . . . . .60 D2
Strathconon Rd MK41 . . . . . .39 C4
Strathmore Ave
Hitchin SG5 . . . . .100 F1
Luton LU3 . . . . .123 F5
Strathmore Ct SG5 . . . . .100 F1
Strathmore Inf Sch SG6 . . . .100 E2
Strathmore Wlk LU1 . . . . . .123 F6
Stratton Bsns Pk SG18 . . . .67 D3
Stratton Cl 7 SG18 . . . . .67 A6
Stratton Gdns LU2 . . . . . . .116 D4
Stratton Mews LU7 . . . . . . .111 B7
Stratton Pk SG18 . . . . .67 A6
Stratton Upper Sch & Com
Coll SG18 . . . . .67 C6
Stratton Way
Bedford MK41 . . . . .39 D3
Biggleswade SG18 . . . . .67 E7
Strawberry Field LU3 . . . . .115 E7
Strawberry Hill Cotts MK44 .9 F7
Straw Plait SG15 . . . . .90 F7
STREATLEY 108 A5
Streatley Rd LU3 . . . . .107 D4
Street Cl MK43 . . . . .25 A3
Streetfield Mid Sch LU5 . .123 A3
Stringfellow Cl MK43 . . . . . .58 E2
Stronnell Cl LU2 . . . . .117 B3
Stuart Cl SG19 . . . . .42 B8
Stuart Pl 8 LU1 . . . . .123 D7
Stuart Rd
Barton-le-C MK45 . . . . .97 C4
Kempston MK42 . . . . .49 E4
Stuart St
Dunstable LU6 . . . . .114 A1
Luton LU1 . . . . .123 D7
Stubbs Cl LU5 . . . . .114 D5
STUDHAM 127 C4
Studham CE Lower Sch
LU6 . . . . .127 B4
Studham La
Dagnall HP4 . . . . .126 D4
Whipsnade LU6 . . . . .127 A7
Studio Ho MK40 . . . . .50 A8
Studley Rd
Luton LU3 . . . . .116 A4
Wootton MK43 . . . . .60 E7
Sturgeon's Rd SG4 . . . . . . .101 B2
Styles Cl LU2 . . . . .117 C2
Sudbury Rd LU3 . . . . .115 B6
Sudeley Wlk MK41 . . . . .39 B4
Suffield Ho 1 PE19 . . . . . . .22 F5
Suffolk Cl LU4 . . . . .115 A3
Suffolk Rd LU5 . . . . .121 F6
Sugden Ct LU6 . . . . .121 A8
Sullivan Cl SG17 . . . . .77 D3
Summerfield Dr MK45 . . . . . .62 F7
Summerfield Rd LU1 . . . . . .122 F8
Summerleys LU6 . . . . .119 E4
Summers Lo SG6 . . . . .101 D5
Summers Rd LU4 . . . . .117 C1
Summer St
Leighton Buzzard LU7 . . . . . .111 B7
Slip End LU1 . . . . .123 C1
Summer Wlk AL3 . . . . .131 A3
Sunbeam Rd MK42 . . . . .49 D1
Sunbower Ave LU6 . . . . .113 F3
Suncote Ave LU6 . . . . .113 E3
Suncote Cl LU6 . . . . .113 E3
Sunderland Cl MK44 . . . . . . .28 F1
Sunderland Hill MK44 . . . . . .29 A4
Sunderland Pl MK42 . . . . . . .51 A2
Sunderland Rd SG19 . . . . . .54 D8
Sundew Cl
Bedford MK42 . . . . .50 F4
St Neots PE19 . . . . .22 B6
Sundon Hills Ctry Pk★
LU3 . . . . .107 C6
Sundon La LU5 . . . . .114 C5
Sundon Lower Sch LU3 . . .107 B4
SUNDON PARK 115 B8
Sundon Park Jun Sch
LU3 . . . . .115 C8
Sundon Park Rd LU3 . . . . . .115 C7
Sundon Rd
Chalton LU3 . . . . .107 A2
Harlington LU5 . . . . .107 B8
Houghton Regis LU5 . . . . . . .114 D7
Streatley LU3 . . . . .107 F5
Sundown Ave LU6 . . . . .121 D7
Sun La AL5 . . . . .131 C2
Sunningdale LU2 . . . . .116 F3
Sunningdale Dr NN10 . . . . . . .8 D8
Sunningdale Wlk MK41 . . . .38 E5
Sunnyside Special Sch
SG18 .67 A6
Sunridge Ave LU2 . . . . .116 E2
Sunrise Est LU2 . . . . .117 A2
Sunset Dr LU2 . . . . .116 F3
Sun St
Biggleswade SG18 . . . . .66 F7
Potton SG19 . . . . .55 A7
Surrey St LU1 . . . . .123 E6
Surrey Street Prim Sch
LU1 . . . . .123 E6
Sursham Ct AL3 . . . . .128 E5
Sussex Cl LU4 . . . . .114 F4
Sussex Pl LU2 . . . . .117 D2
Sussex Rd LU4 . . . . .113 D5
SUTTON 56 A3
Sutton Ave SG18 . . . . .67 B6
Sutton CE Lower Sch
SG19 .56 A3
Sutton Cross Roads SG19 . .55 E4

Sutton Gdns
Caddington LU1 . . . . .122 D3
Luton LU3 . . . . .115 D6
Sutton Mill Rd SG19 . . . . . . .55 F6
Sutton Rd
Eyeworth SG18 . . . . .68 F8
Potton SG19 . . . . .56 C7
Sutton SG19 . . . . .56 B3
Swaden SG19 . . . . .54 E6
Swaffield Cl MK45 . . . . .73 E1
Swale Path MK41 . . . . .38 C7
Swales Dr LU7 . . . . .111 D6
Swallow Cl
Flitwick MK45 . . . . .84 D2
Luton LU4 . . . . .115 A4
Shefford SG17 . . . . .77 C2
Swallow Crest SG19 . . . . . . .42 B2
Swallowfield
Upper Caldecote SG18 . . . . . .66 D8
Wyboston MK44 . . . . .31 F6
Swallowfield Lower Sch
MK17 .81 B5
Swamsholme Garden Ct
SG19 .54 C7
Swanbourne Cl SG18 . . . . . .67 B5
Swan Cl LU7 . . . . .119 A1
Swan La
Guilden Morden SG8 . . . . .69 F4
Luton LU3 . . . . .54 B7
Swan Mead LU4 . . . . .115 B4
Swannells Wood LU6 . . . . .127 C4
Swansholme MK43 . . . . .26 D8
Swansholme Gdns SG19 . . .54 C6
Swansons LU6 . . . . .119 F3
Swanston Grange LU4 . . . .115 B2
Swasedale Rd LU3 . . . . .116 A6
Swift Cl
Bedford MK41 . . . . .38 B4
Flitwick MK45 . . . . .84 D2
Letchworth SG6 . . . . .101 E8
Sandy SG19 . . . . .42 C2
Swifts Green Cl LU2 . . . . . .117 B5
Swifts Green Rd LU2 . . . . .117 B5
Swinburne Ave SG5 . . . . . .100 C1
Swindale MK41 . . . . .38 D6
SWINESHEAD 11 D8
Swiss Garden The★ SG18 . .65 D6
Sworder Cl LU3 . . . . .107 F1
Sybil's Way MK45 . . . . .74 A7
Sycamore Cl
Biggleswade SG18 . . . . .67 A8
Flitwick MK45 . . . . .84 F2
Luton LU3 . . . . .107 C1
Potton SG19 . . . . .55 F7
Sycamore Rd LU5 . . . . .114 C6
Sycamores The
Baldock SG7 . . . . .91 E1
Kempston MK42 . . . . .49 F3
Silsoe MK45 . . . . .86 B5
St Neots PE19 . . . . .22 F6
Sylam Cl LU3 . . . . .115 E7
Sylmond Gdns NN10 . . . . .8 A7
Sylvester St LU7 . . . . .103 A5
Symonds MK41 . . . . .36 F1
Syon Path MK45 . . . . .84 D1

T

Tabor Cl LU5 . . . . .95 F2
Taddy Cl SG18 . . . . .66 B8
Tadlow Rd SG19 . . . . .57 C3
Taft Pl SG17 . . . . .76 E2
Talbot Cl LU7 . . . . .111 A8
Talbot Rd
Bedford MK40 . . . . .38 E1
Luton LU2 . . . . .116 F2
Talbot Way SG6 . . . . .91 B1
Talisman Cl SG19 . . . . .42 B1
Tallents Cres AL5 . . . . .131 D3
Tall Pines LU7 . . . . .102 F2
Tamar Cl MK41 . . . . .38 D5
Tamar Wlk LU7 . . . . .103 B3
Tameton Cl LU2 . . . . .117 F2
Tamworth Rd MK41 . . . . .39 A5
Tancred Rd LU2 . . . . .117 A4
Tandys Cl
Pavenham MK43 . . . . .26 C4
Turvey MK43 . . . . .34 E5
Tanfield Gn LU2 . . . . .117 E1
Tanglewood AL5 . . . . .130 F2
Tannery La MK43 . . . . .15 D1
Tanqueray Ave MK45 . . . . . . .86 C8
Tansur Ct PE19 . . . . .22 F8
Tansy Cl
Bedford MK42 . . . . .50 F4
St Neots PE19 . . . . .22 B6
Tan Yd PE19 . . . . .22 E5
Tarnside Cl LU6 . . . . .121 B6
TARTLETT END 120 E8
Taskers Row LU6 . . . . .119 F4
Taskers Row Cotts LU6 . . .119 F4
Taunton Cl MK41 . . . . .39 A5
Taunton Rd LU2 . . . . .117 B1
Tavistock Ave MK45 . . . . .84 D6
Tavistock Cl MK17 . . . . .81 B6
Tavistock Cres LU1 . . . . . . .123 E5
Tavistock Ct PE19 . . . . .22 E6
Tavistock Rd MK40 . . . . .38 B1
Tavistock St
Bedford MK40 . . . . .38 B1
Dunstable LU6 . . . . .114 A2
Luton LU1 . . . . .123 E5
Taylors Cl SG17 . . . . .88 B5
Taylors End MK45 . . . . .74 B1

Taylor's Rd SG5 . . . . .80 A1
Taylor's Ride LU7 . . . . .102 F2
Taylor St LU2 . . . . .123 F8
Teal Rd SG18 . . . . .66 F5
Teasel Cl
Rushden NN10 . . . . .8 C7
St Neots PE19 . . . . .22 C5
Tebbutts Rd PE19 . . . . .72 B3
Tedworth Rd
Tebworth LU7 . . . . .105 A1
Wingfield LU5, LU7 . . . . .105 E1
Tedder Ave SG16 . . . . .89 B5
Teesdale LU4 . . . . .115 C5
Telford Way
Bedford MK42 . . . . .51 B5
Luton LU1 . . . . .123 D8
Telmere Ind Est 10 LU1 . . .123 E6
Telscombe Way LU2 . . . . . .117 C3
Templars Way MK44 . . . . . . .16 E4
Temple Cl LU2 . . . . .116 E5
Templefield Lower Sch
MK45 .84 E3
Templer Way SG17 . . . . .76 F3
Temple Way MK45 . . . . .84 E2
TEMPSFORD 42 B8
Tempsford Rd
Everton SG19 . . . . .42 E5
Sandy SG19 . . . . .42 A3
Sutton SG19 . . . . .43 C3
Tempsford SG19 . . . . .41 F5
Tempsford St MK42 . . . . .49 E4
Tenby Dr LU4 . . . . .115 E4
Tenby Mews LU6 . . . . .115 E3
Tenby Way PE19 . . . . .22 F1
Tennyson Ave
Biggleswade SG18 . . . . .67 A5
Houghton Regis LU5 . . . . . . .114 D4
Tennyson Ho LU1 . . . . .123 E5
Tennyson Pl PE19 . . . . .22 D6
Tennyson Rd
Bedford MK40 . . . . .50 E8
Luton LU1 . . . . .123 E5
Harpenden AL5 . . . . .131 A2
Luton LU1 . . . . .123 E5
Tennyson Road Prim Sch
LU1 . . . . .123 E5
Tenth Ave LU3 . . . . .115 C7
Tenzing Gr LU1 . . . . .123 C6
Terrace The MK17 . . . . .81 E5
Test Cl MK41 . . . . .38 C7
TETWORTH 43 F7
Tetworth Hill SG19 . . . . .44 A8
Teversham Way PE19 . . . . . .22 C6
Tewkesbury Dr NN10 . . . . .8 D8
Tewkesbury Rd MK42 . . . . . .50 D3
Thames Cl MK45 . . . . .84 D2
Thames Ct LU3 . . . . .116 B3
Thames Ind Est LU6 . . . . . . .121 B8
Thatch Cl LU4 . . . . .114 F4
Thaxted Cl LU2 . . . . .117 F2
THE CITY 20 C3
The Furlong MK43 . . . . .27 A1
The Granary SG15 . . . . .90 A5
The Hawthorns MK45 . . . . . .84 E3
Thelby Cl LU3 . . . . .115 F6
Theobald Bsns Ctr SG4 . . .101 A3
The Orchard
Barton-le-Clay MK45 . . . . .97 A7
Houghton Conquest MK45 . . .74 A8
Therfield Wlk LU6 . . . . .114 E6
The Rickyard MK43 . . . . .60 D2
Thetford Cl MK42 . . . . .49 F4
Thetford Gdns LU2 . . . . .116 E6
Theydon Ave MK17 . . . . .81 B4
Thickthorn La MK45 . . . . . . .62 A3
Thinnings The MK45 . . . . . . .84 E4
Third Ave LU3 . . . . .115 D7
Thirlestone Rd LU4 . . . . . . .115 D1
Thirlmere Cl SG18 . . . . .67 B4
Thirlmere Gdns MK45 . . . . . .84 E2
Thirlmere Rd MK42 . . . . .49 E3
Thistle Rd LU1 . . . . .123 F7
Thistley La MK43 . . . . .36 E1
Thomas Johnson Lower Sch
MK43 .72 B3
Thomas St LU7 . . . . .103 A5
Thomas Whitehead CE Sch
LU5 . . . . .114 B5
Thompsons Cl AL5 . . . . .131 A1
Thompsons Mdw SG8 . . . . . .69 F4
Thomson Ave MK42 . . . . .51 A2
Thor Dr MK41 . . . . .39 D3
THORN 113 E8
Thornage Cl LU2 . . . . .116 D7
Thornbridge Cl NN10 . . . . . . .8 A8
Thornbury
Dunstable LU5 . . . . .114 F2
Harpenden AL5 . . . . .131 D1
Thornbury Ct LU5 . . . . .114 C7
THORNCOTE GREEN 53 E4
Thorncote Rd SG18, SG19 . .53 E4
Thorneycroft Cl LU3 . . . . . .115 F4
Thornhill Cl LU5 . . . . .95 C2
Thornhill Lower Sch
LU5 . . . . .114 D7
Thornhill Rd LU4 . . . . .115 F2
Thorn Rd LU5 . . . . .113 C6
Thorntondale 5 LU4 . . . . . .115 C5
Thornton St MK42 . . . . .49 F5
Thorn View Rd LU5 . . . . .114 B5
Thorpe Cl MK40 . . . . .37 B1
Thorpe Way MK43 . . . . .60 F8
Thrales Cl LU3 . . . . .115 E7
THRALES END 127 D5
Thrales End Rd AL5 . . . . . . .130 E5
Thrapston Rd PE28 . . . . .6 F5
Threave Cl MK41 . . . . .38 F5

Three Closes SG5 . . . . .99 C4
Thresher Cl LU4 . . . . .114 F4
Threshers Ct LU7 . . . . .111 D7
Thricknells Cl LU3 . . . . .115 E7
Thrift Rd LU7 . . . . .103 A5
Thrift View MK43 . . . . .59 C2
Thrupp End MK43 . . . . .72 B3
THURLEIGH 18 C1
Thurleigh Airfield Bsns Pk
MK44 .17 F3
Thurleigh Lower Sch
MK44 .18 C2
Thurleigh Rd
Bolnhurst MK44 . . . . .19 C2
Milton Ernest MK44 . . . . .27 D5
Ravensden MK44 . . . . .28 E2
Thurlestone Cl MK40 . . . . . . .38 F1
Thurlow Cl LU4 . . . . .114 F4
Thurlow St 11 MK43 . . . . . . .50 B8
Thurne Way MK41 . . . . .38 D7
Tibbett Cl LU2 . . . . .121 D7
Tiberius Rd LU3 . . . . .115 F6
Tidbury Cl MK17 . . . . .81 A4
Tiddenfoot Ct LU7 . . . . .110 E5
TILBROOK 6 B7
Tilbrook Rd PE28 . . . . .6 D6
Tilgate LU2 . . . . .117 D3
Tiller Cl LU2 . . . . .111 D7
TILSWORTH 112 F5
Tilsworth Rd LU7 . . . . .112 D5
Timber La MK17 . . . . .92 F7
Timbers Ct AL5 . . . . .132 E2
Times Cl SG5 . . . . .100 D2
Timworth Cl LU2 . . . . .117 D1
Tindall Ave LU7 . . . . .103 B1
Tingey's Cnr SG18 . . . . .54 E1
TINGRITH 94 F5
Tingrith Rd MK17 . . . . .94 D6
Tinker's Cnr MK43 . . . . .48 E1
Tinkers Hill MK42 . . . . .51 A3
Tintagel Cl
Clapham MK41 . . . . .37 C7
Luton LU1 . . . . .123 B5
Tintagel Cl LU3 . . . . .116 B4
Tintagel Ct PE19 . . . . .22 F2
Tintagel Wlk MK41 . . . . .39 B5
Tintern Abbey MK41 . . . . . . .51 A3
Tintern Cl AL5 . . . . .130 C4
Tipcat Cl MK42 . . . . .50 B4
Tippett Dr SG17 . . . . .77 D3
Titan Ct LU4 . . . . .115 F1
Titchfield Dr MK42 . . . . .50 C3
Tithe Barn MK43 . . . . .26 C8
Tithe Barn Rd MK43 . . . . . . .60 F7
TITHE FARM 114 C6
Tithe Farm Cl LU5 . . . . .78 F7
Tithe Farm Lower Sch
LU5 . . . . .114 B6
Tithe Farm Rd LU5 . . . . .114 B6
Tithe Rd MK43 . . . . .48 E4
Tithe The MK43 . . . . .26 C8
Tiverton Rd MK40 . . . . .38 E2
TODDINGTON 105 E8
Toddington Manor★
LU5 . . . . .105 E8
Toddington Rd
Harlington LU5 . . . . .95 D2
Luton LU4 . . . . .115 C6
Tebworth LU7 . . . . .105 C3
Toddington St George
Lower Sch LU5 . . . . .105 F9
Toland Cl LU4 . . . . .115 C1
Tolkien Cl MK41 . . . . .39 E3
Tollers Mews PE19 . . . . .22 E5
Tollfield PE28 . . . . .6 F4
Tollgate Cl MK43 . . . . .36 E1
Tomlinson Ave LU4 . . . . . . .114 F4
Tompions End SG18 . . . . . . .65 E8
TOP END
MK44 .10 F1
MK44 .13 B1
Top End MK41 . . . . .39 F6
Topham Ct PE19 . . . . .17 C1
Torksey Cl LU4 . . . . .115 D1
Tornay Ct LU7 . . . . .118 D6
Torquay Dr LU4 . . . . .115 D4
Torre Abbey MK41 . . . . .51 B8
Torridge Rise MK41 . . . . . . .38 C5
Torrington Cl SG19 . . . . .55 F8
Totnes Cl MK40 . . . . .38 F1
TOTTERNHOE 120 B7
Totternhoe Knolls Nature
Reserve★ LU6 . . . . .120 B8
Totternhoe Lower Sch
LU6 . . . . .120 B7
Totternhoe Rd
Dunstable LU6 . . . . .120 D7
Eaton Bray LU6 . . . . .119 D7
Tower Cl LU2 . . . . .117 A1
Tower Rd LU2 . . . . .124 A8
Tower Way LU2 . . . . .124 A8
Town Cl MK45 . . . . .62 F4
Town Farm Cl SG8 . . . . .69 F4
Town Farm Ct SG16 . . . . .78 D1
Townfield Rd MK45 . . . . .84 F1
Town Lot La MK43 . . . . .26 B8
Town Meadow Dr SG17 . . . .77 C3
Townsend Cl
Cranfield MK43 . . . . .71 A8
Luton LU3 . . . . .115 B1
Townsend Ctr The LU4 . . . .114 B3
Townsend Farm Rd LU5 . . .114 B3
Townsend Ind Est LU5 . . . .114 B3
Townsend La AL5 . . . . .130 F1
Townsend Rd AL5 . . . . .131 A2
Towns End Rd MK44 . . . . . . .16 C4
Townsend Terr LU5 . . . . . . .114 A4

Town Shott MK45 . . . . .75 E1
Townside LU6 . . . . .119 F3
Townsley Cl LU1 . . . . .123 E6
Town The PE19 . . . . .13 E6
Townwell La NN29 . . . . .7 B8
Tracey Cl 15 LU1 . . . . .123 E6
Trafalgar Dr MK45 . . . . .84 E4
Trafalgar Rd PE19 . . . . .22 C5
Trailly Cl MK44 . . . . .4 A3
Trefoil Cl
  Luton LU4 . . . . .114 F4
  Rushden NN10 . . . . .8 C7
Trenchard Ave SG17 . . . . .76 D4
Trenchard La SG17 . . . . .76 E4
Trent Ave MK45 . . . . .84 D2
Trent Rd
  Bedford MK41 . . . . .38 D5
  Luton LU3 . . . . .116 B4
Trent Way LU7 . . . . .111 D5
Trescott Cl LU2 . . . . .117 E2
Trevor Dr MK43 . . . . .36 E2
Trevor St MK40 . . . . .38 A1
Trident Dr LU5 . . . . .114 E6
Triggs Way LU2 . . . . .117 E3
Trilley Fields MK45 . . . . .86 B8
Trimley Cl LU4 . . . . .115 B5
Tring Rd
  Dunstable LU6 . . . . .120 C4
  Dunstable LU6 . . . . .120 E7
Trinity Cl
  Biggleswade SG18 . . . . .66 F6
  Felmersham MK43 . . . . .26 C8
  Roxton MK44 . . . . .31 E2
Trinity Rd
  Bedford MK40 . . . . .49 F7
  Luton LU3 . . . . .116 A4
  Stotfold SG5 . . . . .90 F7
Tristram Rd SG4 . . . . .101 B2
Triumph Way MK42 . . . . .49 E2
Troon Cl MK41 . . . . .38 E5
Troon Gdns LU2 . . . . .116 F7
Trowbridge Gdns LU2 . . . . . .116 E3
Trow Cl MK45 . . . . .63 C7
Trowley Hill Rd AL3 . . . . . . .129 B1
Trowley Hts AL3 . . . . .129 B2
Truemans Rd SG5 . . . . .100 D2
Truman Pl SG17 . . . . .76 E2
Truncals LU1 . . . . .123 D5
Trunk Furlong Est MK17 . .81 D6
Truro Gdns
  Flitwick MK45 . . . . .84 E4
  Luton LU3 . . . . .116 C5
Trust Cotts HP4 . . . . .126 A1
Tudor Cl
  Barton-le-C MK45 . . . . .97 C4
  Bedford MK40 . . . . .38 A1
  Bromham MK43 . . . . .36 F3
Tudor Ct
  Dunstable LU6 . . . . .114 A4
  Kimbolton PE28 . . . . .6 F5
  Leighton Buzzard LU7 . . . . . .110 F7
Tudor Dr LU5 . . . . .114 E4
Tudor Rd LU3 . . . . .116 B2
Tudors The MK44 . . . . .20 B2
Tuffnells Way AL5 . . . . .130 D4
Tulip Cl SG18 . . . . .67 C5
Tulip Dr NN10 . . . . .8 B7
Tulip Tree Cl MK43 . . . . .36 C3
Tunstall Wlk MK41 . . . . .39 C3
Turnberry Wlk MK41 . . . . .38 E5
Turner Cl LU4 . . . . .114 D5
Turner Rd PE19 . . . . .22 C6
Turners Cl AL3 . . . . .131 C4
Turners Rd N LU2 . . . . .117 A2
Turners Rd S LU2 . . . . .117 A2
Turner Way MK41 . . . . .38 A2
Turnham Dr LU7 . . . . .111 C5
Turnpike Cl LU6 . . . . .121 C6
Turnpike Ct MK17 . . . . .81 A5
Turnpike Dr LU3 . . . . .108 C1
Turnpike La SG5 . . . . .100 E3
Turnpike Rd MK43 . . . . .82 B3
Turnpike Way MK41 . . . . .39 B3
TURVEY 34 F6
Turvey Lower Sch MK43 . .34 E6
Turvey Mill MK43 . . . . .34 D5
Turvey Rd
  Astwood MK16 . . . . .46 F6
  Carlton MK43 . . . . .24 E2
Tweedsmuir Rd MK41 . . . . . . .38 F4
Twigden Ct LU3 . . . . .115 F6
Twinwood Arena MK41 . . .27 F2
Twinwood Rd MK41 . . . . .37 C7
Twinwoods Bsns Pk MK44 .27 F5
Twyford Dr LU2 . . . . .117 D1
Tyburn La
  Pulloxhill MK45 . . . . .96 D8
  Westoning MK45 . . . . .95 E6
Tydeman Cl MK41 . . . . .38 C7
Tylecote LU7 . . . . .111 C5
Tylers AL5 . . . . .131 C6
Tylers Mead LU2 . . . . .116 E5
Tyne Cl MK45 . . . . .84 D2
Tyne Cres MK41 . . . . .38 C6
Tyne Rd SG19 . . . . .42 C2
TYRELLS END 94 A6
Tythe Barn Cl MK45 . . . . .95 E6
Tythe
Tythe Cl
  Flitwick MK45 . . . . .85 A2
  Sharnbrook MK44 . . . . .16 E3
Tythe Mews LU6 . . . . .119 E3
Tythe Rd LU4 . . . . .115 C6

U

Ullswater Cl
  Biggleswade SG18 . . . . .67 B4
  Flitwick MK45 . . . . .84 D2
Ullswater Ct MK42 . . . . .49 E3
Ullswater Dr MK42 . . . . .49 E3
Ullswater Dr LU7 . . . . .110 C7
Ullswater Rd LU6 . . . . .121 B6
Ulverston Rd LU6 . . . . .121 A6
Underwood Cl LU3 . . . . .107 F1
Union Chapel Ho 1 LU1 . .123 E6
Union St
  Bedford MK40 . . . . .38 A1
  Dunstable LU6 . . . . .114 A1
  Luton LU1 . . . . .123 E6
University Way MK43 . . . . . . .58 D1
Univ of Bedfordshire
  Bedford MK41 . . . . .38 F1
  Luton LU1 . . . . .123 F7
Univ of Bedfordshire
  (Lansdowne Campus)
  MK40 . . . . .38 A1
Univ of Bedfordshire,
  Putteridge Bury LU2 . . .117 D6
Unwin Cl SG6 . . . . .101 E4
Uplands
  Bedford MK40 . . . . .38 F4
  Luton LU3 . . . . .115 D8
Uplands Ct LU1 . . . . .123 E4
Upper Caldecote 66 F8
UPPER CALDECOTE 66 B7
Upper Coombe LU2 . . . . .110 E8
UPPER DEAN 5 A4
Upper George St LU1 . . . .123 D7
UPPER GRAVENHURST 87 D5
UPPER SHELTON 60 C3
Upper Shelton Rd MK43 . . .60 C3
Upperstone Cl SG5 . . . . .90 F6
UPPER SUNDON 107 A4
Upton Cl LU2 . . . . .116 D1
Upton Dr MK41 . . . . .38 C5
UPTON END 87 F2
Upton End Rd SG5 . . . . .87 F2
Upwell Rd LU7 . . . . .117 B2
Urban Hive LU3 . . . . .115 C7
Urban Way SG18 . . . . .67 A7
Ursula Taylor Lower Sch
  MK41 . . . . .37 E5
Ursula Taylor Wlk MK41 . . .37 E5
Usher Cl MK42 . . . . .50 B7

V

Vadis Cl LU3 . . . . .115 E7
Valarian Cl PE19 . . . . .22 C6
Vale Cl LU3 . . . . .130 D4
Vale Ct MK43 . . . . .59 D2
Valence End LU6 . . . . .121 D6
Valentine Gdns PE28 . . . . .6 F5
Valiant Cl LU4 . . . . .95 F1
Valley Cl
  Studham LU6 . . . . .127 B4
  Whipsnade HP4 . . . . .126 E7
Valley La AL3 . . . . .128 E1
Valley Rd
  Letchworth SG6 . . . . .101 D7
  Studham LU6 . . . . .127 B3
Valley Rise AL4 . . . . .131 F2
Vanbrugh Dr LU5 . . . . .114 D5
Vandyke Cl MK17 . . . . .81 B6
Vandyke Rd LU7 . . . . .103 C2
Vandyke Upper Sch & Com
  Coll LU7 . . . . .103 C1
Vanguard Cl MK42 . . . . .49 D6
Varna Cl LU3 . . . . .116 A3
Vaughan Rd
  Harpenden AL5 . . . . .131 B1
  Stotfold SG5 . . . . .90 E7
Vauxhall Rd LU1, LU2 . . . . . . .124 B5
Vauxhall Way LU2 . . . . .117 B3
Venetia Rd LU2 . . . . .117 A4
Ventnor Gdns LU3 . . . . .116 A7
Verey Rd LU5 . . . . .114 C2
Verne Dr MK45 . . . . .84 F8
Vernon Pl LU5 . . . . .114 B1
Vernon Rd LU1 . . . . .123 C8
Verulam Gdns LU3 . . . . .115 F6
Vespers Cl LU4 . . . . .115 A2
Vestry Cl LU1 . . . . .123 D7
Viaduct Cotts LU1 . . . . .130 F8
Vicarage Cl
  Arlesey SG15 . . . . .90 A8
  Langford SG18 . . . . .78 F8
  Ravensden MK44 . . . . .29 B1
  Shillington SG5 . . . . .98 F8
Vicarage Gdns
  Flamstead AL3 . . . . .129 B1
  Leighton Buzzard LU7 . . . . . .110 E6
Vicarage Gn MK44 . . . . .18 C1
Vicarage Hill MK45 . . . . .84 E1
Vicarage La
  Podington NN29 . . . . .7 E2
  Wilstead MK45 . . . . .62 E3
Vicarage Rd
  Houghton Regis LU5 . . . . . . .114 B5
  Leighton Buzzard LU7 . . . . . .110 E6
  Silsoe MK45 . . . . .86 C4
Vicarage St
  Luton LU1 . . . . .123 F7
  Woburn Sands MK17 . . . . . . .81 C4
Vicarage Wlk PE19 . . . . .13 F6
Vicars Cl MK41 . . . . .49 C8
Vicars Wlk MK41 . . . . .39 B2
Viceroy Cl PE19 . . . . .22 A3

Viceroy Ct LU6 . . . . .121 C8
Victor Cl MK42 . . . . .51 A2
Victoria Cl
  Langford SG18 . . . . .78 E6
  Wrestlingworth SG19 . . . . . . .57 B4
Victoria Cotts LU5 . . . . .114 A4
Victoria Ct 5 SG18 . . . . .67 A6
Victoria Dr
  Houghton Conquest MK45 . . .74 A8
  Stotfold SG5 . . . . .91 A5
Victoria Pl SG18 . . . . .67 A6
Victoria Rd
  Bedford MK42 . . . . .50 B6
  7 Harpenden AL5 . . . . .131 B1
  Leighton Buzzard LU7 . . . . . .110 E6
  Shefford SG17 . . . . .77 D2
Victoria St
  Dunstable LU6 . . . . .114 A1
  Dunstable LU6 . . . . .121 D6
  Luton LU1 . . . . .123 D6
Victoria Terr LU7 . . . . .111 D7
Viking Gr MK42 . . . . .49 D6
Viking Ind Est MK41 . . . . .39 D4
Villa Ct 5 LU2 . . . . .123 D8
Village Cl LU7 . . . . .110 D5
Village Rd MK41 . . . . .36 F3
Villa Park (Mobile Home Pk)
  MK43 . . . . .70 F7
Villa Rd LU2 . . . . .123 D8
Villiers Cl LU4 . . . . .115 D3
Vimy Cl LU7 . . . . .110 F7
Vimy Rd LU7 . . . . .110 F7
Vincent Rd LU4 . . . . .115 A3
Vinegar Hill SG19 . . . . .54 A3
Vines The SG5 . . . . .90 E6
Vineyard Way MK42 . . . . .49 E5
Violet Cl
  Bedford MK42 . . . . .50 F4
  Biggleswade SG18 . . . . .67 B5
Violets Cl MK16 . . . . .58 B6
Virginia Cl LU2 . . . . .116 E5
Viscount Cl LU3 . . . . .116 A5
Viscount Ct
  11 Luton LU2 . . . . .116 D1
  St Neots PE19 . . . . .22 B4
Voyce Way MK42 . . . . .50 C6
Vulcan Cl MK42 . . . . .50 C6
Vulcan Way PE19 . . . . .22 B2
Vyne Cl MK42 . . . . .49 D5

W

Waddesdon Cl LU2 . . . . .117 D2
Wadhurst Ave LU1 . . . . .116 C4
Wagstaffe Cl MK41 . . . . .38 E6
Walcot Ave LU2 . . . . .117 B1
Walcourt Rd MK42 . . . . .50 A5
Waldeck Rd LU3 . . . . .123 C8
Waldegrave Pk AL5 . . . . .131 D1
Waleys Cl LU2 . . . . .115 E8
Walgrave Rd LU5 . . . . .114 F2
Walk House Cl MK43 . . . . .59 B1
Walkley Rd LU5 . . . . .114 B4
Wallace Dr LU6 . . . . .119 E6
Wallace Mews LU6 . . . . .119 E6
Wallace Way SG4 . . . . .101 A2
Waller Ave
  Luton LU4 . . . . .115 F2
  Luton LU4 . . . . .115 F3
Waller Street Mall 3
  LU1 . . . . .123 E7
Wallis Way MK42 . . . . .51 B4
Walmsley House Sch
  MK40 . . . . .38 D2
Walnut Acre LU5 . . . . .105 F6
Walnut Cl
  Biggleswade SG18 . . . . .66 F8
  Blunham MK44 . . . . .41 D3
  Bromham MK43 . . . . .36 D1
  Luton LU2 . . . . .117 B4
  Pavenham MK43 . . . . .26 B3
  Stotfold SG5 . . . . .90 F6
Walnut Gr MK43 . . . . .72 B3
Walnuts The LU7 . . . . .103 B2
Walnut Tree Rd SG5 . . . . .90 F3
Walnut Wlk MK42 . . . . .49 F3
Walsingham Cl LU2 . . . . .116 D7
WALSWORTH 101 A1
Waltham Cl MK41 . . . . .38 F5
Waltham Ct LU2 . . . . .117 C3
Waltham Dr MK42 . . . . .50 D3
Walton Cl SG17 . . . . .77 E3
Wandon Cl LU2 . . . . .117 C4
Wansbeck Rd MK41 . . . . .38 C5
Wantage Pl NN29 . . . . .7 B8
Wantage Rd NN29 . . . . .7 B8
WARDEDGES 84 D7
Warden Abbey MK45 . . . . . . .39 B1
Warden Cl 8 LU2 . . . . .123 E8
WARDEN HILL 116 D7
Warden Hill SG19 . . . . .43 C3
Warden Hill Gdns LU2 . . . . . .116 C8
Warden Hill Inf Sch LU3 . .116 C7
Warden Hill Jun Sch
  LU3 . . . . .116 C7
Warden Hill Rd LU2 . . . . .116 C8
Warden Rd SG18 . . . . .65 D7
WARDEN STREET 64 F5
Wardhedges Rd MK45 . . . . . . .85 E4
Wardown Cres LU2 . . . . .116 D3
Wardown Pk LU3 . . . . .116 D2
Ware Rd MK17 . . . . .22 E6
Waresley Rd SG19 . . . . .44 D7
Warkworth Cl SG19 . . . . .54 C8

Warminster Cl LU2 . . . . .117 F1
Warneford Way LU7 . . . . .111 C5
Warren Cl
  Biggleswade SG18 . . . . .67 A7
  Irchester NN29 . . . . .7 C7
  Letchworth SG6 . . . . .101 D7
  Toddington LU5 . . . . .105 F7
Warren Dr The LU1 . . . . .124 C1
Warren Rd
  Ampthill MK45 . . . . .84 F7
Warren The MK41 . . . . .37 E5
Warton Gn LU2 . . . . .117 E2
Warwick Ave MK40 . . . . .38 A1
Warwick Ct LU5 . . . . .114 A4
Warwick Cl MK45 . . . . .84 D1
Warwick Ct
  Luton LU4 . . . . .123 B8
  St Neots PE19 . . . . .22 C3
Warwick Ho MK40 . . . . .38 A2
Warwick Rd E LU4 . . . . .123 B8
Warwick Rd W LU4 . . . . .123 B8
Washbank Rd PE19 . . . . .22 E4
Washbrook Cl MK45 . . . . .97 C1
Washbrook La MK41 . . . . .38 D6
Washingleys MK43 . . . . .59 C2
Washington Ave SG17 . . . . . . .76 F2
Waterborne Wlk 7 LU7 . .111 A7
Waterdell LU7 . . . . .111 C7
WATER END
  HP1 . . . . .132 F2
  MK17 . . . . .94 C7
  MK44 . . . . .52 A4
  MK45 . . . . .86 A7
  SG19 . . . . .57 B3
Water End
  Cople MK44 . . . . .52 B4
  Workhouse End MK41 . . . . . . .40 A4
  Wrestlingworth SG19 . . . . . . .57 B3
Water End La LU4 . . . . .106 C2
Water End Rd MK45 . . . . .85 F7
WATERHALL 70 C2
Water La
  Chelveston NN9 . . . . .3 B8
  Flitwick MK45 . . . . .85 A2
  Hitchin SG5 . . . . .100 F1
  Kempston MK43 . . . . .49 C3
  Leighton Buzzard LU7 . . . . . .110 F7
Waterloo Cl MK45 . . . . .84 E4
Waterloo Dr PE19 . . . . .22 F3
Waterloo La SG5 . . . . .100 A6
Waterloo Rd
  Bedford MK40 . . . . .50 D8
  Leighton Buzzard LU7 . . . . . .110 E6
Watermead Rd LU3 . . . . .115 F6
Waters End SG5 . . . . .90 E6
Waterside LU5 . . . . .119 F4
Waterslade Gn LU3 . . . . .116 B6
Watery La AL3 . . . . .129 E3
Watkin Wlk SG18 . . . . .66 F7
Watling Ct
  Dunstable LU6 . . . . .114 A2
  1 Houghton Regis LU5 . . . .114 B4
Watling Gdns LU6 . . . . .121 D6
Watling Lower Sch LU6 . .121 C7
Watling St LU6 . . . . .119 D4
Watling St LU6 . . . . .113 E4
Watson Rd MK45 . . . . .62 C6
Watson Way MK43 . . . . .72 D8
Waulud Prim Sch LU3 . . . . . .115 F7
Waulds Bank Dr LU3 . . . . . . .115 E7
Wavell Ct MK41 . . . . .61 D1
Wavendon Ho MK17 . . . . .81 A8
Wavendon House Dr
  MK17 . . . . .81 B8
Wavendon Rd MK17 . . . . .70 C2
Waveney Ave MK41 . . . . .38 C5
Waveney Rd AL3 . . . . .131 C3
Waverly Ave SG19 . . . . .42 B3
Waverley Pre-Prep Sch
  MK45 . . . . .84 E3
Wayside LU6 . . . . .121 D5
Wear The MK41 . . . . .38 C5
Weatherby LU6 . . . . .120 E8
Weatherby Rd LU4 . . . . .115 A3
Weathercock Cl MK17 . . . . . . .81 B5
Weathercock La MK17 . . . . . . .81 C4
Weatherfield Sch LU6 . . . .113 E1
Weaver Cl MK41 . . . . .38 D6
Weavers La LU6 . . . . .113 A4
Weavers Gn SG19 . . . . .42 C2
Weavers Orch SG15 . . . . .90 A4
Webber Cl SG17 . . . . .77 D3
Webbs Cl MK43 . . . . .36 F2
Wedgewood Rd LU4 . . . . .114 F4
Wedgwood Rd MK41 . . . . .38 B3
Weedon Cl SG16 . . . . .89 C5
Welbeck Gdns MK42 . . . . .50 F5
Welbeck Rd 8 LU2 . . . . .123 E8
Welbury Ave LU3 . . . . .115 E8
Weldon Cl LU2 . . . . .117 E1
Welland Ct
  Bedford MK41 . . . . .38 D5
  St Neots PE19 . . . . .22 C4
Wellfield Ave LU5 . . . . .115 C8
Wellfield Rd LU5 . . . . .115 D2
WELL HEAD 120 D5
Well Head Rd LU6 . . . . .120 D5
Wellhouse Cl LU1 . . . . .123 A7
Wellingham Ave SG5 . . . . . . .100 D1
Wellington Cl 3 LU1 . . . . . . .123 D6
Wellington Dr SG17 . . . . .76 F3
Wellington Ho LU7 . . . . .103 A4
Wellington Rd MK42 . . . . .50 F2

Wellington St
  Bedford MK40 . . . . .38 B1
  Luton LU1 . . . . .123 D7
Wellington Terr LU5 . . . . .121 C8
Well La LU7 . . . . .110 A1
Wellpond Cl MK44 . . . . .16 D3
Wells Cl
  Harpenden AL5 . . . . .130 E4
  Kempston MK42 . . . . .49 E6
Wells Ct 1 LU7 . . . . .111 A7
Wellsfield MK44 . . . . .41 E3
Wells Rd MK44 . . . . .10 F2
Weltmore Rd LU3 . . . . .115 E4
Wendover Cl AL5 . . . . .131 D1
Wendover Ct MK41 . . . . .38 F1
Wendover Dr MK41 . . . . .39 A1
Wendover Way LU2 . . . . .116 F3
Wenlock CE Jun Sch
  LU2 . . . . .124 B8
Wenlock Rd MK42 . . . . .49 C3
Wenlock St LU2 . . . . .123 E8
Wensleydale LU7 . . . . .111 C5
Wentworth Ave LU5 . . . . .115 C6
Wentworth Cl LU5 . . . . .105 F7
Wentworth Ct LU5 . . . . .95 F1
Wentworth Dr
  Bedford MK41 . . . . .38 F5
  Leighton Buzzard LU7 . . . . . .111 A8
Wentworth Gdns LU5 . . . . . . .106 A6
Werth Dr MK17 . . . . .81 B2
Wesley Cl SG15 . . . . .90 A4
Wesley Rd
  Markyate AL3 . . . . .128 C5
  Sandy SG19 . . . . .42 C1
West Arc 13 MK40 . . . . .50 B8
Westbourne Rd
  Bedford MK40 . . . . .49 F7
  Luton LU4 . . . . .116 B1
Westbury Cl LU4 . . . . .114 B3
Westbury Ct
  Ampthill MK45 . . . . .84 F8
  Bedford MK41 . . . . .38 C5
Westbury Gdns LU2 . . . . .116 E3
Westbury Pl SG6 . . . . .101 E5
Westbury Prim Sch SG6 . .101 E5
West Cl SG4 . . . . .101 B1
West Ct
  Bedford MK41 . . . . .39 A2
  Leighton Buzzard LU7 . . . . . .110 F7
Westdale Wlk MK42 . . . . .49 F4
West Dene HP2 . . . . .132 F8
Westdown Gdns LU6 . . . . . . .120 F7
West Dr SG15 . . . . .90 A4
WEST END
  MK43 . . . . .36 A8
  MK43 . . . . .70 F8
  MK43 . . . . .13 A2
  MK45 . . . . .86 B4
West End
  Elstow MK42 . . . . .50 B3
  Stevington MK43 . . . . .36 A8
West End La SG19 . . . . .56 A8
West End Rd
  Kempston MK43 . . . . .48 D5
  Silsoe MK45 . . . . .86 B3
Westerdale LU4 . . . . .115 B5
Western Ave SG16 . . . . .89 B3
Western Cl SG6 . . . . .90 E1
Western Rd LU1 . . . . .123 D6
Western St MK40 . . . . .50 B8
Western Way
  Dunstable LU5 . . . . .114 C1
  Letchworth SG6 . . . . .90 E1
  Sandy SG19 . . . . .54 B8
Westfield Ave AL5 . . . . .131 A3
Westfield Dr AL5 . . . . .131 B4
Westfield Gdns LU5 . . . . .114 B5
Westfield Mid Sch MK40 . .49 E8
Westfield Pl AL5 . . . . .131 B4
Westfield Rd
  Bedford MK40 . . . . .49 F8
  Dunstable LU6 . . . . .113 F1
  Harpenden AL5 . . . . .131 B4
  Henlow SG16 . . . . .78 C1
  Oakley MK43 . . . . .36 E8
  Wyboston MK44 . . . . .31 F8
Westgate Ct LU6 . . . . .121 A8
West Gr MK40 . . . . .49 F8
West Hill
  Aspley Guise MK17 . . . . .81 A4
  Dunstable LU6 . . . . .121 C5
West Hill Rd LU1 . . . . .123 E5
Westholme SG6 . . . . .101 F8
West La SG5 . . . . .99 D5
Westlecote Gdns LU2 . . . . . . .116 D4
West Lodge Cotts LU2 . . . . . .117 D5
WESTMILL 100 C2
Westmill La
  Hitchin SG5 . . . . .100 C2
  Ickleford SG5 . . . . .100 C3
Westmill Lawns SG5 . . . . . . .100 D1
Westmill Rd SG5 . . . . .100 D1
Westminster Gdns
  Houghton Regis LU5 . . . . . . .114 D6
  Kempston MK42 . . . . .49 E5
Westmorland Ave LU3 . . . . . .115 F5
Weston Ave LU7 . . . . .111 C6
Weston Ct PE19 . . . . .22 C4
WESTONING 95 F6
Westoning Lower Sch
  MK45 . . . . .95 E6
Westoning Rd
  Greenfield MK45 . . . . .85 B1
  Harlington LU5 . . . . .95 E3
Westoria Ct MK45 . . . . .95 E5

West Par LU6 . . . . **121** A8
West Rd
  Gamlingay SG19 . . . . **44** C4
  Sandy SG19 . . . . **54** B8
  Wharley End MK43 . . . . . . **58** D2
  Woburn Sands MK17 . . . . . **81** B5
Westrope Way MK41 . . . . . . **38** D7
Westside
  Leighton Buzzard LU7 . . . . **110** F7
  Leighton Buzzard LU7 . . . . **111** A7
West St
  Dunstable LU6 . . . . **121** A8
  Leighton Buzzard LU7 . . . . **110** F7
  Lilley LU2 . . . . **109** D1
  St Neots PE19 . . . . **22** E5
West View
  Beeston SG19 . . . . **54** B5
  Langford SG18 . . . . **78** F6
  Letchworth SG6 . . . . **101** E4
  Letchworth SG6 . . . . **101** E5
Westway LU2 . . . . **117** C4
West Way
  Harpenden AL5 . . . . **131** C2
  Moggerhanger MK44 . . . . . **53** C7
West Wlk SG18 . . . . **67** B7
Westwood CI MK42 . . . . . . **51** A2
Wetherne Link LU4 . . . . . . **115** C5
Wexham CI LU3 . . . . **115** E8
Weybourne CI AL5 . . . . . . **131** D2
Weybourne Dr LU2 . . . . . . **116** C7
Wharfdale 7 LU4 . . . . **115** C5
Wharfe The MK41 . . . . **38** C6
Wharf Mews SG18 . . . . **66** F6
WHARLEY END **58** D2
Wheatfield CI LU7 . . . . **111** D7
Wheatfield Ct LU4 . . . . **114** E4
Wheatfield Rd LU4 . . . . **114** E4
Wheat Hill SG6 . . . . **101** F8
Wheathouse CI MK41 . . . . . **38** F4
Wheatlands CI MK45 . . . . . **85** E8
Wheatsheaf Rd PE19 . . . . . **22** C3
Wheel Wright CI SG5 . . . . . **87** F1
Whinnett's Way MK45 . . . . **85** E1
Whipperley Ct LU1 . . . . . . **123** C5
Whipperley Inf Sch LU1 . . . **123** A6
Whipperley Ring LU1 . . . . . **123** A6
Whipperley Way LU1 . . . . . **123** C5
WHIPSNADE **120** F1
Whipsnade Rd LU6 . . . . **120** F7
Whipsnade Tree Cathedral★
  LU6 . . . . **120** F1
Whipsnade Wild Animal
  Park★ LU6 . . . . **126** E7
Whistler Rd PE19 . . . . **22** C5
Whiston Cres SG17 . . . . **78** B3
Whitbread Ave MK42 . . . . . **50** A6
Whitby Rd LU3 . . . . **116** C1
Whitby Way MK42 . . . . **50** C3
White Beam CI MK42 . . . . . **49** F2
Whitechurch CI LU2 . . . . . . **117** D2
Whitecroft Rd LU2 . . . . **124** A8
White Crofts SG5 . . . . **90** F6
Whitefield Ave LU3 . . . . . . **115** C7
Whitefield Inf Sch LU3 . . . . **115** E8
Whitefield Jun Sch LU3 . . . **115** E8
Whitefriars NN10 . . . . **7** F8
Whitefriars Jun & Inf Schs
  NN10 . . . . **7** F8
Whitehall MK43 . . . . **72** B2
Whitehall Wlk PE19 . . . . . . **22** F4
Whitehaven LU3 . . . . **107** F1
Whitehicks SG6 . . . . **91** A1
Whitehill Ave LU1 . . . . **123** D5
White Hill Rd MK45 . . . . . . **97** C3
White Ho PE19 . . . . **22** C4
White Horse CI LU7 . . . . . . **104** E2
White Horse Ct LU7 . . . . . . **111** A7
Whitehorse St SG7 . . . . **91** F1
Whitehorse Vale LU3 . . . . . **107** F1
Whitehouse CI LU5 . . . . **114** B4
Whitehurst Ave SG5 . . . . . . **100** F1
White Lion Ret Pk LU5 . . . . **114** C1
White Lodge CI MK42 . . . . . **49** C3
Whiteman CI SG18 . . . . **78** F5
Whitethorn Way LU1 . . . . . **123** A6
Whitewaybottom La SG4 . . **125** F5
Whitings MK40 . . . . **49** B6
Whitings CI AL5 . . . . **131** D4
Whitley Gn LU2 . . . . **117** D2
Whitley Rd MK42 . . . . **51** A3
Whittingham CI LU2 . . . . . **117** F1
Whittingstall Ave MK42 . . **50** A4
Whittle CI SG16 . . . . **89** B4
Whitwell CI LU3 . . . . **116** B8
Whitworth Ct
  Kempston MK42 . . . . **49** E4
  Shefford SG17 . . . . **77** C3
Whitworth Jones Ave
  SG16 . . . . **89** C5
Whitworth Way MK45 . . . . **62** F3
WICK END **48** B8

Wickets The LU2 . . . . **116** E1
Wick Hill LU6 . . . . **127** F8
Wickmere CI LU2 . . . . **116** C7
Wickstead Ave LU4 . . . . . . **115** E4
Widecombe CI MK40 . . . . . **38** E2
WIGMORE **117** E2
Wigmore La LU2 . . . . **117** D2
Wigmore Park Ctr LU2 . . . . **117** E1
Wigmore PI LU2 . . . . **117** E1
Wigmore Prim Sch LU2 . . . **117** E2
Wigram CI MK42 . . . . **50** B4
Wilbury CI SG6 . . . . **101** C7
Wilbury Dr LU5 . . . . **114** E3
Wilbury Hills Rd SG6 . . . . . **101** C7
Wilbury Jun Sch SG6 . . . . . **101** D6
Wilbury Rd SG6 . . . . **101** E8
Wilbury Way SG4 . . . . **101** A3
Wildber CI PE19 . . . . **22** F4
Wild Cherry Dr LU1 . . . . . . **123** D5
WILDEN **29** F3
Wilden CE Lower Sch
  MK44 . . . . **29** F3
Wilden Rd
  Colmworth MK44 . . . . **30** A6
  Renhold MK41 . . . . **39** C7
Wildflower Way MK42 . . . . **50** F4
Wilhamstead Lower Sch
  MK45 . . . . **62** F4
Wilkinson CI PE19 . . . . **22** B3
Willenhall CI LU3 . . . . **116** A7
William Austin Inf Sch
  LU3 . . . . **116** C4
William Austin Jun Sch
  LU3 . . . . **116** C4
William Dr PE19 . . . . **22** F1
Williams CI SG18 . . . . **67** B8
Williamson CI MK42 . . . . . . **49** C2
Williamson Rd MK42 . . . . . **49** D2
William St 1 LU1 . . . . **123** E7
William St
  Luton LU2 . . . . **116** E1
  Markyate AL3 . . . . **128** E5
William Sutton Ct
  Bedford MK40 . . . . **50** A8
  Luton LU2 . . . . **117** B5
Willian Rd MK45 . . . . **84** D4
Willian Rd SG4, SG6 . . . . . . **101** E1
WILLINGTON **52** C8
Willington Lower Sch
  MK44 . . . . **40** C1
Willington Rd MK44 . . . . . . **52** A6
Williton Rd LU2 . . . . **117** C2
Willmers CI MK41 . . . . **38** E4
Willmott Rd NN10 . . . . **8** C8
Willoughby Ct
  Dunstable LU6 . . . . **121** C7
  Great Barford MK44 . . . . . **40** F5
Willoughby Rd AL5 . . . . . . **131** B4
Willow Bank Wlk LU7 . . . . **111** C8
Willow CI
  Bromham MK43 . . . . **36** F3
  St Neots PE19 . . . . **22** F3
Willow Ct LU3 . . . . **115** E5
Willowfield Lower Sch
  LU1 . . . . **122** F4
Willowgate Trad Est
  LU3 . . . . **115** A8
Willow Gr LU1 . . . . **122** E3
Willow Herb CI NN10 . . . . . **8** C7
Willow Ho LU7 . . . . **110** E7
Willow Rd
  Bedford MK42 . . . . **50** D5
  Potton SG19 . . . . **56** A7
  Shefford SG17 . . . . **77** D2
  Wilstead MK45 . . . . **62** E2
Willow Rise SG19 . . . . **54** D6
Willows La HP1 . . . . **132** F1
Willow Springs MK43 . . . . . **71** A8
Willows The
  Edlesborough LU6 . . . . **119** F3
  Flitwick MK45 . . . . **84** E3
  Leighton Buzzard LU7 . . . . **111** B6
  Wootton MK43 . . . . **61** A8
Willow Tree Way SG5 . . . . **100** E4
Willows CI 1 PE19 . . . . . . **22** E5
Willow Way
  Ampthill MK45 . . . . **84** F7
  Flitwick MK45 . . . . **84** F1
  Harpenden AL5 . . . . **131** C4
  Houghton Regis LU5 . . . . . **114** D6
  Luton LU3 . . . . **115** E5
  Toddington LU5 . . . . **105** F5
Willsheres Rd SG18 . . . . . . **67** A7
Wilman Ct SG18 . . . . **78** F5
Wilshere Cres SG4 . . . . **101** D1
Wilson Ct MK45 . . . . **62** F4
WILSTEAD **62** F3
Wilstead Hill MK45 . . . . . . **74** F7
Wilstead Ind Est MK45 . . . . **62** C6
Wilstead Rd
  Elstow MK45 . . . . **51** C8
  Elstow MK42 . . . . **62** C8
  Wilstead MK45 . . . . **63** C5

Wilton Rd SG5 . . . . **100** E1
Wimborne Rd LU1 . . . . **123** C8
Wimple Rd LU4 . . . . **115** A2
Winchester Gdns LU3 . . . . . **107** E1
Winchester Rd
  Bedford MK42 . . . . **50** F4
  Sandy SG19 . . . . **54** C8
Winchfield LU2 . . . . **122** E4
Winch St LU2 . . . . **116** F1
Windermere CI
  Dunstable LU6 . . . . **121** B7
  Flitwick MK45 . . . . **84** E2
Windermere Cres LU3 . . . . . **115** F5
Windermere Dr SG18 . . . . . **67** A4
Windermere Gdns LU7 . . . . **110** C7
Windermere The MK42 . . . . **49** D3
Windmill CI MK41 . . . . **39** B3
Windmill Ct MK44 . . . . **16** D3
Windmill Hill MK40 . . . . . . **37** D2
Windmill Path 5 LU7 . . . . **111** A7
Windmill Rd
  Flamstead AL3 . . . . **129** B6
  Flitwick MK45 . . . . **84** D4
Windmill Row 6 PE19 . . . . **22** E5
Windmill View SG18 . . . . . **67** A4
Windmill Way MK43 . . . . . **59** C3
Windrush Ave MK45 . . . . . . **38** C5
Windrush CI MK45 . . . . **84** D2
Windsor Ave LU7 . . . . **110** F7
Windsor CI
  Flitwick MK45 . . . . **84** D1
  St Neots PE19 . . . . **22** F2
Windsor Ct 10 LU1 . . . . . . **123** D6
Windsor Dr LU3 . . . . **114** D4
Windsor Gdns MK40 . . . . . . **38** D2
Windsor Par MK45 . . . . **97** C4
Windsor PI LU5 . . . . **114** D5
Windsor Rd
  Barton-le-C MK45 . . . . **97** C4
  Bedford MK42 . . . . **50** D4
  Windsor St LU1 . . . . **123** D6
Windsor Way
  Langford SG18 . . . . **78** F6
  Sandy SG19 . . . . **54** C7
Windsor Wlk 7 LU1 . . . . . **123** D6
Winfield St LU6 . . . . **114** B1
Wingate CI LU4 . . . . **115** F2
Wingate Dr MK45 . . . . **85** A8
Wingate Rd
  Dunstable LU5 . . . . **114** F1
  Harlington LU5 . . . . **95** F2
  Luton LU4 . . . . **115** F2
WINGFIELD **105** E1
Wingfield Ave MK45 . . . . . **74** C1
Wingfield CI MK40 . . . . **49** E7
Wingfield Ct MK45 . . . . **84** F8
Wingfield Dr SG19 . . . . **56** A8
Wingfield Rd
  Bromham MK43 . . . . **36** F4
  Tebworth LU7 . . . . **105** C2
Wing Rd
  Ascott LU7 . . . . **110** B4
  Leighton Buzzard LU7 . . . . **110** D5
  Winhills Prim Sch** PE19 . . . **22** F4
Winifred Rd MK40 . . . . **49** F8
Winkfield CI LU4 . . . . **115** B1
Winsdon CI 1 LU1 . . . . . . **123** D6
Winsdon Rd LU1 . . . . **123** D6
Winslow CI LU3 . . . . **116** C4
Winston CI LU7 . . . . **103** A1
Winston Cres SG18 . . . . **67** A7
Winton CI LU2 . . . . **116** D6
Wintringham Rd 7 PE19 . . **22** F5
Wisdom CI MK43 . . . . **36** D2
Wiseman CI LU2 . . . . **116** E6
Wisteria CI NN10 . . . . **8** B7
Wistow Ct PE19 . . . . **22** C6
Wistow Rd LU3 . . . . **116** A6
Witham CI MK41 . . . . **38** D7
Withybrook MK45 . . . . **84** E3
Withy CI LU4 . . . . **115** B4
Witter Ave SG5 . . . . **100** E4
WITTS END **94** B6
Wivelsfield LU7 . . . . **110** E6
Wiveton CI LU2 . . . . **116** D7
WOBURN **92** F7
Woburn Abbey★ MK17 . . . **93** D6
Woburn CI MK45 . . . . **84** C1
Woburn Ct
  Kempston MK42 . . . . **49** D3
  Leighton Buzzard LU7 . . . . **110** E6
  Luton LU4 . . . . **115** D5
Woburn La MK17 . . . . **81** E4
Woburn Lower Sch MK17 . . **92** F7
WOBURN PARK **93** D7
Woburn PI LU7 . . . . **103** A1
Woburn Rd
  Bedford MK40 . . . . **50** A8
  Heath and Reach LU7 . . . . **103** B7
  Hockliffe LU7 . . . . **104** E3
  Kempston MK42 . . . . **49** D2
  Kempston MK43 . . . . **61** C8

Woburn Rd *continued*
  Marston Moretaine MK43 . . **72** C7
  Millbrook MK45 . . . . **73** B1
  Woburn Sands MK17 . . . . . **81** C1
Woburn Road Ind Est
  MK42 . . . . **49** D1
Woburn Safari Pk★ MK17,
  MK43 . . . . **82** D1
WOBURN SANDS **81** A4
Woburn Sands Sta MK17 . . **81** A5
Woburn St MK45 . . . . **73** D1
Wodecroft Rd LU3 . . . . **116** A7
Wolfsburg Ct 4 LU4 . . . . . **115** C5
Wollaston Rd NN29 . . . . . . **7** A8
Wolseley Bsns Pk MK42 . . . **49** E1
Wolseley Ct MK42 . . . . **49** E1
Wolseley Rd MK42 . . . . **49** E1
Wolston CI LU1 . . . . **123** C7
Woodall CI SG18 . . . . **66** F6
Woodbridge CI LU4 . . . . . . **115** E4
WOODBURY **43** E6
Woodbury Hill LU2 . . . . . . **116** E2
Wood CI
  Biddenham MK40 . . . . **37** C1
  Kensworth LU6 . . . . **121** E1
Woodcock CI SG19 . . . . **42** B2
Woodcock Rd LU2 . . . . **123** A7
Woodcock Wlk MK45 . . . . . **84** F1
Woodcote MK44 . . . . **39** A3
WOOD END
  MK17 . . . . **95** B5
  MK43 . . . . **48** D2
  MK43 . . . . **71** F7
  MK44 . . . . **6** D1
  MK44 . . . . **28** D3
Wood End CI MK44 . . . . **16** B3
Wood End Hill AL5 . . . . . . **130** D3
Wood End JM Sch AL5 . . . . **130** D3
Woodend La MK44 . . . . **31** C2
Wood End La MK43 . . . . . . **48** F2
Wood End Rd
  Cranfield MK43 . . . . **71** B7
  Harpenden AL5 . . . . **130** D3
  Kempston MK43 . . . . **48** D2
Woodfield Gate LU5 . . . . . . **121** E6
Woodfield La MK41 . . . . . . **40** A6
Woodford Rd LU5 . . . . **114** E1
Wood Green CI LU2 . . . . . . **117** B5
Wood Green Rd LU2 . . . . . . **117** C5
Woodhouse La PE19 . . . . . . **21** F6
Woodhurst SG6 . . . . **101** F8
Wood La
  Aspley Guise MK17 . . . . . . **81** D4
  Cotton End MK45 . . . . **63** D7
  Renhold MK41 . . . . **39** E6
  Willington MK44 . . . . **52** D7
Woodland Ave
  Leighton Buzzard LU7 . . . . **102** C2
  Luton LU3 . . . . **116** B2
Woodland Ct
  Heath and Reach LU7 . . . . **103** A5
  Potton SG19 . . . . **56** A8
Woodland Dr MK43 . . . . . . **36** F4
Woodland Mid Sch MK45 . . **84** D2
Woodland Pk LU5 . . . . **62** F2
Woodland Rise LU2 . . . . . . **127** B7
Woodlands
  Bedford MK41 . . . . **38** B6
  Caddington LU1 . . . . **122** E3
  Harpenden AL5 . . . . **130** E3
  Tebworth LU7 . . . . **105** C2
Woodlands Ave LU5 . . . . . . **114** C4
Woodlands CI MK44 . . . . . . **52** A5
Woodlands Rd NN29 . . . . . . **7** A7
Woodlands The SG18 . . . . . **66** C3
Woodland Way MK17 . . . . . **81** B4
Woodlea CI LU7 . . . . **111** B7
Woodmer CI SG5 . . . . **87** E2
Woodmere
  Bedford MK41 . . . . **38** F3
  Luton LU3 . . . . **108** A1
WOODMER END **87** E2
Woodpecker Way SG19 . . . **42** B2
Wood Rd MK43 . . . . **24** F7
WOODSIDE
  LU1 . . . . **123** A2
  MK41 . . . . **39** B4
Woodside
  Aspley Guise MK17 . . . . . . **81** D3
  Eaton Bray LU6 . . . . **119** E6
Woodside Animal Farm &
  Leisure Park★ LU1 . . . . **129** A8
Woodside Ind Est LU5 . . . . **114** D3
Woodside Mid Sch MK41 . . **39** B4
Woodside Park Ind Est
  LU5 . . . . **114** C3
Woodside Rd LU5 . . . . **123** B3
Woodside Way LU7 . . . . . . **110** D6
Wood St
  Dunstable LU6 . . . . **121** C8
  Luton LU1 . . . . **123** F6
  Woburn Sands MK17 . . . . . **81** B5
Woodstock Rd MK40 . . . . . **49** F7
Wood The LU7 . . . . **111** A8

Woodview MK45 . . . . **62** F2
Woodville Dr MK40 . . . . . . **49** B6
Woolfield SG19 . . . . **54** D6
Woolgrove Ct SG4 . . . . **101** B1
Woolgrove Rd SG4 . . . . **101** B1
Woolpack CI LU6 . . . . **121** C7
Wooton Field SG19 . . . . . . **44** D4
WOOTTON **61** A7
WOOTTON BOURNE END . . **48** C1
WOOTTON BROADMEAD . . **60** D4
Wootton CI LU3 . . . . **116** B7
WOOTTON GREEN **60** D4
Wootton Lower Sch MK43 . . **60** F7
Wootton Rd MK43 . . . . **49** A1
Wootton Upper Sch MK43 . . **60** E7
Worboys Ct SG8 . . . . **49** F5
Worcester Rd MK42 . . . . . . **50** F4
Wordsworth Ave PE19 . . . . **22** D5
Wordsworth CI SG18 . . . . . **66** C8
Wordsworth Ct MK40 . . . . . **37** F2
Wordsworth Rd
  Harpenden AL5 . . . . **131** A3
  Luton LU4 . . . . **115** A2
WORKHOUSE END **40** A5
Worthington Rd LU6 . . . . . **120** F8
Wrayfields SG5 . . . . **91** B8
Wraysbury CI LU4 . . . . **115** D3
Wren CI
  Flitwick MK45 . . . . **84** D1
  Luton LU2 . . . . **117** C6
  Sandy SG19 . . . . **42** C1
Wren Wlk LU6 . . . . **119** E4
WRESTLINGWORTH **57** C4
Wrestlingworth CE Lower
  Sch SG19 . . . . **57** B3
Wrestlingworth Rd SG19 . . **56** C6
Wrest Park Gardens★
  MK45 . . . . **86** E3
Wroxham Way
  Bedford MK40 . . . . **49** D7
  Harpenden AL5 . . . . **131** C3
Wulwards CI LU1 . . . . **123** B6
Wulwards Ct LU1 . . . . **123** B6
Wyatt CI SG5 . . . . **100** D4
Wyatt Rd MK42 . . . . **49** D3
WYBOSTON **32** A5
Wyboston Ct PE19 . . . . **22** C4
Wyboston L Pk★ MK44 . . . **32** C7
Wybridge MK44 . . . . **12** B1
Wybridge CI MK44 . . . . **12** B1
Wychwood Ave LU2 . . . . . . **116** E3
Wychwood Rd 2 MK41 . . . **39** B4
Wycklond CI SG5 . . . . **90** E6
Wycliffe CI LU3 . . . . **116** C6
Wycombe Way LU3 . . . . . . **116** C8
Wye MK41 . . . . **38** D5
Wyken CI LU3 . . . . **116** A7
WYMINGTON **8** B5
Wymington Rd
  Podington NN29 . . . . **7** E3
  Rushden NN10 . . . . **8** B8
Wynchwood La SG17 . . . . . **77** B2
Wyndham Rd MK44 . . . . . . **115** C2
Wynd The SG6 . . . . **101** F6
Wyngates LU7 . . . . **110** C5
Wynnefield Wlk SG19 . . . . **54** C8
Wysells Ct SG6 . . . . **101** D7
Wyton CI SG17 . . . . **76** F2
Wyvern CI LU4 . . . . **115** C3

Y

Yardley Ct 14 AL5 . . . . . . **131** B1
Yarrow CI NN10 . . . . **8** C7
Yately CI LU2 . . . . **116** D7
YELDEN **4** B2
Yelnow La MK44 . . . . **16** A3
Yeomans Ave AL5 . . . . **130** D3
Yeomans Gate MK44 . . . . . **51** D4
Yeovil Ct LU2 . . . . **117** B2
Yeovil Rd LU2 . . . . **117** B2
Yew St LU5 . . . . **114** D7
Yew Tree CI
  Eaton Bray LU6 . . . . **119** F5
  Silsoe MK45 . . . . **86** C3
Yew Tree Ct 3 LU7 . . . . . . **111** A7
Yew Tree Wlk LU7 . . . . . . **78** B2
York CI
  Barton-le-C MK45 . . . . **97** D4
  Biggleswade SG18 . . . . **67** B5
York Ct LU7 . . . . **110** F7
York Rd SG5 . . . . **100** E1
York St
  Bedford MK40 . . . . **50** E8
  Luton LU2 . . . . **123** F8
Young Ind Est LU7 . . . . . . **111** D6